PLAYS IN PERIODICALS:

AN INDEX to ENGLISH LANGUAGE SCRIPTS

in TWENTIETH CENTURY JOURNALS

Compiled by

Charlotte A. Patterson

G. K. HALL & CO., 70 LINCOLN STREET, BOSTON, MASS.

1970

This publication is printed on permanent/durable acid-free paper.

PREFACE

With a combination of thirty-five years' experience in theatre, a brand-new library degree, and a position as reference librarian for music and drama at the University of Hawaii, it was inevitable that the need for this sort of index would soon become apparent. *Plays in Periodicals* accumulated gradually over a period of two years to augment the library's services to the active theatre communities of this island state. It proved gratifyingly useful, and when G. K. Hall & Co. realized that many other librarians would appreciate having this type of reference tool, an additional three months of intensive work readied it for publication in this form.

This index gives access to over four thousand plays printed in ninety-seven English language periodicals published from 1900 thru 1968. The broad general coverage encompasses material suitable for all age groups and for every degree of talent and resources, whether for performance or for study.

The main entries in this index are the alphabetically arranged and serially numbered titles of plays. Each title entry includes the author (and translator or adapter where appropriate), the length of the play, the size and mixture of the cast, and the bibliographic location consisting of name of periodical, volume number, date and pagination. The Author Index is cross referenced to the main entries by the key numbers. The Cast Analysis Index is similarly keyed to the main entries, and classifies the plays first according to length and then by the number and distribution of the roles in the cast. The List of Abbreviations used is self-explanatory and probably already familiar to most theatre devotees.

Most plays, wherever published, carry a protective copyright for a stipulated number of years. Small theatre groups, school drama classes and college theatre courses, however, are constantly looking for playscripts to work with as practice pieces for the art and craft of theatre. It is only when public performances are planned that these groups must seek the copyright holder's permission to use his script and possibly pay royalties for that privilege. Copyright information is almost invariably included on the title page of the scripts in the journals, and should be noted whenever any performance is planned outside the classroom or study group.

The compiler of this index must in all candor acknowledge some of its shortcomings. It had been planned to include all the plays appearing in all the nationally circulated journals in the United States within the sixty-nine year period covered. "All" proved to be too ambitious a term and there are many unintended exclusions. Of the more than four thousand entries which have been gathered, almost two hundred have been included for which the author was unable to ascertain the length and cast analysis information within the time limits imposed by publication schedules. Too, there are a few numbering omissions toward the end of the alphabet caused by inadvertently numbering some of the cross references as well as the main entries. These are the known defects. But also, while accuracy of detail was most conscientiously essayed in this compilation, it is realized that some mistakes have undoubtedly escaped the careful proofreading. Your indulgence, please.

Plays in Periodicals could not have become a published reference book at all without the assistance of many friends and co-workers. The author wishes in particular to acknowledge the cooperation of the staff of the Hawaii State Library and of Hamilton Library at the University of Hawaii. She is also especially indebted to Dr. Stanley West, University Librarian, and Miss Virginia Crozier, his Assistant and Head of Public Services, for their encouragement, their active support, and their personal interest in the completion of this project. It could not have been done without them.

CHARLOTTE A. PATTERSON

(née Van Dyke)

Honolulu, Hawaii.
July 4, 1970

TABLE of CONTENTS

PERIODICALS INDEXED

Mlle.	Mademoiselle, New York, N.Y.
Mod. Drama.	Modern International Drama, University Park, Pa.
Musician .	Musician, New York, N.Y.
Nature.	Nature Magazine, Washington, D.C.
Negro History.	Negro History Bulletin, Washington, D.C.
New England.	New England Magazine, Boston, Mass.
New Republic.	New Republic, New York, N.Y.
New Yorker.	New Yorker, New York, N.Y.
19th C.	Nineteenth Century, New York, N.Y. Later: Nineteenth Century and After.
North Amer.	North American Review, New York, N.Y.
Outlook.	Outlook, New York, N.Y.
Overland .	Overland Monthly, San Francisco, Cal.
Pictorial .	Pictorial Review, New York, N.Y.
Playground .	Playground and Recreation, New York, N.Y.
Players.	Plays and Players, London, Eng.
Plays.	Plays, Boston, Mass.
Poet Lore .	Poet Lore, Boston, Mass.
Poetry.	Poetry, Chicago, Ill.
Public Lib.	Public Libraries, Chicago, Ill.
Publish. W.	Publishers' Weekly, New York, N.Y.
Putnam's.	Putnam's Magazine, New York, N.Y.
Queen's.	Queen's Quarterly, Kingston, Can.
Ramparts.	Ramparts Magazine, Berkeley, Cal.
Review.	Review of Reviews, New York, N.Y.
St. Nicholas.	St. Nicholas, New York, N.Y. Later: St. Nicholas Magazine, Columbus, Ohio.
Sat. Evening.	Saturday Evening Post, Philadelphia, Pa.
Sat. Review.	Saturday Review of Literature, New York, N.Y. Later: Saturday Review.
Scholastic.	Senior Scholastic (High School Teacher edition), New York, N.Y.
School Arts.	School Arts Magazine, Worcester, Mass.
Scribner's.	Scribner's Magazine, New York, N.Y.
Speech Educ.	Quarterly Journal of Speech Education, Menasha, Wis.
Sunset.	Sunset: The Pacific Monthly, San Francisco, Cal. Later: Sunset.
Survey.	Survey, New York, N.Y. Later: Survey Graphic.
Theatre .	Theatre Arts Monthly, New York, N.Y. Later: Theatre Arts.
Touchstone.	The Touchstone, New York, N.Y.
Virginia.	Virginia Quarterly Review, Charlottesville, Va.
Vogue.	Vogue, Greenwich, Conn.
Wilson.	Wilson Bulletin for Librarians, New York, N.Y. Later: Wilson Library Bulletin.
Woman's Home.	Woman's Home Companion, Springfield, Ohio.
World Out.	World Outlook, Garden City, N.Y.
Writer.	Writer, Boston, Mass.
Yale Review.	Yale Review, New Haven, Conn.

ABBREVIATIONS USED

Abr.	Abridged.
Adap.	Adapted.
Ed.	Edited.
Trans.	Translated.
Excerpt.	Part of a longer work, usually a scene or two.
Full.	Full length, usually 2 long or 3 regular acts.
Short.	1 act or less. Could be just a skit, short dialog or scene.
Radio.	Usually equivalent to 1 act or a 15 min. show. Cast members may be doubled by changing voices.
b.	boy, young and not fully grown.
c.	child or children of either sex.
ch.	chorus, usually singing.
f.	female, usually adult, though in the children's plays, they may actually be school girls playing adults.
g.	girl, young and not fully grown.
m.	male, usually adult, though in the children's plays, they may actually be school boys playing adults.
un.	unspecified, usually adults.
X.	assorted extras usually in non-speaking roles. Occasionally preceded by m., f., b., g., or c., indicating extras all of one sex or age group.

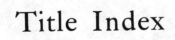

Title Index

1. <u>A B C for Safety</u> by Edrie Pendleton.

   Short. 10 m. 6 f.

   In - Plays. 10: April 1951, 63-66.

2. <u>The A B C's Thanksgiving</u> by Helen Louise Miller.

   Short. 3 m. 2 f. 30 c.

   In - Plays. 21: Nov.1961, 77-80.

3. <u>Abandoned Husbands</u> by Christopher Morley.

   Short. 6 m. 2 f.

   In - Sat. Review. 5: Oct.20,1928, 269-270.

4. <u>Abe Buys a Barrell</u> by Mary Nygaard Peterson.

   Short. 7 m. 3 f.

   In - Plays. 15: Feb.1956, 64-70.

5. <u>Abe Lincoln and Little Joe</u> by Mildred Hark and Noel McQueen.

   Short. 12 m. 3 f.

   In - Plays. 6: Jan.1947, 1-11.

6. <u>Abe Lincoln in Illinois</u> by Robert E. Sherwood.

   Excerpt. 2 m. 1 f. 2 b.

   In - Scholastic. 36: Feb.12,1940, 17-18+.

7. <u>Abe Lincoln Goes to School</u> by Alice Very.

   Short. 5 m. 4 f. +X.

   In - Plays. 16: Feb.1957, 77-80.

8. <u>Abe's Winkin' Eye</u> by Aileen Fisher.

   Short. 4 m. 4 f.

   In - Plays. 11: Feb.1952, 39-49.

9. <u>Abner Crane from Hayseed Lane</u> by Earl J. Dias.

   Short. 4 m. 5 f.

   In - Plays. 16: Oct.1956, 11-24.

10. <u>Abra-Kadabra-Kadoo!</u> by Herbert Ravetch.

    Short. 4 m. 8 f.

    In - Plays. 17: Oct.1957, 35-44.

11. <u>The Abstract Tragedy</u> by Elder Olson.

    Full. 4 m. 1 f.

    In - First Stage. 2: June 1963, 166-186.

12. <u>Ace Navigator</u> by Samuel S. Richmond.

    Short. 4 m. 1 f.

    In - Plays. 4: Nov.1944, 11-15.

<u>The Aching Heart.</u>

   see

<u>Shee Shih, the Aching Heart.</u>

13. <u>Achilles' Heel</u> by Shelley Levi.

    Short. 10 m. 2 f.

    In - Plays. 25: May 1966, 69-72.

14. <u>The Acrobats</u> by Berry Fleming.

    Full. 11 m. 5 f. +X.

    In - First Stage. 1: Dec.1961, 11-40.

15. <u>Across the Jordan</u> by Ernest Howard Culbertson.

    Short. 3 m. 1 f.

    In - Theatre. 13: Dec.1929, 931-939.

16. <u>Adalmina's Pearl</u> by Karin Asbrand.

    Short. 1 m. 3 f.

    In - Plays. 7: March 1948, 44-46.

17. <u>Adam and Eve</u> by Antonio Porras. Trans. from the Spanish by Willis Knapp Jones and Glenn Barr.

    Full. 8 m. 5 f. +X.

    In - Poet Lore. 41: Jan.1930, 1-49.

18. <u>Adjustment</u> by Manta S. Graham.

    Short. 3 m. 3 f.

    In - Plays. 4: April 1945, 17-29.

19. <u>The Admiral and the News</u> by William Morwood.

    Radio. 7 m. 0 f. 1 b.

    In - Scholastic. 51: Oct.13,1947, 22-24.

20. <u>The Admiral Leads On</u> by Fleming Shriner.

    Short. 5 m. 1 f.

    In - Plays. 25: Oct.1965, 79-82.

21. <u>The Admiral's Daughter</u> by Marjorie B. Paradis.

    Short. 0 m. 6 f.

    In - Plays. 11: Jan.1952, 1-8.

22. <u>The Admiral's Daughter</u> by Marjorie B. Paradis.

    Short. 0 m. 6 f.

    In - Plays. 19: Oct.1959, 39-46.

23. <u>The Admiral's Nightmare</u> by Jane McGowan.

    Short. 9 m. 3 f. 1 "sea monster" +m.X.

    In - Plays. 22: Oct.1962, 58-64.

24. Adobe Christmas by Mary Nygaard Peterson.

Short. 3 m. 3 f.

In - Plays. 17: Dec.1957, 45-50.

25. Adored One by Irma Peixotto Sellers. Based on La Mere Michel et Son Chat by E. de la Bedollierre.

In - Drama. 14: May 1924, 253-261.

26. Adventures in Bookland by Florence Lias.

Short. 3 m. 11 f. 4 un

In - Plays. 18: Nov.1958, 61-66.

27. The Adventures of Tom Sawyer by Mark Twain. Adap. by Levy Olfson.

Radio. 4 m. 4 f.

In - Plays. 14: Nov.1954, 91-96.

28. The Adversary by Stephen Phillips.

Short. 4 m. 1 f.

In - Contemporary. 102: Sept.1912, 407-412.

29. Advice to the Lovelorn by Mildred Hark and Noel McQueen.

Short. 3 m. 2 f.

In - Plays. 4: March 1945, 1-9.

30. The Advocate by Robert Noah.

Full. 25 m. 3 f.

In - Theatre. 47: Nov.1964, 33-64.

31. Aesop, Man of Fables by Ernestine Phillips.

Short. 7 m. 1 f. +X.

In - Plays. 22: April 1963, 43-52.

32. The Affair by Ronald Millar. From the novel by C. P. Snow.

Full. 15 m. 2 f.

In - Theatre. 47: March 1963, 25-56.

33. After All by Harriet Monroe.

Short. 1 m. 1 f. +ch.

In - Poet Lore. 12:no.3,1900, 321-326.

34. After Closing by Roy Marz.

Short. 7 m. 3 f. 1 b. 2 c.

In - First Stage. 1: June 1962, 41-51.

35. After Euripides' "Electra" by Maurice Baring.

Short. 6 m. 5 f.

In - Golden. 17: March 1933, 257-261.

36. After Glow by Elizabeth F. Corbett.

In - Poet Lore. 36: June 1925, 311-316.

37. After the Fall by Arthur Miller.

Full. 4 m. 6 f.

In - Sat. Evening. 237: Feb.1,1964, 32-37+.

38. After the Wedding by William Dean Howells.

Short. 1 m. 1 f.

In - Harper's M. 114: Dec.1906, 64-69.

39. After Twenty-Five Years by Oscar W. Firkins.

In - Drama. 15: Feb.1925, 99-101.

40. The Aftermath by H. Glynn-Ward.

Short. 3 m. 1 f.

In - Poet Lore. 37: Dec.1926, 501-511.

41. Afternoon in Arcady by Clarence Stratton.

Short. 0 m. 11 f.

In - House & G. 39: June 1921, 34-35+.

42. Afternoon Orator by Chester T. Crowell.

Short. 4 m. 6 f.

In - New Republic. 39: June 11,1924, 72-75.

43. The Afternoon Walk by Henri Lavedan. Trans. from the French of Les Beaux Dimanches by Sibyl Collar Holbrook.

Short. 1 m. 0 f. 4 b.

In - Poet Lore. 28:no.4,1917, 403-406.

44. Afterwards by Geraldine McGaughan.

Short. 2 m. 2 f.

In - Scholastic. 28: March 7,1936, 7-9.

45. Afterwards by Geraldine E. McGaughan.

Short. 2 m. 2 f.

In - Scholastic. 55: Jan.18,1950, 5-7+.

46. The Age of Accountability by Mody C. Boatright.

Short. 2 m. 7 f.

In - Poet Lore. 40: June 1929, 295-302.

47. The Age of Folly by Henri Lavedon. Trans. from the French by William V. Silverberg.

Short. 1 m. 1 f.

In - Poet Lore. 30:no.1,1919, 1-7.

48. Aglavaine and Selysette by Maurice Maeterlinck. Trans. by Charlotte Porter and Helen A. Clarke.

Full. 2 m. 2 f. 1 g.

In - Poet Lore. 14:no.4,1903, 11-64.

49. <u>Agnes Bernauer</u> by Frederick Hebbel. Trans.
    by Loueen Pattee.

    Full. 20 m. 2 f. +X.

50. <u>Ahasverus</u> by Hermann Heijermans. Trans. by
    Caroline Heijermans-Hauwink and J.J.
    Hauwink.

    Short. 7 m. 3 f.

    In - Drama. 19: Feb.1929, 145-147.

    <u>Aida</u>.

        see

    <u>My Darlin' Aida</u>.

51. <u>The Aino Puku</u> by Tracy Dickinson Mygatt.

    Short. 2 m. 4 f.

    In - World Out. 4: June 1918, 20-21.

52. <u>Air Raid</u> (abr.) by Archibald MacLeish.

    Radio. 4 m. 2 f. 1 b. 1 g. +f.X.

    In - Scholastic. 35: Nov.6,1939, 21E-25E.

53. <u>Aladdin</u> adap. by Deborah Newman.

    Short. 4 m. 4 f. +X.

    In - Plays. 13: April 1954, 36-42.

54. <u>Aladdin and His Wonderful Lamp</u> adap. by Adel*
    Thane from <u>The Arabian Nights</u>.

    Short. 6 m. 4 f. 1 un.

    In - Plays. 23: April 1964, 45-56.

55. <u>Aladdin Incorporated</u> by Mildred Hark and
    Noel McQueen.

    Short. 2 m. 3 f.

    In - Plays. 5: Feb.1946, 33-42.

56. <u>Aladdin Incorporated</u> by Mildred Hark and
    Noel McQueen.

    Short. 2 m. 3 f.

    In - Plays. 24: Feb.1965, 51-60.

57. <u>Aladdin Steps Out</u> by Mildred Hark and Noel
    McQueen.

    Short. 10 m. 4 f.

    In - Plays. 16: Nov.1956, 25-36.

58. <u>Albert Einstein, Schoolboy</u> by Margery C.
    Rutherford.

    Short. 4 m. 1 f. 1 b. 1 g.

    In - Plays. 27: April 1968, 51-57.

59. <u>Albert's Bridge</u> by Tom Stoppard.

    Short. 13 m. 2 f.

    In - Players. 15: Oct.1967, 21-30.

60. <u>An Albino Kind of Logic</u> by Curtis Zahn.

    Short. 2 m. 1 f. +ch.

    In - First Stage. 3: June 1964, 167-173.

61. <u>The Aldrich Family</u> by Clifford H. Goldsmith.

    Radio. 3 m. 5 f.

    In - Scholastic. 35: Jan.22,1940, 19E-21E+.

62. <u>Alexander's Horse</u> by Maurice Baring.

    Short. 1 m. 1 f. 1 b.

    In - Golden. 20: Oct.1934, 419-422.

63. <u>Alias Santa Claus</u> by Percival Wilde.

    Full. 10 m. 4 f.

    In - Pictorial. 28: Dec.1926, 16-17+.

64. <u>Alice in Bookland</u> by Sarah Cauman.

    Short. 1 un. +c.X.

    In - Wilson. 9: Oct.1934, 81-84+.

65. <u>Alice in Bookland</u> by Catherine Urban.

    Short. 2 m. 3 f.

    In - Plays. 22: Nov.1962, 72-74.

66. <u>Alice in Everydayland</u> by Egbert H. Van Delden.

    Short. 3 m. 5 f.

    In - Poet Lore. 38: March 1927, 96-105.

67. <u>Alice in Puzzleland</u> by Aileen Fisher and
    Olive Rabe.

    Short. 4 m. 2 f. +X.

    In - Plays. 14: Jan.1955, 65-70.

68. <u>Alice in Wonderland</u> by Lewis Carroll. Adap.
    by Lewy Olfson.

    Radio. 11 m. 6 f.

    In - Plays. 22: Jan.1963, 85-95.

69. <u>Alice in Wonderland</u> by Lewis Carroll. Adap.
    by Rochelle Hill.

    Short. 7 m. 3 f.

    In - Plays. 26: Jan.1967, 81-91.

70. <u>The Aliens</u> by Charles Hanson Towne.

    Short. 5 m. 4 f.

    In - McClure's. 47: May 1916, 12-13+.

71. <u>Ali's Reward</u> by Margaret C. Hall.

    Short. 7 m. 3 f. 1 b.

    In - Plays. 27: March 1968, 71-74.

72. <u>All Aboard!</u> by Ben Bengal.
    Short. 7 m. 3 f.
    In - Theatre. 28: Sept.1944, 500-504.

73. <u>All Aboard</u> (abr.) by Ben Bengal.
    Short. 7 m. 3 f.
    In - Scholastic. 45: Dec.4,1944, 11-13+.

74. <u>All About Mothers</u> by Claire Boiko.
    Short. 5 m. 11 f. +c.X.
    In - Plays. 24: May 1965, 71-74.

75. <u>An All-American Thank You</u> by Helen Louise Miller.
    Short. 4 m. 3 f.
    In - Plays. 28: Nov.1968, 45-51.

76. <u>The All-American Tour</u> by Deborah Newman.
    Short. 5 m. 5 f. +X.
    In - Plays. 23: May 1964, 71-75.

77. <u>All Because of a Scullery Maid</u> by Marguerite Kreger Phillips.
    Short. 3 m. 5 f.
    In - Plays. 21: March 1962, 15-24.

78. <u>All Blood is Red</u> by Eugene Lavine.
    Radio. 7 m. 0 f. +X.
    In - Education. 66: Jan.1946, 292-296.

79. <u>All God's Chillun Got Wings</u> by Eugene O'Neill.
    Full. 4 m. 3 f. +X. (white & Negro).
    In - American Merc. 1: Feb.1924, 129-148.

80. <u>All Hands on Deck</u> by Claire Boiko.
    Short. 6 m. 5 f.
    In - Plays. 26: Jan.1967, 35-43.

81. <u>All Houses Are Haunted</u> by Alice Woster.
    Short. 4 m. 1 f. 13 un.
    In - Plays. 9: Dec.1949, 71-74.

82. <u>All In Favor</u> by Morton K. Schwartz.
    Short. 4 m. 3 f.
    In - Plays. 5: March 1946, 47-53.

83. <u>All Is Not Gold</u> by Mildred Hark and Noel McQueen.
    Short. 3 m. 2 f.
    In - Plays. 9: Oct.1949, 25-35.

84. <u>All My Own Work</u> by Romilly Cavan.
    Full. 7 m. 5 f.
    In - Players. 6: March & April 1959, 25-30, 25-29.

85. <u>All on a Day in May</u> by Aileen Fisher.
    Short. 2 m. 2 f. +c.X.
    In - Plays. 14: May 1955, 73-76.

86. <u>All or None</u> by Franklin Kent Gifford.
    Short. 1 m. 3 f. +f.X.
    In - Drama. 16: March 1926, 207-209.

87. <u>All Points West</u> by Claire Boiko.
    Short. 8 m. 1 f. 5 b. 1 g. +X.
    In - Plays. 26: Nov.1966, 41-52.

88. <u>All Summer Long</u> by Robert Anderson.
    Full. 3 m. 3 f. 1 b.
    In - Theatre. 39: Aug.1955, 32-63.

89. <u>All the Way Home</u> by Tad Mosel.
    Full. 13 m. 7 f.
    In - Theatre. 46: Oct.1962, 25-56.

90. <u>All This and Alan, Too</u> by Joan Allred.
    Short. 0 m. 5 f.
    In - Plays. 5: Oct.1945, 9-15.

91. <u>All This and Alan, Too</u> by Joan Allred.
    Short. 0 m. 5 f.
    In - Plays. 12: May 1953, 74-80.

92. <u>All This and Alan, Too</u> by Joan Allred.
    Short. 0 m. 5 f.
    In - Plays. 23: April 1964, 37-44.

93. <u>Allons Enfants!</u> by Ivo Vojnovich. Trans. from the Croatian by John J. Batistich and George Rapall Noyes.
    Full. 23 m. 4 f. 2 b.
    In - Poet Lore. 56:no.2,1951, 103-142.

94. <u>Almost Everyman</u> by Helen H. Austin.
    Short. 8 m. 4 f. +X.
    In - Speech Educ. 5: Jan.1919, 45-53.

95. <u>Aloha, Mother</u> by Jane McGowan.
    Short. 5 m. 7 f. 1 un. +X.
    In - Plays. 21: May 1962, 61-64.

96. Along the Quays by Henri Lavedan. Trans.
     from the French by Sibyl Collar Holbrook.

     Short. 2 m. 0 f.

     In - Poet Lore. 28: no.4,1917, 385-390.

97. Alpha Kappa by Marjorie B. Paradis.

     Short. 0 m. 8 f.

     In - Plays. 12: Oct.1952, 12-23.

98. Alumni Dinner by Mildred Hark and Noel
     McQueen.

     Short. 6 m. 3 f. +X.

     In - Plays. 7: May 1948, 10-18.

99. America Is a Song by Paul T. Nolan.

     Short. 11 m. 3 f. +X.

     In - Plays. 22: March 1963, 61-68.

100. America the Beautiful by Leslie Hollings-
     worth.

     Radio. 4 m. 3 f. +X.

     In - Plays. 4: Oct.1944, 80-86.

101. American Answer by Perry Birnbaum.

     Short. 4 m. 1 f.

     In - Scholastic. 36: Feb.12,1940, 23-24+.

102. An American Dream by Edward Albee.

     In - Mlle. 52: Nov.1960, 86-89+.

103. An American Grandfather by Marian Spencer
     Smith.

     Short. 4 m. 1 f. +X.

104. The American Way by Anne Coulter Martens.

     Short. 6 m. 8 f. +X.

     In - Plays. 23: Feb.1964, 13-24.

105. Among Ourselves by Sol Panitz.

     Radio. 17 m. 4 f. 2 un.

     In - Scholastic. 52: Feb.23,1948, 15-19.

106. Anastasia by Marcelle Maurette. English adap.
     by Guy Bolton.

     Full. 9 m. 4 f.

     In - Theatre. 40: May 1956, 34-61.

107. And Christmas Is Its Name by Paul T. Nolan.

     Short. 16 m. 9 x.

     In - Plays. 19: Dec.1959, 87-95.

108. And Pippa Dances by Gerhart Hauptmann.
     Trans. from the German by Mary Harned.

     Full. 13 m. 2 f. +X.

     In - Poet Lore. 18:no.3,1907, 289-341.

109. And Sew On by Karin Asbrand.

     Short. 1 m. 7 f.

     In - Plays. 4: Nov.1944, 47-48.

110. And the Stars Heard by Jean M. Byers.

     Short. 1 m. 2 f. 6 b. 2 g. +c.X.

     In - Jl., N.E.A. 30: Nov.1941, 243-246.

111. Anders Paints a Picture by Karin Asbrand.

     Short. 5 m. 6 f.

     In - Plays. 25: Jan.1966, 55-60.

112. The Andersonville Trial by Saul Levitt.

     Full. 28 m. 0 f.

     In - Theatre. 45: May 1961, 27-53.

113. Androcles and the Lion by George Bernard Shaw.

     Full. 14 m. 2 f. +X.

     In - Everybody's. 31: Sept.1914, 289-311.

114. Angel in the Looking-Glass by Aileen Fisher.

     Short. 3 m. 5 f.

     In - Plays. 9: Dec.1949, 33-39.

115. Angel in the Looking Glass by Aileen Fisher.

     Short. 3 m. 5 f.

     In - Plays. 16: Dec.1956, 51-57.

116. Angel of Mercy by Esther Lipnick.

     Short. 4 m. 4 f.

     In - Plays. 5: Nov.1945, 28-34.

117. The Angel on the Ship by Thornton Wilder.

     Short. 2 m. 1 f.

     In - Harper's M. 157: Oct.1928, 564-565.

118. Animal Crackers by Karin Asbrand.

     Short. 10 m. 15 f.

     In - Plays. 7: Dec.1947, 69-71.

119. The Animals' Christmas Tree by O.J. Robertson.

     Short. 1 m. 0 f. 14 c.

     In - Plays. 27: Dec.1967, 67-69.

120. The Animals' Thanksgiving by June Barr.
     Short. 5 m. 4 f.
     In - Plays. 8: Nov.1948, 42-45.

121. Anne of the Thousand Days by Maxwell Anderson.
     Full. 25 m. 6 f.
     In - Theatre. 33: June 1949, 57-92

122. Anniversary Waltz by Jerome Chodorov and Joseph Fields.
     Full. 7 m. 5 f.
     In - Theatre. 39: Feb.1955, 33-58.

123. Another Cinderella by Robert Fontaine.
     Short. 1 m. 5 f.
     In - Plays. 25: Jan.1966, 91-95.

124. Another Man's Family by Harold Cable.
     Short. 9 m. 4 f. +X.
     In - Plays. 25: Dec.1965, 1-14.

125. An Anton Chekhov Sort of Evening by Paul T. Nolan.
     Short. 4 m. 3 f.
     In - Plays. 27: March 1968, 1-12.

126. Antonio by Roberto Zerboni.
     Short. 1 m. 2 f.
     In - First Stage. 4: Dec.1965, 226-231.

127. Antony and Cleopatra by William Shakespeare.
     Excerpts. 11 m. 1 f.
     In - Scholastic. 52: April 19,1948, 15-18.

128. Anyone for the Moon? by Elinor R. Alderman.
     Short. 7 m. 3 f. +m.X.
     In - Plays. 19: March 1960, 1-10.

129. Anywhere and Everywhere by Claire Boiko.
     Short. many c.
     In - Plays. 22: Jan.1963, 73-76.

130. The Apostle by George Moore.
     Full. 18 m. 3 f.
     In - Dial. 74 & 75: June & July 1923, 537-561, 43-72.

131. The Apparition by Richard Eberhart.
     Short. 3 m. 3 f. 1 g.
     In - Poetry. 77: March 1951, 311-321.

132. An Apple From Coles County by Graham DuBois.
     Short. 8 m. 1 f.
     In - Plays. 8: Jan.1949, 1-10.

133. The Apple of Contentment by Howard Pyle.
     Short. 4 m. 5 f.
     In - Plays. 23: Nov.1963, 57-65.

134. The Appointment by Melvin Irving Weisburd.
     Short. 2 m. 0 f.
     In - Poet Lore. 57: March 1952, 61-79.

135. The Apprentices by Peter Terson.
     Full. 15 m. 4 f. +X.
     In - Players. 16: Oct.1968, 27-55.

136. The April Elves by Josef A. Elfenbein.
     Short. 3 m. 3 f.
     In - Plays. 14: April 1955, 63-69.

137. April Fool by Marion Wefer.
     Short. 5 m. 5 f.
     In - Plays. 8: April 1949, 55-59.

138. An April Fool Surprise by June Barr.
     Short. 6 m. 3 f.
     In - Plays. 11: April 1952, 59-62.

139. April Fool's Day by Lucille Miller Duvall.
     Short. 6 m. 2 f. +X.
     In - Plays. 19: April 1960, 47-52.

140. April Showers by Claribel Spamer.
     Short. 4 m. 1 f. +c.X.
     In - Plays. 9: April 1950, 62-65.

141. April's Lady by Carolyn Wells.
     Short. many g.
     In - Ladies' Home. 33: April 1916, 38.

142. Arabella by Richard Strauss. English version of the Hugo von Hofmannsthal libretto by John Gutman.
     Full (opera). 16 m. 5 f. +X.
     In - Theatre. 41: Jan.1957, 42-63.

143. The Argument by Phoebe-Lou Adams.
     Short. 15 un.
     In - Plays. 4: April 1945, 49-50.

144. Ariadne Exposed by E.M. Nightingale.

Short. 4 m. 1 f.

In - Plays. 25: Jan.1966, 15-20.

145. Around the World in Eighty Days by Jules Verne. Adap. by Levy Olfson.

Radio. 18 m. 1 f.

In - Plays. 18: Oct.1958, 85-95.

146. The Arrow by June E. Downey.

Short. 4 m. 3 f. +X.

In - Poet Lore. 38: June 1927, 297-306.

147. Arthur Bones, the Reading Dog by Frances B. Watts.

Short. 3 m. 3 f. 3 b. 3 g. 1 "dog".

In - Plays. 26: Nov.1966, 63-69.

148. Arts and Parts by Betty Tracy Huff.

Short. 6 m. 7 f. +X.

In - Plays. 28: Dec.1968, 19-29.

149. As Grandmother Told It by Fannie R. Ross.

Short. 8 m. 4 f.

In - Plays. 3: Nov.1943, 58-62.

150. As You like It by William Shakespeare. Adap. by Levy Olfson.

Radio. 5 m. 2 f.

In - Plays. 17: Feb.1958, 87-96.

151. Ashes by Eleanor C. Whiting.

Short. 2 m. 1 f.

In - Poet Lore. 33: Sept.1922, 423-438.

152. Ask the Library Lady by Marguerite Kreger Phillips.

Short. 4 m. 4 f. +X.

In - Plays. 14: April 1955, 31-40.

153. The Ass and the Lap Dog by Rowena Bennett.

Short. 6 m. 0 f.

In - Plays. 8: Jan.1949, 42-45.

154. The Assumption of Hannele by Gerhart Hauptmann. Trans. by G.S. Bryan.

Short. 9 m. 1 f.

In - Poet Lore. 20:no.3,1909, 161-191.

155. At the Cleaners by Samuel S. Richmond.

Short. 4 m. 3 f.

In - Plays. 6: Oct.1947, 76-81.

156. At the Eleventh Hour by Edith V. Brander Matthews.

In - Harper's B. 38: March 1904, 232-239.

157. At the End of the Rainbow by Mary Warner Howard.

Short. 2 m. 4 f.

In - Plays. 18: Oct.1958, 59-64.

158. At the Flowing of the Tide by Edward J. O'Brien.

Short. 1 m. 2 f.

In - Forum. 52: Sept.1914, 375-386.

159. At the Jolly Spot by Alexander Ostrovsky. Trans. from the Russian.

In - Poet Lore. 36: March 1925, 1-44.

160. At the Little Pipe by Lillian Sutton Pelée.

In - Poet Lore. 31: Sept.1920, 422-431.

161. At the Mulligans' Reception by Edward Harrigan.

Excerpt. 1 m. 2 f.

In - Theatre. 22: Sept.1938, 684-685.

162. At the Shrine by Stark Young.

Short. 1 m. 1 f.

In - Theatre. 3: July 1919, 196-203.

163. At the Shrine by Stark Young.

Short. 1 m. 1 f.

In - Golden. 16: July 1932, 77-82.

164. At the Sign of the Bible and Sun by Emma Lee.

Short. 6 m. 2 f. 2 b. 1 g.

In - Wilson. 9: Nov.1934, 120-124.

165. At the Wakehouse by Frank O'Connor.

Short. 3 m. 3 f.

In - Theatre. 10: June 1926, 412-414.

166. At Whitsuntide by Leverett D.G. Bentley.

In - New England. 42(n.s.): May 1910, 331-339.

167. Atla by Kunigunde Duncan.

Short. 4 m. 5 f. 1 g.

In - Poet Lore. 60: March 1965, 3-19.

168. The Atom and Oak Ridge, Tennessee by Marcus Konick.

Radio. 3 m. 1 f.

In - Plays. 5: May 1946, 71-75.

169. **Atomic Insight** by Norman DeMarco.
     Radio. 7 m. 2 f.
     In - Plays. 6: April 1947, 71-75.

170. **Atonement** by James H. Parke.
     Short. 3 m. 1 f.
     In - Poet Lore. 41: Jan.1930, 59-71.

171. **Attic Treasure** by Jean Gould.
     Short. 4 m. 1 f.
     In - Plays. 11: Feb.1952, 81-84.

172. **Attic Treasure** by Helen Louise Miller.
     Short. 4 m. 5 f.
     In - Plays. 24: Jan.1965, 1-13.

173. **Attorney for the Defense** by Graham DuBois.
     Short. 3 m. 4 f.
     In - Plays. 7: March 1948, 21-29.

174. **The Au Pair Man** by Hugh Leonard.
     Full. 1 m. 1 f.
     In - Players. 16: Dec.1968, 35-50+.

175. **The Auction** by Morton Schwartz.
     Short. 5 m. 0 f.
     In - Plays. 10: April 1951, 53-58.

176. **Auf Wiedersehen** by Sada Cowan. Ed. by Margaret
     Mayorga.
     Short. 4 m. 2 f.
     In - Scholastic. 33: Oct.8,1938, 17E-19E.

177. **August for the People** by Nigel Dennis.
     Full. 14 m. 9 f.
     In - Players. 9: Nov. & Dec.1961, 25-33, 25-32.

178. **Aunt Columbia's Dinner Party** by Mary R. Gamble.
     Short. many c.
     In - Ladies' Home. 34: June 1917, 28.

179. **Aunt Lasmi** by Sree Basudeb.
     Short. 6 m. 2 f.
     In - Poet Lore. 35: March 1924, 101-113.

180. **Auntie Mame** by Jerome Lawrence and Robert E.
     Lee. Based on the novel by Patrick Dennis.
     Full. 26 m. 11 f. 2 b. +X.
     In - Theatre. 42: Nov.1958, 27-62.

181. **Author of Liberty** by Mildred Hark and Noel
     McQueen.
     Short. 6 m. 2 f.
     In - Plays. 11: Jan.1952, 20-32.

182. **The Autocrat of the Coffee Stall** by Harold
     Chapin.
     Short. 7 m. 0 f.
     In - Theatre. 5: April 1921, 125-141.

183. **The Autumn Garden** by Lillian Hellman.
     Full. 5 m. 7 f.
     In - Theatre. 35: Sept.- Nov.1951, 62-71,
     62-73, 56-64.

184. **Autumn's Visit** by Lucille Duvall.
     Short. 1 m. 1 f. 11 c. +X.
     In - Plays. 17: Oct.1957, 75-78.

185. **The Awakening** by Francis Adolf Subert.
     Trans. from the Bohemian by Beatrice
     M. Mekota.
     Full. 14 m. 3 f. +X.
     In - Poet Lore. 33:no.2,1922, 159-227.

186. **The Awakening of Ebenezer Scrooge** by Mildred E.
     Myers and Margaretta E. Hoover. Adap. from
     Charles Dickens' A Christmas Carol.
     Short. 14 m. 4 f. 5 b.
     In - Etude. 56: Nov.1938, 709-710.

187. **Ay, There's the Rub** by Graham DuBois.
     Short. 8 m. 2 f.
     In - Plays. 9: Feb.1950, 10-19.

188. **Babe Wins Her Wings** by Leslie Hollingsworth.
     Radio. 2 m. 2 f.
     In - Plays. 6: Oct.1946, 73-77.

189. **Babes in the Wood (as Maeterlinck Would Have
     Written It)** by Winifred Duncan Ward.
     Short. 1 m. 3 f. 1 b. 1 g.
     In - Touchstone. 5: July 1919, 281-285.

190. **The Baby Liked "Greensleeves"** by Margaret
     Widdemer.
     Short. 1 m. 4 f.
     In - Plays. 3: Dec.1943, 35-38.

191. **Background for Nancy** by Susan Manning.
     Short. 3 m. 4 f.
     In - Plays. 7: Jan.1948, 19-27.

192. Background for Nancy by Susan Manning.

   Short. 3 m. 4 f.

   In - Plays. 27: Jan.1968, 27-35.

193. The Backward Jumping Frog by Vernon Howard.

   Short. 6 m. 6 f. +X.

   In - Plays. 15: April 1956, 73-74.

194. Bad Day at Bleak Creek by Elinor R. Alderman.

   Short. 6 m. 4 f.

   In - Plays. 17: Oct.1957, 23-34.

195. Bad News by Henri Lavedan. Trans. from
   the French by William V. Silverberg.

   Short. 1 m. 1 f.

   In - Poet Lore. 30:no.1,1919, 19-24.

196. The Bad Penny by Rachel Field.

   Short. 0 m. 4 f.

   In - Scholastic. 24: March 24,1934, 7-10+.

197. The Bad Seed by Maxwell Anderson. From the
   novel by William March.

   Full. 7 m. 4 f. 1 g.

   In - Theatre. 39: Dec.1955, 35-59.

198. Badlands Ballyhoo by John Murray.

   Short. 7 m. 3 f. +X.

   In - Plays. 21: Jan.1962, 1-13.

199. Bake a Cherry Pie by Mildred Hark and Noel
   McQueen.

   Short. 4 m. 3 f.

   In - Plays. 12: Feb.1953, 1-10.

200. The Baker's Dozen by Hector H. Munro.

   Short. 1 m. 2 f.

   In - Golden. 15: June 1932, 553-556.

201. The Baking Contest by Shirley Simon.

   Short. 3 m. 6 f. +X.

   In - Plays. 18: Feb.1959, 49-54.

202. Balaustion's Euripides by Helen Archibald
   Clarke. (A dramatic version of
   "Balaustion's Adventure" and "Aris-
   tophanes' Apology".

   Full. 26 m. 1 f. +X.

   In - Poet Lore. 26:no.1,1915, 1-37.

203. The Balcony by Gunnar Heiberg. Trans. from
   the Norwegian by Edwin Johan Vickner
   and Glen Hughes.

   Short. 4 m. 1 f.

   In - Poet Lore. 33:no.4,1922, 475-496.

204. A Ballad for the Shy by Earl J. Dias.

   Short. 4 m. 8 f.

   In - Plays. 26: Dec.1966, 21-31.

205. The Balloon by Amos Kenan. Trans. by
   Rosette Lamont.

   Short. 4 m. 2 f.

   In - First Stage. 2: June 1963, 187-193.

206. Band Aid by Helen Louise Miller.

   Short. 5 m. 4 f.

   In - Plays. 4: Oct.1944, 58-66.

207. Bandit Ben Rides Again by Helen Louise
   Miller.

   Short. 12 m. 8 f.

   In - Plays. 21: March 1962, 65-71.

208. The Bar-None Trading Post by Helen Louise Miller

   Short. 7 m. 6 f. +X.

   In - Plays. 23: April 1964, 77-85.

209. Barefoot in Athens by Maxwell Anderson.

   Full. 17 m. 2 f.

210. The Barefoot Trader by Frances B. Watts.

   Short. 2 m. 2 f. 1 b. 1 g.

   In - Plays. 26: Nov.1966, 79-85.

211. A Bargain in Sheets by Mary Elizabeth Rust.

   Short. 0 m. 3 f.

   In - Jl. Home Econ. 27: Jan.1935, 26-28.

212. Bargains in Bonds by Betty Bridgman.

   Short. 0 m. 4 f.

   In - Plays. 4: Jan.1945, 64-71.

213. Baron Barnaby's Box by J.G. Colson.

   Short. 5 m. 4 f.

   In - Plays. 14: March 1955, 73-78.

214. Bath Road by Francis Neilson.

   In - Drama. 13: Feb.- April 1923,
   175-183, 222-228, 260-266.

215. Bartholomew's Joyful Noise by Helen Louise
   Miller.

   Short. 4 m. 4 f.

   In - Plays. 22: Nov.1962, 65-71.

216. The Bashful Bunny by Helen Louise Miller.
      Short. 3 m. 3 f.
      In - Plays. 15: March 1956, 53-60.

217. A Basket of Acorns by Alan S. Feinstein.
      Short. 3 m. 4 f. 2 c. +f.X.
      In - Plays. 17: March 1958, 68-71.

218. Baskets or Bonnets by Helen Louise Miller.
      Short. 8 m. 17 f. 6 c.
      In - Plays. 21: April 1962, 77-83.

219. A Battle of Samurai and Christian Spirits by
             Kido Okamoto.
      Short. 6 m. 4 f. 1 b. 2 g.
      In - Living Age. 314: Aug.26,1922, 532-541.

220. Be Good Sweet Maid by C. E. Webber.
      Full. 6 m. 4 f.
      In - Players. 6: Nov. & Dec.1958, 27-31, 26-31.

221. Be My Ghost by John Murray.
      Short. 5 m. 5 f.
      In - Plays. 14: Oct.1954, 27-38.

222. Be My "Valentine" by Helen Louise Miller.
      Short. 5 m. 5 f. +X.
      In - Plays. 7: Feb.1948, 1-11.

223. Beany's Private Eye by Helen Louise Miller.
      Short. 6 m. 4 f.
      In - Plays. 15: Jan.1956, 1-13.

224. Bears, Bears, Bears by Patricia Goodell.
      Short. 7 m. 4 f. +c.X.
      In - Plays. 15: Feb.1956, 81-85.

225. The Beat of the Wing by François de Curel.
             Trans. from the French by Alice Van
             Kaathoven.
      Full. 5 m. 5 f.
      In - Poet Lore. 20:no.5,1909, 321-375.

226. Beat That Bongo by Betty Tracy Huff.
      Short. 5 m. 7 f. +X.
      In - Plays. 24: Nov.1964, 13-21.

227. The Beatnik and the Bard by Earl J. Dias.
      Short. 3 m. 4 f.
      In - Plays. 20: Oct.1960, 1-12.

228. Beatrice and Benedick by Margaret Mantle.
      Short. 2 m. 3 f. 1 un.
      In - Plays. 14: May 1955, 13-18.

229. A Beau for Nora by Jessie Nicholson.
      Short. 6 m. 7 f.
      In - Plays. 25: March 1966, 1-14.

230. Beauty and the Ballot by Earl J. Dias.
      Short. 4 m. 9 f.
      In - Plays. 26: Nov.1966, 29-39.

231. Beauty and the Beast by Michael T. Leech.
      Short. 2 m. 4 f. 1 "beast".
      In - Plays. 27: March 1968, 85-94.

232. Beauty and the Jacobin by Booth Tarkington.
      Full. 3 m. 2 f.
      In - Harper's M. 125: Aug. & Sept.1912, 390-399,
             539-553.

233. The Bed by Jack Adler.
      Short. 2 m. 1 f.
      In - First Stage. 2: Sept.1963, 390-396.

234. Bedroom Suite by Christopher Morley.
      Short. 2 m. 1 f.
      In - Outlook. 133: Jan.10,1923, 79-82.

235. The Bee by Lilian Saunders.
      In - Drama. 14: Feb.1924, 170-172.

236. Before Breakfast by Eugene O'Neill.
      In - Golden. 15: Feb.1932, 151-156.

237. Before Dawn by Gerhart Hauptmann. Trans.
             by Leonard Bloomfield.
      Full. 10 m. 9 f.
      In - Poet Lore. 20:no.4,1909, 242-315.

238. The Beggars by José Ruibal. Trans. by
             John Pearson.
      Short. 13 un. +X.
      In - First Stage. 7: Sept.1968, 56-63.

239. Belcher's Luck by David Mercer.
      Full. 3 m. 2 f.
      In - Players. 14: Feb.1967, 31-46.

240. Bell, Book and Candle by John Van Druten.
      Full. 3 m. 2 f. 1 cat.
      In - Theatre. 36: June 1952, 50-75.

241. The Bell of Dolores by Camilla Campbell.

   Short. 13 m. 3 f. +X.

   In - Plays. 11: Oct.1951, 17-26.

242. The Bell of Freedom by Peter Sydney Salt.

   Full. 14 m. 5 f. +X.

   In - Poet Lore. 59: March 1964, 3-32.

243. The Belles of Horsefly Gulch by John Murray.

   Short. 7 m. 4 f.

   In - Plays. 21: April 1962, 31-43.

244. Bells Are Ringing by Betty Comden and Adolph Green. Music by Jule Styne.

   Full (musical). 22 m. 7 f.

   In - Theatre. 43: April 1959, 24-51.

245. Beloved Hedgerose by Andreas Gryphius. Trans. by John T. Krumpelmann.

   In - Poet Lore. 39: Dec.1928, 544-572.

246. Beloved It Is Morn by Adelaide Corinne Rowell.

   In - Poet Lore. 36: March 1925, 101-125.

247. Ben Franklin and the King by Paul Green. Abr. by Hermann Hagedorn.

   Short. 8 m. 1 f. +X.

   In - Scholastic. 35: Jan.8,1940, 21E-24E+.

248. Ben Franklin, Peace-Maker by Helen L. Howard.

   Short. 3 m. 1 f.

   In - Plays. 6: Oct.1947, 71-73.

249. Benefit for the Seamen by Charles Angoff.

   In - North Amer. 248: Dec.1939, 234-243.

250. Benjamin West by Ralph Brown and Charles Andes.

   Radio. 6 m. 1 f. 1 b.

251. Bernardine by Mary Chase.

   Full. 12 m. 5 f.

   In - Theatre. 38: March 1954, 34-65.

252. The Best-Dressed Snowman by Claribel Spamer.

   Short. 8 m. 1 f.

   In - Plays. 6: Jan.1947, 55-57.

253. Best Friends by Esther MacLellan and Catherine V. Schroll.

   Short. 2 m. 4 f.

   In - Plays. 16: March 1957, 61-66.

254. The Best Man by Gore Vidal.

   Full. 14 m. 6 f.

   In - Theatre. 45: Sept.1961, 25-56.

255. The Best of All Possible Worlds by Antonio Martínez Ballesteros. English version by Sevilla Gross and Henry F. Salerno.

   Full. 18 m. 2 f. +X.

   In - First Stage. 5: Sept.1966, 172-193.

256. The Best of Sports by Harold Cable.

   Short. 5 m. 3 f.

   In - Plays. 26: May 1967, 1-14.

257. The Best Part of Christmas by Deborah Newman.

   Short. 6 m. 8 f. 8 un. +ch.

   In - Plays. 16: Dec.1956, 58-62.

258. The Best Policy by Helen Louise Miller.

   Short. 5 m. 2 f. +X.

   In - Plays. 11: Feb.1952, 1-11.

259. The Best Year by Mildred Hark and Noel McQueen.

   Short. 8 m. 6 f. +X.

   In - Plays. 16: Jan.1957, 57-62.

260. Bethlehem by Arthur Ketchum.

   Short. 8 m. 1 f. 1 b.

   In - Horn Book. 19: Nov.1943, 435-443.

261. Bethlehem by Laurence Housman.

   Short. 11 m. 1 f.

   In - Scholastic. 47: Dec.10,1945, 17-20.

262. Betsy Ross by Helen M. Roberts.

   Short. 3 m. 2 f. +X.

   In - Plays. 3: Jan.1944, 33-38.

263. Betty Blue's Shoe by Helen Littler Howard.

   Short. 4 m. 2 f.

   In - Plays. 5: May 1946, 58-60.

264. Between Book Covers by Anna Louise Stump and M.M. Heller.

   Radio. 3 un.

   In - Library Jl. 77: Feb.15,1952, 286-289.

265. Between Two Trains by D.C. Pedder.

   Short. 6 m. 3 f.

   In - 19th C. 58: Oct.1905, 649-656.

266. <u>Beware of Rumors</u> by Mildred Hark and Noel McQueen.

Short. 4 m. 0 f. 16 c. +X.

In - Plays. 3: Nov.1943, 76-80.

267. <u>Bewitched and Bewildered</u> by Helen Louise Miller.

Short. 3 m. 7 f. +X.

In - Plays. 10: Oct.1950, 1-11.

268. <u>Beyond Mutiny</u> by Mary Nygaard Peterson.

Short. 10 m. 0 f. +m.X.

In - Plays. 16: Oct.1956, 57-62.

269. <u>Beyond the Horizon</u> by Eugene O'Neill.

Excerpt. 5 m. 1 f.

In - Scholastic. 45: Oct.9,1944, 13-15+.

270. <u>Beyond Thule</u> by Lida Lisle Greene.

Short. 7 m. 1 f.

In - Plays. 9: Oct.1949, 41-48.

271. <u>Beyond Ultraviolet</u> by Cora Burlingame.

Short. 3 m. 3 f.

In - Plays. 7: April 1948, 12-20.

272. <u>The Bible Salesman</u> by Jay Thompson.

Short (musical). 1 m.(white) 1 m. 1 f.(Negro).

In - Theatre. 45: July 1961, 34-39.

273. <u>Big Banker</u> by Samuel S. Richmond.

Short. 5 m. 1 f.

In - Plays. 9: Nov.1949, 74-79.

274. <u>The Big Difference</u> by Herbert Ravatch.

Short. 3 m. 2 f. 8 un.

In - Plays. 18: March 1959, 64-68.

275. <u>Big Fish, Little Fish</u> by Hugh Wheeler.

Full. 5 m. 2 f.

In - Theatre. 46: Sept.1962, 25-56.

276. <u>The Big Idea</u> by Samuel S. Richmond.

Short. 4 m. 2 f.

In - Plays. 5: Oct.1945, 76-82.

277. <u>Big News from Little America</u> by Dorothy Deming.

Short. 5 m. 2 f.

In - Plays. 7: Feb.1948, 56-60.

278. <u>The Big Shoo</u> by Claire Boiko.

Short. 8 m. 1 f. +c.X.

In - Plays. 24: Oct.1964, 41-46.

279. <u>The Biggest Thief in Town</u> by Dalton Trumbo.

Full. 10 m. 2 f.

In - Theatre. 34: Jan.1950, 59-88.

280. <u>Billy Budd</u> by Louis O. Coxe and Robert Chapman. From the novel by Herman Melville

Full. 24 m. 0 f.

In - Theatre. 36: Feb.1952, 50-69.

281. <u>Billy Liar</u> by Keith Waterhouse and Willis Hall.

Full. 3 m. 5 f.

In - Players. 8: March & April,1961, 24-30, 23-31.

282. <u>Billy Liar</u> by Keith Waterhouse and Willis Hall.

Full. 3 m. 5 f.

In - Theatre. 46: May 1962, 27-56.

283. <u>Billy's Train Ride</u> by Mildred L. McLarrin.

Short. 2 m. 1 f. +X.

In - Plays. 8: March 1949, 57-59.

284. <u>Bimbo, the Pirate</u> by Booth Tarkington.

Short. 5 m. 1 f.

In - Ladies. 41: June 1924, 18-19+.

285. <u>Bind Up the Nation's Wounds</u> by Graham DuBois.

Short. 3 m. 4 f.

In - Plays. 16: Feb.1957, 13-22.

286. <u>The Bird Court</u> by Vernon Howard.

Short. 7 m. 5 f.

In - Plays. 15: Nov.1955, 62-64.

287. <u>The Bird Who Couldn't Sing</u> by Hilda Adam Kring.

Short. 2 m. 1 f. 12 un. +X.

In - Plays. 16: April 1957, 65-66.

288. <u>The Birds' Christmas Carol</u> by Kate Douglas Wiggin. Adap. by Helen Louise Miller.

Short. 8 m. 10 f. 1 un. +ch.

In - Plays. 13: Dec.1953, 40-48.

289. <u>The Birds' Christmas Carol</u> by Kate Douglas Wiggin. Adap. by Levy Olfson.

Radio. 10 m. 7 f.

In - Plays. 17: Dec.1957, 87-94.

290. The Birds' Christmas Carol by Kate Douglas
     Wiggin. Adap. by Helen Louise Miller.

     Short. 8 m. 10 f. +c.X.

     In - Plays. 25: Dec.1965, 87-95.

291. Birthday Candles by Margaret Colby Getchell.

     In - Woman's Home. 44: Aug.1917, 23.

292. Birthday Gift by Esther MacLellan and
     Catherine V. Schroll.

     Short. 4 m. 3 f.

     In - Plays. 9: Feb.1950, 75-78.

293. The Birthday of the Infanta by Oscar Wilde.
     Adap. by Paul T. Nolan.

     Short. 9 m. 2 f. +X.

     In - Plays. 24: April 1965, 85-95.

294. Birthday Party for UNICEF by Aileen Fisher and
     Olive Rabe.

     Short. 12 m. 8 f. +X.

     In - Plays. 26: Oct.1966, 47-58.

295. The Birthday Pie by Jane McGowan.

     Short. 6 m. 6 f.

     In - Plays. 23: Feb.1964, 79-83.

296. Birthdays of Frances Willard by Jane Ashman.

     Radio. 7 m. 8 f. +X.

     In - Scholastic. 35: Sept.25,1939, 29-31.

297. Birthplace for a King by Graham DuBois.

     Short. 6 m. 3 f. +X.

     In - Plays. 22: Dec.1962, 15-24.

298. The Bishop Misbehaves by Frederick Jackson.
     Ed. by Margaret Mayorga

     Short. 7 m. 3 f.

     In - Scholastic. 32: May 21,1938, 17E-19E.

299. The Bishop's Candlesticks adap. by Levy
     Olfson from Victor Hugo's Les Miserables.

     Radio. 7 m. 6 f.

     In - Plays. 16: Feb.1957, 89-96.

300. The Bishop's Candlesticks by Victor Hugo. Adap.
     from Les Miserables by Levy Olfson.

     Short. 6 m. 2 f.

     In - Plays. 22: Dec.1962, 25-33.

301. The Bitterly Reviled by Lucy Lowe.

     Short. 1 m. 4 f. 1 baby. +X.

     In - Poet Lore. 33:no.2,1922, 300-307.

302. Black Beauty by Anna Sewell. Adap. by Levy
     Olfson.

     Radio. 17 m. 4 f. 1 b. 1 g.

     In - Plays. 17: March 1958, 89-96.

303. Black Blizzard by Aileen Fisher.

     Short. 3 m. 2 f.

     In - Plays. 10: Oct.1950, 39-44.

304. The Black Bottle by Seumas O'Brien.

     Short. 5 m. 2 f. +X.

     In - Scholastic. 50: March 17,1947, 17-18+.

305. Black Comedy by Peter Shaffer.

     Short. 5 m. 3 f.

     In - Players. 15: April 1968, 42-46+.

306. The Black Indies by Jules Verne. Adap. by Levy
     Olfson.

     Short. 7 m. 4 f.

     In - Plays. 25: April 1966, 81-91.

307. Black Ivo by John G. Colson.

     Short. 8 m. 0 f.

     In - Plays. 12: Jan.1953, 40-50.

308. Black Sheep by John Markey.

     In - Canadian M. 48: Feb.1917, 345-348.

309. The Blackbird by Vernon Howard.

     Short. 5 m. 0 f.

     In - Plays. 14: Jan.1955, 84-87.

310. The Blaumilch Canal by Ephraim Kishon.

     Radio. 15 m. 3 f. +X.

     In - Gambit. 3: no.12, 69-88.

311. Blind Alley by M.C. Richmond.

     Short. 7 m. 0 f. +m.X.

     In - Indus. Arts. 17: July 1928, 238-241.

312. Blithe Spirit by Noel Coward.

     Excerpt. 1 m. 2 f.

     In - Life. 11: Dec.8,1941, 91-92+.

313. Blockade by Olivia Howard Dunbar.

     Short. 3 m. 2 f. 1 g.

     In - Theatre. 7: April 1923, 127-142.

314. Blockhead by Ludwig Fulda. Trans. by Anna
     Emilia Bagdad.

     In - Poet Lore. 39: March 1928, 3-92.

     The Blow of Thunder.

              see

     Two Milords.

315. The Blue Serge Suit by Vernon Howard.

     Short. 6 m. 0 f.

     In - Plays. 13: Oct.1953, 64-66.

316. The Blue Toadstool by Melanie Bellah.

     Short. 6 un.

     In - Plays. 9: March 1950, 65-68.

317. Bluebird's Children by Samuel S. Richmond.

     Short. 3 m. 3 f.

     In - Plays. 4: May 1945, 70-73.

318. The Blushing Bunny by Claribel Spamer.

     Short. 3 m. 2 f.

     In - Plays. 17: April 1958, 78-80.

319. Bo-Peep's Valentine by Helen L. Howard.

     Short. 6 m. 3 f.

     In - Plays. 5: Feb.1946, 61-63.

320. The Boat Club Dance by Christina Robinson.

     Short. 3 m. 6 f.

     In - Plays. 22: April 1963, 11-22.

321. The Boat in the Forest by Nicolai Haitov.
     Trans. from the Polish by Donna and
     Kevin Ireland.

     Short. 1 m. 1 f.

     In - Gambit. 3: no.12, 15-38.

322. Bob and the Indians by Ernestine Horvath and
     Florence Horvath.

     Short. 0 m. 0 f. 6 b.

     In - Etude. 59: May 1941, 356.

323. Bobby and the Lincoln Speech by Edrie
     Pendleton.

     Short. 3 m. 3 f.

     In - Plays. 14: Feb.1955, 56-65.

324. Bob's Armistice Parade by Lucille Streacker.

     Short. 7 m. 5 f. +X.

     In - Plays. 5: Nov.1945, 44-47.

325. The Bogie Men by Lady Gregory.

     Short. 2 m. 0 f.

     In - Fortnightly. 98: Dec.1912, 1165-1174.

326. The Bogie Men By Lady Gregory.

     Short. 2 m. 0 f.

     In - Forum. 49: Jan.1913, 28-40.

327. Bohboh, Beebee, and Booboo by Helen L. Howard.

     Short. 6 m. 2 f.

     In - Plays. 5: March 1946, 54-56.

328. La Boheme by Giacomo Puccini. English Adap.
     by Howard Dietz.

     Full (opera). 8 m. 2 f. +ch.

     In - Theatre. 37: Dec.1953, 34-60.

329. A Bolt From the Blue by Harry Major Paull.

     Short. 3 m. 2 f.

     In - 19th C. 94: Dec.1923, 843-855.

330. Bonds of Affection by Graham DuBois.

     Short. 3 m. 3 f.

     In - Plays. 15: Jan.1956, 14-24.

331. Bondwomen by Alexander Ostrovsky.

     In - Poet Lore. 36: Dec.1925, 475-541.

332. Bonnie Annie by Helen Q. Lathers.

     Radio. 6 m. 1 f.

     In - Plays. 7: April 1948, 81-86.

333. The Boo-Hoo Princess by Ruth Jaeger Buntain.

     Short. 2 m. 2 f. +X.

     In - Plays. 12: Jan.1953, 63-67.

334. The Booby Trap by Helen Louise Miller.

     Short. 2 m. 2 f.

     In - Plays. 3: April 1944, 63-72.

335. The Book Hospital by Jean Brabham McKinney.

     Short. 4 m. 4 f.

     In - Plays. 21: Nov.1961, p.73-76.

336. The Book Revue by Mildred Hark and Noel
     McQueen.

     Short. 17 m. 13 f. 3 c.

     In - Plays. 14: Nov.1954, 85-89.

337. The Book that Saved the Earth by Claire Boiko.

Short. 6 m. 0 f.

In - Plays. 27: Jan.1968, 37-42.

338. Book Week Birthday Party by Mary Anne Kernan.

Short. 3 m. 6 f. 1 un.

In - Wilson. 15: Oct.1940, 154-156.

339. Books à la Mode by Mildred Hark and Noel McQueen.

Short. 7 m. 6 f.

In - Plays. 17: Nov.1957, 80-94.

340. Books Are Bridges by Mildred Hark and Noel McQueen.

Short. 2 m. 3 f.

In - Plays. 6: Nov.1946, 60-67.

341. Books Have Wings by Benjamin P. Indick.

Short. 9 m. 5 f. 6 c.X.

In - Plays. 24: Nov.1964, 63-66.

342. Books in the Woods. (Anon.)

Short. 3 m. 0 f. 2 b. 2 g.

In - Wilson. 10: Oct.1935, 114-117.

343. Books to the Rescue by Mildred Hark and Noel McQueen.

Short. 4 m. 3 f.

In - Plays. 14: Nov.1954, 73-84.

344. The Bookworm by Gwen Chaloner.

Short. 4 m. 4 f. 8 un.

In - Plays. 20: Nov.1960, 35-40.

345. Boomerang by Helen Louise Miller.

Short. 2 m. 2 f.

In - Plays. 9: Jan.1950, 1-10.

346. Boomerang by Helen Louise Miller.

Short. 2 m. 1 f.

In - Plays. 16: April 1957, 25-33.

347. The Boor by Anton Chekhov. Trans. by Hilmar Baukage.

Short. 4 m. 1 f. +X.

In - Golden. 2: Nov.1925, 654-660.

348. Borga Gard by Tor Hedberg. Trans. from the Swedish.

In - Poet Lore. 32: Sept.1921, 317-374.

349. Boris Godunov by Modest Mussorgsky. From the play by Pushkin. English text by John Gutman.

Full (opera). 17 m. 4 f.

In - Theatre. 43: March 1959, 25-43.

350. Born to the Soil by Samuel S. Richmond.

Short. 5 m. 1 f.

In - Plays. 4: Dec.1944, 72-78.

351. Boshibari and the Two Thieves by Paul T. Nolan.

Short. 3 m. 0 f.

In - Plays. 19: Oct.1959, 82-86.

352. Bos'n by Dorothy Kaucher.

In - Poet Lore. 36: Dec.1925, 583-599.

353. Boston Tea-Party by Constance D'Arcy Mackay.

In - Woman's Home. 38: June 1911, 13.

354. The Boston Tea Party by Lindsey Barbee.

Short. 3 m. 4 f.

In - Plays. 5: May 1946, 42-47.

355. Bottled in Bond by Glenn Hughes.

In - Drama. 13: Feb.1923, 170-173.

356. Bow to the Queen by J.G. Colson.

Short. 7 m. 1 f.

In - Plays. 11: April 1952, 47-54.

357. The Bow-Wow Blues by Earl J. Dias.

Short. 4 m. 3 f.

In - Plays. 19: Oct.1959, 17-28.

358. The Boy Bowditch by Riley Hughes.

Radio. 8 m. 0 f.

In - Plays. 3: May 1944, 77-81.

359. The Boy Dreamer by Helen Roberts.

Short. 6 m. 2 f.

In - Plays. 3: Oct.1943, 25-32.

360. The Boy From Nebraska by Millard Lampell.

Radio. 10 m. 0 f.

In - Scholastic. 49: Oct.14,1946, 17-19.

Boy Gets Book.

see

The Masque of Tomes.

361. The Boy Next Door by John Murray.
Short. 2 m. 3 f.
In - Plays. 14: Nov.1954, 25-38.

362. The Boy Who Could Not Tell a Lie by Alice Very.
Short. 6 m. 2 f. +X.
In - Plays. 6: Feb.1947, 69-71.

363. The Boy Who Didn't Belong by Helen Louise Miller.
Short. 9 m. 4 f. +X.
In - Plays. 8: Dec.1948, 1-11.

364. Boy With a Future by Mildred Hark and Noel McQueen.
Short. 4 m. 6 f. +X.
In - Plays. 5: Jan.1946, 39-44.

365. The Boy with the Bagpipe by Louise Metcalfe Isom.
Short. 7 m. 0 f.
In - Plays. 18: May 1959, 49-54.

366. Boys in Books by Helen Louise Miller.
Short. 15 m. 0 f. +m.X.
In - Plays. 13: Nov.1953, 77-83.

367. Brave Admiral by Bernard Hirshberg.
Short. 2 m. 1 f. +X.
In - Plays. 4: Oct.1944, 27-31.

368. The Brave But Once by Graham DuBois.
Short. 4 m. 5 f.
In - Plays. 5: April 1946, 10-18.

369. Brave Little Indian Brave by Rose M. Holler.
Short. 6 m. 2 f.
In - Plays. 11: April 1952, 36-46.

370. The Brave Little Tailor adap. by Adele Thane from Grimms' Fairy Tales.
Short. 8 m. 4 f. 7 c.
In - Plays. 26: Feb.1967, 49-57.

371. The Bravest Flower by Claribel Spamer.
Short. 3 m. 5 f.
In - Plays. 6: May 1947, 57-58.

372. Bread and Butter by Cecil P. Taylon
Full. 2 m. 2 f.
In - Players. 14: Oct.1966, 31-46+.

373. The Bread and Butter Shop by Helen Louise Miller.
Short. 12 m. 10 f.
In - Plays. 24: Jan.1965, 69-77.

374. Breadline by Philip Ketchum.
Short. 22 m. 0 f.
In - Survey. 22: Aug.1933, 414-416.

375. The Bremen Town Musicians by Mildred Hark McQueen.
Short. 4 m. 4 un.
In - Plays. 21: Jan.1962, 79-84.

376. The Bridal Dinner by A.R. Gurney, Jr.
Full. 12 m. 7 f. 1 b. 1 g.
In - First Stage. 4: March 1965, 33-56.

377. The Bride's Christmas Tree by Beatrice Herford.
Short. 4 m. 4 f.
In - Ladies' Home. 28: Dec.1911, 14+.

378. Bridging the Gap by Geneva C. Turner and Jessie H. Roy.
In - Negro History. 20: March 1957, 133-137.

379. Briefly Speaking by Paul S. McCoy.
Short. 2 m. 2 f.
In - Plays. 17: Feb.1958, 81-86.

380. Brigadoon by Alan Jay Lerner. Music by Frederick Loewe.
Full (musical). 10 m. 5 f. +ch.
In - Theatre. 36: Aug.1952, 48-65.

381. Bright Corner by Karin Asbrand.
Short. 5 m. 14 f.
In - Plays. 5: March 1946, 43-46.

382. Bright Stream by Mary Thurman Pyle.
Short. 4 m. 5 f.
In - Plays. 11: March 1952, 55-62.

383. Bringing Up Father by Aileen Fisher and Olive Rabe.
Short. 3 m. 3 f.
In - Plays. 15: Nov.1955, 51-55.

384. A Broadway Turkey by Jane McGowan.
Short. 4 m. 3 f.
In - Plays. 20: Nov.1960, 1-12.

385. The Broken Broomstick by Helen Louise Miller.
Short. 5 m. 3 f. 6 c. +X.
In - Plays. 18: Oct.1958, 69-73.

386. The Broken Doll by Claribel Spamer.
Short. 12 m. 4 f.
In - Plays. 7: Jan.1948, 51-53.

387. Broken Pines by Charles Hilton.
Short. 5 m. 1 f.
In - Poet Lore. 40: Sept.1929, 461-473.

388. The Brooding Calves by Hans Sachs. Trans.
by John T. Krumpelmann.
Short. 2 m. 1 f.

389. Broom Market Day by Lida Lisle Greene.
Short. 5 m. 4 f.
In - Plays. 6: Oct.1947, 37-43.

390. The Broomstick Beauty by Helen Louise Miller.
Short. 2 m. 4 f.
In - Plays. 6: Oct.1947, 1-10.

391. The Broth of Christkindle by Eleanore Leuser.
Short. 5 m. 3 f. +ch.
In - Plays. 9: Dec.1949, 50-54.

392. Brother Bill by Alfred Kreymborg.
Short. 1 m. 1 f.
In - Theatre. 11: April 1927, 299-306.

393. Brother Wolf by Laurence Housman.
Short. 7 m. 0 f.
In - 19th C. 88: Nov.1920, 813-823.

394. Brothers-In-Arms by Walter Frith.
Short. 3 m. 0 f.
In - Living Age. 281: April 18,1914, 166-175.

395. The Brownie Who Found Christmas by Adele Thane.
Short. 7 m. 4 f. +m.X.
In - Plays. 20: Dec.1960, 53-58.

396. Brushes for Benjy by Eleanore Leuser.
Short. 9 m. 2 f. +X.
In - Plays. 12: Nov.1952, 52-57.

397. Bud for President by Mildred Hark and Noel
McQueen.
Short. 3 m. 2 f.
In - Plays. 6: Nov.1946, 21-28.

398. Bud on Nantucket Island by Thomas Beer.
Short. 5 m. 4 f.
In - Scribner's. 91: Jan.1932, 43-47.

399. The Builder of the Wall by Helen Roberts.
Short. 6 m. 3 f.
In - Plays. 4: May 1945, 41-48.

400. The Bull Terrier and the Baby by Helen M.
Givens.
Short. 2 m. 2 f.
In - Ladies' Home. 23: Oct.1906, 15.

401. Bumblepuppy by John William Rogers, Jr.
Short. 3 m. 0 f.
In - Theatre. 10: Sept.1926, 604-612.

402. A Bunch of Keys by Mildred Hark and Noel
McQueen.
Short. 3 m. 3 f.
In - Plays. 5: Nov.1945, 60-66.

403. Bunnies and Bonnets by Helen Louise Miller.
Short. 6 m. 9 f. +g.X.
In - Plays. 12: April 1953, 77-86.

404. Bunnies and Bonnets by Helen Louise Miller.
Short. 6 m. 9 f. +g.X.
In - Plays. 25: April 1966, 43-52.

405. Bunny Comes to Town by Graham DuBois.
Short. 3 m. 2 f.
In - Plays. 6: Dec.1946, 30-39.

406. Bunny of the Year by Deborah Newman.
Short. 8 m. 2 f. +X.
In - Plays. 9: April 1950, 59-62.

407. Bunny Picnic by Esther MacLellan and
Catherine V. Schroll.
Short. 2 m. 3 f.
In - Plays. 8: April 1949, 63-65.

408. The Bunny Who Was Always Late by Claribel
Spamer.
Short. 3 m. 1 f. +c.X.
In - Plays. 9: April 1950, 57-59.

409.   The Bunnyland Brigade by Claribel Spamer.
       Short. 7 m. 1 f.
       In - Plays. 8: April 1949, 69-72.

410.   The Burial Committee by Otway Crockett.
       Full. 6 m. 0 f.
       In - First Stage. 5: Dec.1966, 199-220.

411.   Buried Treasure by June Barr.
       Short. 7 m. 3 f.
       In - Plays. 12: Feb.1953, 58-61.

412.   Buried Treasure by June Barr.
       Short. 7 m. 3 f.
       In - Plays. 24: March 1965, 77-80.

413.   Bury the Dead by Irwin Shaw.
       Excerpt. 8 m. 6 f.
       In - Scholastic. 31: Nov.6,1937, 8-10+.

414.   Bus Stop by William Inge.
       Full. 5 m. 3 f.
       In - Theatre. 40: Oct.1956, 33-56.

415.   Bus Trip by Robert St. Clair.
       Short. 2 m. 3 f. +X.
       In - Plays. 19: Feb.1960, 25-36.

416.   Business is Business by Samuel S. Richmond.
       Short. 7 m. 4 f.
       In - Plays. 4: Jan.1945, 72-79.

417.   A Business Meeting by Arlo Bates.
       Short. 0 m. 10 f.
       In - Ladies' Home. 20: March 1903, 15.

418.   The Buskers by Kenneth Jupp.
       Full. 8 m. 3 f.
       In - Players. 6: May & June 1959, 27-31, 27-32.

419.   Buster Picks a Winner by Samuel S. Richmond.
       Short. 2 m. 3 f.
       In - Plays. 10: April 1951, 73-78.

420.   The Busy Barbers by Helen Louise Miller.
       Short. 14 m. 23 f.
       In - Plays. 17: March 1958, 63-67.

421.   The Busy Martyr by George Hitchcock.
       Full. 17 m. 8 f. +X.
       In - First Stage. 2: Dec.1962, 46-68.

422.   But One Life to Give by Graham DuBois.
       Short. 4 m. 3 f.
       In - Plays. 8: Nov.1948, 9-18.

423.   The Butterfly by Lucine Finch.
       Short. 1 m. (a faun) 3 f.
       In - Poet Lore. 21:no.5,1910, 401-414.

424.   By Order of the King by Aileen Fisher.
       Short. 8 m. 4 f. +X.
       In - Plays. 13: Nov.1953, 47-57.

425.   By the Sumida River by Colin Campbell Clements.
       In - Poet Lore. 31: June 1920, 166-175.

426.   C. C. by Mody C. Boatright.
       Short. 8 m. 1 f. +m.X.
       In - Poet Lore. 41: Jan.1930, 124-131.

427.   Cabana Blues by Mildred Hark and Noel
             McQueen.
       Short. 4 m. 3 f.
       In - Plays. 14: April 1955, 20-30.

428.   Caesar and Cleopatra by George Bernard Shaw.
       Full. 23 m. 4 f.
       In - Theatre. 34: Sept.1950, 53-88.

429.   Calculated Risk by Joseph Hayes.
       Full. 11 m. 3 f.
       In - Theatre. 47: Dec.1963, 20-54.

430.   Caleb Stone's Death Watch by Martin A. Flavin.
       In - Drama. 14: Jan.1924, 143-147.

431.   Ca'line by Bernice Kelly Harris.
       Short. 4 m. 3 f. +X.
       In - Carolina. 5: Sept.1932, 74-88.

432.   The Caliph's Journey by Adele Thane.
       Short. 4 m. +c.X.
       In - Plays. 21: Jan.1962, 62-68.

433.   Call Washington 1776 by Helen Louise Miller.
       Short. 7 m. 7 f.
       In - Plays. 24: Feb.1965, 3-15.

434. The Callers by Alice Very.
Short. 2 m. 4 f.
In - Plays. 7: Dec.1947, 63-66.

435. Callie Goes to Camp by Ella Williams Porter.
Short. 0 m. 4 f.
In - Plays. 9: May 1950, 52-58.

436. Calling All Christmases by Aileen Fisher.
Short. 7 m. 5 f. +c.ch.
In - Plays. 21: Dec.1961, 89-96.

437. Calling All Planets by Florence E. Dennler.
Short. 1 m. 8 c.
In - Plays. 19: Feb.1960, 79-82.

438. The Camelia Costumes by Marcella Rave.
Short. 5 m. 6 f.
In - Plays. 20: March 1961, 27-38.

439. Camino Real by Tennessee Williams.
Full. 26 m. 12 f.
In - Theatre. 38: Aug.1954, 36-65.

440. The Canary by Josephine Henry Whitehouse.
Short. 4 m. 1 f.
In - Poet Lore. 37: Dec.1926, 589-596.

441. Candaules, Commissioner by Daniel C. Gerould.
Short. 2 m. 1 f.
In - First Stage. 4: Sept.1965, 150-167.

442. Candles for Christmas by Helen L. Howard.
Short. 2 m. 0 f. 2 b. 2 g.
In - Plays. 13: Dec.1953, 75-76.

443. Candy Canes by Claribel Spamer.
Short. 4 m. 1 f.
In - Plays. 6: Dec.1946, 74-76.

444. The Canterbury Tales by Geoffrey Chaucer.
Adap. by Lewy Olfson
Radio. 18 m. 6 f.
In - Plays. 22: May 1963, 97-107.

445. The Canterville Ghost by Oscar Wilde. Adap.
by Walter Hackett.
Radio. 8 m. 4 f.
In - Plays. 7: Feb.1948, 75-84.

446. The Canterville Ghost by Oscar Wilde.
Adap. by Walter Hackett
Radio. 6 m. 4 f.
In - Plays. 23: March 1965, 85-94.

447. The Cape of Feathers by Esther E. Ziegler.
Short. 9 m. 4 f. +X.
In - Plays. 13: May 1954, 46-58.

448. A Caprice by Alfred de Musset. Trans. from
the French by Anne Grace Wirt.
Short. 1 m. 2 f.
In - Poet-Lore. 33: Sept.1922, 395-419.

449. Captain Castaway's Captives by Helen Louise
Miller.
Short. 13 m. 4 f.
In - Plays. 27: May 1968, 59-68.

450. Captains Courageous by Rudyard Kipling.
Adap. by Lewy Olfson.
Radio. 9 m. 3 f.
In - Plays. 15: April 1956, 79-87.

451. The Car Lover by Bruce Jay Friedman.
Short. 2 m. 0 f.
In Esquire. 69: June 1968, 120+.

452. The Cardboard Star by Olive Phillips.
Short. 4 m. 2 f.
In - Plays. 27: Dec.1967, 1-11.

453. Career by James Lee.
Full. 11 m. 4 f.
In - Theatre. 41: Nov.1957, 36-61.

454. Careless Ness the Dragon by Bernice McMahon.
Short. 4 m. 1 f. 1 "dragon" +ch.
In - Plays. 27: March 1968, 81-84.

455. Carfare Home by Helen Diehl Olds.
Radio. 3 m. 7 f.
In - Plays. 7: Jan.1948, 60-66.

456. Carlos Among the Candles by Wallace Stevens.
Short. 1 m. 0 f.
In - Poetry. 11: Dec.1917, 115-123.

457. Carnival Saturday by Anton Arrufat.
Short. 1 m. 2 f.
In - Américas. 10: Oct.1958, 20-25.

458. A Carol for Santa ed. by Elizabeth A. Gest.
     Short. 1 m. 4 b. 4 g.
     In - Etude. 68: Dec.1950, 54.

459. Carol's Christmas Cards by Robert St.Clair.
     Short. 2 m. 4 f.
     In - Plays. 20: Dec.1960, 25-36.

460. The Case for Books by Mildred Hark and Noel
     McQueen.
     Short. 4 m. 3 f.
     In - Plays. 10: Nov.1950, 57-69.

461. The Case for Books by Mildred Hark and Noel
     McQueen.
     Short. 4 m. 3 f.
     In - Plays. 26: Nov.1966, 15-28.

462. A Case for Mrs. Hudson by John Murray.
     Short. 3 m. 3 f.
     In - Plays. 11: April 1952, 1-14.

463. A Case for Two Detectives by John Murray.
     Short. 6 m. 6 f.
     In - Plays. 15: April 1956, 13-22.

464. A Case for Two Detectives by John Murray.
     Short. 6 m. 6 f.
     In - Plays. 18: Oct.1958, 25-34.

465. A Case of Mistaken Identity by John Murray.
     Short. 4 m. 4 f.
     In - Plays. 22: March 1963, 13-24.

466. The Case of Mr. X by Samuel S. Richmond.
     Short. 3 m. 3 f.
     In - Plays. 9: April 1950, 66-71.

467. The Case of the Easter Bonnet by Helen Louise
     Miller.
     Short. 3 m. 4 f.
     In - Plays. 7: April 1948, 1-11.

468. The Case of the Forgetful Easter Rabbit by
     Helen Louise Miller.
     Short. 9 m. 7 f. 7 c.
     In - Plays. 24: April 1965, 63-69.

469. The Case of the Frustrated Corpse by Ruth
     Wallace.
     Short. 2 m. 2 f.
     In - Plays. 19: Feb.1960, 88-90.

470. The Case of the Giggling Goblin by Helen
     Louise Miller.
     Short. 11 m. 7 f. 8 c.
     In - Plays. 28: Oct.1968, 47-54.

471. The Case of the Missing Masterpiece by
     Betty Tracy Huff.
     Short. 3 m. 6 f.
     In - Plays. 21: Jan.1962, 15-24.

472. The Case of the Missing Parents by John A.
     Campbell.
     Short. 9 m. 0 f.
     In - Plays. 17: March 1958, 61-62.

473. The Case of the Missing Pearls by Earl J.
     Dias.
     Short. 6 m. 4 f.
     In - Plays. 16: March 1957, 37-47.

474. The Case of the Missing Poet by John Murray.
     Short. 5 m. 3 f.
     In - Plays. 12: April 1953, 27-37.

475. The Case of the Silent Caroler by Helen
     Louise Miller.
     Short. 4 m. 4 f. +X.
     In - Plays. 11: Dec.1951, 1-11.

476. The Case of the Silent Caroler by Helen
     Louise Miller.
     Short. 4 m. 4 f. +X.
     In - Plays. 17: Dec.1957, 33-43.

477. The Case of the Wall Street Bear by John
     Murray.
     Short. 4 m. 4 f.
     In - Plays. 20: Jan.1961, 21-33.

478. Cash - $2,000 by Nathan G. Chatterton.
     Short. 2 m. 2 f.
     In - Drama. 15: Jan.1925, 78-80.

479. Cassandra Singing by David Madden.
     Full. 8 m. 6 f.
     In - First Stage. 2: March 1963, 99-132.

480. Cast Up by the Sea by Earl J. Dias.
     Short. 5 m. 3 f.
     In - Plays. 20: May 1961, 33-43.

481. A Castle in Spain by Jessie Nicholson.
     Short. 4 m. 4 f.
     In - Plays. 21: Nov.1961, 1-12.

482. The Cat by Otto F. Walter. Trans. by Derk
     Wynand.
     Full. 2 m. 2 f.
     In - Gambit. 4: no.15, 5-64.

483. The Cat and the Moon by William Butler Yeats.
     Short. 3 m. 0 f.
     In - Dial. 77: July 1924, 23-30.

484. Cat and the Queen by Lida Lisle Molloy.
     Short. 2 m. 8 f.
     In - Plays. 6: Nov.1946, 42-46.

485. The Cat and the Queen by Rowena Bennett.
     Short. 8 m. 1 f. +X.
     In - Plays. 22: Feb.1963, 72-74.

486. A Cat for Halloween by Esther McLellan and
     Catherine V. Schroll.
     Short. 3 m. 5 f. +X.
     In - Plays. 12: Oct.1952, 48-52.

487. A Cat Has Not Always Carnival by Alexander
     Ostrovsky. Trans. by Jane Paxton
     Campbell and George Rapall Noyes.
     Full. 2 m. 4 f.
     In - Poet Lore. 40: Sept.1929, 317-372.

     A Cat in the Ghetto.
        see
     The Windows of Heaven.

488. Cat on a Hot Tin Roof by Tennessee Williams.
     Full. 10 m. 7 f.
     In - Theatre. 41: June 1957, 33-71.

489. The Cat Who Wanted to Ride on a Broom by
     Alice Very.
     Short. 2 m. 1 f. +X.
     In - Plays. 4: Oct.1944, 49-51.

490. Catastrophe Clarence by Maxine Shore.
     Short. 6 m. 0 f.
     In - Plays. 15: March 1956, 43-52.

491. Catch as Catch Can by Aileen Fisher.
     Short. 1 m. 9 un.
     In - Plays. 13: Jan.1954, 65-70.

492. The Catnip Patch by Gladys V. Smith.
     Short. 20 c.
     In - Plays. 20: March 1961, 75-78.

493. The Cats and the Cheese by June Barr.
     Short. 3 un.
     In - Plays. 8: March 1949, 59-61.

494. Caught at the Narrows by Aileen Fisher.
     Short. 3 m. 3 f.
     In - Plays. 9: Jan.1950, 45-52.

495. Caught - One Snipe by Samuel S. Richmond.
     Short. 6 m. 0 f. 1 b.
     In - Plays. 5: Jan.1946, 67-71.

496. Cause for Gratitude by Graham DuBois.
     Short. 2 m. 6 f.
     In - Plays. 15: Nov.1955, 14-20.

497. A Cause to Serve by Graham DuBois.
     Short. 5 m. 4 f.
     In - Plays. 4: Dec.1944, 20-27.

498. Cavalcade of Human Rights by Aileen Fisher
     and Olive Rabe.
     Short. 30 m. 8 f. +ch. +X.
     In - Plays. 15: Oct.1955, 63-85.

499. Cavalcade of Human Rights by Aileen Fisher
     and Olive Rabe.
     Pageant. 30 m. 8 f. +X.
     In - Plays. 24: May 1965, 99-122.

500. The Cave by Edmund B. Hennefeld.
     Full. 2 m. 2 f.
     In - First Stage. 4: June 1965, 108-136.

501. The Cave at Machpelah by Paul Goodman.
     Short. 13 m. 1 f. 1 b.
     In - Commentary. 25: June 1958, 512-517.

502. The Cave Dwellers by William Saroyan.
     Full. 9 m. 5 f.
     In - Theatre. 42: Dec.1958, 27-42.

503. Cave Man, Brave Man by Juliet Garver.
     Short. 2 m. 3 f.
     In - Plays. 19: May 1960, 13-22.

504. Cave of Precious Things by Alice Wangenheim.
     Short. 3 m. 1 f. 4 b. 1 g. +m.X.
     In - Jl. Home Econ. 11: May 1919, 215-220.

505. Caves of the Earth by Aileen Fisher.

      Short. 5 m. 2 f. +X.

      In - Plays. 6: May 1947, 11-15.

506. Cecily Entertains the Enemy by Helen E.
           Waite.

      Short. 2 m. 4 f.

      In - Plays. 14: Feb.1955, 32-42.

507. The Century Plant by Frank J. Conboy.

      Short. 7 m. 2 f.

      In - Plays. 17: Jan.1958, 43-49.

508. Cesaire by Jean Schlumberger.

      Short. 3 m. 0 f.

      In - Living Age. 312: Jan.14,1922, 106-115.

509. The Chairs by Eugene Ionesco.

      Short. 2 m. 1 f.

      In - Theatre. July 1958, 26-38.

510. The Chalk Garden by Enid Bagnold.

      Full. 2 m. 6 f.

      In - Players. 4: April & May 1957, 23-31,
           24-31.

511. A Challenge to Young America by Jane L.
           Baker.

      Short. 3 m. 1 f.

      In - Plays. 3: Oct.1943, 65-69.

512. A Change of Mind by Russell F. Speirs.

      Short. 1 m. 2 f.

      In - Drama. 20: Oct.1929, 13-14.

513. Changing of the Guard by Raúl Ruiz. Trans.
           by Miller Williams.

      Short. 2 m. 0 f. 1 b.

      In - First Stage. 5: Dec.1966, 238-243.

514. Charivari by Nan Bagby Stephens.

      Short. 3 m. 2 f.

      In - Theatre. 12: Nov.1928, 814-822.

515. Charles! Charles! by Laurence Housman.

      Short. 8 m. 0 f.

      In - 19th C. 105: Jan.1929, 127-142.

516. Charlie Barringer by John Joseph Martin.

      Short. 3 m. 0 f.

      In - Theatre. 5: July 1921, 242-248.

517. Cheers for Miss Bishop. From movie based on
           story by Bess Streeter Aldrich.

      Excerpt. 7 m. 4 f.

      In - Scholastic. 38: March 3,1941, 17-19+.

518. Cherry-Blossom River by Colin Campbell
           Clements.

      In - Poet Lore. 31: June 1920, 159-165.

519. Chicken Soup With Barley by Arnold Wesker.

      Full. 6 m. 4 f.

      In - Players. 7 & 8: Sept. & Oct.1960,
           23-29, 25-31.

520. Chief Halloween Spirit by Ann Muni.

      Short. 5 m. 3 f.

      In - Plays. 17: Oct.1957, 66-68.

521. Chi-fu by William Justema, Jr.

      In - Drama. 13: Aug.1923, 356.

522. A Child is Born by Stephen Vincent Benét.

      Radio. 8 m. 3 f. +ch.

      In - Sat. Review. 25: Dec.26,1942, 7-9.

523. A Child of Destiny by Graham DuBois.

      Short. 7 m. 2 f.

      In - Plays. 5: Oct.1945, 16-24.

524. Child of Her Spirit by Graham DuBois.

      Short. 3 m. 3 f.

      In - Plays. 6: Jan.1947, 12-20.

525. The Child Who Was Made of Snow adap. by
           Rowena Bennett from a Russian folk tale.

      Short. 1 m. 2 f. many c.

      In - Plays. 26: Dec.1966, 72-74.

526. Childhood by Thornton Wilder.

      Short. 1 m. 1 f. 1 b. 2 g.

      In - Atlantic. 206: Nov.1960, 78-84.

527. Childhood and Youth of Edvard Grieg by
           James F. Cooke.

      Short. 7 m. 3 f.

      In - Etude. 62: Oct.1944, 561-562.

528. The Children by C. Hutchinson Ruthenburg.

      Short. 1 m. 2 f.

      In - Drama. 15: March 1925, 131-132.

529. Children is All by James Purdy.

      Short. 2 m. 3 f.

      In - Mlle. 56: Nov.1962, 108-109+.

530. The Children of Chocolate Street by Eleanora
     Bowling Kane.
     Short. 2 m. 8 f.
     In - Plays. 10: Dec.1950, 54-59.

531. Children of the Calendar by Carol Hartley.
     Short. 7 m. 6 f.
     In - Plays. 6: Jan.1947, 50-53.

532. The Children of the Sun by Maxim Gorki.
     Trans. from the Russian by Archibald
     John Wolfe.
     Full. 10 m. 6 f.
     In - Poet Lore. 17:no.2,1906, 1-77.

533. Children of the Sun by Charles Rittenhouse.
     Short. 16 m. 7 f.
     In - Plays. 5: April 1946, 57-66.

534. Children of the Sunrise by Julia P. Dabney.
     Full. 9 m. 7 f. +X.
     In - Poet Lore. 26:no.6,1915, 653-693.

535. The Children's Hour by Lillian Hellman.
     Full. 2 m. 14 f.
     In - Theatre. 37: May 1953, 34-63.

536. China Comes to You by Karin Asbrand.
     Short. 8 m. 8 f. 2 "lions' 1 "dragon".
     In - Plays. 3: April 1944, 41-46.

537. The China Pig by Evelyn Emig.
     Short. 1 m. 2 f.
     In - Poet Lore. 33:no.3,1922, 439-450.

538. Chinese Incident by Pearl S. Buck.
     Radio. 6 m. 1 f. 2 b. 1 c.
     In - Scholastic. 41: Oct.26,1942, 17-19.

539. Chinese Lily by Paula Jakobi.
     Short. 1 m. 7 f.
     In - Forum. 54: Nov.1915, 551-566.

540. A Chinese Rip Van Winkle by Anna Curtis
     Chandler.
     Short. 9 m. 3 f. +X.
     In - Plays. 5: Jan.1946, 51-56.

541. The Chinese Wall by Max Frisch. Trans. by
     James S. Rosenberg.
     Full. 17 m. 5 f. +X.
     In - Theatre. 47: Aug.1963, 32-60.

542. The Chinese Water Wheel by Edna Higgins
     Strachan.
     Short. 3 m. 2 f.
     In - Drama. 21: Oct.1930, 15-16+.

543. La Chinita by Rafael M. Saavedra y Bessey.
     Trans. from the Spanish by Lilian
     Saunders.
     Short. 5 m. 1 f. +X.
     In - Poet Lore. 37: March 1926, 107-119.

544. Chips With Everything by Arnold Wesker.
     Full. 20 m. 0 f.
     In - Players. 10: Dec.1962, 34-48.

545. Chips with Everything by Arnold Wesker.
     Full. 20 m. 0 f.
     In - Theatre. 47: Oct.1963, 33-57.

546. Chit-Chat on a Rat by Camille Skrivanek
     Atherton.
     Short. 1 m. 1 f.
     In - First Stage. 2: Dec.1962, 37-41.

547. The Choice of Gianetta by Allita Applegate.
     In - Poet Lore. 36: Sept.1925, 405.

548. The Choosing of Easter Rabbit by Sally
     Werner.
     Short. 0 m. 1 f. +c.X.
     In - Plays. 14: April 1955, 77-80.

549. The Chorus Girl by John A. Stone. Based on
     the story by Anton Chekhov.
     Short. 1 m. 2 f.
     In - First Stage. 1: Dec.1961, 41-49.

550. The Chosen One by Lucille M. Duvall.
     Short. 7 m. 3 f. +X.
     In - Plays. 16: Dec.1956, 41-50.

551. Chrissy In Christmasland by Carolyn Wells.
     In - Harper's B. 46: Nov.1912, 553-554.

552. Christ is Born by A. Eulalia Gough.
     Short. 7 m. 1 f.
     In - School Arts. 37: Nov.1937, 7a-8a.

553. Christmas at the Cratchits adap. by Deborah
     Newman.
     Short. 2 m. 3 f. 2 b. 1 g.
     In - Plays. 12: Dec.1952, 45-50.

554. The Christmas Bear by Mildred Hark McQueen.
Short. 4 m. 5 f. +c.X.
In - Plays. 23: Dec.1923, 69-74.

555. The Christmas Bug by Edith Larson.
Short. 1 m. 5 f.
In - Plays. 13: Dec.1953,1-10.

556. The Christmas Cake by Aileen Fisher.
Short. 2 m. 1 f. 1 b.
In - Plays. 10: Dec.1950, 60-61.

557. A Christmas Carol by George S. Kaufman and
Marc Connelly.
Short. 5 m. 2 f.
In - Bookman. 56: Dec.1922, 409-419.

558. A Christmas Carol by Charles Dickens.
Adap. for radio by Walter Hackett.
Radio. 9 m. 3 f. 3 b. +ch. +X.
In - Plays. 7: Dec.1947, 77-86.

559. A Christmas Carol by Charles Dickens. Adap.
by Walter Hackett.
Short. 19 m. 5 f. +m.X.
In - Plays. 10: Dec.1950, 65-77.

560. A Christmas Carol by Charles Dickens. Adap.
by Lewy Olfson.
Radio. 9 m. 2 f. 3 b. 3 g.
In - Plays. 16: Dec.1956, 87-95.

561. A Christmas Carol by Charles Dickens. Adap.
by Walter Hackett.
Short. 19 m. 5 f. +m.X.
In - Plays. 22: Dec.1962, 83-95.

562. A Christmas Carol by Charles Dickens. Adap.
by Walter Hackett.
Radio. 11 m. 4 f. 4 b. +X.
In - Plays. 27: Dec.1967, 81-90.

563. The Christmas Cat by Bob Anglund.
Short. 4 b. 3 g.
In - Better Homes. 39: Dec.1961, 44-45:.

564. A Christmas Chime by Margaret Cameron.
Short. 2 m. 2 f.
In - McClure's. 22: Dec.1903, 174-184.

565. Christmas Coast to Coast by Lewy Olfson.
Short. 9 m. 4 f. +X.
In - Plays. 21: Dec.1961, 23-32.

566. Christmas Comes to Hamelin by Grace Evelyn
Mills.
Short. 13 m. 13 f. +X.
In - Plays. 4: Dec.1944, 36-44.

567. Christmas Conspiracy by Anna Steese
Richardson.
In - Woman's Home. 37: Dec.1910, 25.

568. Christmas Conspiracy by Elizabeth Woodbridge.
In - St. Nicholas. 39: Dec.1911, 163-169.

569. The Christmas Cowboy by Helen Louise Miller.
Short. 4 m. 4 f. +X.
In - Plays. 10: Dec.1950, 26-35.

570. A Christmas Criss Cross by Helen L. Howard.
Short. 3 m. 1 f.

571. Christmas Eve in Pine Cone Forest by Frances
B. Watts.
Short. 3 m. 3 f. 4 c.
In - Plays. 26: Dec.1966, 75-79.

572. Christmas Eve Letter by Mildred Hark and
Noel McQueen.
Short. 3 m. 4 f. +X.
In - Plays. 7: Dec.1947, 1-12.

573. Christmas Eve Letter by Mildred Hark and
Noel McQueen.
Short. 3 m. 4 f. +X.
In - Plays. 18: Dec.1958, 21-32.

574. Christmas Eve News by Mildred Hark and
Noel McQueen.
Short. 18 m. 9 f. +X.
In - Plays. 10: Dec.1950, 43-49.

575. Christmas Eve News by Mildred Hark and
Noel McQueen.
Short. 13 m. 8 f. +X.
In - Plays. 28: Dec.1968, 61-67.

576. Christmas Every Day by William Dean Howells.
Adap. by Jane McGowan.
Radio. 9 m. 7 f. 5 b.
In - Plays. 12: Dec.1952, 68-76.

577. Christmas Every Day by William Dean Howells.
Adap. by Adele Thane.
Short. 5 m. 4 f.
In - Plays. 59: Dec.1959, 57-65.

578. Christmas Every Day by William Dean Howells. Adap. by Jane McGovan.

    Radio. 16 m. 7 f.

    In - Plays. 23: Dec.1963, 87-95.

579. Christmas for Cosette adap. by Levy Olfson from Victor Hugo's Les Miserables.

    Radio. 6 m. 4 f.

    In - Plays. 20: Dec.1960, 87-95.

580. Christmas Gifts of All Nations by Carolyn Wells.

    Short. 1 m. 1 f. many c.

    In - Ladies' Home. 29: Dec.1912, 86+.

581. Christmas House by Helen E. Waite and Elbert M. Hoppenstedt.

    Short. 4 m. 6 f.

    In - Plays. 4: Dec.1944, 28-35.

582. Christmas House by Helen E. Waite and Elbert M. Hoppenstedt.

    Short. 4 m. 6 f.

    In - Plays. 25: Dec.1965, 15-22.

583. Christmas in Court by Aileen Fisher.

    Short. 4 m. 3 f. +12 or more X.

    In - Plays. 22: Dec.1962, 47-52.

584. Christmas in Old Boston by Alice Very.

    Short. 4 m. 5 f. +X.

    In - Plays. 14: Dec.1954, 71-74.

585. Christmas in Old New England by Patricia Clapp.

    Short. 3 m. 3 f.

    In - Plays. 23: Dec.1963, 37-44.

586. Christmas in the Woods by Mildred Hark and Noel McQueen.

    Short. 4 m. 3 f.

    In - Plays. 16: Dec.1956, 75-78.

587. Christmas Joy by Alice Very.

    Short. 5 m. 6 f.

    In - Plays. 3: Dec.1943, 53-55.

588. The Christmas Nutcracker adap. by Adele Thane from story by E.T.A. Hoffman.

    Short. 9 m. 4 f.

    In - Plays. 22: Dec.1962, 35-45.

589. The Christmas Oboe by Helen Louise Miller.

    Short. 5 m. 2 f.

    In - Plays. 14: Dec.1954, 1-12.

590. Christmas Party by Mildred Hark and Noel McQueen.

    Short. 7 m. 5 f.

    In - Plays. 9: Dec.1949, 63-67.

591. The Christmas Peppermints by Helen Louise Miller.

    Short. 9 m. 5 f.

    In - Plays. 23: Dec.1963, 49-57.

592. A Christmas Promise by Helen Louise Miller.

    Short. 3 m. 3 f.

    In - Plays. 12: Dec.1952, 1-12.

593. Christmas Quest by Helen V. Runnette.

    Short. 13 m. 10 f. +X.

    In - Plays. 28: Dec.1968, 41-49.

594. The Christmas Question by Deborah Newman.

    Short. 2 m. +X.

    In - Plays. 21: Dec.1961, 85-88.

595. Christmas Recaptured by Mildred Hark and Noel McQueen.

    Short. 4 m. 4 f.

    In - Plays. 11: Dec.1951, 20-31.

596. Christmas Recaptured by Mildred Hark and Noel McQueen.

    Short. 4 m. 4 f.

    In - Plays. 19: Dec.1959, 25-36.

597. The Christmas Revel by Claire Boiko.

    Short. 8 m. 8 f. +X.

    In - Plays. 24: Dec.1964, 39-50.

598. The Christmas Runaways by Helen Louise Miller.

    Short. 4 m. 2 f.

    In - Plays. 14: Dec.1954, 63-70.

599. The Christmas Sampler by Eleanore Leuser.

    Short. 6 m. 4 f. +m.X.

    In - Plays. 11: Dec.1951, 57-61.

600. The Christmas Shoe by Lucille Miller Duvall.

    Short. 5 m. 1 f. ch. +X.

    In - Plays. 19: Dec.1959, 67-71.

601.   Christmas Shopping Early by Mildred Hark and
       Noel McQueen.

       Short. 3 m. 3 f. +X.

       In - Plays. 8: Dec.1948, 12-22.

602.   Christmas Shopping Early by Mildred Hark
       and Noel McQueen.

       Short. 2 m. 2 f. 1 b. 1 g. +X.

       In - Plays. 27: Dec.1967, 49-58.

603.   The Christmas Snowman by Mildred Hark and
       Noel McQueen.

       Short. 4 m. 3 f.

       In - Plays. 9: Dec.1949, 39-50.

604.   The Christmas Snowman by Mildred Hark and
       Noel McQueen.

       Short. 2 m. 1 f. 2 b. 2 g.

       In - Plays. 25: Dec.1965, 41-50.

605.   Christmas Spirit by Earl J. Dias.

       Short. 4 m. 4 f.

       In - Plays. 13: Dec.1953, 23-32.

606.   The Christmas Starlet by Earl J. Dias.

       Short. 5 m. 6 f.

       In - Plays. 23: Dec.1963, 15-26.

607.   Christmas Stockings by Arthur Guiterman.

       Short. 1 m. 1 b. 1 g.

       In - Ladies' Home. 22: Dec.1904, 28.

608.   The Christmas Table Cloth by Aileen Fisher.

       Short. 2 m. 3 f.

       In - Plays. 23: Dec.1963, 45-48.

609.   The Christmas Train by Helen L. Howard.

       Short. 8 m. 2 f. +X.

       In - Plays. 8: Dec.1948, 59-60.

610.   A Christmas Tree for Kitty by Aileen Fisher.

       Short. 0 m. 1 f. 2 b. 3 g. +c.X.

       In - Plays. 19: Dec.1959, 84-86.

611.   The Christmas Tree Surprise by Deborah
       Newman.

       Short. 3 m. 3 f. +X.

       In - Plays. 11: Dec.1951, 73-76.

612.   The Christmas Tryst by Katharine Metcalf
       Roof.

       Short. 2 m. 3 f. 1 b. +X.

       In - Touchstone. 6: Dec.1919, 83-89+.

613.   The Christmas Umbrella by Jane McGowan.

       Short. 7 m. 7 f. 10 c.

       In - Plays. 14: Dec.1954, 43-52.

614.   The Christmas Umbrella by Jane McGowan.

       Short. 7 m. 7 f. 10 c.

       In - Plays. 24: Dec.1964, 51-60.

615.   The Christmas Visitor by Anne Howard Bailey.

       Short. 2 m. 2 f. 2 b. +X.

       In - Plays. 28: Dec.1968, 1-10.

616.   Cicero the Great by Paul S. McCoy.

       Short. 2 m. 1 f.

       In - Plays. 17: Oct.1957, 79-86.

617.   The Ci-Devant by Michael Arlen.

       Short. 1 m. 2 f.

       In - Dial. 69: August 1920, 125-131.

618.   Cinder-Rabbit by Constance Whitman Baher.

       Short. 3 m. 5 f. 4 c.

       In - Plays. 26: March 1967, 61-69.

619.   Cinder-Riley by Claire Boiko.

       Short. 2 m. 5 f. 3 b. +X.

       In - Plays. 20: March 1961, 51-56.

620.   Cinderella by Edith Nesbit.

       Short. 4 m. 5 f. +X.

       In - Delineator. 74: Dec.1909, 504-505+.

621.   Cinderella by Alice D'Arcy.

       Short. 17 m. 9 f.

       In - Plays. 3: Dec.1943, 45-52.

622.   Cinderella by June Barr.

       Short. 4 m. 4 f. +m.X.

       In - Plays. 7: Oct.1948, 63-67.

623.   Cinderella by Deborah Newman.

       Short. 10 m. 5 f.

       In - Plays. 18: April 1959, 65-73.

624.   Cinderella adap. by Adele Thane.

       Short. 5 m. 7 f. 3 b. +X.

       In - Plays. 27: Oct.1967, 57-68.

625.   Circumventin' Saandy by Zellah MacDonald.

       Short. 3 m. 2 f.

       In - Drama. 17: Feb.1927, 145-146+.

626. <u>Circus Parade</u> by Esther MacLellan and
     Catherine V. Schroll.

Short. 9 m. 4 f. +X.

In - Plays. 11: May 1952, 52-55.

627. <u>Circus Daze</u> by Helen Louise Miller.

Short. 12 m. 3 f.

In - Plays. 26: May 1967, 49-57.

628. <u>Circus Magic</u> by Rod Vahl.

Short. 6 m. 0 f.

In - Plays. 25: Jan.1966, 63-66.

629. <u>Citizenship</u> by James M. Cain.

Short. 6 m. 0 f.

In - American Merc. 18: Dec.1929, 403-408.

630. <u>The City: A Grotesque Adventure</u> by David
     Novak.

In - Poet Lore. 36: June 1925, 208-221.

631. <u>The City Mouse and the Country Mouse</u> by
     Rowena Bennett.

Short. 3 m. 2 f.

In - Plays. 5: Dec.1945, 56-59.

632. <u>City of Fear</u> by John Murray.

Short. 6 m. 2 f.

In - Plays. 19: May 1960, 1-12.

633. <u>Civilians Stay Put</u> by Mildred Hark and Noel
     McQueen.

Short. 9 m. 1 f.

In - Plays. 4: April 1945, 59-66.

634. <u>Clarence</u> by Booth Tarkington.

Excerpt. 3 m. 3 f.

In - Scholastic. 46: Feb.19,1945, 13-15.

635. <u>The Classic Dancing School</u> by Winifred Duncan.

Short. 1 m. 10 f.

In - Drama. 17: May 1927, 235-242.

636. <u>The Clean Up</u> by Barbara Abel.

Short. 0 m. 3 f.

In - Survey. 74: Sept.1938, 274-277.

637. <u>The Clean-Up Club</u> by Aileen Fisher and
     Olive Rabe.

Short. 2 m. 2 f. +X.

In - Plays. 16: Jan.1957, 82-84.

638. <u>Clean Up, Shine Up</u> by Mildred Hark and Noel
     McQueen.

Short. 1 m. 1 f. 7 un. +X.

In - Plays. 7: Oct.1948, 70-72.

639. <u>The Cleanest Town in the West</u> by Earl J.
     Dias.

Short. 6 m. 3 f.

In - Plays. 20: Nov.1960, 13-24.

640. <u>Cleopatra In Judaea</u> by Arthur Symons.

Short. 7 m. 3 f.

In - Forum. 55: June 1916, 643-660.

641. <u>Clerambard</u> by Marcel Ayme. Trans. by
     Norman Denny and Alvin Sapinsley.

Full. 9 m. 5 f.

In - Theatre. 42: June 1958, 26-51.

642. <u>The Clever Peasant</u> adap. by Hazel W. Corson
     from a folk tale.

Short. 11 m. 5 f. +X.

In - Plays. 28: Oct.1968, 63-68.

643. <u>Clever Peter</u> by Mary Thurman Pyle.

Short. 9 m. 6 f. +X.

In - Plays. 6: Feb.1947, 53-64.

644. <u>The Climate of Eden</u> by Moss Hart.

Full. 8 m. 5 f. 1 b. 1 g. +X.

In - Theatre. 38: May 1954, 34-65.

645. <u>Climb the Greased Pole</u> by Vincent Longhi.

Full. 5 m. 5 f.

In - Players. 15: Feb.1968, 21-36.

646. <u>The Clock's Secret</u> by Esther MacLellan and
     Catherine V. Schroll.

Short. 2 m. 4 f.

In - Plays. 6: April 1947, 43-48.

647. <u>Cloey</u> by Loretto Carroll Bailey.

Short. 1 m. 3 f.

In - Carolina. 4: March 1931, 15-31.

648. <u>Close to the Wind</u> by Eleanor Barnes.

Short. 0 m. 1 f. 1 b. 1 g.

In - Poet Lore. 40: Dec.1929, 588-596.

649. <u>The Closing Door</u> by Alexander Knox.

Full. 9 m. 3 f.

In - Theatre. 34: May 1950, 62-88.

650. The Clouds by Jaroslav Kvapil. Trans. from
      the Bohemian by Charles Recht.
      Full. 3 m. 2 f.
      In - Poet Lore. 21:no.6,1910, 417-466.

651. The Club Bedroom by Louis Auchincloss.
      Short. 0 m. 3 f.
      In - Esquire. 66: Dec.1966, 226-229.

652. The Coach Scores by Samuel S. Richmond.
      Short. 8 m. 0 f.
      In - Plays. 7: April 1948, 65-71.

653. The Cock and the Fox by Alice Very.
      Short. 3 m. 4 f. +X.
      In - Plays. 7: Feb.1948, 65-68.

654. Cockade 1 - Prisoner and Escort by Charles
      Wood.
      Short. 3 m. 3 f.
      In - Players. 11: Dec.1963, 23-30+.

655. Cockade 2 - John Thomas by Charles Wood.
      Short. 2 m. 0 f.
      In - Players. 11: Jan.1964, 23-27.

656. Cockade 3 - Spare by Charles Wood.
      Short. 6 m. 0 f.
      In - Players. 11: Jan.1964, 27-30+.

657. Cockcrow by L. M. Taylor. Based on the old
      Scottish ballad Clerk Saunders.
      Short. 4 m. 1 f.
      In - Poet Lore. 33: March 1922, 118-127.

658. The Codicil by Paul Ferrier. Trans. by
      Elizabeth Lester Mullin.
      Short. 3 m. 1 f.
      In - Poet Lore. 19: no.2,1908, 193-206.

659. Collector's Item by Earl J. Dias.
      Short. 4 m. 3 f.
      In - Plays. 22: Jan.1963, 1-12.

660. The Colonnade by Stark Young.
      Full. 5 m. 3 f.
      In - Theatre. 8: Aug.1924, 521-560.

661. Color Fairies by Adeline M. Storts.
      In - School Arts. 27: Oct.1927, 98-99.

662. Color Fantasy by Ruth Horwood.
      In - School Arts. 27: Oct.1927, 77-80.

663. Color Play by Joysa Gaines.
      Short. 0 m. 0 f. 2 b. 2 g. +c.X.
      In - School Arts. 30: April 1931, 513-517.

664. Colors Mean So Much by Karin Asbrand.
      Short. 1 m. 16 f.
      In - Plays. 5: May 1946, 63-65.

665. Colossal, Stupendous! by John Murray.
      Short. 6 m. 3 f.
      In - Plays. 16: April 1957, 13-24.

666. Columbus Sails the Sea by Lindsey Barbee.
      Short. 4 m. 1 f. +m.X.
      In - Plays. 4: Oct.1944, 44-48.

667. The Combat by Georges Duhamel. Trans. from
      the French by Sasha Best.
      Full. 11 m. 3 f. 1 c. +X.
      In - Poet Lore. 26:no.4,1915, 409-487.

668. Come Back, Little Sheba by William Inge.
      Full. 8 m. 3 f.
      In - Theatre. 34: Nov.1950, 60-88.

669. Come What May by Anatole France. Trans. by
      F. Chapman and J. Lewis May.
      Short. 3 m. 2 f.
      In - Golden. 6: Nov.1927, 631-641.

670. Comedietta by Marion Smith.
      Short. 0 m. 2 f. 1 g.
      In - Canadian M. 19: May 1902, 40-42.

671. Comedy in Ancient Rome by Edith Hamilton.
      Short. 11 m. 3 f.
      In - Theatre. 16: May 1932, 400-406.

672. A Comedy of Danger by Richard Hughes.
      Radio. 2 m. 1 f. +X.
      In - Golden. 14: Aug.1931, 82-87.

673. Comedy of Death by George Edward Harris.
      In - Poet Lore. 36: March 1925, 63-75.

674. The Comedy of the Dead by José Cid Pérez.
Trans. by John P. Dyson.

Short. 10 m. 5 f. +X.

In - First Stage. 6: March 1967, 68-80.

675. A Comedy of the Exile by Isabella Howe Fiske.

Short. 3 m. 2 f. 1 dog.

In - Poet Lore. 17:no.1,1906, 51-58.

676. Comes the Dreamer by John Wexley.

Full. 15 m. 8 f. +X.

In - First Stage. 2: Dec.1962, 7-36.

677. Comic Strip Antics by Charles F. Wilde.

Short. 3 m. 1 f.

In - Plays. 6: Oct.1946, 30-38.

678. The Coming of the Prince by Eugene Field.
Adap. by Jane McGowan.

Short. 7 m. 2 f. 2 c. +X.

In - Plays. 14: Dec.1954, 88-94.

679. Command Decision by Wister Haines.

Full. 18 m. 0 f.

In - Theatre. 32: Summer 1948, 61-89.

680. The Committee On Matrimony by Margaret
Cameron.

Short. 1 m. 1 f.

In - McClures. 21: Oct.1903, 659-665.

681. A Common for All Saints by Gregory Ziegelmaier.

Short. (Plainsong).

In - First Stage. 4: Sept.1965, 168-175.

682. Common Ground by Eleanor Whiting.

In - Poet Lore. 32: March 1921, 140-148.

683. A Compass for Christopher by Celia Gordon.

Short. 6 m. 4 f.

In - Plays. 12: Oct.1952, 61-64.

684. A Compass for Christopher by Deborah
Newman.

Short. 6 m. 4 f.

In - Plays. 24: Oct.1964, 73-76.

685. The Concert at Saint Ovide by Antonio Buero
Vallejo. Trans. from the Spanish by
Farris Anderson.

Full. 14 m. 9 f.

In - Mod. Drama. 1: Sept.1967, 9-61.

686. Conchita by Rosemary Shirley DeCamp.

Short. 8 m. 8 f. +X.

In - Carolina. 4: Sept.1931, 76-84.

687. Conditioned Reflex by Curtis Zahn.

Short. 2 m. 0 f.

In - First Stage. 4: June 1965, 97-107.

688. Confab With Crockett by Carl Carmer.

Radio. 3 m. 0 f.

In - Scholastic. 41: Oct.12,1942, 17-19.

689. Confidence by Elizabeth D. Jordan.

In - Harper's B. 43: May 1909, 447-450.

690. A Connecticut Yankee in King Arthur's Court
by John Grant Fuller. From the novel by
Mark Twain.

Excerpt. 5 m. 3 f. 1 b.

In - Scholastic. 40: March 9,1942, 17-19.

691. A Connecticut Yankee in King Arthur's Court
by Mark Twain. Adap. by Lewy Olfson.

Radio. 7 m. 3 f.

In - Plays. 14: May 1955, 84-92.

692. The Conspiracy of Feelings by Yurii Olyesha.
English version by Daniel C. Gerould
and Eleanor S. Gerould.

Full. 13 m. 5 f. 3 un. +X.

In - First Stage. 7: Sept.1968, 20-38.

693. The Conspirators by Ralph Henry Barbour.

In - New England. 37(n.s.): Dec.1907,
425-432.

694. The Conspirators by Prosper Mérimée.

Short. 9 m. 2 f.

In - Golden. 1: April 1925, 537-553.

695. The Constant Lover by St.John Hankin.

Short. 1 m. 1 f.

In - Theatre. 3: April 1919, 67-77.

696. Contrary Mary by Karin Asbrand.

Short. 1 m. 12 f.

In - Plays. 6: Nov.1946, 55-57.

697. Cookbook by Mary Ruth Parsons.

Short. 4 m. 3 f.

In - Mlle. 64: Nov.1966, 164-165.

698. <u>Cooking Up a Storm</u> by Joe Feinstein.

Short. 4 m. 6 f.

In - Plays. 26: Jan.1967, 13-23.

699. <u>The Copper Farthing</u> by Betty Tracy Huff.

Short. 12 m. 4 f. +f.X.

In - Plays. 19: March 1960, 73-76.

700. <u>The Copperhead</u> by Augustus Thomas. Ed. by Margaret Mayorga.

Excerpt. 9 m. 3 f.

In - Scholastic. 36: Feb.5,1940, 17-19.

701. <u>Copy</u> by Edith Wharton.

Short. 1 m. 2 f.

In - Scribner's. 27: June 1900, 657-663.

702. <u>Copy</u> by Edith Wharton.

Short. 1 m. 2 f.

In - Outlook. 87: Oct.26,1907, 441-449.

703. <u>Cordia</u> by Hyacinth Stoddart Smith.

Short. 2 m. 4 f.

In - Poet Lore. 19:no.2,1908, 165-192.

704. <u>Corinna Goes A-Maying</u> by Claire Boiko.

Short. 6 m. 7 f. +X.

In - Plays. 27: May 1968, 85-92.

705. <u>Corn Meal and Poetry</u> by Graham DuBois.

Short. 2 m. 5 f.

In - Plays. 9: Feb.1950, 31-39.

706. <u>The Corner Store</u> by Samuel S. Richmond.

Short. 7 m. 2 f.

In - Plays. 5: March 1946, 65-72.

707. <u>Cornerstone of Freedom</u> by Karin Asbrand.

Short. 6 m. 5 f.

In - Plays. 7: May 1948, 31-40.

708. <u>Cosi Fan Tutte</u> by Wolfgang Amadeus Mozart. English version of the Lorenzo DaPonte libretto by Ruth and Thomas Martin.

Full (opera). 4 m. 3 f. ch. +X.

In - Theatre. 40: Jan.1956, 36-57.

709. <u>The Costume Caper</u> by Anne Coulter Martens.

Short. 2 m. 4 f. 1 b. 1 g.

In - Plays. 27: Oct.1967, 1-12.

710. <u>Cottie Mourns</u> by Patricia McMullan.

Short. 3 m. 1 f.

In - Carolina. 8: March 1935, 7-21.

711. <u>The Count of Monte Cristo</u> by Alexandre Dumas. Adap. by Lewy Olfson.

Radio. 12 m. 1 f.

In - Plays. 18: May 1959, 97-105.

712. <u>The Country Girl</u> by Clifford Odets.

Full. 7 m. 1 f.

In - Theatre. 36: May 1952, 58-86.

713. <u>The Country Store Cat</u> by Helen Louise Miller.

Short. 15 m. 6 f. +X.

In - Plays. 19: March 1960, 77-83.

714. <u>The Courage Piece</u> by Eleanore Leuser.

Short. 6 m. 3 f.

In - Plays. 8: April 1949, 43-50.

715. <u>The Court of King Arithmetic</u> by Gwen Chaloner.

Short. 8 m. 4 f. 10 c.

In - Plays. 23: March 1964, 35-40.

716. <u>The Courters</u> by Paul T. Nolan.

Short. 5 m. 1 f.

In - Plays. 22: Jan.1963, 27-34.

717. <u>The Courting of Marie Jenvrin</u> by Gwen Pharis Ringwood.

Short. 5 m. 2 f.

In - Carolina. 14: Dec.1941, 101-116.

718. <u>Courting Trouble</u> by Aileen Fisher.

Short. 4 m. 3 f. +X.

In - Plays. 13: March 1954, 63-69.

719. <u>The Courtroom of Terror</u> by Betty Gray Blaine.

Short. 8 m. 6 f.

In - Plays. 18: Oct.1958, 74-78.

720. <u>The Covetous Councilman</u> by J.H. Bealmear.

Short. 2 m. 2 f.

In - Plays. 27: May 1968, 53-58.

721. <u>Crabbed Youth and Age</u> by Lennox Robinson.

Short. 3 m. 4 f.

In - Theatre. 8: Jan.1924, 51-63.

722.   <u>A Crack in the Universe</u> by Elder Olson.

Full. 6 m. 2 f.

In - First Stage. 1: March 1962, 9-33.

723.   <u>The Cracked Easter Egg</u> by Sylvia Lee.

Short. 1 m. 1 f. 8 un.

In - Plays. 13: April 1954, 63-65.

724.   <u>Cranford</u> by Marguerite Merington.

Full. 1 m. 9 f.

In - Ladies' Home. 18: Feb.1901, 5-6+.

725.   <u>Crawling Arnold</u> by Jules Feiffer.

Short. 2 m. 2 f.

In - Horizon. 4: Nov.1961, 49-56.

726.   <u>The Crazy Locomotive</u> by Stanislaw Ignacy Witkiewicz. English version by C.S. Durer and Daniel C. Gerould.

Short. 9 m. 5 f. +X.

In - First Stage. 6: Dec.1967, 206-215.

727.   <u>The Cresta Run</u> by N.F. Simpson.

Full. 4 m. 2 f.

In - Players. 13: Feb.1966, 29-43.

728.   <u>Criminals</u> by Gustaf of Geijerstam. Trans. from the Swedish by Roy W. Swanson.

Full. 2 m. 3 f.

In - Poet Lore. 34: June 1923, 186-209.

729.   <u>The Crimson Feather</u> by Frances B. Watts.

Short. 6 m. 4 f.

In - Plays. 22: March 1963, 81-85.

730.   <u>The Crimson Glory Rose</u> by Marguerite Kreger Phillips.

Short. 2 m. 5 f.

In - Plays. 12: May 1953, 23-31.

731.   <u>Crisscross Streets</u> by Dorothy Deming.

Short. 1 m. 4 un. 4 c. +c.X.

In - Plays. 10: May 1951, 58-61.

732.   <u>Cristina's Journey Home</u> by Hugo von Hofmannsthal. Trans. from the German by Roy Temple House.

Full. 9 m. 7 f. +X.

In - Poet Lore. 28:no.2,1917, 129-186.

733.   <u>The Critical Year</u> by Paul Green.

Short. 9 m. 1 f. +X.

In - Scholastic. 49: Oct.28 & Nov.4,1946, 17-19+, 17-19+.

734.   <u>Crocus</u> by Claribel Spamer.

Short. 6 m. 6 f.

In - Plays. 7: April 1948, 58-60.

735.   <u>The Crocus Who Couldn't Bloom</u> by Claire Boiko.

Short. 9 m. 10 f.

In - Plays. 20: May 1961, 77-82.

736.   <u>The Crooked Jar</u> by Ronald Lackmann.

Short. 2 m. 3 f. +X.

In - Plays. 17: Feb.1958, 77-80.

737.   <u>Cross My Palm With Silver</u> by Florence King.

Short. 1 un. 4 b. 3 g. +c.X.

In - Wilson. 11: Oct.1936, 119-120.

738.   <u>The Cross of Gold</u> by Donald Andersson and Sid Dimond.

Radio. 10 m. 2 f.

In - Plays. 11: Oct.1951, 69-74.

739.   <u>The Cross Princess</u> by Esther MacLellan and Catherine V. Schroll.

Short. 4 m. 6 f.

In - Plays. 12: Feb.1953, 35-40.

740.   <u>Cross-Roads</u> by Julian Sturgis.

Short. 3 m. 1 f.

In - Blackwood's. 171: Feb.1902, 194-204.

741.   <u>Crosspatch and Cupid</u> by Jane McGowan.

Short. 7 m. 6 f.

In - Plays. 16: Feb.1957, 71-76.

742.   <u>The Crowded House</u> by Eva Jacob.

Short. 6 m. 6 f. 8 un.

In - Plays. 16: April 1957, 59-64.

743.   <u>The Crowning of King Arthur</u> adap. by Levy Olfson from Sir Thomas Malory's <u>Morte d'Arthur.</u>

Radio. 12 m. 3 f.

In - Plays. 24: Dec.1964, 87-96.

744.   <u>Crows</u> by Betti Primrose Sandiford.

In - Canadian M. 58: March 1922, 397-405.

745.   <u>The Crucible</u> by Arthur Miller.

Full. 11 m. 10 f.

In - Theatre. 37: Oct.1953, 35-67.

746. <u>Crusade for Liberty</u> by Manta S. Graham.
      Short. 3 m. 4 f.
      In - Plays. 3: Oct.1943, 38-45.

747. <u>Crusoe Islanders</u> by Clare Johnson Marley.
      Short. 3 m. 2 f.
      In - Carolina. 17: March 1944, 7-16.

748. <u>Crusts</u> by Paul Claudel. Trans. from the
         French by John Heard.
      Full. 6 m. 0 f.
      In - Poet Lore. 50: July 1944, 195-258.

      <u>Cry, the Beloved Country.</u>
         see
      <u>Lost in the Stars.</u>

749. <u>Cry Witch</u> by Marion L. Miller.
      Short. 7 m. 7 f.
      In - Plays. 10: Jan.1951, 1-11.

750. <u>Cry Witch</u> by Marion L. Miller.
      Short. 7 m. 7 f.

751. <u>The Crying Clown</u> by Mary Ann Nicholson.
      Short. 4 m. 0 f.
      In - Plays. 14: Nov.1954, 69-71.

752. <u>The Crystal Flask</u> by Karin Astrand.
      Short. 2 m. 6 f.
      In - Plays. 5: Oct.1945, 43-47.

753. <u>Cub Reporter</u> by Samuel S. Richmond.
      Short. 5 m. 1 f.
      In - Plays. 4: March 1945, 67-71.

754. <u>The Cuckoo</u> by Marion Murdoch.
      Short. 1 m. 6 f.
      In - Plays. 5: March 1946, 11-27.

755. <u>The Cuckoo</u> by Marion Murdoch.
      Short. 0 m. 7 f.
      In - Plays. 14: April 1955, 1-19.

756. <u>A Cue for Cleopatra</u> by Anne Coulter Martens.
      Short. 6 m. 6 f.
      In - Plays. 23: Oct.1963, 1-15.

757. <u>Cupid and Company</u> by Cecelia C. Callanan.
      Short. 2 m. 2 f.
      In - Plays. 12: Feb.1953, 11-18.

758. <u>The Cupid Computer</u> by Anne Coulter Martens.
      Short. 6 m. 6 f. +X.
      In - Plays. 27: Feb.1968, 1-12.

759. <u>Cupid in Command</u> by Jane McGowan.
      Short. 6 m. 5 f.
      In - Plays. 23: Feb.1924, 71-74.

760. <u>Cupid on the Loose</u> by Helen Louise Miller.
      Short. 3 m. 2 f.
      In - Plays. 14: Feb.1955, 13-20.

761. <u>Cupid's Partner</u> by Marjorie B. Paradis.
      Short. 2 m. 8 f.
      In - Plays. 14: May 1955, 30-38.

762. <u>Cupies and Hearts</u> by Mildred Hark and Noel
         McQueen.
      Short. 2 m. 4 f.
      In - Plays. 14: Feb.1955, 47-55.

763. <u>Cupivac</u> by Claire Boiko.
      Short. 9 m. 6 f. +X.
      In - Plays. 26: May 1927, 59-63.

764. <u>Cure for a King</u> by Shirley Simon.
      Short. 8 m. 3 f.
      In - Plays. 18: May 1959, 61-66.

765. <u>The Curious Quest</u> by Helen Louise Miller.
      Short. 6 m. 3 f.
      In - Plays. 14: March 1955, 49-56.

      <u>The Curse of the Pyncheons.</u>
         see
      <u>Nathaniel Hawthorne and the Curse of the
      Pyncheons.</u>

766. <u>Cyrano de Bergerac</u> by Edmond Rostand.
         Adap. by Lewy Olfson.
      Radio. 7 m. 4 f.
      In - Plays. 15: Oct.1955, 87-96.

767. <u>Curtain</u> by Hallie F. Flanagan.
      In - Drama. 13: Feb.1923, 167-169.

768. The Curtains by Cloyd Head and Mary Gavin.

Short. 8 m. 3 f.

In - Poetry. 16: April 1920, 1-11.

769. The Dagger of the Goth by Jose Zorrilla.
Trans. by Willis Knapp Jones.

Short. 4 m. 0 f.

In - Poet Lore. 40: Sept.1929, 426-442.

770. Daily Bread by Josephine Henry Whitehouse.

Short. 1 m. 4 f.

In - Poet Lore. 40: March 1929, 129-140.

771. Dame Fortune and Don Money adap. by Hazel
W. Corson from a Spanish folk tale.

Short. 7 m. 5 f. +X.

In - Plays. 26: April 1967, 55-61.

772. Dame Julian's Window by Edith Lyttleton.

Short. 6 m. 3 f. 3 c. +X.

In - 19th C. 73: Feb.1913, 435-449.

773. Damn Yankees by George Abbott and Douglas
Wallop. Music and lyrics by Richard
Adler and Jerry Ross.

Full (musical). 13 m. 7 f. +ch.

In - Theatre. 40: Nov.1956, 34-59.

774. Damsels in Distress by Jane McGowan.

Short. 9 m. 6 f. 1 un.

In - Plays. 17: Nov.1957, 71-79.

775. The Dancing Children by Alice Very.

Short. 10 m. 7 f.

In - Plays. 11: Oct.1951, 55-57.

776. The Dancing Princesses adap. by Caroline
H. Corey.

Short. 4 m. 15 f.

In - Plays. 12: May 1953, 49-54.

777. Danger - Pixies at Work by Vernon Howard.

Short. 7 m. 0 f.

In - Plays. 14: May 1955, 80-83.

778. The Dangerous Game by Stephanie Miller.

Short. 3 m. 5 f.

In - Plays. 27: March 1968, 48-58.

779. Dangling From Two Second Rate Tragedies by
Nicilas Cooke.

Short. 10 m. 4 f.

In - Poet Lore. 59: Sept.1964, 222-246.

780. Dare All for Liberty by Eleanor Sickels.

Short. 5 m. 1 f. +m.X.

In - Plays. 4: Jan.1945, 43-49.

781. The Dark at the Top of the Stairs by
William Inge.

Full. 8 m. 3 f.

In - Theatre. 43: Sept.1959, 33-60.

782. Dark Roses by Louis F. Doyle.

Short. 7 m. 2 f. 1 b. 1 g. +X.

In - Cath. World. 121: May 1925, 158-162.

783. The Darkest Hour by Graham DuBois.

Short. 3 m. 4 f.

In - Plays. 5: Nov.1945, 34-39.

784. Darkness at Noon by Sydney Kingsley. Based
on the novel by Arthur Koestler.

Full. 18 m. 3 f.

In - Theatre. 37: April 1953, 34-64.

785. A Date with Washington by Mildred Hark and
Noel McQueen.

Short. 3 m. 2 f.

In - Plays. 26: Feb.1967, 33-42.

786. The Daughter-In-Law by D.H. Lawrence.

Full. 2 m. 3 f.

In - Players. 14: June 1967, 23-38.

787. The Daughter of Jorio by Gabriele D'Annunzio.
Trans. from the Italian by Charlotte
Porter, Pietro Isola and Alice Henry.

Full. 10 m. 16 f. +X.

In - Poet Lore. 18:no.1,1907, 1-88.

788. A Daughter of the Gods by Graham DuBois.

Short. 3 m. 4 f.

In - Plays. 9: Oct.1949, 11-21.

789. David Copperfield and Uriah Heep by Charles
Dickens. Adap. by Lewy Olfson.

Radio. 6 m. 3 f.

In - Plays. 17: Jan.1958, 77-86.

790. Davy Crockett: Half Horse, Half Alligator by
John Philip Milhous.

Short. 7 m. 5 f.

In - Carolina. 6: March 1933, 7+.

791. Dawn, Day, Night by Dario Niccodemi. English
version by Robert Rietty.

Full. 3 m. 4 f.

In - Gambit. 2: no.6, 3-32.

792. The Day After Tomorrow by Frederick Lonsdale.

  Full. 9 m. 5 f.

  In - Theatre. 35: April 1951, 59-88.

793. The Day Before Christmas by Carolyn Wells.

  Short. 7 m. 6 f. +c.X.

  In - Ladies' Home. 21: Dec.1903, 16.

794. The Day Education Stood Still by William C. Miller.

  Short. 6 m. 2 f. 2 un.

  In - Scholastic. 73: Nov.7,1958, 11T-12T.

795. A Day for Trees by Mildred Hark and Noel McQueen.

  Short. 5 m. 5 f.

  In - Plays. 12: May 1953, 66-69.

  A Day in Everygirl's Life.

    see

  Wohelo.

796. Day of Destiny by Aileen Fisher.

  Short. 10 m. 0 f.

  In - Plays. 13: Oct.1953, 11-16.

797. A Day of Thanks by Edrie Pendleton.

  Short. 5 m. 3 f.

  In - Plays. 6: Nov.1946, 29-35.

798. The Day of the Dragon by Ethel McFarlan.

  Short. 2 m. 3 f. 3 c.

  In - Plays. 20: Nov.1960, 51-57.

799. The Day That Baseball Died by Irving Teitel.

  Radio. 12 m. 2 f.

  In - Scholastic. 50: April 14,1947, 21-23+.

800. The Day the Indians Came by Helen Ramsey.

  Short. 8 m. 7 f. +X.

  In - Plays. 20: Nov.1960, 71-76.

801. The Day the Moonmen Landed by Rose Kacherian Rybak.

  Short. 11 m. 5 f. +X.

  In - Plays. 22: Oct.1962, 45-50.

802. The Day the Shoemaker Came by Mary Thurman Pyle.

  Short. 5 m. 6 f.

  In - Plays. 7: Oct.1948, 20-29.

803. A Day to Remember by Helen Louise Miller.

  Short. 4 m. 2 f.

  In - Plays. 9: May 1950, 15-23.

804. Daylight Wishing Time by Margaret C. Richardson.

  Short. 3 m. 3 f.

  In - Plays. 14: April 1955, 58-62.

805. Days in the Trees by Marguerite Duras. Trans. by Sonia Orwell.

  Full. 6 m. 6 f.

  In - Players. 14: Nov.1966, 31-43.

806. Dead End by Sidney Kingsley.

  Excerpt. 3 m. 0 f. 10 b. 1 g.

  In - Scholastic. 47: Nov.26,1945, 19-24.

807. Dead End by Sidney Kingsley.

  Excerpt. 3 m. 0 f. 10 b. 1 g.

  In - Scholastic. 51: Dec.15,1947, 18-20.

808. The Dead Nephew by August Von Kotzebue. Trans. from the German by Beatrice B. Beebe.

  Short. 5 m. 1 f.

  In - Poet Lore. 38: June 1927, 160-176.

809. Dead of Night by John Murray.

  Short. 3 m. 3 f.

  In - Plays. 15: March 1956, 11-21.

810. A Dead Secret by Rodney Ackland.

  Full. 8 m. 6 f.

  In - Players. 4 & 5: Sept.-Nov.1957, 22-32, 22-28, 23-29.

811. Dear Lottie by Earl J. Dias.

  Short. 3 m. 3 f.

  In - Plays. 19: April 1960, 13-23.

812. Death Knocks by Woody Allen.

  Short. 2 m. 0 f.

  In - New Yorker. 44: July 27,1968, 31-33.

813. Death of a Salesman by Arthur Miller.

  Full. 8 m. 5 f.

  In - Theatre. 35: March 1951, 49-91.

814. The Death of Aunt Aggie by Ranald Macdougall.

  Radio. 13 m. 1 f. +X.

  In - Theatre. 27: Sept.1943, 538-554.

815. The Death of Columbine by Walter J. Vail.

Full. 12 m. 5 f. +X.

In - First Stage. 4: June 1965, 62-89.

816. Death of Mohammed by Tawfiq el-Hakim.
Trans. by William R. Polk.

Short. 8 m. 2 f.

In - Atlantic. 198: Oct.1956, 186-189.

817. The Death of Nero by Herbert S. Gorman.

Short. 4 m. 0 f. 1 b. 1 g.

In - Theatre. 8: March 1924, 195-204.

818. The Death of the Duc D'Enghien by Leon
Hennique. Trans. from the French by
F. Cridland Evans.

Short. 21 m. 2 f. +X.

In - Poet Lore. 20:no.6,1909, 401-431.

819. Debit and Credit by August Strindberg. Trans.
from the German of Emil Schering by
Mary Harned.

Short. 6 m. 3 f.

In - Poet Lore. 17:no.3,1906, 28-44.

820. A December Evening, 1817 by Clive Sansom.

Short. 7 m. 0 f.

In - Fortnightly. 172(n.s.166): Dec.1949,
400-407.

821. December's Gifts by Frances Duggar.

Short. 1 m. 1 f. 12 c. +c.X.

In - Plays. 12: Dec.1952, 60-64.

822. The Deep Blue Sea by Terence Rattigan.

Full. 5 m. 3 f.

In - Theatre. 37: July 1953, 34-59.

823. The Deerslayer by Robert St.Clair. Based
on episode from the novel by James
Fenimore Cooper.

Short. 3 m. 3 f.

In - Scholastic. 37: Sept.23,1940, 17-19.

824. The Defense Never Rests by Dorothy Deming.

Short. 8 m. 5 f.

In - Plays. 9: Jan.1950, 31-36.

825. Deirdre of the Sorrows by John Millington
Synge.

Full. 8 m. 3 f.

In - Theatre. 34: Aug.1950, 69-88.

826. The Demon's Shell. Trans. from the Japanese
by Yone Noguchi.

Short. 2 m. 0 f.

In - Poet Lore. 17:no.3,1906, 44-49.

827. The Departures by Jacques Languirand. Trans.
from the French by Albert Bermel.

Full. 3 m. 3 f.

In - Gambit. 2: no.5, 41-74.

828. A Deputy for Broken Bow by Harold Cable.

Short. 4 m. 5 f.

In - Plays. 27: Nov.1967, 13-22.

829. The Derelict by Clarendon Ross.

Short. 2 m. 1 f.

In - Poet Lore. 30:no.4,1919, 601-607.

830. The Desert Blooms by Gladys L. Schmitt.

Radio. 4 m. 2 f. 1 b.

In - Scholastic. 51: Nov.17,1947, 18-20.

831. The Deserter by Lascelles Abercrombie.

Short. 5 m. 3 f. 1 g. +X.

In - Theatre. 6: July 1922, 237-254.

832. The Deserter by August von Kotzebue.
Trans. by Beatrice B. Beebe.

Short. 4 m. 1 f. +m.X.

In - Golden. 7: Feb.1928, 193-202.

833. The Devil and Daniel Webster by Stephen
Vincent Benét.

Excerpt. 7 m. 0 f. + jury (1 voice).

In - Scholastic. 39: Sept.22,1941, 17-19+.

834. The Devil Comes to Alcaraz by William H.
Fulham.

Short. 5 m. 5 f.

In - Theatre. 14: Sept.1930, 797-803.

835. Dial "M" for Mother by Helen Louise Miller.

Short. 5 m. 3 f.

In - Plays. 21: May 1962, 13-24.

836. Dial "M" for Murder by Frederick Knott.

Full. 5 m. 1 f.

In - Theatre. 39: March 1955, 32-63.

837. Dialogue of the Dead by Lucian.

Short. 8 m. 0 f.

In - Golden. 13: Jan.1931, 61-62.

838. The Diamond Earring by Marjorie B. Paradis.

Short. 4 m. 4 f. +X.

In - Plays. 16: Jan.1957, 1-13.

839. Dick Whittington and His Cat adap. by
Helen Louise Miller.

Radio. 11 m. 2 f. 1 b. +ch.

In - Plays. 15: Jan.1956, 83-89.

840. Dick Whittington and His Cat by Adele Thane.

Short. 3 m. 4 f. 1 cat +X.

In - Plays. 21: April 1962, 45-53.

841. Dickens' Christmas Carol adap. by Frederick
Garrigue.

Radio. 13 m. 3 f. 2 b.

In - Scholastic. 51: Dec.8,1947, 17-20.

842. Dingo by Charles Wood.

Full. 12 m. 0 f.

In - Players. 14: July 1967, 23-38.

843. Dinner With the Family by Jean Anouilh.
Trans. by Edward Owen Marsh.

Full. 6 m. 6 f.

In - Players. 5: Feb.& March 1958, 25-30,
25-30.

844. Directive for Democracy by Marion A. Roberts.

Radio. 3 m. 4 f. 6 un.

In - Scholastic. 49: Jan.20,1947, 13-14.

The Discomfited Husband.

see

George Dandin.

845. The Disenchanted by Budd Schulberg and
Harvey Breit.

Full. 19 m. 12 f.

In - Theatre. 44: Aug.1960, 22-47.

846. A Dish for the Colonel by Nina Brown Baker.

Short. 6 m. 2 f.

In - Plays. 3: Nov.1943, 18-25.

847. A Dish for the King by Mildred Hark and
Noel McQueen.

Short. 11 m. 7 f. +m.X.

In - Plays. 17: Jan.1958, 35-42.

848. A Dish of Green Peas by Aileen Fisher and
Olive Rabe.

Short. 3 m. 2 f.

In - Plays. 15: Feb.1956, 55-63.

849. Dissolution by Arthur Schnitzler.

In - Golden. 16: Aug.1932, 175-180.

850. Distress by Henri Lavedan. Trans. from the
French by William V. Silverberg.

Short. 1 m. 1 f.

In - Poet Lore. 30:no.1,1919, 24-29.

851. The Do-Nothing Frog by Patricia Clapp.

Short. 1 m. 0 f. 9 b. 6 g. + c.X.

In - Plays. 27: April 1968, 69-73.

852. Do You Know the Milky Way? by Karl
Wittlinger.

Full. 2 m. 1 f.

In - Theatre. 47: June 1963, 37-60.

853. Dobromila Rettig by Alois Jirásek. Trans.
from the Bohemian.

In - Poet Lore. 31: Dec.1920, 475-537.

854. The Doctor and the Patient by William
Saroyan.

Short. 2 m. 0 f.

In - Atlantic. 211: April 1963, 51.

855. Doctor Farmer by Shirley Simon.

Short. 7 m. 3 f. 4 un.

In - Plays. 18: April 1959, 75-80.

856. A Doctor for Lucinda by Margaret Mantle.

Short. 4 m. 2 f.

In - Plays. 14: Jan.1955, 59-64.

857. The Doctor in Spite of Himself by Molière.
Adap. by Lewy Olfson.

Radio. 6 m. 3 f.

In - Plays. 16: April 1957, 73-80.

858. Doctor Know All by Helen L. Howard.

Short. 8 m. 4 f.

In - Plays. 9: Oct.1949, 54-58.

859. Doctor Know-It-All adap. by Margaret C. Hall
from Grimms' Fairy Tales.

Short. 9 m. 1 f.

In - Plays. 27: April 1968, 65-68.

860. Dr. Leviticus and the Wicked Imp by J.H.
Bealmear.

Short. 6 m. 4 f. 3 b. 1 g.

In - Plays. 26: Jan.1967, 57-64.

861. <u>Dr. McGrath</u> by Edmund Wilson

Short. 5 m. 0 f.

In - Commentary. 43: May 1967, 60-67.

862. <u>Doctor Manners</u> by Mildred Hark and Noel McQueen.

Short. 3 m. 4 f.

In - Plays. 10: April 1951, 67-72.

863. <u>Dr. Manners</u> by Mildred Hark and Noel McQueen.

Short. 1 m. 1 f. 2 b. 3 g.

In - Plays. 26: Jan.1967, 75-80.

864. <u>Doctor Time's Office</u> by Alice Very.

Short. 5 m. 2 f. 22 un.

In - Plays. 4: Jan.1945, 57-60.

865. <u>The Doctor Turns Into a Poet</u> by Gladys L. Schmitt.

Short. 3 m. 1 f.

In - Scholastic. 24: May 5,1934, 7-8.

866. <u>The Doctor Who Wore Skirts</u> by Laura Kerr.

Radio. 5 m. 7 f.

In - Plays. 6: Feb.1947, 79-84.

867. <u>Doctor's Daughter</u> by Helen Louise Miller.

Short. 2 m. 3 f.

In - Plays. 4: May 1945, 27-35.

868. <u>Doctor's Daughter</u> by Helen Louise Miller.

Short. 2 m. 3 f.

In - Plays. 15: May 1956, 83-91.

869. <u>Doll Shop Window</u> by Catherine Urban.

Short. 3 m. 6 f.

In - Plays. 6: April 1947, 59-61.

870. <u>The Dolls</u> by Mildred Hark and Noel McQueen.

Short. 1 m. 6 f.

In - Plays. 7: April 1948, 53-57.

871. <u>Dolly Saves the Picture</u> by Lindsey Barbee.

Short. 4 m. 5 f.

In - Plays. 5: Feb.1946, 49-57.

872. <u>Dolly's Little Bills</u> by Henry Arthur Jones.

Short. 2 m. 1 f.

In - Golden. 8: Nov.1928, 641-649.

873. <u>Don Juan in Hell</u> by George Bernard Shaw. From his <u>Man and Superman</u>.

Excerpt. 3 m. 1 f.

In - Theatre. 36: April 1952, 50-66.

874. <u>Don Juan's Failure</u> by Maurice Baring.

Short. 1 m. 2 f.

In - Golden. 13: April 1931, 69-71.

875. <u>Don Pedro II of Brazil</u> by Samuel S. Ullman.

Short. 16 m. 2 f.

In - Plays. 6: April 1947, 32-38.

876. <u>Don Quixote</u> by Miguel de Cervantes. Adap. by Lewy Olfson.

Radio. 11 m. 3 f.

In - Plays. 20: March 1961, 85-94.

877. <u>Don't Call Us - We'll Call You</u> by John Murray.

Short. 6 m. 3 f.

In - Plays. 21: Feb.1962, 11-22.

878. <u>Don't Send for Hector</u> by Margaret E. Slattery.

Short. 5 m. 4 f.

In - Plays. 25: Jan.1966, 1-13.

879. <u>Don't Tell the Folks Back Home</u> by Earl J. Dias.

Short. 0 m. 12 f.

In - Plays. 23: Jan.1964, 27-37.

880. <u>The Door</u> by Charles W. Stokes.

In - Canadian M. 58: April 1922, 498-502.

881. <u>The Door</u> by John Murray.

Short. 1 m. 2 f.

In - Plays. 10: March 1951, 10-18.

882. <u>Door Mats</u> by Stella Dunaway Whipkey.

Short. 2 m. 2 f.

In - Poet Lore. 40: March 1929, 92-109.

883. <u>A Door Must be Either Open or Shut</u> by Alfred de Musset. Trans. by S.L. Gwynn.

Short. 2 m. 0 f.

In - Golden. 4: July 1926, 67-74.

<u>Double Entry</u>.

see

<u>The Bible Salesman</u>.

and

<u>The Oldest Trick in the World</u>.

884. Double Exposure by Mildred Hark and Noel McQueen.

Short. 3 m. 2 f.

In - Plays. 4: Oct.1944, 1-9.

885. The Double Miracle by Robert Garland.

Short. 6 m. 2 f.

In - Forum. 53: April 1915, 511-527.

886. The Double Nine of Chih Yuan by Paul T. Nolan.

Short. 4 m. 2 f.

In - Plays. 23: Oct.1963, 78-84.

887. Double Talk by Paul S. McCoy.

Short. 2 m. 1 f.

In - Plays. 20: Jan.1961, 84-89.

888. The Dragon's Head by Don Ramon del Valle Inclan. Trans. from the Spanish by May Heywood Broun.

Short. 16 m. 4 f. +X.

In - Poet Lore. 29:no.4,1918, 531-564.

889. The Dralda Bloom by Leon Cunningham.

Short. 9 m. 3 f.

In - Poet Lore. 30:no.4,1919, 553-566.

890. The Dreadful Dragon by Margaret Wylie Brydon and Esther Ziegler.

Short. 7 m. 8 f. +X.

In - Plays. 10: Jan.1951, 35-47.

891. The Dreadful Dragon by Margaret Wylie Brydon and Esther Ziegler.

Short. 7 m. 8 f. +X.

In - Plays. 18: Feb.1959, 63-75.

892. A Dream by Alice Thornbery Smith.

Short. 0 m. 1 g. + c.X.

In - Etude. 53: May 1935, 318.

893. The Dream by Herbert Edward Mierow.

Short. 6 m. 1 f.

In - Poet Lore. 58: June 1963, 123-145.

894. The Dream Comes True by Lindsey Barbee.

Short. 0 m. 8 f.

In - Plays. 3: May 1944, 56-57.

895. The Dream of a Spring Morning by Gabriele D'Annunzio. Trans. from the Italian by Anna Schenck.

Short. 2 m. 5 f.

In - Poet Lore. 14:no.1,1902, 6-36.

896. The Dream of an Autumn Sunset by Gabriele D'Annunzio. Trans. from the Italian by Anna Schenck.

Short. 0 m. 9 f.

In - Poet Lore. 15:no.1,1904, 6-29.

897. Dream On, Soldier by Moss Hart and George S. Kaufman.

Short. 11 m. 2 f.

In - Theatre. 27: Sept.1943, 533-535.

898. The Dreammaker's Tree by Mary B. Huber.

Short. 1 m. 8 f.

In - Plays. 5: Dec.1945, 55-56.

899. The Dreamy Kid by Eugene O'Neill.

Short. 0 m. 3 f. 1 b.

In - Theatre. 4: Jan.1920, 41-56.

900. Drums in the Dusk by Katherine Lauré.

Short. 3 m. 2 f.

In - Plays. 10: April 1951, 17-30.

901. The Drums of Father Ned by Sean O'Casey.

Full. 15 m. 4 f.

In - Theatre. 44: May 1960, 23-52.

902. The Drums of Oude by Austin Strong.

Short. 7 m. 1 f.

In - Golden. 10: Oct.1929, 103-110.

903. The Drunken Sisters by Thornton Wilder.

Short. 1 m. 3 f.

In - Atlantic. 200: Nov.1957, 92-95.

904. Dryad by George Sterling.

Short. 1 m. 2 f.

In - Overland. 84(n.s.): Sept.1926, 293-294.

905. The Duel adap. by Jack Holton from the novel by Anton Chekhov.

Full. 8 m. 3 f.

In - Players. 15: June 1968, 27-43.

906. The Duke and the Actress by Arthur Schnitzler. Trans. from the German by Hans Weysz.

Short. 14 m. 4 f. +X.

In - Poet Lore. 21:no.4,1910, 257-284.

907. The Dulce Man by Catherine Blanton.

Short. 3 m. 2 f. +X.

In - Plays. 7: Jan.1948, 36-41.

908. The Dulce Man by Catherine Blanton.
Short. 4 m. 2 f. +X.
In - Plays. 22: Jan.1963, 55-60.

909. Dummling and the Golden Goose adap. by
Adele Thane from Grimms' Fairy Tales.
Short. 15 m. 9 f. 4 c. +g.X.
In - Plays. 25: Jan.1966, 35-43.

910. Dusky Singing by Gladys L. Schmitt.
Radio. 2 m. 2 f.
In - Scholastic. 32: Apr.30,1938, 21E-22E+.

911. Dust of the Road by Kenneth S. Goodman.
Short. 3 m. 1 f.
In - Scholastic. 27: Dec.14,1935, 7-8+.

912. The Dwarfs' Beards by Claribel Spamer.
Short. 5 m. 0 f.
In - Plays. 5: April 1946, 70-73.

913. Dyer Day by Jackson Burgess.
Short. 0 m. 2 f.
In - First Stage. 4: Dec.1965, 222-225.

914. The Ear of Malchus by Peter de Prins.
Trans. by Calvin Evans.
Full. 5 m. (1 Negro). 2 f.
In - Gambit. 4: no.13, 5-97.

915. Early Snow by Komparu Zembo Motoyazu.
Trans. from the Japanese by Arthur Waley.
Short. 0 m. 5 f. +ch.
In - Poetry. 15: March 1920, 317-320.

916. East of Eden, Genesis iv. 16. by Christopher
Morley.
Short. 2 m. 2 f. 1 baby.
In - New Republic. 39: Aug.13,1924, 318-323.

917. Easter Bunny Magic by June Barr.
Short. 5 m. 4 f. 1 un.
In - Plays. 13: April 1954, 52-56.

918. Easter Bunny on Pleasant Street by Gladys
V. Smith.
Short. 4 m. 9 f. 7 c.
In - Plays. 19: March 1960, 69-72.

919. Easter Egg Magic by Mary Stansbury.
Short. 6 m. 3 f.
In - Plays. 16: April 1957, 41-46.

920. Easter Egg Rolling by Alice Very.
Short. 15 m. 4 f. +X.
In - Plays. 5: March 1946, 61-64.

921. The Easter Hop by Mildred Hark and Noel
McQueen.
Short. 4 m. 3 f.
In - Plays. 13: April 1954, 1-12.

922. Easter Lily by Walter King.
Short. 3 m. 2 f.
In - Plays. 7: April 1948, 34-37.

923. Easter Reminders by Violet Hummell.
Short. 7 m. 7 f.
In - Plays. 16: April 1957, 56-58.

924. Ebenezer Neverspend by John G. Colson.
Short. 2 m. 2 f.
In - Plays. 12: Dec.1952, 65-67.

925. Edward and Agrippina by René de Obaldia.
Trans. from the French by Donald Watson.
Short. 2 m. 1 f.
In - Gambit. 1: no.2, 59-67.

926. Edward, My Son by Robert Morley and Noel
Langley.
Full. 10 m. 3 f.
In - Theatre. 33: Sept.1949, 58-96.

927. The Efficiency Expert by Robert Fontaine.
Short. 4 m. 3 f.
In - Plays. 24: Oct.1964, 77-81.

928. Eglantina by Mary E. Wilkins Freeman.
Full. 3 m. 3 f.
In - Ladies' Home. 27: July 1910, 13.

929. The Egyptian Cinderella by Lowell Swortzell.
Short. 6 m. 3 f. 12 c.
In - Plays. 21: Feb.1962, 47-52.

930. Eight Column Streamer by Salvador Novo.
Trans. from the Spanish by Willis
Knapp Jones.
Full. 4 m. 2 f.
In - Poet Lore. 62: March 1967, 25-80.

931. Eight Hundred Rubles by John G. Nuhardt.
Short. 1 m. 2 f.
In - Forum. 53: March 1915, 393-402.

932. Eight-Thirty Sharp by Jasmine S. Van Dresser.

Short. 1 m. 2 f. 2 b. 1 dog.

In - Delineator. 99: Jan.1922, 20-21.

933. Elaine by Mildred Weinberger.

Short. 6 m. 5 f.

In - Poet Lore. 34: March 1923, 72-110.

934. Election Day in Spooksville by Rose
      Kacherian Rybak.

Short. 11 m. 5 f. 3 un. +X.

In - Plays. 24: Oct.1964, 29-39.

935. The Election of Lincoln by Robert E.
      Sherwood. Abr. from his Lincoln in
      Illinois.

Excerpt. 6 m. 1 f. +X.

In - Scholastic. 42: Feb.8,1943, 19-20.

936. The Election of the Roulette by William
      Byron Mowery.

Short. 4 m. 1 f. 2 c.

In - Poet Lore. 33:no.4,1922, 525-536.

937. Electra by Euripides. Trans. by Gilbert
      Murray.

Excerpt. 4 m. 4 f.

In - Golden. 15: Jan.1932, 82-88.

938. Eleven Million. (Anon.)

Short. 4 m. 3 f.

In - Jl., N.E.A. 26: Dec.1937, 283.

939. The Elf in the Woods by Mary Nygaard
      Peterson.

Short. 8 m. 3 f.

In - Plays. 18: March 1959, 79-86.

940. Elga by Gerhart Hauptmann. Trans. from the
      German by Mary Harned.

Short. 10 m. 4 f.

In - Poet Lore. 17:no.1,1906, 1-35.

941. Elijah Lovejoy by George Jennings.

Radio. 13 m. 1 f.

In - Scholastic. 40: March 23,1942, 17-19+.

942. The Elixir by James De Felice.

Short. 6 m. 2 f. +X.

In - First Stage. 3: Dec.1963, 46-58.

943. Ellen Comes Through by Priscilla Kent.

Radio. 2 m. 4 f.

In - Scholastic. 43: Sept.27,1943, 15-16.

944. Elopements While You Wait by Caroline D.
      Stevens.

Short. 2 m. 2 f.

In - Drama. 13: Feb.1923, 184-187.

945. The Elves and the Shoemaker by E.B. Kane.

Radio. 3 m. 3 f. 3 b. 1 g. +X.

In - Plays. 7: Dec.1947, 86-91.

946. The Elves and the Shoemaker adap. by Adele
      Thane from Grimms' Fairy Tales.

Short. 2 m. 3 f. 1 b. 1 g. 9 c.

In - Plays. 25: Dec.1965, 33-40.

947. Emilia Viviani by Charmion Von Wiegand.

In - Poet Lore. 36: Dec.1925, 552-568.

948. The Emperor and the Nightingale by Hans
      Christian Andersen. Adap. by Michael
      T. Leech.

Short. 7 m. 2 f.

In - Plays. 26: April 1967, 49-54.

949. The Emperor Jones by Eugene O'Neill.

Full. 3 m. 1 f. +X.

In - Theatre. 5: Jan.1921, 29-59.

950. The Emperor Jones by Eugene O'Neill.

Full. 3 m. 1 f. +X.

In - Golden. 3: April 1926, 517-530.

951. The Emperor's Daughters by Cena Christopher
      Draper.

Short. 7 m. 4 f.

In - Plays. 10: May 1951, 43-54.

952. The Emperor's New Clothes by Hans Christian
      Andersen. Adap. by Deborah Newman.

Short. 5 m. 3 f. +X.

In - Plays. 12: April 1953, 61-65.

953. The Emperor's New Robes by Marie Agnes Foley.

Short. 5 m. 4 f. 3 c. +X.

In - Plays. 23: March 1964, 41-51.

954. The Emperor's Nightingale by Hans Christian
      Anderson. Adap. by Adele Thane.

Short. 7 m. 5 f. 2 c.

In - Plays. 22: Nov.1962, 41-50.

955. The Empire Builders by Boris Vian.

Full. 3 m. 3 f.

In - Players. 10: Oct.1962, 31-42.

956. The Empty Room by Graham DuBois.
Short. 9 m. 3 f.
In - Plays. 7: Dec.1947, 12-20.

957. The Empty Room at the Inn by Graham DuBois.
Short. 9 m. 3 f. +1m.1f.X.
In - Plays. 25: Dec.1965, 23-31.

958. The Enchanted by Jean Giraudoux. Adap. by
Maurice Valency.
Full. 9 m. 3 f. 7 g.
In - Theatre. 34: Oct.1950, 57-88.

959. The Enchanted Bicycle by John Carroll.
Short. 5 m. 9 un.
In - Plays. 27: Oct.1967, 83-88.

960. The Enchanted Broom by Georgiana Lieder Lanr.
Short. 9 m. 9 f. (not all human).
In - Plays. 26: Oct.1966, 72-80.

961. The Enchanted Chimney by Mary T. Hart.
In - Woman's Home. 37: Dec.1910, 46-47.

962. The Enchanted Christmas Tree by Percival
Wilde.
Full. 3 m. 1 f. + many c.
In - Pictorial. 26: Dec.1924, 14-15+.

963. The Enchanted Cottage by Deborah Newman.
Short. 0 m. 16 f.
In - Plays. 20: Oct.1960, 63-67.

964. Enchanted, I'm Sure by James R. Chisholm.
Short. 4 m. 2 f.
In - Plays. 18: Jan.1959, 35-44.

965. The Enchanted Island by Mabel S. Van Tassell.
Short. 3 m. 3 f. 1 g. +X.
In - St. Nicholas. 60: May 1933, 338-339+.

966. The Enchanted Princess by Constance Whitman
Baher.
Short. 9 m. 4 f. +c.X.
In - Plays. 24: May 1965, 55-64.

967. The End of Chipi Gonzalez by Jose Maria
Rivarola Matto. Trans. by Willis
Knapp Jones.
Full. 12 m. 3 f.
In - Poet Lore. 60: June 1965, 99-146.

968. The End of the Line by John Murray.
Short. 5 m. 3 f. +X.
In - Plays. 16: Oct.1956, 25-36.

969. The End of the Road by Graham DuBois.
Short. 3 m. 4 f.
In - Plays. 4: Jan.1945, 27-35.

970. The End of the Row by Paul Green.
Short. 1 m. 4 f.
In - Poet Lore. 35: March 1924, 58-74.

971. The End of the Story by Margaret Barbrick
Purcell.
Short. 0 m. 3 f.
In - Poet Lore. 61: Dec.1966, 387-394.

972. The End of the Trail by Ernest Howard
Culbertson.
Short. 2 m. 1 f.
In - Theatre. 8: May 1924, 326-340.

973. The Enemy - A Monologue by I.J. Alexander.
Short. 0 m. either 6 f. or one actress.
In - Theatre. 28: Sept.1944, 529-533.

974. Engineering a Bid by Samuel S. Richmond.
Short. 3 m. 1 f.
In - Plays. 9: Jan.1950, 70-75.

975. English as She is Spoke by Tristan Bernard.
Trans. by J. Harris Gable.
Short. 5 m. 2 f. 1 b.
In - Golden. 7: May 1928, 677-683.

976. Enoch Arden by Alfred, Lord Tennyson.
Adap. by Lewy Olfson.
Radio. 3 m. 3 f.
In - Plays. 17: March 1958, 79-88.

977. Enter Dora; Exit Dad by Freeman Tilden.
Short. 4 m. 1 f.
In - Ladies' Home. 39: May 1922, 15+.

978. Enter George Washington by Mildred Hark
and Noel McQueen.
Short. 2 m. 3 f.
In - Plays. 7: Feb.1948, 41-49.

979. Enter George Washington by Mildred Hark and
Noel McQueen.
Short. 2 m. 3 f.
In - Plays. 22: Feb.1963, 53-61.

980. Enter Juliet by Lindsey Barbee.

Short. 3 m. 5 f.

In - Plays. 8: Nov.1948, 18-24.

981. Entertaining Mr. Sloane by Joe Orton.

Full. 3 m. 1 f.

In - Players. 11 & 12: Aug.& Sept.1964, 17-24,
17-24.

982. Entremes of the Cave of Salamanca by
Miguel de Cervantes Saavedra. Trans.
by Willis Knapp Jones.

In - Poet Lore. 39: March 1928, 120-131.

983. Ephraim by Allan Knee.

Short. 2 m. 0 f.

In - First Stage. 5: March 1966, 23-29.

984. Ephraim's Breite by Cerl Hauptmann. Trans.
by Mary Harned.

Full. 10 m. 10 f. +X.

In - Poet Lore. 12:no.4,1900, 465-536.

985. Epilogue by Henri Lavedan. Trans. from the
French by William V. Silverberg.

Short. 4 m. 1 f.

In - Poet Lore. 30:no.1,1919, 29-34.

986. Episode by Arthur Schnitzler.

Short. 2 m. 1 f.

In - Golden. 17: Jan.1933, 70-77.

987. Epitaph for George Dillon by John Osborne
and Anthony Creighton.

Full. 5 m. 4 f.

In - Theatre. 46: March 1962, 25-56.

988. Equals by August Strindberg.

Short. 2 m. 0 f.

In - Golden. 7: Jan.1928, 85-91.

989. L'Eroica by Cesare Lodovici. Trans. from
the Italian by Petronelle Sombart.

Short. 4 m. 6 f.

In - Poet Lore. 34: June 1923, 159-176.

990. The Eternal Presence by André Dumas. Trans.
by Carrie Horton Blackman.

Short. 1 m. 1 f.

In - Poet Lore. 29:no.4,1918, 459-468.

991. Eve Has Seven Faces by Eisig Silberschlag.

Short. 8 m. 3 f.

In - Poet Lore. 49: Jan.1943, 50-76.

992. Evening Dress Indispensable by Roland Pertwee.

Short. 2 m. 3 f.

In - Ladies' Home. 4: Nov.1924, 10-11+.

993. An Evening in an Important Asylum by Louis
Stettner.

Short. 12 m. 1 f. +X.

In - First Stage. 6: June 1967, 119-132.

994. An Evening of Mozart by Jean Sanders.

Short. 5 m. 12 f. 4 g. 2 b.

In - Etude. 52: Jan.1934, 9-10.

995. An Evening With the Older Set by Kenneth
Lewis Roberts.

Short. 4 m. 5 f. 1 b. 1 g.

In - Sat. Evening. 199: May 28,1927, 10+.

996. Events While Guarding the Bofors Gun by
John McGrath.

Full. 11 m. 0 f.

In - Players. 13: June 1966, 31-46+.

997. Ever Since Eve by Florence Ryerson and Colin
C. Clements. Ed. by Margaret Mayorga.

Excerpt. 3 m. 3 f.

In - Scholastic. 40: April 13,1942, 17-19.

998. Ever' Snitch by Irene Fussler.

Short. 2 m. 2 f. 1 b.

In - Carolina. 4: June 1931, 43-58.

999. The Ever Womanly by Newell Dunbar.

Short. 3 m. 1 f.

In - Arena. 31: Feb.1904, 180-198.

1000. Evergreen by Ethel Mahar.

Short. 11 un. +X.

In - Plays. 5: Dec.1945, 40-43.

1001. Every Day is Thanksgiving by Graham Du Bois.

Short. 4 m. 5 f.

In - Plays. 20: Nov.1960, 41-50.

1002. Every Room with Bath by John Murray.

Short. 5 m. 6 f.

In - Plays. 19: Nov.1959, 11-22.

1003. Everybody Join Hands by Owen Dodson.

Short. 1 m. +ch.

In - Theatre. 27: Sept.1943, 555-565.

1004. Everyday Fairies by Jessica Beatty.
    Short. 0 m. 1 f. 4 b. 4 g. 8 c.
    In - Woman's Home. 42: May 1915, 38+.

1005. Everygirl by Rachel Lyman Field.
    In - St. Nicholas. 40: Oct.1913, 1115-1117.

1006. Everywhere Christmas by Alice Very.
    Short. 15 m. 9 f. +X.
    In - Plays. 4: Dec.1944, 56-60.

1007. The Evolution of the Iris by Annye Allison.
    Short. 6 m. 4 f. 8 b. 14 g.
    In - School Arts. 26: March 1927, 406-410.

1008. Excitement at the Circus by Irving A. Leitner.
    Short. 9 m. 2 f. 5 b. 5 g. 1 "lion".
    In - Plays. 27: Nov.1967, 79-82.

1009. The Exile by Amy Josephine Klauber.
    Short. 7 m. 1 f.
    In - Poet Lore. 33:no.2,1922, 246-254.

1010. The Experiment by Samuel S. Richmond.
    Short. 5 m. 3 f.
    In - Plays. 7: May 1948, 69-76.

1011. Express to Valley Forge by Earl J. Dias.
    Short. 2 m. 4 f.
    In - Plays. 9: Feb.1950, 54-63.

1012. Express to Valley Forge by Earl J. Dias.
    Short. 2 m. 4 f.
    In - Plays. 17: Feb.1958, 51-59.

1013. Exterior (pantomime) by Elmer Rice.
    Short. 12 m. 7 f. 1 b. 1 baby.
    In - Scholastic. 29: Nov.14,1936, 11-12.

1014. The Exterior Decorator by Claire Boiko.
    Short. 3 m. 1 f. 16 un.
    In - Plays. 23: March 1964, 60-64.

1015. Eyes Right! by Dorothy Deming.
    Short. 3 m. 4 f. +X.
    In - Plays. 12: March 1953, 67-70.

1016. A Fable by Ralph Scholl.
    Short. 5 m. 1 f. +X.
    In - First Stage. 6: Sept.1967, 177-186.

1017. Fabre's Little World by John Murray.
    Short. 3 m. 3 f.
    In - Plays. 11: March 1952, 17-27.

1018. The Face is Familiar by Earl J. Dias.
    Short. 9 m. 3 f. +m.X.
    In - Plays. 19: Jan.1960, 1-13.

1019. Facing Reality by Floy Pascal.
    Short. 2 m. 2 f.
    In - Poet Lore. 33:no.3,1922, 451-457.

1020. Facing the Future by Walter Hackett.
    Short. 4 m. 2 f.
    In - Plays. 5: Oct.1945, 56-65.

1021. Fads and Frills by M.C. Richmond.
    Short. 4 m. 1 f.
    In - Indus. Arts. 19: March 1930, 91-93.

1022. The Fair-God (Malinche) by Josephina Niggli.
    Excerpt. 5 m. 2 f.
    In - Carolina. 9: Dec.1936, 101-104.

1023. Fair Today, Followed by Tomorrow by Robert Fontaine.
    Short. 4 m. 1 f.
    In - Plays. 24: April 1965, 81-84.

1024. The Fairest Pitcher of Them All by Harold Cable.
    Short. 12 m. 12 f.
    In - Plays. 25: March 1966, 27-41.

1025. The Fairest Spirit by Carolyn Wells.
    Short. 0 m. 16 f. +f.ch.
    In - Ladies' Home. 32: May 1915, 15+.

1026. Fairy Gold by Alexander Nicolaievich Ostrovsky. Trans. by C.C. Daniels and G.R. Noyes.
    Full. 8 m. 3 f. 1 b. +X.
    In - Poet Lore. 40: March 1929, 1-80.

1027. Fairy Gold by Mary Nygaard Peterson.
    Short. 4 m. 1 f. +X.
    In - Plays. 17: March 1958, 55-60.

1028. The Fairy Prince by Sydney K. Phelps.
    Short. 0 m. 3 f.
    In - 19th C. 63: Jan.1908, 138-143.

1029. Faith by Margaret Evans.

Short. 2 m. 1 f.

In - Poet Lore. 33:no.1,1922, 132-137.

1030. The Fall of the City by Archibald MacLeish.

Radio. 7 m. 1 f. +ch. +X.

In - Scholastic. 31: Nov.13,1937, 17E-23E.

1031. Fame and the Poet by Lord Dunsany.

Short. 2 m. 1 f.

In - Atlantic. 124: Aug.1919, 175-184.

1032. Fame and the Poet by Lord Dunsany.

Short. 2 m. 1 f.

In - Golden. 12: Nov.1930, 87-89.

1033. A Family Affair by Muriel Ward.

Short. 5 m. 4 f.

In - Plays. 25: Jan.1966, 21-34.

1034. A Family in Space by Charles Rittenhouse.

Short. 16 m. 7 f.

In - Plays. 18: March 1959, 49-58.

1035. Famous Nickname by Aileen Fisher and Olive Rabe.

Short. 0 m. 0 f. 9 b. 9 g. 1 un.

In - Plays. 15: Jan.1956, 77-78.

1036. Fanghorn by David Pinner.

Full. 2 m. 3 f.

In - Players. 15: Jan.1968, 23-37.

1037. Fanny's Consent by José Moratin. Trans. by A.E. Bagstad.

Full. 4 m. 3 f.

In - Poet Lore. 40: June 1929, 159-214.

1038. The Far-Away Princess by Hermann Sudermann. Trans. by Grace Frank.

Short. 2 m. 7 f.

In - Golden. 5: May 1927, 625-633.

1039. A Far Country by Henry Denker.

Full. 5 m. 5 f.

In - Theatre. 46: Dec.1962, 25-56.

1040. The Farce of the Worthy Master Pierre Patelin, the Lawyer trans. from the Mediaeval French by Maurice Relonde.

Short. 4 m. 1 f.

In - Poet Lore. 28:no.3,1917, 343-364.

1041. Farewell to Calvin by Paul S. McCoy.

Short. 3 m. 4 f.

In - Plays. 19: March 1960, 11-22.

1042. Farmyard Frolic by Karin Asbrand.

Short. 8 m. 1 f. 8 un.

In - Plays. 6: May 1947, 59-61.

1043. The Fascinating Mr. Denby by Selwin Sage and Howard Mumford Jones.

Short. 0 m. 4 f.

In - Drama. 14: Feb.1924, 175-177.

1044. Fashion by Anna Cora Mowatt.

Excerpt. 2 f.

In - Theatre. 22: Sept.1938, 683-684.

1045. Fashion Show by Dorothy Deming.

Short. 4 m. 3 f. +X.

In - Plays. 9: March 1950, 25-30.

1046. The Fatal French Dentist by Oscar Mandel.

Short. 3 m. 3 f.

In - First Stage. 4: June 1965, 90-96.

1047. Father by Colin Campbell Clements.

In - Poet Lore. 31: June 1920, 187-196.

1048. Father Hits the Jackpot by Juliet Garver.

Short. 3 m. 6 f.

In - Plays. 15: April 1956, 55-62.

1049. Father Hits the Jackpot by Juliet Garver.

Short. 4 m. 6 f.

In - Plays. 26: May 1967, 65-72.

1050. Father Keeps House by Mildred Hark and Noel McQueen.

Short. 5 m. 4 f. +m.X.

In - Plays. 14: May 1955, 19-29.

1051. Father of the Year by Juliet Garver.

Short. 2 m. 9 f.

In - Plays. 15: Jan.1956, 35-44.

1052. Father Talks Turkey by Helen Louise Miller.

Short. 3 m. 4 f.

In - Plays. 4: Nov.1944, 1-10.

1053. Father Talks Turkey by Helen Louise Miller.

Short. 3 m. 4 f.

In - Plays. 7: Nov.1947, 10-19.

1054. Father Talks Turkey by Helen Louise Miller.

Short. 3 m. 4 f.

In - Plays. 28: Nov.1968, 25-34.

1055. Father's Easter Hat by Mildred Hark and Noel McQueen.

Short. 3 m. 3 f.

In - Plays. 14: April 1955, 41-48.

1056. Fear by Hugo von Hofmannsthal. Trans. by Mariana Scott.

Short. 3 m. 0 f.

In - Poet Lore. 60: Sept.1965, 244-250.

1057. The Fearless Knight and the Dragon by Elizabeth Brenner.

Short. 8 m. 3 f. 4 un. +X.

In - Plays. 19: Feb.1960, 59-66.

1058. The Fearless One by Mary Ann Nicholson.

Short. 5 m. 2 f.

In - Plays. 17: Jan.1958, 57-62.

1059. The Feast of the Thousand Lanterns by Betty Tracy Huff.

Short. 5 m. 3 f. +X.

In - Plays. 19: April 1960, 60-64.

1060. The Feather Fisher by Zellah K. Macdonald.

Short. 4 m. 1 f.

In - Touchstone. 4: Nov.1918, 120-128.

1061. The Feathered Dream by Helen Ramsey.

Short. 5 m. 3 f.

In - Plays. 20: April 1961, 23-30.

1062. A February Failure by Helen Louise Miller.

Short. 1 m. 1 f. +c.X.

In - Plays. 14: Feb.1955, 43-46.

1063. February Frenzy by Helen Louise Miller.

Short. 4 m. 4 f. +f.X.

In - Plays. 13: Feb.1954, 1-11.

1064. February Heroes by Mildred Hark and Noel McQueen.

Short. 4 m. 4 f.

In - Plays. 20: Feb.1961, 39-48.

1065. A February Play by Sally Werner.

Short. 1 m. 12 un. +X.

In - Plays. 13: Feb.1954, 60-62.

1066. Fern's Friends by Janice Auritt Oser.

Short. 3 m. 5 f.

In - Plays. 15: Jan.1956, 67-73.

1067. Fetters and Dreams by Graham DuBois.

Short. 9 m. 0 f.

In - Plays. 6: Oct.1947, 10-18.

1068. Feudin' Fun by Earl J. Dias.

Short. 5 m. 3 f.

In - Plays. 15: Nov.1955, 21-30.

1069. The Field of Honor by George Hamilton.

Short. 4 m. 3 f.

In - Plays. 11: Feb.1952, 21-29.

1070. Fiesta by Jean McArthur.

Short. 7 m. 10 f. 1 "horse". +X.

In - Plays. 16: May 1957, 53-59.

1071. Fiesta for Juanita by Gladys L. Schmitt.

Radio. 4 m. 2 f.

1072. Fiesta the First by Jean McArthur.

Short. 7 m. 7 f. +X.

In - Plays. 19: May 1960, 47-51.

1073. The Fifth Column by Ernest Hemingway. Adap. by Benjamin F. Glazer.

Excerpt. 4 m. 0 f.

In - Theatre. 24: Oct.1940, 750-751.

1074. The Fifth Season by Sylvia Regan.

Full. 5 m. 7 f.

In - Theatre. 38: July 1954, 34-63.

1075. The Fighting Cock by Jean Anouilh. Trans. by Lucienne Hill.

Full. 10 m. 3 f.

In - Players. 13: July 1966, 31-46+.

1076. Fill 'Er Up by Pauline Gibson and Martin Rudd.

Radio. 11 m. 1 f.

In - Scholastic. 31: Oct.16,1937, 17E-18E+.

1077. Filumena Marturano by Eduardo de Filippo. Trans. by Eric Bentley.

Excerpt. 4 m. 1 f.

In - Theatre. 35: Feb.1951, 34-36.

1078. The Final Curtain by John Murray.

Short. 6 m. 5 f.

In – Plays. 17: Oct.1957, 1-13.

1079. Final Edition by George Wallace Sayre.

Short. 8 m. 0 f.

In – Plays. 15: April 1956, 1-12.

1080. Finally I Am Born by Madeline Davidson.

Full. 8 m. 5 f.

In – First Stage. 1: March 1962, 49-78.

1081. Finders – Keepers by George Kelly.

Short. 1 m. 2 f.

In – Scholastic. 26: March 16 & 23,1935, 8-10, 10-13.

1082. Finding and Holding a Job. Editorial.

Short. 13 m. 0 f.

In – Indus. Educa. 33 & 34: June-Aug.1932, 310-311, 9-10, 32-33.

1083. The Finding of the First Arbutus by Agnes Miller.

Short. 1 m. 1 f. 4 c.

In – St. Nicholas. 47: April 1920, 550-553.

Fine Wagon.

see

A Start in Life.

1084. Finger Fairies by Edith Jennings.

Short. 0 m. 2 f. 10 un. 12 c.

In – Wilson. 15: Oct.1940, 152-153.

1085. A Finger in Art by Marjorie B. Paradis.

Short. 2 m. 9 f. +f.X.

In – Plays. 6: Jan.1947, 21-29.

1086. Finian's Rainbow by Fred Saidy and E.Y. Harburg. Music by Burton Lane.

Full (musical). 20 m. 4 f. +ch.

In – Theatre. 33: Jan.1949, 55-76.

1087. Finn McCool by May Lynch.

Short. 2 m. 4 f. 3 b. 2 g.

In – Plays. 26: March 1967, 55-59.

1088. Fiorello! by Jerome Weidman and George Abbott. Music by Jerry Block; lyrics by Sheldon Harnick.

Full (musical). 30 m. 8 f.

In – Theatre. 45: Nov.1961, 25-56.

1089. Fire Bug by Marjorie B. Paradis.

Short. 4 m. 4 f.

In – Plays. 7: Nov.1947, 1-9.

1090. Fire in a Paper by Loleta Hagy.

Short. 0 m. 5 f.

In – Plays. 3: Jan.1944, 39-42.

1091. Fires at Valley Forge by Harold Harper.

Short. 8 m. 0 f.

In – Scholastic. 36: Feb.19,1940, 17-20.

1092. Firm Foundations by Charlotte K. Brooks.

Radio. 1 m. 1 f. 5 b. 4 g.

In – Negro History. 17: March 1954, 128-131.

1093. Firm Foundations by Charlotte K. Brooks.

Radio. 1 m. 1 f. 5 b. 4 g.

In – Negro History. 23: April 1960, 157-160.

1094. First! by Lindsey Barbee.

Radio. 4 m. 6 f. 4 un.

In – Plays. 4: April 1945, 72-76.

1095. The First Butterfly by Claribel Spamer.

Short. 9 un. +X.

In – Plays. 16: March 1957, 77-78.

1096. The First Cat on Mars by James Macpherson Harper.

Short. 9 m. 0 f.

In – Plays. 15: Feb.1956, 47-54.

1097. First Christmas by Marjorie Marquis.

Short. 16 m. 1 f. 5 c. +f.X.

In – Ladies' Home. 47: Dec.1930, 14-15+.

1098. The First Christmas Tree by Loretta Camp Capell.

Short. 2 m. 3 f. +X.

In – Plays. 6: Dec.1946, 51-55.

1099. The First Day of April by Lindsey Barbee.

Short. 0 m. 5 f.

In – Plays. 8: April 1949, 50-55.

1100. The First Day of April by Lindsey Barbee.

Short. 0 m. 5 f.

In – Plays. 27: April 1968, 45-50.

1101. The First Day of School by Lindsey Barbee.
Short. 0 m. 7 f.
In - Plays. 6: Oct.1946, 45-48.

1102. The First Easter Eggs by Rowena Bennett.
Short. 3 m. 5 f. +X.
In - Plays. 11: April 1952, 55-58.

1103. The First Flowers by Marie Lyon Wilson.
Short. 3 m. 11 f.
In - Plays. 3: March 1944, 50-52.

1104. The First New England Christmas Tree by
Ella Stratton Colbo.
Short. 6 m. 2 f. +m.X.
In - Plays. 7: Dec.1947, 41-48.

1105. The First of October by Josephine Daskam
Bacon.
Short. 9 m. 2 f.
In - Harper's M. 109: Oct.1904, 721-733.

1106. The First Ride of Willow Witch by Barbara
A. Steiner.
Short. 3 m. 14 f. +X.
In - Plays. 28: Oct.1968, 69-72.

1107. First Sorrow by Betty Smith.
Short. 2 m. 1 f.
In - Plays. 3: Jan.1944, 1-3.

1108. The First Thanksgiving by Amelia D. White.
Short. 5 m. 6 f. +X.
In - School Arts. 24: Nov.1924, 167-173.

1109. The First Thanksgiving by Deborah Newman.
Short. 6 m. 6 f.
In - Plays. 13: Nov.1953, 58-60.

1110. First Thanksgiving Day by Agnes Miller.
In - St. Nicholas. 40: Nov.1912, 61-64.

1111. The First Year by Frank Craven. Ed. by
Margaret Mayorga.
Short. 5 m. 4 f.
In - Scholastic. 35: Oct.30,1939, 19E-21E.

1112. Fish in the Forest adap. by Hazel W. Corson
from a Russian folk tale.
Short. 8 m. 5 f. +X.
In - Plays. 27: Oct.1967, 43-49.

1113. The Fisherman and His Wife adap. by Lovell
Swortzell from Grimms' Fairy Tales.
Short. 2 m. 1 f. +X.
In - Plays. 25: May 1966, 62-68.

1114. Fit to be Tied by Anne Coulter Martens.
Short. 3 m. 4 f.
In - Plays. 27: Nov.1967, 1-11.

1115. Fitness is the Fashion by Anne Coulter
Martens.
Short. 7 m. 7 f. +X.
In - Plays. 23, April 1964, 1-11.

1116. The Five Brothers by Eleanore Leuser.
Short. 6 m. 0 f.
In - Plays. 12: Jan.1953, 68-69.

1117. The Five Buttons by John Murray.
Short. 3 m. 4 f.
In - Plays. 14: March 1955, 35-48.

1118. Five Finger Exercise by Peter Schaffer.
Full. 3 m. 1 f. 1 g.
In - Players. 5 & 6: Sept.& Oct.1958, 25-30,
26-31.

1119. Five Finger Exercise by Peter Schaffer.
Full. 3 m. 1 f. 1 g.
In - Theatre. 45: Feb.1961, 27-56.

1120. The Five Senses by Mildred Hark and Noel
McQueen.
Short. 2 m. 5 f.
In - Plays. 8: Jan.1949, 51-54.

1121. Five Weeks in a Balloon by Jules Verne.
Adap. by Levy Olfson.
Radio. 8 m. 0 f.
In - Plays. 23: April 1964, 87-95.

1122. The Fixer by Warren Sullivan.
Short. 7 m. 3 f.
In - Scholastic. 26: April 27,1935, 8-11.

1123. Flag Stop by Marcus Bach.
Short. 4 m. 2 f.
In - Scholastic. 52: April 5,1948, 18-21.

1124. Flag Stop by Marcus Bach.
Short. 4 m. 2 f.
In - Scholastic. 60: March 19,1952, 36-37+.

1125. Flag the Limited by Samuel S. Richmond.

Short. 6 m. 0 f.

In - Plays. 5: Nov.1945, 67-70.

1126. A Flair for Fashion by Marguerite Kreger
         Phillips.

Short. 0 m. 6 f.

In - Plays. 11: Oct.1951, 1-9.

1127. Flatlanders by Kathleen Millay.

Short. 4 m. 0 f.

In - Scholastic. 26: April 6,1935, 9+.

1128. Flibber Turns the Table by Lee Knight.

Short. 3 m. 1 f.

In - Plays. 9: Nov.1949, 63-68.

1129. Flight Completed by Samuel S. Richmond.

Short. 4 m. 0 f.

In - Plays. 7: Dec.1947, 72-76.

1130. A Flight of Fancy by Parke Cummings.

Short. 2 m. 1 f.

In - Scholastic. 33: Nov.19,1938, 11+.

1131. The Flight of the Herons by Marietta C.
         Kennard.

Short. 3 m. 2 f.

In - Drama. 14: Dec.1923, 97-98.

1132. The Flight of the Moon Witches by Florence
         Reiter Flanders.

Short. 6 m. 12 f.

In - Plays. 26: Oct.1966, 67-71.

1133. Flittermouse by Mary Katherine Reely.

In - Drama. 14: Dec.1923, 104-107.

1134. The Floor by May Swenson.

Short. 2 m. 0 f.

In - First Stage. 6: June 1967, 112-118.

1135. Flora Macdonald's Farewell to America. Scene
         from Paul Green's The Highland Call.

Excerpt. 4 m. 4 f.

In - Carolina. 13: Sept.1940, 125-127.

1136. Flora of the Flower Shop by Betty Tracy Huff.

Short. 5 m. 6 f.

In - Plays. 26: Feb.1967, 23-32.

1137. A Flower for Mother's Day by Esther MacLellan
         and Catherine V. Schroll.

Short. 0 m. 3 f. 9 g. 2 c.

In - Plays. 12: May 1953, 70-73.

1138. The Flower Garden by Alice Very.

Short. 0 m. 0 f. 1 b. 23 c.

In - Plays. 3: April 1944, 55-57.

1139. Flowering Cherry by Robert Bolt.

Full. 4 m. 2 f.

In - Players. 6: Jan.& Feb.1959, 24-30, 28-31.

1140. Flowers for Mother by Marjorie Ann York.

Short. 6 m. 10 f. +X.

In - Plays. 13: May 1954, 67-70.

1141. Flowers in May by Estelle Ritchie.

Short. 3 m. 2 f. +ch.

In - Plays. 3: May 1944, 49-51.

1142. Flowers, Music and Sunbeams by Maud S.
         Bariteau.

Short. 3 m. 2 f. 2 b. 7 g. +c.X.

In - Etude. 48: June 1930, 397-398.

1143. Flying Doctor by Molière.

Short. 4 m. 3 f.

In - Golden. 1: May 1925, 672-677.

1144. Flying High by Samuel S. Richmond.

Short. 3 m. 6 f.

In - Plays. 8: Jan.1949, 62-68.

1145. The Flying Horseshoe by May Emery Hall.

Short. 6 m. 0 f.

In - Plays. 3: Nov.1943, 1-6.

1146. Fool of God by Charles Phillips.

In - Cath. World. 108: Dec.1918, 358-377.

1147. The Foolish Mouse by Carolyn Sherwin Bailey.

Short. 3 c. +c.X.

In - Delineator. 75: June 1910, 557.

1148. Football Hero by Helen Louise Miller.

Short. 3 m. 3 f.

In - Plays. 8: Nov.1948, 1-9.

1149. Footprints by Lucile E. Langston.
Short. 7 m. 5 f.
In - Plays. 19: Feb.1960, 73-78.

1150. For Art's Sake by Samuel S. Richmond.
Short. 4 m. 1 f.
In - Plays. 9: March 1950, 74-82.

1151. For Ever and Ever by Henri Lavedan. Trans.
from the French of Les Beaux Dimanches
by Sibyl Collar Holbrook.
Short. 1 m. 1 f.
In - Poet Lore. 28:no.4,1917, 391-396.

1152. For France by Stuart Benson and Mercedes
de Acosta.
Short. 1 m. 1 f.
In - Outlook. 116: July 25,1917, 482-483.

1153. For Heaven's Sake by Lynn Starling.
Short. 16 m. 2 f.
In - Plays. 3: Oct.1943, 70-77.

1154. For Love of the King by Oscar Wilde.
Short. 7 m. 1 f.
In - Century. 103: Dec.1921, 225-242.

1155. For the Glory of Spain by Helen Roberts.
Short. 5 m. 1 f.
In - Plays. 4: Oct.1944, 37-44.

1156. For the Welfare of All by Samuel S. Richmond.
Short. 2 m. 4 f.
In - Plays. 10: May 1951, 66-73.

1157. The Foreign Girl by Florencio Sanchez.
Trans. by Alfred Coester.
Full. 14 m. 5 f. +X.
In - First Stage. 6: March 1967, 51-67.

1158. Forest Bride by Paul Scott Mowrer.
Short. 6 m. 2 f.
In - Poet Lore. 60: Sept.1965, 219-242.

1159. Forest Fantasy by Mildred Hark and Noel
McQueen.
Short. 11 m. 4 f. +X.
In - Plays. 3: May 1944, 43-49.

1160. The Forest of Arden by Elizabeth George Speare.
Short. 4 m. 1 f. +X.
In - Plays. 11: April 1952, 14-19.

1161. Forfeit by Corrie Crandall Howell.
In - Poet Lore. 36: March 1925, 136-141.

1162. The Forgotten Hero by Helen Louise Miller.
Short. 5 m. 5 f.
In - Plays. 17: Nov.1957, 41-47.

1163. The Form by N.F. Simpson.
Short. 2 m. 2 f.
In - Players. 9: May 1962, 31-35.

1164. The Formation Dancers by Frank Marcus.
Full. 2 m. 2 f.
In - Players. 11: June & July 1964, 19-25,
19-26+.

1165. The Fortunes of Merrylegs and Tawny-Whiskers
by Lida Lisle Molloy.
Short. 11 m. 0 f.
In - Plays. 7: April 1948, 48-52.

1166. A Fountain for a Duke by Cora Burlingame.
Short. 3 m. 2 f.
In - Plays. 6: Oct.1947, 28-36.

1167. The Four Extra Valentines by Lindsey Barbee.
Short. 1 m. 6 f.
In - Plays. 5: Feb.1946, 42-46.

1168. Four Letters Home by Elizabeth Brenner.
Short. 7 m. 6 f. +X.
In - Plays. 18: Nov.1958, 54-60.

1169. The Fox's Grave. Translated from the ancient
Japanese farce Kitsune Zuka by Michio
Itow and Louis V. Ledoux.
Short. 3 m. 0 f.
In - Outlook. 133: Feb.14,1923, 306-308.

1170. Fragments of a Play by Kate Douglas Wiggin.
Short. 1 m. 3 f.
In - Poet Lore. 40: June 1929, 281-287.

1171. France by Louis F. Doyle.
Short. 6 m. 1 f.
In - Cath. World. 124: March 1927, 788-797.

1172. The Franklin Reversal by Claire Boiko.
Short. 3 m. 2 f. +4 c.X.
In - Plays. 24: Nov.1964, 47-53.

1173. The Freedom Train by Walter Hackett.
       Radio. 25 m. 2 f.
       In - Plays. 7: Jan.1948, 67-77.

1174. The French Cabinetmaker by Paul T. Nolan.
       Short. 3 m. 5 f.
       In - Plays. 22: Oct.1962, 37-44.

1175. The French Doll's Surprise by Rowena Bennett.
       Short. 1 m. 2 f.
       In - Plays. 25: May 1966, 85-86.

1176. The Friday Foursome Packs a Box by Lindsey
       Barbee.
       Short. 0 m. 7 f.
       In - Plays. 7: Dec.1947, 48-54.

1177. A Friend by Henri Lavedan. Trans. from
       the French by William V. Silverberg.
       Short. 1 m. 1 f.
       In - Poet Lore. 30:no.1,1919, 15-19.

1178. A Friend in Need by Maude Morrison Frank.
       Short. 2 m. 1 f. 1 b. 1 g.
       In - St. Nicholas. 42: March 1915, 447-451.

1179. Friend of His Youth by Edmond Sée. Trans.
       from the French.
       In - Poet Lore. 36: June 1925, 159-187.

1180. Friendly As Can Be by Karin Asbrand.
       Short. 5 m. 4 f.
       In - Plays. 8: Nov.1948, 48-50.

1181. The Friendship Bracelet by Patricia Clapp.
       Short. 3 m. 2 f.
       In - Plays. 23: Nov.1963, 43-50.

1182. Frightened Men by Cora Burlingame.
       Short. 2 m. 3 f.
       In - Plays. 6: Dec.1946, 19-29.

1183. The Frightful Forest by John N. Sumner.
       Short. 2 m. 2 f. +X.
       In - Plays. 11: Oct.1951, 40-49.

1184. The Frog and the Mouse by Alice Very.
       Short. 4 m. 2 f. 5 c.
       In - Plays. 5: Feb.1946, 63-66.

1185. The Frolic of the Leaves by Claribel Spamer.
       Short. 6 m. 5 f.
       In - Plays. 6: Oct.1947, 73-75.

1186. From Morn to Midnight by Georg Kaiser.
       In - Poet Lore. 31: Sept.1920, 317-363.

1187. From Where I Sit ... by Lucille Coleman.
       Short. 5 m. 4 f. 1 b. 1 cow.
       In - Poet Lore. 56:no.4,1951, 345-359.

1188. The Front Page by Ben Hecht and Charles
       MacArthur.
       Excerpt. 6 m. 0 f.
       In - Theatre. 22: Sept.1938, 689-690.

1189. Full Measure of Devotion by Graham DuBois.
       Short. 4 m. 3 f.
       In - Plays. 20: Feb.1961, 1-11.

1190. A Full Moon in March by William Butler Yeats.
       Short. 4 m. 1 f.
       In - Poetry. 45: March 1935, 299-310.

1191. Full of the Moon by Gertrude Herrick.
       In - Poet Lore. 31: Sept.1920, 379-393.

1192. Funeral Flowers for the Bride by Beverly
       DuBose Hamer.
       Short. 2 m. 2 f.
       In - Carolina. 10: Sept.1937, 67-77.

1193. Funeral March of a Marionette by Arthur H.
       Nethercot.
       In - Poet Lore. 31: June 1920, 232-242.

1194. G for Gettysburg by Mildred Hark and Noel
       McQueen.
       Short. 5 m. 5 f.
       In - Plays. 14: Feb.1955, 21-31.

1195. Gainsborough Lady by Marguerite Merington.
       Short. 1 m. 1 f.
       In - Scribner's. 31: Jan.1902, 65-67.

1196. Galileo by Michael T. Leech.
       Short. 14 m. 3 f. +X.
       In - Plays. 27: Oct.1967, 13-27.

1197. Gallant Cassian by Arthur Schnitzler. Trans.
       by Moritz A. Jagendorf.
       Short. 3 m. 1 f.
       In - Poet Lore. 33:no.4,1922, 507-520.

1198. Gallop Away! by Helen Littler Howard.
       Short. 2 m. 2 f.
       In - Plays. 4: May 1945, 60-62.

1199. Galloping Steeds by Karin Asbrand.
Short. 10 m. 6 f.
In - Plays. 6: April 1947, 54-56.

1200. Gambetta's Love Story by Sir Thomas Barclay.
Full. 4 m. 3 f.
In - Fortnightly. 120: Aug.1923, 215-232.

1201. Game of Adverbs by Thomas Anstey Guthrie.
Short. 3 m. 5 f. 1 b. 1 g.
In - Golden. 10: Dec.1929, 99-102.

1202. A Game of Chess by John Murray.
Short. 2 m. 3 f.
In - Plays. 12: Oct.1952, 23-32.

1203. A Game of Hearts by Mildred Hark and Noel McQueen.
Short. 3 m. 2 f.
In - Plays. 6: Feb.1947, 18-27.

1204. The Gang's All Here by Jerome Lawrence and Robert E. Lee.
Full. 14 m. 4 f.
In - Theatre. 44: Nov.1960, 25-56.

1205. Garden Hold-Up by Helen Louise Miller.
Short. 18 un.
In - Plays. 18: May 1959, 55-59.

1206. The Garden of the Christmas Fairy by Horace Varney.
Short (musical). 1 m. 1 f. many c.
In - Ladies' Home. 29: Dec.1912, 85.

1207. The Gardener by Vera I. Arlett.
Short. 4 m. 0 f. 1 b.
In - Poet Lore. 41: April 1930, 305-313.

1208. The Gas Tank by Peter J. Smith.
Short. 3 m. 1 f.
In - First Stage. 6: Dec.1967, 216-229.

1209. The Gates of Dinkelsbuehl by Paul T. Nolan.
Short. 7 m. 1 f. +c.X.
In - Plays. 20: April 1961, 89-96.

1210. Gathering Sticks by Helen Louise Miller.
Short. 5 m. 4 f.
In - Plays. 21: May 1962, 85-98.

1211. The Gay Pretenders by Robert St.Clair.
Short. 4 m. 3 f.
In - Plays. 20: Jan.1961, 1-13.

1212. The General and the Christmas Tree by Jane McGowan.
Radio. 18 m. 19 f. 3 b. 2 g. 4 c.
In - Plays. 13: Dec.1953, 77-86.

1213. General Audax by Oscar Mandel.
Full. 16 m. 1 f. +X.
In - First Stage. 6: Sept.1967, 146-168.

1214. General Gage's Chowder by Earl J. Dias.
Short. 3 m. 3 f.
In - Plays. 7: March 1948, 8-20.

1215. General George by Alice Very.
Short. 9 m. 2 f.
In - Plays. 18: Feb.1959, 76-78.

1216. The General Goes Home by Lucy Barton.
Short. 0 m. 11 f.
In - Playground. 20: Jan.1927, 568-571.

1217. The General Returns by Jane McGowan.
Short. 6 m. 4 f.
In - Plays. 7: Feb.1948, 22-31.

1218. The General's Letter by Earl J. Dias.
Short. 5 m. 4 f.
In - Plays. 18: Feb.1959, 1-10.

1219. The Genie of the Bottle by Helene Whittaker.
Short. 1 m. 1 f. 5 b. 2 g.
In - Plays. 25: Nov.1965, 79-84.

1220. The Gentle Giant Killer by Helen Louise Miller.
Short. 2 m. 4 f. 5 b. 6 g.
In - Plays. 26: Oct.1966, 59-66.

1221. The Gentleman from Philadelphia by Beth Harber.
Radio. 4 m. 1 f.
In - Plays. 10: Jan.1951, 72-78.

1222. Gentleman from Virginia by Walter Hackett.
Radio. 3 m. 1 f.
In - Plays. 4: March 1945, 72-75.

1223. George Dandin or The Discomfited Husband by
      Molière. Trans. by Stark Young.

      Full. 5 m. 3 f.

      In - Theatre. 8: Sept.1924, 604-621.

1224. George Moore and Granville Barker by
      George Moore.

      Short. 2 m. 1 f.

      In - Fortnightly. 120: July 1923, 40-54.

1225. George Moore and Granville Barker by George
      Moore.

      Short. 3 m. 1 f.

      In - Dial. 75: Aug.1923, 135-150.

1226. George Moore and John Freeman by George
      Moore.

      Short. 2 m. 0 f.

      In - Dial. 75: Oct.1923, 341-362.

1227. George Washington Carver by Mildred Hark
      and Noel McQueen.

      Short. 7 m. 3 f.

      In - Plays. 8: April 1949, 27-42.

1228. George Washington Comes to Town by Eleanor
      Leuser.

      Short. 3 m. 2 f.

      In - Plays. 13: Feb.1954, 63-64.

1229. Germs by H. Sutton Sharp.

      Short. 3 m. 2 f.

      In - Drama. 16: Feb.1926, 167-168+.

1230. Gertie, the Greeting Card Girl by Betty
      Tracey Huff.

      Short. 4 m. 5 f.

      In - Plays. 26: May 1967, 37-47.

1231. Getting Ready for Winter by Alice V. Brown.

      Short. 9 um. +X.

      In - Plays. 5: Jan.1946, 63-66.

1232. The Ghost From Genoa by Earl J. Dias.

      Short. 2 m. 2 f.

      In - Plays. 15: Oct.1955, 23-31.

1233. Ghost in the House by Helen Louise Miller.

      Short. 3 m. 4 f.

      In - Plays. 7: Oct.1948, 1-13.

1234. Ghost in the House by Helen Louise Miller.

      Short. 3 m. 4 f.

      In - Plays. 12: Oct.1952, 70-81.

1235. Ghost-Layers, Incorporated by Dorothy Deming.

      Short. 4 m. 2 f.

      In - Plays. 9: Nov.1949, 49-54.

1236. The Ghost Story by Booth Tarkington.

      Short. 5 m. 5 f.

      In - Ladies' Home. 39: March 1922, 6-7+.

1237. The Ghost Walks Tonight by Jessie Nicholson.

      Short. 9 m. 3 f.

      In - Plays. 11: Oct.1951, 27-35.

1238. The Ghost Walks Tonight by Jessie Nicholson.

      Short. 9 m. 3 f.

      In - Plays. 18: Oct.1958, 45-53.

1239. Ghosts in the Library by Edrie Pendleton.

      Short. 7 m. 6 f.

      In - Plays. 9: Nov.1949, 21-32.

1240. Ghosts in the Library by Edrie Pendleton.

      Short. 6 m. 6 f. 1 um.

      In - Plays. 12: Nov.1952, 70-81.

1241. Ghosts on Guard by Aileen Fisher.

      Short. 4 m. 3 f.

      In - Plays. 9: Oct.1949, 36-41.

1242. Gibson by Marguerite Merington.

      Full. 6 m. 4 f.

      In - Ladies' Home. 18: March 1901, 7-8+.

1243. Gideon by Paddy Chayefsky.

      Full. 15 m. 7 f. +X.

      In - Esquire. 56: Dec.1961, 215-230+.

1244. The Gift by Ronald Duncan.

      Short. 3 m. 2 f.

      In - Gambit. 3: no.11, 93-110.

1245. A Gift for Hans Brinker by Adele Thane.

      Short. 8 m. 7 f.

      In - Plays. 27: Jan.1968, 61-66.

1246. A Gift for the World by Deborah Newman.

      Short. 7 m. 11 f.

      In - Plays. 15: Nov.1955, 57-61.

1247. A Gift From Johnny Appleseed by Helene
      Whittaker.

      Short. 3 m. 2 f. 1 b. 3 g.

      In - Plays. 25: Feb.1965, 71-77.

1248. The Gift Horse by Betty Gray Blaine.
Short. 7 m. 4 f.
In - Plays. 20: April 1961, 31-44.

1249. The Gift of Gifts by Marion Keep Patton.
Short. 7 m. 4 f. +X.
In - Delineator. 85: Dec.1914, 20-21.

1250. The Gift of Laughter by Earl J. Dias.
Short. 4 m. 4 f.
In - Plays. 19: Feb.1960, 1-12.

1251. A Gift of Pottery by Recene Ashton.
Short. 0 m. 1 f. 1 b. 1 g. +c.X.
In - School Arts. 38: Dec.1938, 144.

1252. The Gift of the Fairies by Alice Very.
Short. 1 m. 1 f. 15 c.
In - Plays. 6: Jan.1947, 53-55.

1253. The Gift That Changed by Ernestine Horvath
and Florence Horvath.
In - Etude. 59: Feb.1941, 140.

1254. The Gift That Won the Princess by Mary
Nygaard Peterson.
Short. 7 m. 3 f.
In - Plays. 19: March 1960, 59-67.

1255. Gifts for the New Year by Helen Louise
Miller.
Short. 3 m. 16 f. +X.
In - Plays. 23: Jan.1964, 69-74.

1256. Gigi by Anita Loos. From the novel by
Colette.
Full. 2 m. 5 f.
In - Theatre. 36: July 1952, 41-47+.

1257. Gilt Edges by Russell Speirs.
Short. 2 m. 1 f.
In - Poet Lore. 41: Oct.1930, 525-535.

1258. The Ginger Man by J.P. Donleavy.
Full. 2 m. 2 f.
In - Players. 9: Sept.1962, 27-41+.

1259. The Gioconda Smile by Aldous Huxley.
Full. 4 m. 5 f.
In - Theatre. 36: May 1951, 53-88.

1260. The Girl by Edward Peple.
Short. 3 m. 0 f.
In - Golden. 7: April 1928, 495-500.

1261. The Girl and the Gold Mine by Betty Tracy
Huff.
Short. 6 m. 4 f. +X.
In - Plays. 26: Oct.1966, 29-39.

1262. The Girl From the Sea adap. by Dorothy
Heiderstadt.
Short. 2 m. 4 f.
In - Plays. 13: March 1954, 38-50.

1263. Girl Wanted by Marguerite Fellows Melcher.
Short. 0 m. 8 f.
In - Plays. 6: Dec.1946, 77-82.

1264. The Girl Who Slipped by Lawton Campbell.
Short. 5 m. 1 f.
In - Drama. 17: April 1927, 203-205.

1265. The Girl Whose Fortune Sought Her by
Patricia Clapp.
Short. 3 m. 3 f.
In - Plays. 14: May 1955, 53-60.

1266. Girls in Books by Helen Louise Miller.
Short. 0 m. 12 f. +f.X.
In - Plays. 13: Nov.1953, 69-76.

1267. Girls In Books by Helen Louise Miller.
Short. 0 m. 13 f. +f.X.
In - Plays. 24: Nov.1964, 55-62.

1268. Give the Book a Chance by Mary Malone.
Short. 7 m. 4 f. +X.
In - Plays. 8: Nov.1948, 51-58.

1269. Glamour and Grease by Samuel S. Richmond.
Short. 2 m. 2 f.
In - Plays. 5: Dec.1945, 60-64.

1270. The Glass Slippers by Helen Louise Miller.
Short. 7 m. 5 f. 8 un.
In - Plays. 21: March 1962, 77-83.

1271. Glendale Plantation by Tom Loy.
Short. 2 m. 3 f.
In - Carolina. 4: Dec.1931, 108-122.

1272. The Glittering Gate by Lord Dunsany.

Short. 2 m. 0 f.

In – Golden. 16: Nov.1932, 464-468.

1273. The Glittering Highway by Enrique de
Meneses. Trans. from the Spanish by
Gustav Davidson.

Full. 6 m. 3 f.

In – Poet Lore. 38: Sept.1927, 317-357.

1274. Gloriana by Britton B. Cooke.

In – Canadian M. 46: March 1916, 403-406.

1275. The Glorious Whitewasher by Mark Twain.
Adap. by Walter Hackett.

Short. 6 m. 1 f.

In – Plays. 8: March 1949, 44-49.

1276. The Glorious Whitewasher adap. by Walter
Hackett from Mark Twain's Adventures
of Tom Sawyer.

Short. 6 m. 1 f.

In – Plays. 27: Jan.1968, 55-60.

1277. The Glory and The Dream by Graham DuBois.

Short. 4 m. 4 f.

In – Plays. 11: Feb.1952, 12-21.

1278. The Glory He Deserves by Mildred Hark and
Noel McQueen.

Short. 11 m. 3 f. +X.

In – Plays. 5: Oct.1945, 35-39.

1279. Glory Road by Graham DuBois.

Short. 6 m. 4 f.

In – Plays. 5: Jan.1946, 19-28.

1280. Gloves by Gilbert Cannan.

Short. 1 m. 1 f.

In – Theatre. 4: April 1920, 160-165.

1281. The Gnädiges Fräulein by Tennessee Williams.

Short. 2 m. 2 f.

In – Esquire. 64: Aug.1965, 102+.

1282. The Go-Go Gophers by Anne Coulter Martens.

Short. 7 m. 7 f. +f.X.

In – Plays. 26: March 1967, 1-12.

1283. The Goal by Henry Arthur Jones.

Short. 4 m. 2 f.

In – American. 63: March 1907, 451-461.

1284. God and Texas by Robert Ardrey.

Short. 9 m. 0 f.

In – Theatre. 27: Sept.1943, 524-532.

1285. Godbug by Kenneth Cavander.

Short. 7 m. 1 f.

In – First Stage. 6: Dec.1967, 249-259.

1286. God's Little Tumbler by Louise C. Willcox.

Short. 2 m. 3 f. 1 b. 1 g. +X.

In – Delineator. 89: Dec.1916, 8-9+.

1287. Going Steady by Paul T. Nolan.

Short. 4 m. 4 f.

In – Plays. 23: March 1964, 27-34.

1288. Going Up by Mildred Hark and Noel McQueen.

Short. 3 m. 3 f.

In – Plays. 4: May 1945, 63-69.

1289. Gold in Your Garden by Karin Asbrand.

Short. 3 m. 4 f.

In – Plays. 22: March 1963, 77-80.

1290. The Gold Machine by Eugene Selnick.

Short. 3 m. 1 f.

In – Drama. 20: March 1930, 173-175.

1291. The Gold Mine at Jeremiah Flats by Robert A.
Anderson.

Short. 7 m. 3 f.

In – Plays. 23: Oct.1963, 17-30.

1292. Gold Mohur Tune: "To Remember" by Cornelia
Sorabji.

Short. 1 m. 4 f. +X.

In – 19th C. 106: July 1929, 133-142.

1293. A Golden Bell for Mother by Alice Very.

Short. 7 m. 7 f.

In – Plays. 3: May 1944, 52-55.

1294. The Golden Bird adap. by Frances Mapp from
Grimms' Fairy Tales.

Short. 14 m. 3 f.

In – Plays. 28: Dec.1968, 51-60.

1295. The Golden Door by Katherine Lauré.

Short. 2 m. 2 f.

In – Plays. 4: Dec.1944, 48-52.

1296. The Golden Hearts by Margaret E. Slattery.
Short. 6 m. 5 f. +X.
In - Plays. 22: Feb.1963, 63-71.

1297. The Golden Voice of Little Erik by Paul T.
Nolan.
Short. 6 m. 3 f. +X.
In - Plays. 21: Nov.1961, 81-86.

1298. Golem by H. Leivick. Trans. by J.C.
Augenlicht.
In - Poet Lore. 39: June 1928, 159-288.

1299. Gone by Dannie Abse.
Short. 2 m. 0 f.
In - Gambit. 1: no.1, 70-83.

1300. Gone for a Soldier by Nicholas Biel.
Full. 20 m. 3 f.
In - Gambit. 3: no.10, 3-66.

1301. Gone Tomorrow by Richard Harrity.
Short. 5 m. 2 f.
In - Theatre. 30: Aug.1946, 472+.

1302. The Good and Obedient Young Man by Betty
Barr and Gould Stevens.
Short. 4 m. 2 f. 3 musicians. +X.
In - Theatre. 15: Feb.1931, 134-139.

1303. Good-Bye by Arlo Bates.
Short. 0 m. 2 f.
In - Ladies' Home. 20: Jan.1903, 8.

1304. A Good Dinner by Mary Stewart Cutting.
Short. 4 m. 4 f.
In - Ladies' Home. 22: Feb.1905, 5+.

1305. The Good Egg by Graham DuBois.
Short. 3 m. 4 f.
In - Plays. 11: April 1952, 20-29.

1306. The Good Egg by Graham DuBois.
Short. 3 m. 4 f.
In - Plays. 27: April 1968, 27-36.

1307. Good Enough for Lincoln by Helen Louise Miller.
Short. 4 m. 5 f.
In - Plays. 9: Feb.1950, 1-9.

1308. Good Enough for Lincoln by Helen Louise
Miller.
Short. 4 m. 5 f.
In - Plays. 17: Feb.1958, 25-33.

1309. Good Friday by John Masefield.
Full. 7 m. 1 f. +X.
In - Fortnightly. 104: Dec.1915, 993-1018.

1310. Good Health Trolley by John F. Lehman.
Short. 2 m. 10 un.
In - Plays. 4: Oct.1944, 53-55.

1311. Good Morning, Mr. Rabbit by Rowena Bennett.
Short. 2 m. 1 f.
In - Plays. 17: April 1958, 72-74.

1312. Good Neighbors by Mildred Hark and Noel
McQueen.
Short. 6 m. 2 f.
In - Plays. 6: Dec.1946, 46-51.

1313. The Good Neighbors by Lucia Turnbull.
Short. 4 m. 2 f. 6 un.
In - Plays. 18: May 1959, 42-48.

1314. Good Night by Marian Spencer Smith.
Short. 1 m. 1 f.
In - Drama. 16: Feb.1926, 174+.

1315. Good Old Summer Time by Nina Reay.
Short. 4 m. 3 f.
In - Plays. 14: May 1955, 61-64.

1316. Good Out of Nazareth by Graham DuBois.
Short. 5 m. 4 f. 6 or 7 m.X.
In - Plays. 18: Dec.1958, 13-20.

1317. The Good Sainte Anne by Helen Gilbert.
Short. 1 m. 3 f.
In - Poet Lore. 35: Dec.1924, 576-586.

1318. Good Theatre by Christopher Morley.
Short. 4 m. 1 f.
In - Sat. Review. 2: April 10,1926, 695-697.

1319. Good Theatre by Christopher Morley.
Short. 4 m. 1 f.
In - Scholastic. 25: Oct.13,1934, 7-9.

1320. <u>Good Words for a Stirring Tune</u> by Katherine Little Bakeless.

    Radio. 6 m. 2 f.

    In - Plays. 4: May 1945, 74-79.

1321. <u>Gool and Bahar</u> by Inar Prakas Baunevji.

    Short. 5 m. 1 f. +X.

    In - New England. 52(n.s.): Sept.1914, 19-30.

1322. <u>Governor Bradford's Scissors</u> by Graham DuBois.

    Short. 5 m. 4 f.

    In - Plays. 21: Nov.1961, 25-35.

1323. <u>The Governor's Lady</u> by David Mercer.

    Short. 3 m. 3 f.

    In - Players. 12: April 1965, 25-30.

1324. <u>Goya in the Cupola</u> by Thomas Walsh.

    Short. 3 m. 0 f.

    In - Century. 89: March 1915, 701-704.

1325. <u>Graduation Present</u> by Frank Orme.

    Short. 8 m. 1 f.

    In - Plays. 3: May 1944, 21-27.

1326. <u>A Gram of Radium</u> by Cora Burlingame.

    Short. 6 m. 1 f.

    In - Plays. 3: April 1944, 1-7.

1327. <u>The Grandfather</u> by Perez Galdós. Trans. from the Spanish by Elizabeth Wallace.

    Full. 7 m. 4 f.

    In - Poet Lore. 21: no.3,1910, 161-233.

1328. <u>Granny from Killarney</u> by Anne Coulter Martens.

    Short. 2 m. 4 f.

    In - Plays. 23: March 1964, 1-14.

1329. <u>The Grass Harp</u> by Truman Capote.

    Full. 10 m. 8 f.

    In - Theatre. 36: Sept.1952, 32-64.

1330. <u>The Grass's Springing</u> by Theodore Labrenz.

    Full. 11 m. 6 f.

    In - First Stage. 2: Sept.1963, 365-389.

1331. <u>The Grateful Gobbler</u> by Helen Ramsey.

    Short. 4 m. 2 f. +X.

    In - Plays. 16: Nov.1956, 64-66.

1332. <u>The Grave</u> by Russell F. Speirs.

    Short. 3 m. 0 f.

    In - Poet Lore. 40: March 1929, 113-117.

1333. <u>Gray Flannel Blues</u> by John Murray.

    Short. 6 m. 6 f.

    In - Plays. 24: May 1965, 1-13.

1334. <u>The Great Adventure</u> by Gustav Davidson.

    Full. 42 m. 9 f. +X.

    In - Poet Lore. 51: July 1945, 195-255.

1335. <u>Great Beginning</u> by Margaret Goff Clark.

    Short. 10 m. 0 f. +m.X.

    In - Plays. 6: Oct.1947, 60-66.

1336. <u>Great Catherine</u> by George Bernard Shaw.

    Short. 4 m. 4 f.

    In - Everybody's. 32: Feb.1915, 193-212.

1337. <u>Great Choice</u> by Fred Eastman.

    Excerpt. 3 m. 1 f.

    In - Christian C. 49: Oct.12,1932, 1240-1243.

1338. <u>The Great Contest</u> by Betty Tracy Huff.

    Short. 4 m. 4 f.

    In - Plays. 26: April 1967, 15-27.

1339. <u>The Great Dark</u> by Dan W. Totheroh.

    Short. 0 m. 6 f. +f.X.

    In - Drama. 21: Feb.1931, 19-20+.

1340. <u>Great Expectations</u> by Charles Dickens. Adap. by Edward Golden.

    Radio. 4 m. 4 f. 1 b.

    In - Plays. 13: Oct.1953, 67-78.

1341. <u>Great Expectations</u> by Charles Dickens. Adap. by Edward Golden.

    Radio. 5 m. 4 f.

    In - Plays. 21: March 1962, 85-96.

1342. <u>The Great Freeholder</u> by Frantisek Adolf Subert. Trans. from the Bohemian by Beatrice M. Mekota.

    Full. 19 m. 4 f.

    In - Poet Lore. 35: Sept.1924, 317-379.

1343. <u>The Great Gift</u> by Mildred Hark and Noel McQueen.

    Short. 4 m. 1 f.

    In - Plays. 7: Nov.1947, 59-66.

1344. The Great Golden Nugget by Francis L. Kroll.

Short. 5 m. 2 f.

In - Plays. 21: March 1962, 58-64.

1345. The Great Middle Class by Rudolfo Usigli.
Trans. by Edna Lue Furness.

Full. 9 m. 4 f.

In - Poet Lore. 63: June 1968, 156-232.

1346. The Great One by Ethel McFarlan.

Short. 7 m. 1 f. +X.

In - Plays. 14: March 1955, 79-83.

1347. The Great Sebastians by Howard Lindsay and
Russel Crouse.

Full. 15 m. 6 f.

In - Theatre. 41: July 1957, 34-69.

1348. The Great Stone Face by Nathaniel Hawthorne.
Adap. by Walter Hackett.

Radio. 13 m. 1 f. +X.

In - Plays. 8: Nov.1948, 68-77.

1349. The Great Stone Face by Nathaniel Hawthorne.
Adap. by Walter Hackett.

Radio. 9 m. 2 f. 1 b. +X.

In - Plays. 25: Nov.1965, 85-94.

1350. The Greatest Day In the Year by Carolyn
Wells.

Short. many c.

In - Ladies Home. 28: Dec.1911, 85-86.

1351. The Greatest Gift by Carolyn Wells.

Short. 0 m. 1 f. many c.

In - Ladies' Home. 30: Dec.1913, 32+.

1352. The Grecian Urn by Arthur H. Nethercot.

Short. 5 m. 1 f. +X.

In - Poet Lore. 33: March 1922, 142-147.

1353. The Greedy Goblin by Helen Louise Miller.

Short. 6 m. 3 f.

In - Plays. 13: Oct.1953, 35-43.

1354. The Green Cockatoo by Arthur Schnitzler.
Trans. by G.I. Colbron.

Short. 16 m. 5 f. +X.

In - Golden. 4: Nov.1926, 637-653.

1355. The Green-Eyed Monster by Graham DuBois.

Short. 9 m. 2 f.

In - Plays. 7: May 1948, 19-31

1356. The Green Glass Ball adap. by Hazel W.
Corson from an Irish folk tale.

Short. 7 m. 3 f. 1 b. 1 g.

In - Plays. 27: Jan.1968, 43-49.

1357. The Green Helmet by William Butler Yeats.

Short. 6 m. 2 f. +X.

In - Forum. 46: Sept.1911, 301-321.

1358. Green Leaf's Lesson by Deborah Newman.

Short. 2 m. 0 f. 5 c.

In - Plays. 9: Oct.1949, 66-69.

1359. The Green Pastures by Marc Connelly.

Excerpt. 4 m. 2 f.

In - Theatre. 22: Sept.1938, 691-692.

1360. The Green Piper by Sylvia Lee.

Short. 4 m. 4 f. +c.X.

In - Plays. 15: April 1956, 75-78.

1361. The Green Thumb by Marguerite Kreger Phillips.

Short. 5 m. 4 f.

In - Plays. 14: May 1955, 65-68.

1362. Greetings from the Fultons by Paul S. McCoy.

Short. 3 m. 3 f.

In - Plays. 17: Dec.1957, 11-22.

1363. Grey Ghosts by Dorothy Deming.

Short. 4 m. 2 f.

In - Plays. 7: Oct.1948, 53-58.

1364. Grey Squirrel and the White Buffalo by
Augusta Hutson Privacky.

Short. 10 m. 7 f.

In - Plays. 16: May 1957, 61-68.

1365. Grief (La Pena) by Serafín and Joaquín
Alvarez Quintero. Trans. by Ane Lee Utt.

Short. 1 m. 2 f.

In - Poet Lore. 41: July 1930, 391-402.

1366. The Groundhog's Shadow by Mary Malone.

Short. 2 m. 3 f. +X.

In - Plays. 16: Feb.1957, 66-70.

1367. Grouse Out of Season by Marguerite Merington.

In - Harper's B. 37: Nov.1903, 1018-1027.

1368. Growing Old Together by Colin Campbell Clements.

In - Poet Lore. 31: June 1920, 176-180.

1369. Growing Pains by Aurania Rouverol. Ed. by Margaret Mayorga.

Short. 9 m. 9 f. +X.

In - Scholastic. 33: Jan.21,1939, 21E-24E.

1370. Grown-Up Children by Mattie Frances Simmonds.

In - Poet Lore. 36: Sept.1925, 434-440.

1371. Guaranteed Forever by Gretta Baker.

Radio. 5 m. 1 f. 2 un.

In - Scholastic. 45: Dec.11,1944, 17-18.

1372. Guard for the King by Estelle Ritchie.

Short. 7 m. 1 f. +X.

In - Plays. 6: Jan.1947, 46-49.

1373. Du Guesclin by Theodore Botrel. Trans. from the French by Elizabeth S. Dickerman.

Full. 17 m. 0 f.

In - Poet Lore. 30:no.2,1919, 159-207.

1374. Guest House by Reby Edmond. Ed. by Margaret Mayorga.

Short. 2 m. 4 f. 2 b. 2 g.

In - Scholastic. 31: Dec.18,1937, 17E-19E+.

1375. Guest of Honor by Josephine E. Campbell.

Short. 2 m. 3 f.

In - Plays. 4: May 1945, 20-27.

1376. Gulliver's Travels in Lilliput Land by Jonathan Swift. Adap. by Edward Golden.

Radio. 15 m. 1 f.

In - Plays. 18: Jan.1959, 83-96.

1377. Gunther Groundhog by Lucille Miller Duvall.

Short. 6 m. 2 f. 2 un. +X.

In - Plays. 17: Feb.1958, 60-66.

1378. A Gust of Wind by Giovacchino Foranzo. English version by Robert Rietty.

Full. 13 m. 5 f. 1 b.

In - Gambit. 2: no.7, 58-105.

1379. Gustavus Vasa by August Strindberg. Trans. by Edwin Bjorkman.

Excerpt. 6 m. 1 f.

In - Scholastic. 48: Feb.18,1946, 13-15.

1380. The Guy Upstairs by Egbert H. Van Delden.

Short. 4 m. 1 f.

In - Poet Lore. 40: June 1929, 251-263.

1381. The Gypsies' Secret by Betty Tracy Huff.

Short. 3 m. 6 f. +X.

In - Plays. 27: Dec.1967, 23-32.

1382. Gypsy by Arthur Laurents. Music by Jule Styne; lyrics by Stephen Sondheim.

Full (musical). 12 m. 17 f. 3 g. 6 b. +ch.

In - Theatre. 46: June 1962, 25-56.

1383. The Gypsy Look by Anna Lenington Heath.

Short. 3 m. 3 f.

In - Plays. 12: Jan.1953, 33-39.

1384. Hadrian the Seventh by Peter Luke.

Full. 13 m. 2 f. +X.

In - Players. 15: May 1968, 27-42.

1385. Hail and Farewell And Howdy Do! by Arthur Royce MacDonald.

In - System. 51: Jan.1927, 40.

1386. Half Brother by Daisy Lee Worthington Worcester.

Short. 1 m. 1 f. 1 b.

In - Survey. 64: April 15,1930, 82-85.

1387. The Half Pint Cowboy by Helen Louise Miller.

Short. 23 m. 0 f.

In - Plays. 18: Jan.1959, 67-72.

1388. Halfway to Concord by Marcella Rowe.

Short. 6 m. 2 f.

In - Plays. 18: April 1959, 13-22.

1389. Hall-Marked by John Galsworthy.

Short. 4 m. 4 f. 2 dogs.

In - Atlantic. 113: June 1914, 845-851.

1390. Halloween Brew by Dorothy M. Compton, et al.

Short. 0 m. 3 f. 7 un. 5 c.

In - Nature. 32: Oct.1939, 463-465.

1391. Halloween Brew by Francis L. Kroll.

Short. 4 m. 4 f.

In - Plays. 16: Oct.1956, 82-86.

1392. Halloween Gets A New Look by Mary Thurman Pyle.

Short. 10 m. 0 f.

In - Plays. 10: Oct.1950, 31-38.

1393. Halloween Luck by Mildred Hark and Noel McQueen.

Short. 3 m. 3 f.

In - Plays. 13: Oct.1953, 1-10.

1394. Halloween Magic by Mildred Hark and Noel McQueen.

Short. 6 m. 2 f. +X.

In - Plays. 16: Oct.1956, 68-74.

1395. Halloween Scarecrow by Claribel Spamer.

Short. 2 m. 3 f.

In - Plays. 15: Oct.1955, 60-61.

1396. The Halloween Spell by Deborah Newman.

Short. 3 m. 6 f. +X.

In - Plays. 19: Oct.1959, 47-52.

1397. Halloween Spirits Go Musical by Esther Stinehart.

In - Etude. 54: Oct.1936, 612+.

1398. The Halloween Wishes by Esther MacLellan.

Short. 2 m. 6 f. +ch.

In - Plays. 6: Oct.1946, 59-62.

1399. Hamburger King by Marian Spencer Smith.

In - Drama. 15: March 1925, 125-127.

1400. Hamlet by William Shakespeare. Adap. by Levy Olfson.

Radio. 10 m. 2 f.

In - Plays. 18: Nov.1958, 86-96.

1401. Hand-Me-Down Hildy by Sara E. Sagoff.

Short. 0 m. 14 f.

In - Plays. 21: Dec.1961, 51-56.

1402. Hands Across the Sea by Kenneth Lewis Roberts.

Short. 5 m. 3 f.

In - Sat.Evening. 201: April 27,1929, 49-50+.

1403. The Handshakers by William Saroyan.

Short. 3 m. 0 f.

In - Atlantic. 211: April 1963, 50-51.

1404. The Handwriting on the Wall by Lawrence Wight.

Short. 4 m. 4 f.

In - Plays. 11: Feb.1952, 58-69.

1405. The Handy Man by Richard D. Elton.

Short. 1 m. 1 f. 1 b. 1 g.

In - Indus. Educa. 33: June 1944, 226.

1406. Hang By Their Shoelaces by Karl A. Tunberg.

Full. 9 m. 2 f. +X.

In - First Stage. 7: Sept.1968, 64-87.

1407. The Hanger Back by Elizabeth F. Corbett.

Short. 2 m. 1 f.

In - Poet Lore. 41: Jan.1930, 91-104.

1408. Hansel and Gretel by Natalie Simonds.

Short. 2 m. 3 f.

In - Plays. 3: Dec.1943, 58-61.

1409. Hansel and Gretel by Natalie Simonds.

Short. 2 m. 3 f.

In - Plays. 21: April 1962, 73-76.

1410. Hansel and Gretel adap. by Adele Thane from Grimms' Fairy Tales.

Short. 3 m. 3 f. +c.X.

In - Plays. 24: Feb.1965, 41-50.

1411. Hansel and Gretel Go Back to School by George Creegan.

Short. 0 m. 1 f. 1 un. 1 b. 1 g.

In - Plays. 25: Feb.1966, 89-92.

1412. Happy Christmas to All by Jeannette Covert Nolan.

Short. 3 m. 3 f.

In - Plays. 3: Dec.1943, 27-34.

1413. Happy Christmas to All by Jeannette Covert Nolan.

Short. 3 m. 3 f.

In - Plays. 18: Dec.1958, 63-70.

1414. Happy Days by Samuel Beckett.

Full. 1 m. 1 f.

In - Players. 10: Nov.1962, 34-42.

1415. Happy Easter to Margy by Mildred Hark and Noel McQueen.

Short. 3 m. 6 f.

In - Plays. 15: March 1956, 79-83.

1416. Happy Ending by Paul T. Nolan.
Short. 7 m. 4 f.
In - Plays. 27: April 1968, 17-26.

1417. Happy Family by Giles Cooper.
Full. 2 m. 2 f.
In - Players. 14: May 1967, 27-42+.

1418. The Happy Gardener by Bessie F. Collins.
Short. 1 m. 1 f. 4 c.
In - Plays. 15: May 1956, 57-58.

1419. Happy Haunts by Mildred Hark and Noel
McQueen.
Short. 4 m. 3 f.
In - Plays. 10: Oct.1950, 20-30.

1420. Happy Hearts by Mildred Hark and Noel
McQueen.
Short. 3 m. 3 f.
In - Plays. 9: Feb.1950, 20-30.

1421. Happy Holidays by Deborah Newman.
Short. 12 m. 5 f. 12 c. +X.
In - Plays. 12: Jan.1953, 59-63.

1422. The Happy Journey by Thornton Wilder. Ed.
by Margaret Mayorga.
Short. 3 m. 3 f.
In - Scholastic. 33: Sept.17,1938, 17E-20E.

1423. Happy New Year by Lindsey Barbee.
Short. 6 m. 6 f.
In - Plays. 4: Jan.1945, 60-63.

1424. Happy New Year by Mildred Hark and Noel
McQueen.
Short. 3 m. 2 f.
In - Plays. 9: Jan.1950, 19-30.

1425. The Happy Poet by Vernon Howard.
Short. 3 m. 3 f. 2 un.
In - Plays. 15: Feb.1956, 86-88.

1426. The Happy Prince by Oscar Wilde. Adap. by
Edward Golden.
Radio. 10 m. 4 f. 2 b. 1 g. 2 c.
In - Plays. 14: Feb.1955, 85-93.

1427. The Happy Prince by Oscar Wilde. Adap. by
Virginia Bartholome.
Short. 7 m. 7 f.
In - Plays. 19: March 1960, 51-58.

1428. The Happy Time by Samuel Taylor.
Full. 8 m. 4 f.
In - Theatre. 35: Feb.1951, 53-90.

1429. The Happy Valentine by Lavinia R. Davis.
Short. 7 m. 4 f. +X.
In - Plays. 21: Feb.1962, 59-62.

1430. Happy Valentine's Day by Juliet Garver.
Short. 3 m. 2 f. 1 un.
In - Plays. 13: Feb.1954, 12-18.

1431. Hardy Perennials by Arthur Meeker, Jr.
Short. 2 m. 3 f.
In - Drama. 13: May 1923, 292-296.

1432. The Hare and the Tortoise by Rowena Bennett.
Short. 3 un.
In - Plays. 5: Jan.1946, 60-63.

1433. A Hat for Mother by Marguerite Kreger
Phillips.
Short. 0 m. 6 f.
In - Plays. 13: May 1954, 39-44.

1434. A Hat For Mother by Marguerite Kreger
Phillips.
Short. 0 m. 6 f.
In - Plays. 24: May 1965, 65-70.

1435. The Hat Rack by George Herman.
Short. 1 m. 1 f.
In - First Stage. 1: Sept.1962, 50-52.

1436. A Hatful of Rain by Michael Vincente Gazzo.
Full. 6 m. 3 f.
In - Theatre. 40: Dec.1956, 33-57.

1437. Hats and Rabbits by Mildred Hark and Noel
McQueen.
Short. 3 m. 2 f.
In - Plays. 9: April 1950, 11-21.

1438. Hattie by Elva DePue.
Short. 2 m. 3 f.
In - Touchstone. 1: Aug.1917, 361-369.

1439. The Haunted Bookshop by Jessie Nicholson.
Short. 12 m. 1 f. +X.
In - Plays. 12: Nov.1952, 40-48.

1440. The Haunted Bookshop by Jessie Nicholson.
Short. 5 m. 1 f. 7 b. +X.
In - Plays. 27: Nov.1967, 55-63.

1441. The Haunted Clothesline by Helen Louise
Miller.
Short. 4 m. 3 f.
In - Plays. 9: Oct.1949, 1-10.

1442. The Haunted Clothesline by Helen Louise
Miller.
Short. 4 m. 3 f.
In - Plays. 22: Oct.1962, 27-36.

1443. The Haunted High School by Helen Louise
Miller.
Short. 9 m. 0 f. +m.X.
In - Plays. 16: Oct.1956, 87-93.

1444. Haunts for Hire by Helen Louise Miller.
Short. 8 m. 6 f.
In - Plays. 18: Oct.1958, 1-12.

1445. Haym Salomon by Mildred June Janusch.
Radio. 17 m. 2 f. 1 g.
In - Scholastic. 34: May 6,1939, 33-35+.

1446. He is Something! by John William Andrews.
Short. 9 m. 2 f. 2 c.
In - Poet Lore. 58: Sept.1963, 258-270.

1447. He Lives by A. Holdas.
Short. 2 m. 1 f.
In - Poet Lore. 52: April 1945, 117-126.

1448. He, the One Who Gets Slapped by Leonid
Andreyev.
Full. 8 m. 5 f. +X.
In - Dial. 70: March 1921, 247-300.

1449. The Head-Ax of Ingfell by Anne B. Walters.
Short. 4 m. 2 f. 1 b. +X.
In - Carolina. 6: Dec.1933, 106-118.

1450. Hear No Evil, Speak No Evil by John Murray.
Short. 3 m. 3 f.
In - Plays. 23: March 1964, 15-25.

1451. Heart of Oak by Rose Netzorg Kerr.
Short. 4 m. 2 f. 5 b.
In - School Arts. 27: June 1928, 587-593.

1452. The Heart of Youth by Hermann Hagedorn.
Short. 8 m. 3 f. +X.
In - Outlook. 111: Nov.24,1915, 744-756.

1453. Heart Throbs by Helen Louise Miller.
Short. 1 m. 15 f.
In - Plays. 16: Feb.1957, 1-12.

1454. Heart Trouble by Mildred Hark and Noel
McQueen.
Short. 3 m. 2 f.
In - Plays. 10: Feb.1951, 1-10.

1455. Heart Trouble by Mildred Hark and Noel
McQueen.
Short. 2 m. 2 f. 1 b.
In - Plays. 18: Feb.1959, 11-20.

1456. Hearts and Flowers by Helen Louise Miller.
Short. 4 m. 4 f.
In - Plays. 8: April 1949, 1-10.

1457. Hearts and Flowers for Mother by Edrie
Pendleton.
Short. 4 m. 3 f.
In - Plays. 12: May 1953, 32-39.

1458. Hearts and Flowers For Mother by Mildred
Hark and Noel McQueen.
Short. 4 m. 3 f.
In - Plays. 18: May 1959, 81-88.

1459. Hearts, Tarts, and Valentines by Aileen
Fisher.
Short. 6 m. 3 f. +X.
In - Plays. 9: Feb.1950, 48-54.

1460. Heidi by Johanna Spyri. Adap. by Adele Thane.
Short. 4 m. 7 f.
In - Plays. 26: March 1967, 85-96.

1461. Heidi Finds the Way by Johanna Spyri.
Adap. by Karin Asbrand.
Short. 7 m. 4 f. 3 un. +X.
In - Plays. 18: Jan.1959, 51-59.

1462. Helen Retires by John Erskine.
Short. 10 m. 1 f. +m.X.
In - Golden. 19: May 1934, 537-548.

1463. Hello, Mr. Groundhog by Helen Louise Miller.
Short. 18 m. 13 f.
In - Plays. 24: Feb.1965, 65-74.

1464. **Heloise** by James Forsyth.

Full. 7 m. 2 f.

In - Theatre. 43: Jan.1959, 26-49.

1465. **Help Wanted for Easter** by Esther MacLellan and
Catherine V. Schroll.

Short. 4 m. 5 f.

In - Plays. 12: April 1953, 70-73.

1466. **The Helpful Cats** by Phoebe-Lou Adams.

Short. 0 m. 1 f. 4 "cats".

In - Plays. 3: April 1944, 60-62.

1467. **Helpless Herberts** by Alfred Kreymborg.

Short. 1 m. 1 f.

In - Theatre. 8: Feb.1924, 119-132.

1468. **Hemp** by James M. Cain.

Short. 3 m. 0 f.

In - American Merc. 10: April 1927, 404-409.

1469. **Her Old Sweethearts** by Ethel H. Porter.

Short. 1 m. 1 f. (+8 m. 1 b., silent).

In - Ladies' Home. 27: April 1910, 17.

1470. **Her Opinion of His Story** by William Dean
Howells.

In - Harper's B. 41: May 1907, 429-437.

1471. **Here Comes the Interesting Part** by Stuart
M. Kaminsky.

Short. 6 m. 2 f.

In - First Stage. 6: Sept.1967, 169-176.

1472. **Hermes and the Two Woodsmen** by Rowena Bennett.

Short. 3 m. 0 f.

In - Plays. 7: May 1948, 52-57.

1473. **The Hero** by James M. Cain.

Short. 3 m. 0 f.

In - American Merc. 6: Sept.1925, 52-57.

1474. **Herod Play From America** by Frederick Samuel
Boas.

In - Contemporary. 144: Nov.1933, 575-580.

1475. **The Heroine of Wren** by Ella Stratton Colbo.

Short. 4 m. 2 f.

In - Plays. 7: April 1948, 43-47.

1476. **A Hero's Homecoming** by Helen Louise Miller.

Short. 3 m. 5 f.

In - Plays. 15: Nov.1955, 81-94.

1477. **Hi Down There** by Paul T. Nolan.

Short. 4 m. 4 f.

In - Plays. 28: Oct.1968, 21-31.

1478. **Hi, Neighbor** by Karin Asbrand.

Short. 9 m. 9 f.

In - Plays. 3: May 1944, 58-60.

1479. **Hidden Meanings** by Aileen Fisher.

Short. 1 un. 4 b. 4 g. +X.

In - Plays. 24: Feb.1965, 79-80.

1480. **The Hidden Spring** by Roberto Bracco. Trans.
by Dirce St. Cyr.

Full. 7 m. 3 f.

In - Poet Lore. 18:no.2,1907, 143-186.

1481. **The Hiding Place** by Francis L. Kroll.

Short. 3 m. 3 f.

In - Plays. 19: April 1960, 53-59.

1482. **The High Heart** by Adelaide C. Rowell.

Short. 7 m. 2 f.

In - Drama. 17: March 1927, 173-176+.

1483. **High Street China** by Robin Chapman and Richard
Kane.

Full. 10 m. 4 f.

In - Players. 10: March 1963, 28-42.

1484. **The Highland Call** by Paul Green.

Excerpt. 5 m. 1 f. 1 b.

In - Carolina. 12: Sept.1939, 102-107.

1485. **The Highland Fling** by Paul T. Nolan.

Short. 4 m. 4 f. +X.

In - Plays. 20: Feb.1961, 89-96.

1486. **Highland Lad** by Alice Very.

Short. 3 m. 2 f.

In - Plays. 4: Oct.1944, 20-26.

1487. **The Highway Trail** by Samuel S. Richmond.

Short. 7 m. 0 f.

In - Plays. 9: Oct.1949, 70-74.

1488. **Hilarion** by Josephine Howell-Carter.

Short. 5 m. 1 f.

In - Poet Lore. 26: no.3,1915, 374-392.

1489. The Hill by Herbert Edward Mierow.

Short. 6 m. 3 f. +X.

In - Poet Lore. 52: Jan.1945, 3-29.

1490. Hillbilly Blues by Betty Tracy Huff.

Short. 8 m. 7 f. +X.

In - Plays. 27: Jan.1968, 1-10.

1491. Hilltop House by Samuel S. Richmond.

Short. 3 m. 5 f.

In - Plays. 5: April 1946, 76-81.

1492. Him by E.E. Cummings.

Excerpts. 3 m. 0 f.

In - Dial. 83: Aug.1927, 101-127.

1493. Hip Hip Ho by Helen L. Howard.

Short. 5 m. 1 f.

In - Plays. 5: Jan.1946, 57-60.

1494. Hippocrates Dying by N.G. Flokos.

Short. 3 m. 0 f.

In - Poet Lore. 58: Dec.1963, 328-331.

1495. His and Hers by John Murray.

Short. 3 m. 4 f.

In - Plays. 18: Feb.1959, 35-48.

1496. His First Patient by Samuel S. Richmond.

Short. 5 m. 0 f.

In - Plays. 4: Nov.1944, 66-71.

1497. His First Patient by Samuel S. Richmond.

Short. 5 m. 0 f.

In - Plays. 24: April 1965, 29-34.

1498. His Imitation Sweetheart by Elliott Flower.

Short. 1 m. 2 f.

In - Ladies' Home. 25: Feb.1908, 12+.

1499. His Melted Majesty by Luise and Norman DeMarco.

Radio. 11 m. 1 f. 1 g.

In - Plays. 6: Oct.1946, 77-82.

1500. His Old Sweethearts by G.T. Palmer.

Short. 1 m. (8 f. 2 g., silent).

In - Ladies' Home. 26: Nov.1909, 13+.

1501. His Son by Tracy Dickinson Mygatt.

In - Poet Lore. 39: Dec.1928, 605-630.

1502. His Superior in Command by Walter Lewis Bissell.

Short. 6 m. 0 f.

In - Scholastic. 34: Feb.25,1939, 21E-24E.

1503. His Widow's Husband by Jacinto Benavente y Martinez. Trans. by J.G. Underhill.

Short. 5 m. 2 f.

In - Golden. 3: March 1926, 342-354.

1504. The Hitch Hiker by Lucille Fletcher.

Radio. 4 m. 5 f.

In - Scholastic. 51: Oct.20,1947, 18-21.

1505. Hogan's Successor by Russell F. Speirs.

Short. 3 m. 1 f.

In - Drama. 19: May 1929, 233-234.

1506. Hold Back the Redskins by Earl J. Dias.

Short. 10 m. 3 f.

In - Plays. 19: Nov.1959, 23-34.

1507. Hold Your Hat! by Paul S. McCoy.

Short. 2 m. 4 f.

In - Plays. 17: March 1958, 1-11.

1508. The Hole by N.F. Simpson.

Short. 4 m. 2 f.

In - Players. 5: June 1958, 25-30.

1509. The Holiday by Emile Mazaud. Trans. by Ralph Roeder.

Short. 4 m. 1 f.

In - Theatre. 6: Jan.1922, 33-61.

1510. Holiday for Santa by Jessie Nicholson.

Short. 8 m. 1 f. +X.

In - Plays. 17: Dec.1957, 51-58.

1511. The Holly Hangs High by Lindsey Barbee.

Short. 3 m. 4 f.

In - Plays. 5: Dec.1945, 34-40.

1512. Home for Christmas by Helen Louise Miller.

Short. 3 m. 3 f.

In - Plays. 6: Dec.1946, 1-11.

1513. Home Sports by James Heath.

Short. 2 m. 2 f.

In - Indus. Educa. 30: May 1941, 199-200.

1514. The Homecoming by Mildred Hark and Noel
       McQueen.

       Short. 2 m. 4 f.

       In - Plays. 10: Jan.1951, 12-22.

1515. The Homecoming by Mildred Hark and Noel
       McQueen.

       Short. 2 m. 3 f. 1 g.

       In - Plays. 25: Oct.1965, 37-47.

1516. Homemakers Have A Way by Samuel S. Richmond.

       Short. 0 m. 7 f.

       In - Plays. 8: Dec.1948, 66-71.

1517. Hometown Halloween by Mildred Hark and
       Noel McQueen.

       Short. 2 m. 3 f. 1 g.

       In - Plays. 12: Oct.1952, 1-11.

1518. Hometown Halloween by Mildred Hark and Noel
       McQueen.

       Short. 2 m. 4 f.

       In - Plays. 23: Oct.1963, 31-41.

1519. Homework by Helen Louise Miller.

       Short. 3 m. 3 f.

       In - Plays. 4: Jan.1945, 1-10.

1520. Homework by Helen Louise Miller.

       Short. 3 m. 3 f.

       In - Plays. 11: March 1952, 85-93.

1521. The Homiest Room by Mildred Hark and Noel
       McQueen.

       Short. 3 m. 2 f.

       In - Plays. 3: March 1944, 1-9.

1522. Honest Abe Lincoln by Aileen Fisher and
       Olive Rabe.

       Short. 4 m. 4 f.

       In - Plays. 16: Feb.1957, 37-42.

1523. Honest Injun! by John Murray.

       Short. 8 m. 2 f.

       In - Plays. 16: March 1957, 1-13.

1524. The Honeymoon by Arnold Bennett.

       Full. 6 m. 2 f.

       In - McClure's. 36: Mar.& April 1911,
          501-513, 688-706.

1525. Honor -- and the Girl by Grace S. Richmond.

       Short. 1 m. 1 f.

       In - Ladies' Home. 20: Feb.1903, 13.

1526. The Honored One by Eleanore Leuser.

       Short. 8 m. 4 f. 1 c.

       In - Plays. 22: Nov.1962, 35-39.

1527. A Hooky Holiday by Helen Louise Miller.

       Short. 5 m. 5 f.

       In - Plays. 13: April 1954, 13-25.

1528. A Hooky Holiday by Helen Louise Miller.

       Short. 4 m. 5 f. 1 b.

       In - Plays. 25: March 1966, 15-26.

1529. Hop, Jump and Skip by Claribel Spamer.

       Short. 9 m. 0 f. +X.

       In - Plays. 9: May 1950, 68-70.

1530. Hope Is the Thing with Feathers by Richard
       Harrity.

       Short. 9 m. 0 f.

       In - Theatre. 29: Sept.1945, 502-514.

1531. Horace Mann, American Educator by Bernard
       J. Reines.

       Short. 14 m. 3 f.

       In - Plays. 3: Nov.1943, 7-18.

1532. Horn of Plenty by Helen Louise Miller.

       Short. 6 m. 4 f.

       In - Plays. 24: Nov.1964, 1-12.

1533. The Horrible Humpy Dragon by Doris McBride.

       Short. 4 m. 1 f. 1 "dragon" (2 or 3 c.)

       In - Plays. 20: Jan.1961, 77-80.

1534. Horrors Incorporated by Helen Louise Miller.

       Short. 3 m. 5 f.

       In - Plays. 6: Oct.1946, 13-21.

1535. Horrors, Incorporated by Helen Louise Miller.

       Short. 3 m. 2 f. 6 un. +X.

       In - Plays. 28: Oct.1968, 11-19.

1536. The Host by Ferenc Molnar. Trans. by J.
       Szebenyei.

       Short. 6 m. 4 f. +X.

       In - Golden. 7: June 1928, 781-786.

1537. The Hostage by Paul Claudel. Trans. from
       the French by John Heard.

       Full. 6 m. 0 f. +X.

       In - Poet Lore. 50: April 1944, 100-175.

1538. The Hostage by Brendan Behan.

Full. 9 m. 5 f. +X.

In - Players. 6: July & Aug.1959, 27-31, 27-32.

1539. The Hostage by Brendan Behan.

Full. 8 m. 5 f. +X.

In - Theatre. 46: Nov.1962, 25-56.

1540. Hot Iron by Paul Green.

Short. 1 m. 1 f. 3 c.

In - Poet Lore. 35: March 1924, 48-57.

1541. Hotel Santa Claus by Helen Louise Miller.

Short. 10 m. 4 f. +X.

In - Plays. 23: Dec.1963, 1-13.

1542. The Hound of the Maskervilles by Helen Louise Miller.

Short. 7 m. 7 f. +X.

In - Plays. 26: Oct.1966, 15-27.

1543. The Hour-Glass by William Butler Yeats.

Short. 3 m. 1 f. 2 c. +X.

In - North Amer. 177: Sept.1903, 445-456.

1544. The Hour-Glass by William Butler Yeats.

Short. 3 m. 1 f. 2 c. +X.

In - Golden. 3: May 1926, 641-646.

1545. The Hour of Prospero by C.E. Lawrence.

Short. 4 m. 3 f.

In - 19th C. 92: Oct.1922, 685-696.

1546. House and Home by Josephine Miles.

Short. 2 m. 1 f. 3 c.

In - First Stage. 4: Sept.1965, 196-202.

1547. House Beautiful by Tacie May Hanna.

In - Drama. 15: Feb.1925, 112-114.

1548. The House by the Lake by Hugh Mills.

Full. 4 m. 5 f.

In - Players. 4: June-Aug.1957, 25-32, 25-30, 25-31.

1549. The House by the Side of the Road by August von Kotzebue. Trans. and adap. by Beatrice B. Beebe.

Short. 2 m. 1 f.

In - Golden. 10: July 1929, 89-93.

1550. House for Rent by Esther MacLellan and Catherine V. Schroll.

Short. 4 m. 8 f.

In - Plays. 16: Jan.1957, 63-68.

1551. House Gnomes by John Chipman Farrar.

Short. 1 b. 1 g. 6 c. +m.&f.X.

In - Bookman. 56: Dec.1922, 449-459.

1552. The House Into Which We Are Born by Jacques Copeau. Trans. by Ralph Roeder.

Full. 6 m. 2 f.

In - Theatre. 8: July 1924, 459-488.

1553. The House Is Haunted by Mildred Hark and Noel McQueen.

Short. 5 m. 6 f. +X.

In - Plays. 7: Oct.1948, 40-46.

1554. The House is Haunted by Mildred Hark and Noel McQueen.

Short. 1 m. 1 f. 4 b. 5 g.

In - Plays. 27: Oct.1967, 50-56.

1555. The House of Bernarda Alba by Federico Garcia Lorca. Trans. by James Graham Lujan and Richard L. O'Connell.

Full. 0 m. 11 f. 2 g.

In - Theatre. 36: March 1952, 52-68.

1556. A House of Cards by William Gilbert Van Tassal Sutphen.

Short. 3 m. 1 f.

In - Harper's M. 109: Nov.1904, 901-910.

1557. The House of Oedipus by Ferdinando Fontana. Trans. by Arthur Stringer.

Full. 18 m. 10 f. +X.

In - Canadian M. 38: Feb.-April 1912, 341-356, 423-436, 520-536.

1558. The House of Rimmon by Henry Van Dyke.

Full. 9 m. 4 f. +X.

In - Scribner's. 44: Aug.& Sept.1908, 129-147, 283-300.

1559. The House of Seven Gables by Nathaniel Hawthorne. Adap. by Lewy Olfson.

Radio. 7 m. 7 f.

In - Plays. 14: March 1955, 87-95.

1560. The House of the Setting Suns by Rene Marques. Trans. from the Puerto Rican by Willis Knapp Jones.

Full. 0 m. 3 f.

In - Poet Lore. 59: June 1964, 99-131.

1561. The House That Jack Built by Samuel S.
       Richmond.

       Short. 4 m. 2 f.

       In - Plays. 5: May 1946, 66-70.

1562. A Houseful of Elves by Betty Tracy Huff.

       Short. 5 m. 8 f. 3 c. +X.

       In - Plays. 19: Jan.1960, 65-68.

1563. How Christmas Was Saved by Catherine Markham.

       In - St. Nicholas. 36: Dec.1908, 153-157.

1564. How Hi Is Your Fi? by John Murray.

       Short. 7 m. 5 f.

       In - Plays. 18: April 1959, 23-37.

1565. How Much Land Does a Man Need? by Leo
       Tolstoy. Adap. by Michael T. Leech.

       Short. 5 m. 3 f. +X.

       In - Plays. 27: Jan.1968, 75-85.

       How the West Was Lost.
             see
       Roamin' Jo and Juli.

1566, How the World Began by Jocelyn Moore and
       Heather G. Thorpe.

       Short. 1 m. 8 un. +4X.

       In - Horn Book. 17: March 1941, 130-138.

1567. How To Choose a Boy by Claire Boiko.

       Short. 9 m. 5 f.

       In - Plays. 27: Jan.1968, 67-70.

1568. How We Got Our Numbers by Eleanora Bowling
       Kane.

       Short. 7 m. 2 f.

       In - Plays. 7: March 1948, 39-43.

1569. Howard's Forward Pass by Dorothy Deming.

       Short. 3 m. 2 f.

       In - Plays. 9: Oct.1949, 21-25.

1570. A Howling Success by Juliet Garver.

       Short. 5 m. 5 f.

       In - Plays. 15: May 1956, 1-10.

1571. A Howling Success by Juliet Garver.

       Short. 4 m. 3 f. 1 b. 2 g.

       In - Plays. 24: Jan.1965, 15-24.

1572. How's The World Treating You? by Roger
       Milner.

       Full. 3 m. 3 f.

       In - Players. 13: March 1966, 31-46+.

1573. Hubbub on the Bookshelf by Alice Woster.

       Short. 7 m. 2 f.

       In - Plays. 3: Nov.1943, 42-53.

1574. Hubbub on the Bookshelf by Alice Woster.

       Short. 6 m. 3 f.

       In - Plays. 28: Nov.1968, 61-72.

1575. Huckleberry Finn by Mark Twain. Adap. by
       Graham DuBois.

       Radio. 3 m. 1 f. 1 b.

       In - Plays. 13: Feb.1954, 77-87.

1576. The Human Accident by Charles Frink.

       Full. 13 m. 3 f. +m.X.

       In - First Stage. 1: June 1962, 53-67.

1577. The Humiliation of the Father by Paul
       Claudel. Trans. from the French
       by John Heard.

       Full. 7 m. 1 f.

       In - Poet Lore. 50: Oct.1944, 291-360.

1578. Humpty Dumpty by Bertram Bloch.

       In - Poet Lore. 32: March 1921, 76-97.

1579. A Hundred Years of Lovemaking ed. by
       Lauraine Field. (11 scenes by 11
       authors from 1820 to 1920.)

       Full. 1 m. 1 f. each

       In - Theatre. 14: June 1930, 499-514.

1580. Hunt for the Violet by Lindsey Barbee.

       Short. 0 m. 11 f.

       In - Plays. 4: May 1945, 36-40.

1581. Hurrah for Books by Frances B. Watts.

       Short. 6 m. 6 f.

       In - Plays. 27: March 1968, 41-47.

1582. I Am A Camera by John Van Druten.

       Full. 3 m. 4 f.

       In - Theatre. 37: Jan.1953, 34-64.

1583. I Am A Camera by John Van Druten.

       Full. 3 m. 4 f.

       In - Players. 3: June & July 1956, 20-29,
       21-26.

1584. I Can Get Along by Karin Asbrand.

Short. 4 m. 6 f. +X.

In - Plays. 9: May 1950, 58-63.

1585. I Can't Imagine Tomorrow by Tennessee Williams.

Short. 1 m. 1 f.

In - Esquire. 65: Mar.1966, 76-79.

1586. I Did But Jest by Godfrey P. Schmidt, Jr.

Short. 2 m. 1 f.

In - Poet Lore. 35: March 1924, 130-139.

1587. I Love You, Mr. Klotz by John Murray.

Short. 4 m. 4 f.

In - Plays. 21: March 1962, 25-38.

1588. I Shall Sail Again by Graham DuBois.

Short. 8 m. 1 f.

In - Plays. 6: Oct.1946, 21-29.

1589. I Remember Mama by John Van Druten. From the novel Mama's Bank Account by Kathryn Forbes.

Excerpt. 3 m. 5 f.

In - Scholastic. 51: Sept.22,1947, 22-24.

1590. I Rise in Flame, Cried the Phoenix by Tennessee Williams.

In - Ramparts. 6: Jan.1968, 14-19.

1591. I Thank You by Mary Cornell.

In - Canadian F. 12: Sept.1932, 454-456.

1592. I Too Have Lived in Arcadia by V.R. Lang.

Short. 2 m. 1 f.

In - Poetry. 86: April 1955, 27-40.

1593. I Want to Report a Murder by John Murray.

Short. 4 m. 4 f.

In - Plays. 19: Jan.1960, 15-28.

1594. Ichabod Rides Again by Charles F. Wilde.

Radio. 13 m. 2 f.

In - Plays. 6: Oct.1947, 82-92.

1595. The Idealists by Helen R. Hull.

Short. 2 m. 1 f.

In - Touchstone. 1: Sept.1917, 457-463.

1596. The Ides of March by Mildred Hark and Noel McQueen.

Short. 3 m. 2 f.

In - Plays. 8: March 1949, 1-12.

1597. The Idiot by Cesare Ludovici. Trans. from the Italian by Petronelle Sombart.

Full. 4 m. 3 f.

In - Poet Lore. 30:no.3,1919, 317-355.

1598. Idyl by Hugo von Hofmannsthal.

Short. 1 m. 1 f. 1 centaur(!)

In - Poet Lore. 51: March 1945, 117-120.

1599. Idyll by Martinez Sierra. Trans. from the Spanish by Charlotte Marie Lorenz.

Short. 6 un. +X.

In - Poet Lore. 37: March 1926, 63-72.

1600. Idyll by Mary Grahn.

In - Drama. 16: April 1926, 255-256.

Idylls of the King.

see

Launcelot and Elaine.

1601. If Shakespeare Lived Today by Lord Dunsany.

Short. 5 m. 0 f.

In - Atlantic. 126: Oct.1920, 497-508.

1602. If Wishes Were Horses by Bertha Nathan.

Short. 5 m. 3 f.

In - Plays. 5: April 1946, 33-39.

1603. Ile by Eugene O'Neill

Short. 5 m. 1 f. +m.X.

In - Golden. 9: Feb.1929, 87-93.

1604. Ile by Eugene O'Neill.

Short. 5 m. 1 f. +m.X.

In - Scholastic. 28: Feb.15,1936, 4-6+.

1605. The Iliad by Homer. Adap. by Lewy Olfson.

Radio. 11 m. 0 f.

In - Plays. 19: April 1960, 88-96.

1606. I'll Eat My Hat by Helen Louise Miller.

Short. 6 m. 4 f. +X.

In - Plays. 15: Nov.1955, 69-80.

1607. I'll Share My Fare by Helen L. Howard.

Short. 4 m. 2 f.

In - Plays. 7: Nov.1947, 53-54.

1608. I'll Try by Elinor Murphy.

Short. 0 m. 3 f. 15 c.

In - St. Nicholas. 48: Jan.1921, 256-260.

1609. I'm Not Complaining by Alfred Kreymborg.

Short. 0 m. 2 f.

In - Theatre. 15: June 1931, 493-498.

1610. I'm Not Complaining by Alfred Kreymborg.
Ed. by Margaret Mayorga.

Short. 0 m. 2 f.

In - Scholastic. 32: April 2,1938. 21E-23E.

1611. I'm Talking About Jerusalem by Arnold Wesker.

Full. 8 m. 4 f.

In - Players. 8: Nov.& Dec.1960. 25-31, 25-30.

1612. An Imaginary Trial of George Washington by
Diana Wolman.

Short. 15 m. 3 f. +X.

In - Plays. 20: Feb.1961, 26-38.

1613. Immortal by Carl Glick and Bernard Sobel.

In - Poet Lore. 32: Sept.1921, 441-453.

1614. Immortal Hour by Fiona Macleod.

In - Fortnightly. 74: Nov.1900, 867-896.

1615. Immortality by Charles Pattison MacInnis.

Short. 4 m. 2 f.

In - Drama. 16: April 1926, 258-260.

1616. The Immortals by Charles Caldwell Dobie.

Short. 3 m. 3 f.

In - Overland. 84 n.s.: March 1926, 74-76.

1617. The Importance of Being Earnest by Oscar
Wilde.

Excerpt. 0 m. 2 f.

In - Theatre. 22: Sept.1938, 685-686.

1618. The Importance of Being Earnest by Oscar
Wilde. Adap. by Lewy Olfson.

Radio. 6 m. 3 f.

In - Plays. 14: Oct.1954, 87-95.

1619. The Importance of Being Earnest by Oscar
Wilde. Adap. by Lewy Olfson.

Short. 5 m. 4 f.

In - Plays. 21: Jan.1962, 85-95.

1620. The Impossible by William Dean Howells.

Short. 2 m. 1 f.

In - Harper's M. 122: Dec.1910, 116-125.

1621. The Impossible Room by John Murray.

Short. 4 m. 4 f.

In - Plays. 13: Jan.1954, 13-26.

1622. Impromptu by Dana Burnet.

Short. 4 m. 2 f. +X.

In - Bookman. 57: May 1923, 267-273.

1623. Impromptu de Paris by Jean Giraudoux.
Trans. by Rosamond Gilder.

Short. 11 m. 2 f.

In - Theatre. 22: March 1938, 217-230.

1624. Improving a Husband by Helen M. Givens.

Short. 1 m. 1 f.

In - Ladies' Home. 24: Mar.1907, 10+.

1625. Improvisation; or The Shepherd's Chameleon
by Eugene Ionesco.

Short. 4 m. 0 f.

In - Horizon. 3: May 1961, 92+.

1626. Il Improvisatore by Paul Scott Mowrer.

Short. 7 m. 2 f.

In - Poet Lore. 62: June 1967, 144-148.

1627. In Chains by Paul Hervieu. Trans. by
Ysidor Asckenasy.

Short. 5 m. 2 f.

In - Poet Lore. 20:no.2,1909, 81-112.

1628. In County Mayo by W.M. Conacher.

Short. 8 m. 2 f.

In - Queen's. 40: Nov.1933, 599-611.

1629. In Garrison by C.E. Freyhe.

Short. 5 m. 0 f.

In - Poet Lore. 26:no.4,1915, 499-511.

1630. In Gotham Meadow by Marion Wefer.

Short. 6 m. 3 f.

In - Plays. 5: May 1946, 48-54.

1631. In Gremio Deorum: A Super-Historical
Phantasy by Thomas Barclay.

Short. 9 m. 1 f. +X.

In - 19th C. 79: March 1916, 554-568.

1632. The In-Group by Paul T. Nolan.

Short. 12 un.

In - Plays. 27: May 1968, 93-103.

1633. In Honor of Trees by Deborah Newman.

Short. 4 m. 7 f. 7 c. +c.X.

In - Plays. 10: May 1951, 61-65.

1634. In Honor of Washington by Edrie Pendleton.
Short. 3 m. 2 f. +X.
In - Plays. 9: Feb.1950, 63-70.

1635. In Honor of Washington by Edrie Pendleton.
Short. 3 m. 2 f. +X.
In - Plays. 19: Feb.1960, 37-44.

1636. In My Father's House by David Madden.
Short. 3 m. 2 f.
In - First Stage. 5: June 1966, 119-131.

1637. In Savoy by Gertrude Stein.
Excerpt. 4 m. 3 f.
In - Sat. Review. 28: May 5,1945, 5-7.

1638. In the Andes by Herbert Parrish.
Full. 3 m. 1 f. +X.
In - Atlantic. 140: Aug.1927, 231-238.

1639. In the Fog by Homer King Gordon.
In - Sunset. 58: Feb.1927, 28-31.

1640. In the Jungle of Cities by Bertolt Brecht.
Trans. by Gerhard Nellhaus.
Full. 14 m. 5 f. +X.
In - Theatre. 45: Aug.1961, 25-56.

1641. In the Light of the Star by Agnes Emelie Peterson.
Short. 12 m. 2 f. 1 b. +ch. +X.
In - Drama. 21: Nov.1930, 19-20+.

1642. In the Morgue by Sada Cowan.
Short. 2 m. 0 f. +X.
In - Forum. 55: April 1916, 399-407.

1643. In the Name of Miles Standish by Helen Ramsey.
Short. 7 m. 4 f. +m.X.
In - Plays. 14: Nov.1954, 39-44.

1644. In the Secret Places by Elsa Behaim Nessenson.
Short. 4 m. 4 f. +m.X.
In - Drama. 17: Nov.1926, 43-45+.

1645. In the Sky Village by Melicent H. Lee.
Short. 2 m. 1 f. +X.
In - School Arts. 33: Sept.1933, 40-43.

1646. In the Witch's House by Rowena Bennett.
Short. 1 m. 2 f.
In - Plays. 4: March 1945, 47-50.

1647. In the Zone by Eugene O'Neill.
Short. 9 m. 0 f.
In - Scholastic. 38: Jan.27,1941, 17-21+.

1648. In Time to Come (abr.) by Howard Koch and John Huston.
Excerpt. 4 m. 0 f.
In - Scholastic. 40: Feb.23,1942, 17-19+.

1649. In Wedlock by Henri Lavedan. Trans. from the French by William V. Silverberg.
Short. 1 m. 1 f.
In - Poet Lore. 30:no.1,1919, 7-14.

1650. Incident at Valley Forge by Walter Hackett.
Short. 6 m. 2 f.
In - Plays. 3: Jan.1944, 4-12.

1651. The Inconveniences of Being Neutral by Laurence Vail.
Short. 17 m. 3 f.
In - Forum. 59: Jan.1918, 85-100.

1652. The Indian Boy Without a Name by Rod Vahl.
Short. 2 m. 1 f. 3 b. 2 g.
In - Plays. 25: Oct.1965, 55-60.

1653. Indian Brave by Nathalie F. Gross.
Short. 5 m. 5 f.
In - Plays. 14: Jan.1955, 75-78.

1654. Indian Summer by Josephine Henry Whitehouse.
In - Poet Lore. 39: Sept.1928, 455-466.

1655. Indians for Thanksgiving by Dorothy Heiderstadt.
Short. 4 m. 3 f. +m.X.
In - Plays. 8: Nov.1948, 37-41.

1656. In'ependence by Esther Marion Alger.
Short. 5 m. 4 f. 2 b. 2 g. 2 babies.
In - Poet Lore. 41: Jan.1930, 140-149.

1657. The Inexperienced Ghost by H.G. Wells.
Adap. by Paul T. Nolan.
Short. 3 m. 2 f.
In - Plays. 25: Oct.1965, 87-96.

1658. The Informer by Bertolt Brecht. Trans. by
      Ruth Norden.

      Short. 1 m. 2 f. 1 b.

      In - Living Age. 355: Sept.1938, 35-42.

1659. The Informer by Dudley Nichols. Ed. by John
      Gassner from the movie based on the
      novel by Liam O'Flaherty.

      Full. 14 m. 5 f.

      In - Theatre. 35: Aug.1951, 58-83.

1660. Inherit the Wind by Jerome Lawrence and
      Robert E. Lee.

      Full. 23 m. 7 f. +X.

      In - Theatre. 41: Aug.1957, 34-62.

1661. The Inheritors or The Part You Can't Get in
      Your Mouth by Richard Cook.

      Short. 2 m. 3 f.

      In - First Stage. 7: Dec.1968, 159-172.

1662. The Inn at Bethlehem by Aileen Fisher.

      Short. 11 m. 5 f. +X.

      In - Plays. 19: Dec.1959, 47-56.

1663. The Inn of Return by Don C. Jones. Ed. by
      Margaret Mayorga.

      Short. 6 m. 2 f.

      In - Scholastic. 34: May 20,1939, 19E-21E.

1664. The Inn of the Blue Rose by Marguerite
      Kreger Phillips.

      Short. 8 m. 3 f. +X.

      In - Plays. 21: Dec.1961, 13-22.

1665. The Innocents by William Archibald. Based
      on the story The Turn of the Screw.

      Full. 0 m. 2 f. 1 b. 1 g.

      In - Theatre. 35: Jan.1951, 59-88.

1666. The Insatiable Dragon by Claire Boiko.

      Short. 6 m. 1 f. +X.

      In - Plays. 25: April 1966, 63-68.

1667. Inside a Kid's Head by Jerome Lawrence and
      Jerome L. Schwartz.

      Radio. 16 un. 4 c.

      In - Scholastic. 48: March 18,1946, 17-19.

1668. An Inspector Calls by J.B. Priestly.

      Full. 4 m. 3 f.

      In - Theatre. 33: April 1949, 65-85.

1669. Instructions for Gary by Paul S. McCoy.

      Short. 2 m. 3 f.

      In - Plays. 13: March 1954, 13-26.

1670. An International Affair by John Murray.

      Short. 4 m. 3 f. +X.

      In - Plays. 13: April 1954, 26-35.

1671. Interpolated by Katherine Barron Brookman.

      Short. 3 m. 2 f. 8 un.

      In - Poet Lore. 35: March 1924, 78-88.

1672. The Interrupted Act by Tadeusz Rozewicz.
      Trans. from the Polish by Adam
      Czerniawski.

      Short. 5 m. 3 f.

      In - Gambit. 3: no.12, 39-67.

1673. An Interrupted Proposal by Arlo Bates.

      Short. 3 m. 4 f.

      In - Ladies' Home. 23: Feb.1906, 10.

1674. Interruption by Margarita Spalding Gerry.

      In - Harper's B. 40: May 1906, 398-403.

1675. The Intimate Strangers by Booth Tarkington.

      Full. 4 m. 4 f.

      In - Harper's M. 144: April & May 1922,
      599-610, 761-773, and 145: June 1922,
      75-86.

1676. Into the Everywhere by Edith Heal.

      Short. 2 m. 2 f. 1 c.

      In - Poet Lore. 38: Sept.1927, 466-472.

1677. Into the Tents of Men by M.G. Jacobs.

      Short. 3 m. 0 f.

      In - Poet Lore. 58: Dec.1963, 336-351.

1678. The Intruder by Maurice Maeterlinck.

      Short. 4 m. 3 f.

      In - Golden. 16: Dec. 1932, 543-553.

1679. The Invasion by Arthur Adamov. Trans. from
      the French L'Invasion by Robert J. Doan.

      Short. 3 m. 4 f. 1 b.

      In - Mod. Drama. 2: Sept.1968, 59-75.

1680. Invasion from the Stratosphere by Aileen
      Fisher and Olive Rabe.

      Short. 5 m. 2 f. +m.X.

      In - Plays. 13: March 1954, 51-56.

1681. The Invisible Dragon of Winn Sinn Tu by
Rosemary G. Musil.

Short. 3 m. 1 f. 1 un.

In - Plays. 19: March 1960, 37-49.

1682. Invisible Inventions, Incorporated by John
Murray.

Short. 7 m. 2 f.

In - Plays. 23: April 1964, 13-26.

1683. The Invisible Man by H.G. Wells. Adap. by
Levy Olfson.

Radio. 8 m. 4 f.

In - Plays. 24: Nov.1964, 83-93.

1684. Invitation to a March by Arthur Laurents.

Full. 3 m. 4 f. 1 b.

In - Theatre. 46: Jan.1962, 25-56.

1685. Is Santa Claus a Fraud? by Carolyn Wells.

Short. Large cast of c.

In - Ladies' Home. 27: Dec.1909, 9-10+.

1686. Is There Life on Other Planets? by Marion
Lane.

Short. 6 m. 0 f.

In - Plays. 24: March 1965, 60.

1687. Isaiah and the United Nations by Stanley H.
Silverman.

Radio. 10 m. 1 f. +X.

In - Scholastic. 51: Oct.6,1947, 19-21.

1688. It Happened in Egypt by Fannie R. Ross.

Short. 8 m. 5 f.

In - Plays. 10: March 1951, 41-46.

1689. It Happened Tomorrow by Dudley Nichols and
Rene Clair.

Excerpt. 10 m. 2 f. +X.

In - Theatre. 28: June 1944, 375-381.

1690. It Takes a Thief adap. by William Kozlenko.
From the story of Michael Zoschenko.

Short. 6 m. 0 f.

In - First Stage. 4: Dec.1965, 232-236.

1691. The Italian Girl by Iris Murdoch and James
Saunders.

Full. 3 m. 4 f.

In - Players. 15: March 1968, 27-42+.

1692. It's a Date. Excerpt from the movie.

Excerpt. 5 m. 2 f.

In - Scholastic. 36: April 22, 1940, 15-17+.

1693. It's A Magic Time by Lindsey Barbee.

Short. 1 m. 3 f.

In - Plays. 5: Oct.1945, 53-55.

1694. It's All Wrong by Ogden Nash.

Short. 2 m. 0 f.

In - Golden. 17: Feb.1933, 137-138.

1695. It's Greek to Me by Mildred Hark and Noel
McQueen.

Short. 3 m. 2 f.

In - Plays. 5: April 1946, 1-10.

1696. It's So Complex by Mildred Hark and Noel
McQueen.

Short. 3 m. 2 f.

In - Plays. 13: Jan.1954, 1-11.

1697. It's So Peaceful by Muriel Ward.

Short. 6 m. 2 f.

In - Plays. 5: May 1946, 12-23.

1698. It's So Peaceful by Muriel Ward.

Short. 6 m. 2 f.

In - Plays. 16: March 1957, 25-36.

1699. The Ivory Tower by Elizabeth Macintire and
Colin C. Clements.

Short. 3 m. 1 f.

In - Poet Lore. 30:no.1,1919, 127-137.

1700. J.B. by Archibald MacLeish.

Excerpt. 4 m. 0 f.

In - Sat. Review. 39: Sept.1,1956, 7-10.

1701. J.B. by Archibald MacLeish.

Excerpt. 6 m. 4 f.

In - Life. 46: May 18,1959, 126-132.

1702. J.B. by Archibald MacLeish.

Full. 12 m. 10 f.

In - Theatre. 44: Feb.1960, 33-64.

1703. Jack and Jill adap. by S. Decatur Smith Jr.
From the story by Louisa May Alcott.

Short. 1 m. 2 f. 6 b. 6 g. +c.X.

In - Ladies' Home. 24: Dec.1906, 14+.

1704. <u>Jack and the Beanstalk</u> by Alice Very.

Short. 4 m. 4 f. +X.

In - Plays. 8: Jan.1949, 57-61.

1705. <u>Jack and the Magic Beanstalk</u> adap. by
Adele Thane.

Short. 5 m. 4 f. 1 "cow" +X.

In - Plays. 24: Jan.1965, 55-63.

1706. <u>Jack Frost and Technicolor</u> by Catherine
Urban.

Short. 6 m. 1 f.

In - Plays. 6: Jan.1947, 57-59.

1707. <u>Jack Frost and the Scarecrow</u> by Marilyn C.
Nadin.

Short. 3 m. 20 c.

In - Plays. 28: Nov.1968, 83-85.

1708. <u>Jack Frost's Goodbye Gift</u> by Claribel
Spamer.

Short. 4 m. 4 f.

In - Plays. 14: March 1955, 84-86.

1709. <u>Jack-O-Lantern</u> by Claribel Spamer.

Short. 2 m. 1 f. 4 c.

In - Plays. 9: Oct.1949, 63-66.

1710. <u>Jack Straw</u> by Aileen Fisher.

Short. 2 m. 1 f.

In - Plays. 9: Nov.1949, 71-73.

1711. <u>The Jackass</u> by José Ruibal. Trans. from
the Spanish by Thomas Seward.

Full. 14 m. 3 f.

In - Mod. Drama. 2: Sept.1968, 33-56.

1712. <u>Jackie the Jumper</u> by Gwyn Thomas.

Full. 13 m. 3 f. +ch.

In - Players. 10: Feb.1963, 26-44.

1713. <u>Jack's Friends</u> by Claribel Spamer.

Short. 3 m. 1 f. +X.

In - Plays. 11: Jan.1952, 64-66.

1714. <u>Jan Výrava</u> by Frantisek Adolf Subert.
Trans. from the Bohemian by Sarka B.
Hrbkova.

Full. 21 m. 11 f. +X.

In - Poet Lore. 26:no.3,1915, 281-350.

1715. <u>Jane Eyre</u> by Helen B. Jerome. From the novel
by Charlotte Brontë.

Excerpt. 10 m. 11 f. 1 g.

In - Scholastic. 35: Sept.18,1939, 25E-27E.

1716. <u>Jane Eyre</u> by Charlotte Brontë. Adap. by
Lewy Olfson.

Radio. 4 m. 3 f.

In - Plays. 13: May 1954, 85-92.

1717. <u>Jane Eyre</u> by Charlotte Brontë. Adap. by
Lewy Olfson.

Short. 2 m. 2 f.

In - Plays. 19: Oct.1959, 29-38.

1718. <u>Jane Eyre</u> adap. by Lewy Olfson. From the
novel by Charlotte Brontë.

Radio. 3 m. 3 f.

1719. <u>Jane's Visit to the Museum</u> by Beulah
Breckinridge.

Short. 1 m. 1 f. 1 b. 1 g.

In - School Arts. 49: Feb.1950, 204-205+.

1720. <u>Janus</u> by Carolyn Green.

Full. 3 m. 2 f.

In - Theatre. 41: Oct.1957, 34-58.

1721. <u>Jasmine and the Poet</u> by Charmion Von Wiegand.

Short. 3 m. 1 f.

In - Poet Lore. 37: Sept.1926, 418-431.

1722. <u>Jeanne d'Arc at Vancouleurs</u> by Will Hutchins.

Full. 6 m. 3 f.

In - Poet Lore. 21:no.2,1910, 101-148.

1723. <u>Jenny-By-The-Day</u> by Lida Lisle Molloy.

Short. 4 m. 3 f.

In - Plays. 8: Jan.1949, 27-33.

1724. <u>Jerry Makes a Discovery</u> by Lillian Alverson.

Short. 5 m. 0 f. +X.

In - Plays. 6: Jan.1947, 36-40.

1725. <u>The Jest of Hahalaba</u> by Lord Dunsany.

Short. 4 m. 1 f.

In - Atlantic. 139: Jan.1927, 58-62.

1726. <u>The Jester and the King's Tarts</u> by Francis L.
Kroll.

Short. 4 m. 2 f.

In - Plays. 17: Feb.1958, 72-76.

1727. <u>The Jesuit</u> by José de Alencar. Trans. from
the Portuguese by Edgardo R. DeBritto.

Full. 9 m. 2 f.

In - Poet Lore. 30:no.4,1919, 475-547.

1728. The Jew of Constance by Wilhelm von Scholz. Trans. from the German by Lee M. Hollander.

Full. 26 m. 1 f. 1 b. +X.

In - Poet Lore. 57: Dec.1962, 387-472.

1729. The Jewel Merchants by James Branch Cabell.

Short. 2 m. 1 f.

In - Golden. 12: Sept.1930, 88-96.

1730. Jezebel by Robert Gilbert Welsh.

Short. 6 m. 3 f. +X.

In - Forum. 53: May 1915, 647-660.

1731. Jill-in-the-Box by Frances B. Watts.

Short. 6 m. 5 f. 2 un.

In - Plays. 23: Dec.1963, 75-80.

1732. Jiminy Cinders by Helen Louise Miller.

Short. 8 m. 0 f.

In - Plays. 16: Jan.1957, 49-56.

1733. Jimmy Columbus by Alice Very.

Short. 8 m. 5 f. +m.X.

In - Plays. 7: Oct.1948, 46-53.

1734. Jimmy Six by Robert Downing.

Short. 2 m. 3 f.

In - Plays. 13: Nov.1953, 21-30.

1735. Jimmy Six by Robert Downing.

Short. 2 m. 3 f.

In - Plays. 22: Nov.1962, 25-34.

1736. Jingle Bells by Mildred Hark and Noel McQueen.

Short. 3 m. 4 f.

In - Plays. 8: Dec.1948, 37-46.

1737. Joan of Arc by Julia H. Chadwick.

In - Woman's Home. 39: May 1912, 35.

1738. Joan of Lorraine by Maxwell Anderson.

Full. 18 m. 4 f.

In - Theatre. 32: Spring 1948, 61-92.

1739. Johan Ulfstjerna by Tor Hedberg.

In - Poet Lore. 32: March 1921, 1-63.

1740. John Brown of Pottawatomie by John F. Alexander.

Short. 11 m. 1 f.

In - Carolina. 7: March 1934, 15-28.

1741. John Crown's Legacy by Ernst H. Suerken.

Short. 26 m. 0 f.

In - Plays. 12: Nov.1952, 12-22.

1742. John Grumlie by Alice Very.

Short. 3 m. 4 f.

In - Plays. 5: Oct.1945, 48-50.

John Thomas.

see

Cockade 2.

1743. Johnny Appleseed by Bernard C. Schoenfeld.

Radio. 5 m. +ch.

In - Scholastic. 37: Sept.16,1940, 17-19.

1744. Johnny Appleseed by Paul T. Nolan.

Short. 6 m. 3 f.

In - Plays. 21: March 1962, 39-46.

1745. Johnny Appleseed's Vision by Aileen Fisher and Olive Rabe.

Short. 3 m. 3 f. +ch.

In - Plays. 24: Jan.1965, 64-68.

1746. Johnny Did Try by Marguerite Kreger Phillips.

Short. 2 m. 4 f.

In - Plays. 11: March 1952, 48-54.

1747. Johnny Has a Design Dream by Ruth C. Merry.

Short. 0 m. 1 f. 3 b. 2 g. 5 c.

In - School Arts. 26: Jan.1927, 304+.

1748. Johnny Nightmare by Paul S. McCoy.

Short. 3 m. 4 f.

In - Plays. 18: Jan.1959, 1-11.

1749. Johnny On the Spot by Aileen Fisher and Olive Rabe.

Short. 3 m. 1 f. 2 b. 1 g. +X.

In - Plays. 25: March 1966, 75-80.

1750. Johnny So Long by Vivienne C. Welburn.

Full. 3 m. 3 f.

In - Gambit. 2: no.8, 3-67.

1751. Jonah in the Bible Country by Charles Lee Snider.

Short. 5 m. 0 f. +X.

In - American Merc. 30: Oct.1933, 165-171.

1752. Jose San Martin, South American Hero. (anon.)
       Radio. 16 m. 3 f.
       In - Plays. 3: April 1944, 73-77.

1753. Journey for Margaret, M.G.M. movie.
       Excerpt. 1 m. 2 f. 1 b. 1 g.
       In - Scholastic. 41: Jan.11,1943, 17-19.

1754. Journey to Jerusalem by Maxwell Anderson.
       Excerpt. 5 m. 1 f.
       In - Scholastic. 37: Jan.13,1941, 17-20.

1755. Journeys End in Lovers' Meeting by Paula
       Mendel and Arthur Guiterman.
       Short. 1 m. 2 f.
       In - Ladies' Home. 19: Feb.1902, 9.

1756. Joy Giver by Elizabeth Stuart Phelps Ward.
       In - Harper's B. 38: Jan.1904, 25-31.

1757. Joy Lady by Upton Close.
       In - Drama. 18: May 1928, 250-252.

1758. Joy of Giving Thanks by Florence Liss and
       Nova G. Nestrick.
       Short. 8 m. 13 f. +X.
       In - Plays. 19: Nov.1959, 55-60.

1759. Joyzelle by Maurice Maeterlinck. Trans. by
       Clarence Stratton.
       Full. 2 m. 2 f.
       In - Poet Lore. 16:no.2,1905, 1-45.

1760. Juan Moriera by Eduardo Gutierrez and Jose
       J. Podesta. Trans. by Willis Knapp
       Jones and Carlos Escudero. Ed. by
       John Heard.
       Short. 15 m. 0 f. +m.X.
       In - Poet Lore. 51: April 1945, 101-117.

1761. Jubilee by Anton Chekhov.
       In - Poet Lore. 31: Dec.1920, 616-628.

1762. Jubilee by Herman Heijermans.
       In - Drama. 13: July 1923, 325-331.

1763. Judge Monkey by Mildred Colbert.
       Short. 4 m. 0 f.
       In - Plays. 14: May 1955, 77-79.

1764. The Judge's Diary by Helen Louise Miller.
       Short. 5 m. 5 f.
       In - Plays. 11: May 1952, 10-20.

1765. The Judge's Diary by Helen Louise Miller.
       Short. 5 m. 5 f.
       In - Plays. 18: May 1959, 13-22.

1766. Judgment Comes to Dan'l by Bernice Kelly
       Harris.
       Short. 1 m. 4 f.
       In - Carolina. 6: Sept.1933, 76-88.

1767. The Judgment of Paris by Lucian. Trans. by
       A.M. Harmon.
       Short. 3 m. 3 f.
       In - Golden. 6: July 1927, 49-52.

1768. Judith's Father by Margaret Widdemer.
       Short. 7 m. 5 f.
       In - Plays. 3: April 1944, 24-33.

1769. The Juggler of Our Lady by Anatole France.
       Adap. by Walter Hackett.
       Radio. 9 m. 0 f. 2 b. 2 g. +ch.
       In - Plays. 9: Dec.1949, 78-83.

1770. Julius Caesar by William Shakespeare. Adap.
       by Lewy Olfson.
       Radio. 12 m. 3 f.
       In - Plays. 14: Jan.1955, 88-96.

1771. Jump for George by Helen Louise Miller.
       Short. 6 m. 11 f. +X.
       In - Plays. 15: Feb.1956, 1-12.

1772. Jump for Joy by Albert Schaaf.
       Short. 7 m. 7 f.
       In - Plays. 19: March 1960, 23-35.

1773. Junction Santa Claus by Mildred Hark and
       Noel McQueen.
       Short. 5 m. 5 f.
       In - Plays. 11: Dec.1951, 43-52.

1774. Junction Santa Claus by Mildred Hark and Noel
       McQueen.
       Short. 5 m. 5 f.
       In - Plays. 20: Dec.1960, 37-46.

1775. June Mad by Florence Ryerson and Colin
       Campbell Clements.
       Excerps. 4 m. 3 f.
       In - Scholastic. 38: April 28,1941, 17-19.

1776. Junior Prom by Charles F. Wilde.

Short. 4 m. 4 f.

In - Plays. 8: Jan.1949, 10-18.

1777. Junior Prom by Charles F. Wilde.

Short. 4 m. 4 f.

In - Plays. 12: Jan.1953, 70-77.

1778. A Just and Lasting Peace by Graham DuBois.

Short. 3 m. 3 f.

In - Plays. 23: Feb.1964, 25-34.

1779. Just in Time by Esther E. Ziegler.

Short. 9 m. 7 f. +X.

In - Plays. 12: April 1953, 38-46.

1780. Just Like Us by Dorothy Deming.

Short. 4 m. 3 f.

In - Plays. 8: Jan.1949, 33-38.

1781. Just Relax, Mother by Mildred Hark and Noel McQueen.

Short. 8 m. 4 f.

In - Plays. 17: May 1958, 35-45.

1782. Just What the Doctor Ordered by Helen Louise Miller.

Short. 14 m. 3 f.

In - Plays. 9: Nov.1949, 11-20.

1783. Just What the Doctor Ordered by Helen Louise Miller.

Short. 14 m. 3 f.

In - Plays. 16: Nov.1956, 1-10.

1784. Kachoo! by Deborah Newman.

Short. 4 m. 4 f. +X.

In - Plays. 11: Jan.1952, 61-64.

1785. Kataki by Shimon Wincelberg.

Full. 2 m. 0 f.

In - Gambit. 2: no.5, 3-40.

1786. The Keep by Gwyn Thomas.

Full. 7 m. 2 f.

In - Players. 9: March & April 1962, 31-38, 31-40.

1787. Keep It Under Cover by Paul S. McCoy.

Short. 2 m. 4 f.

In - Plays. 18: May 1959, 23-33.

1788. The Keeper of the Gate by Hermann Hagedorn.

Short. 2 m. 1 f.

In - Outlook. 107: Aug.29,1914, 1056-1060.

1789. Keeping Christmas by Mary Peacock.

Short. 4 m. 5 f.

In - Plays. 10: Dec.1950, 50-53.

1790. A Kettle of Brains by Gweneira M. Williams.

Short. 2 m. 2 f.

In - Plays. 3: Nov.1943, 69-72.

1791. A Kettle of Brains by Gweneira M. Williams.

Short. 2 m. 2 f.

In - Plays. 24: April 1965, 77-80.

1792. Key Largo by Maxwell Anderson.

Excerpt. 2 m. 0 f.

In - Theatre. 24: Oct.1940, 749-750.

1793. The Key to the Music Room by Hermia Harris Fraser.

Short. 2 m. 0 f. 1 b. 1 g.

In - Etude. 52: July 1934, 445-446.

1794. The Key to Understanding by Louise Biggs.

Short. 7 m. 3 f. 18 c.

In - Plays. 21: Nov.1961, 48-52.

1795. The Keys to Peace by Deborah Newman.

Short. 3 m. 8 f.

In - Plays. 12: Nov.1952, 61-65.

1796. The Keys to Peace by Deborah Newman.

Short. 3 m. 8 f.

In - Plays. 18: Nov.1958, 67-70.

1797. Kid Avalanche by John Murray.

Short. 3 m. 8 f.

In - Plays. 20: Feb.1961, 13-25.

1798. Kidnapped by the Indians by Ruth Perlmutter.

Short. 2 m. 3 f.

In - Plays. 5: Jan.1946, 29-38.

1799. The Kidnapping of David Balfour by Robert Louis Stevenson. Adap. by Lewy Olfson.

Radio. 8 m. 2 f.

In - Plays. 15: April 1956, 88-96.

1800. Killed by Merry Christmas by Julia M. Street.
Radio. 9 m. 1 f. +X.
In - Plays. 8: Dec.1948, 81-84.

1801. Killer on the Prowl by Robert Combs.
Short. 4 m. 3 f.
In - Plays. 18: March 1959, 36-48.

1802. The Killing of Sister George by Frank Marcus.
Full. 0 m. 4 f.
In - Players. 12 & 13: Sept.& Oct.1965, 23-30+, 23-30+.

1803. The Killing of Sister George by Frank Marcus.
Full. 0 m. 4 f.
In - Esquire. 66: Nov.1966, 118-129.

1804. Killing Them All by Frederick Palmer.
Full. 7 m. 1 f.
In - Colliers. 68: Oct.22,1921, 9-10+.

1805. Kills-With-Her-Man by Hartley Alexander.
Short. 2 m. 1 f.
In - Theatre. 12: June 1928, 439-446.

1806. King Alfred and the Cakes adap. by Adele Thane from an old English folktale.
Short. 4 m. 1 f. 2 b. 2 g.
In - Plays. 25: May 1966, 79-84.

1807. The King and the Bee by Virginia Payne Whitworth.
Short. 4 m. 2 f.
In - Plays. 18: Jan.1959, 73-76.

1808. The King and the Vowels. (anon.)
Short. 6 m. 2 f.
In - Plays. 3: Jan.1944, 50-52.

1809. King Arthur and His Sword by Lynne Sharon Schwartz.
Short. 8 m. 3 f. +X.
In - Plays. 21: March 1962, 51-57.

1810. King Cole's Blues by Claribel Spamer.
Short. 9 m. 6 f.
In - Plays. 3: Oct.1943, 62-64.

1811. King Horn by Margaret C. Hall.
Short. 3 m. 3 f.
In - Plays. 18: Jan.1959, 60-66.

1812. The King in the Kitchen by Margaret E. Slattery.
Short. 4 m. 4 f.
In - Plays. 11: March 1952, 62-68.

1813. The King in the Kitchen by Margaret E. Slattery.
Short. 4 m. 4 f.
In - Plays. 23: March 1965, 53-59.

1814. A King Is Born by Lewy Olfson.
Radio. 10 m. 2 f.
In - Plays. 18: Dec.1958, 87-94.

1815. The King Is Here by Graham DuBois.
Short. 6 m. 4 f.
In - Plays. 6: Dec.1946, 12-19.

1816. King Lear by William Shakespeare. Adap. by Lewy Olfson.
Radio. 6 m. 3 f.
In - Plays. 21: Nov.1961, 87-96.

1817. King of Hearts by Jean Kerr and Eleanor Brooke.
Full. 10 m. 1 f. 1 dog.
In - Theatre. 39: July 1955, 34-62.

1818. The King of Spain's Daughter by Teresa Deevy.
Short. 3 m. 2 f.
In - Theatre. 19: June 1935, 459-465.

1819. The King of the Golden River by John Ruskin.
Radio. 7 m. 0 f. 1 b. +X.
In - Plays. 11: Jan.1952, 71-77.

1820. The King, the Greatest Alcalde by Lope Felix De Vega Carpio. Trans. from the Spanish by John Garrett Underhill.
Full. 11 m. 4 f. +X.
In - Poet Lore. 29:no.3,1918, 379-446.

1821. King Thrushbeard adap. by Adele Thane from Grimms' Fairy Tales.
Short. 14 m. 5 f. 3 b.
In - Plays. 27: Nov.1967, 45-54.

1822. The King Who Couldn't Be Fooled by Josef A. Elfenbein.
Short. 4 m. 5 f.
In - Plays. 14: March 1955, 57-66.

1823. The King Who Scoffed by Oscar Williams and Jack Brady.
Short. 5 m. 0 f. +X.
In - Poet Lore. 34: March 1923, 139-144.

1824. Kingdom of Earth by Tennessee Williams.
Short. 3 m. 2 f.
In - Esquire. 67: Feb.1967, 98-100+.

1825. The Kingdom of Hearts by Claribel Spamer.
Short. 4 m. 4 f.
In - Plays. 6: Feb.1947, 73-75.

1826. The Kingdom of Oceanus by Irene Moran.
Short. 4 m. 3 f. +X.
In - Plays. 17: April 1958, 45-50.

1827. The King's Bean Soup by Sally Werner.
Short. 3 m. 11 un.
In - Plays. 14: Jan.1955, 71-74.

1828. The King's Calendar by Janice Auritt Oser.
Short. 8 m. 5 f.
In - Plays. 13: March 1954, 57-62.

1829. The King's Creampuffs by Martha Swintz.
Short. 5 m. 4 f.
In - Plays. 5: April 1946, 46-56.

1830. The King's Creampuffs by Martha Swintz.
Short. 5 m. 4 f.
In - Plays. 15: April 1956, 43-53.

1831. The King's Creampuffs by Martha Swintz.
Short. 3 m. 4 f. 2 b. +f.X.
In - Plays. 27: March 1968, 59-69.

1832. The King's Jester by Eleanore Leuser.
Short. 6 m. 1 f. +f.X.
In - Plays. 12: April 1953, 66-70.

1833. Kings of Nomania by Percival Wilde.
Short. 4 m. 1 f. +many c. +X.
In - Pictorial. 27: Dec.1925, 6-7+.

1834. The King's Son by Margaret Scott Oliver.
Short. 7 m. 4 f.
In - Drama. 16: May 1926, 297-298.

1835. The King's Toothache by Aileen Fisher.
Short. 7 m. 1 f. 6 un.
In - Plays. 13: April 1954, 43-50.

1836. The King's Weather by Janice Auritt Oser.
Short. 8 m. 5 f.
In - Plays. 16: March 1957, 49-54.

1837. Kiri No Meijiyama by S. Foster Damon.
Short. 3 m. 2 f.
In - Dial. 68: Feb.1920, 205-213.

1838. Kiss Me, Kate by Sam and Bella Spewack.
Lyrics by Cole Porter.
Full (musical). 14 m. 3 f. +ch.
In - Theatre. 39: Jan.1955, 33-57.

1839. Kissing Goes By Favor by Laura Norton Brown.
Short. 1 m. 1 f.
In - Drama. 16: Oct.1925, 14-15+.

1840. The Kitchen by Arnold Wesker.
Full. 18 m. 12 f.
In - Players. 9: Jan.& Feb.1962, 29-36, 31-36.

1841. Kitten Capers by Claire Boiko.
Short. 2 m. 3 f. +X.
In - Plays. 22: Oct.1962, 81-84.

1842. Kitty Hawk - 1903 by Lyda M. Ickler.
Radio. 5 m. 1 f.
In - Plays. 5: Feb.1946, 72-76.

1843. The Knack by Ann Jellicoe.
Full. 3 m. 1 f.
In - Players. 9: June & July 1962, 23-30, 25-31.

1844. The Knights of the Square Table by Earl J. Dias.
Short. 5 m. 4 f. 1 b.
In - Plays. 25: Dec.1965, 51-62.

1845. Known But to God by Graham DuBois.
Short. 6 m. 5 f.
In - Plays. 6: Nov.1946, 11-20.

1846. Known But to God by Graham DuBois.
Short. 6 m. 5 f.
In - Plays. 16: Nov.1956, 79-88.

1847. Laboremus by Bjornstjerne Bjornson.
In - Fortnightly. 75 sup: May 1901, 1-32.

1848. Lacey's Last Garland by Helen Louise Miller.
Short. 2 m. 5 f.
In - Plays. 16: May 1957, 45-52.

1849. The Lady Compassionate by Katherine Kirker.
Short. 1 m. 1 f. 2 b. 1 baby.
In - Poet Lore. 33: June 1922, 239-245.

1850. <u>Lady Hosokawa</u> by Kido Okamoto. Trans. from the Japanese by Asataro Miyameri.

Full. 6 m. 5 f. 1 b. 1 g. +X.

In - Poet Lore. 37: March 1926, 1-23.

1851. <u>Lady Jane's Highwayman</u> by Frances Aymar Mathews.

In - Harper's W. 47: Dec.12,1903, 1979-1981.

1852. <u>Lady Moon and the Thief</u> by Claire Boiko.

Short. 11 m. 1 f. 2 b. +X.

In - Plays. 27: Oct.1967, 77-82.

1853. <u>A Lady of Eternal Springtime</u> by Bernard Sabath.

Full. 7 m. 6 f. +X.

In - First Stage. 2: March 1963, 81-97.

1854. <u>The Lady of the Lake</u> by Sir Walter Scott. Adap. by Edward Golden.

Radio. 7 m. 3 f. +X.

In - Plays. 16: Jan.1957, 85-94.

1855. <u>The Lady or the Tiger</u> by Frank R. Stockton. Adap. by Lewy Olfson.

Radio. 5 m. 2 f. 3 un.

In - Plays. 21: May 1962, 99-107.

1856. <u>The Lady With the Dagger</u> by Arthur Schnitzler. Trans. from the German by Helen Tracy Porter.

Short. 3 m. 2 f.

In - Poet Lore. 15:no.2,1904, 1-18.

1857. <u>Lammas Eve</u> by Edith Randolph.

In - Poet Lore. 33: June 1921, 288-306.

1858. <u>The Lamp in the Forest</u> by Esther MacLellan and Catherine V. Schroll.

Short. 4 m. 2 f.

1859. <u>Lamplighter</u> by Charles Dickens.

Short. 5 m. 3 f.

In - Golden. 3: Jan.1926, 69-80.

1860. <u>Land Ho!</u> by Esther Hill Lamb.

Short. 1 m. 3 f.

In - Drama. 21: June 1931, 13-14+.

1861. <u>The Land of Make Believe</u> by Blanche G. Williams.

Short. 1 un. many c.

In - Wilson. 9: Oct.1934, 78.

1862. <u>A Land of Nobody</u> by Lee Chin-Yang.

Short. 3 m. 1 f.

In - Theatre. 29: Sept.1945, 532-535+.

1863. <u>Landslide for Shakespeare</u> by Earl J. Dias.

Short. 8 m. 8 f.

In - Plays. 16: April 1957, 1-11.

1864. <u>The Language Shop</u> by Mazie Hall.

Short. 12 m. 5 f.

In - Plays. 3: March 1944, 32-36.

1865. <u>The Language Shop</u> by Mazie Hall.

Short. 16 m. 6 f.

In - Plays. 24: Jan.1965, 49-54.

1866. <u>The Lantern</u> by Aloïs Jirásek. Trans. from the Bohemian.

In - Poet Lore. 36: Sept.1925, 317-398.

1867. <u>The Lark</u> by Jean Anouilh. Adap. by Lillian Hellman.

Full. 21 m. 8 f.

In - Theatre. 41: March 1957, 33-56.

1868. <u>Last Boat</u> by D.H. Johnson.

Radio. 3 m. 1 f.

In - Scholastic. 40: April 27,1942, 17-19.

1869. <u>The Last Frontier</u> by Adelaide Corinne Rowell.

In - Drama. 15: April 1925, 157-160.

1870. <u>The Last Laugh</u> by Graham DuBois.

Short. 3 m. 4 f.

In - Plays. 9: March 1950, 13-24.

1871. <u>The Last Man In</u> by Vera I. Arlett.

Short. 2 m. 3 f.

In - Poet Lore. 41: July 1930, 410-418.

1872. <u>The Last of Mr. Weekney</u> by Edwin Elliott Willoughby.

Short. 4 m. 2 f. +ch.

In - Wilson. 9: May 1935, 484-488.

1873. <u>The Last Rising</u> by Sir Andrew Macphail.

In - Queen's. 37: April 1930, 246-258.

1874. <u>Last Sacrifice</u> by Alexander Ostrovsky. Trans. by E. Korvin-Kroukovsky and G.R. Noyes.

In - Poet Lore. 39: Sept.1928, 317-410.

1875. The Last Snake in Ireland by Mary Malone.
Short. 6 m. 1 f. 1 un. +X.
In - Plays. 16: March 1957, 55-60.

1876. Last Stop by Harold Cable.
Short. 3 m. 5 f.
In - Plays. 24: May 1965, 15-29.

1877. The Late Christopher Bean by Sidney Howard.
Abr. by Margaret Mayorga.
Short. 5 m. 2 f.
In - Scholastic. 38: March 31,1941, 17-19+.

1878. The Late Christopher Bean by Sidney Howard.
Excerpts. 3 m. 4 f.
In - Scholastic. 52: March 15,1948, 16-18.

1879. Late Spring by Ruth I. Petersen.
Short. 3 m. 4 f.
In - Plays. 14: May 1955, 69-72.

1880. A Late Spring by Ralph Bobb. Suggested by
Henry James' novel The Wings of the Dove.
Full. 2 m. 2 f.
In - First Stage. 2: June 1963, 202-231.

1881. Latent Heterosexual by Paddy Chayefsky.
Full. 7 m. 3 f.
In - Esquire. 68: Aug.1967, 49-56+.

1882. The Laughing Princess by Mary Ann Nicholson.
Short. 5 m. 3 f. +X.
In - Plays. 15: April 1956, 69-72.

1883. The Laughter of the Gods by Lord Dunsany.
Short. 9 m. 4 f. +X.
In - Golden. 8: Oct.1928, 496-507.

1884. Launcelot and Elaine adap. from Idylls of
the King by Alfred, Lord Tennyson.
Short. 2 m. 3 f.
In - Delineator. 94: May 1919, 51.

1885. The Laurence Boy by Louisa May Alcott.
Adap. by Walter Hackett.
Radio. 3 m. 5 f.
In - Plays. 8: Jan.1949, 69-77.

1886. Law by Lester Luther.
Short. Indef.un.
In - Forum. 53: June 1915, 776-779.

1887. The Law Takes It's Toll by Robert Blake.
Short. 6 m. 0 f. +X.
In - American Merc. 17: July 1929, 263-270.

1888. The Law Takes It's Toll by Robert Blake.
Excerpts. 6 m. 0 f. +X.
In - Review. 80: Aug.1929, 88-90.

1889. The Laziest Man in the World by Erik
Barnouw.
Radio. 6 m. 3 f.
In - Scholastic. 39: Oct.6,1941, 17-19.

1890. A Lazy Afternoon by Morton K. Schwartz.
Short. 5 m. 1 f.
In - Plays. 7: Nov.1947, 42-49.

1891. The Lazy Fox by Vernon Howard.
Short. 7 un.
In - Plays. 15: Jan.1956, 74-76.

1892. The Lazy Little Raindrop by June Barr.
Short. 2 m. 0 f. 1 c. +c.X.
In - Plays. 9: March 1950, 68-71.

1893. The Leading Lady by Ruth Gordon.
Full. 11 m. 8 f.
In - Theatre. 34: Feb.1950, 57-88.

1894. A Leak in the Dike by Paul T. Nolan.
Short. 4 m. 4 f.
In - Plays. 19: May 1960, 79-84.

1895. The Least Gift by Adele Thane.
Short. 7 m. 3 f.
In - Plays. 21: Dec.1961, 67-75.

1896. A Leave-Taking by Ferenc Molnar.
Short. 1 m. 1 f.
In - Golden. 15: May 1932, 449-451.

1897. Leavin's by Janie Malloy Britt.
Short. 2 m. 3 f.
In - Carolina. 10: March 1937, 7-19.

1898. 'Lection by Ellsworth P. Conkle.
Short. 5 m. 1 f.
In - Scholastic. 32: March 19,1938, 17E-18E+.

1899. The Legend of Sleepy Hollow by Washington
       Irving. Adap. by Walter Hackett.

       Radio. 5 m. 1 f. 1 b.

       In - Plays. 10: Oct.1950, 67-78.

1900. The Legend of the Christmas Rose by Eleanore
       Leuser.

       Short. 7 m. 3 f. +f.X.

       In - Plays. 16: Dec.1956, 83-86.

1901. A Leghorn Hat by Eugene Labiche and Marc
       Michel. Trans. from the French by
       Clair Vincent Chesley.

       Full. 9 m. 5 f. +X.

       In - Poet Lore. 28:no.1,1917, 1-53.

1902. The Leprechaun Shoemakers by Frances B. Watts.

       Short 4. b. 8 g.

       In - Plays. 25: March 1966, 43-48.

1903. The Leprechaun's Pot of Gold by Frances B.
       Watts.

       Short. 5 m. 5 f.

       In - Plays. 24: March 1965, 43-50.

1904. The Lesson by Eugene Ionesco. Trans. by
       Donald Watson.

       Short. 1 m. 2 f.

       In - Theatre. 42: July 1958, 39-48.

1905. A Lesson In Thrift by Modzy DeJong.

       Short. 7 b. 8 g.

       In - School Arts. 28: Jan.1929, 299-300.

1906. Let George Do It by Mildred Hark and Noel
       McQueen.

       Short. 3 m. 3 f.

       In - Plays. 6: Feb.1947, 40-49.

1907. Let George Do It by Mildred Hark and Noel
       McQueen.

       Short. 3 m. 2 f. 1 g.

       In - Plays. 25: Feb.1966, 61-70.

1908. Let It Snow by Betty Gray Blaine.

       Short. 4 m. 4 f.

       In - Plays. 16: Jan.1957, 69-73.

1909. Let Sleeping Beauties Lie by Robert Fontaine.

       Short. 6 m. (incl."Beauty") 0 f.

       In - Plays. 24: Feb.1965, 91-95.

1910. Let the Next Generation Be My Client by
       Eleanor Craven and Mildred Sandison.

       Short. 4 m. 2 f.

       In - Jl., N.E.A. 26: Feb.1937, 45-46.

1911. Let's Go Formal by Mildred Hark and Noel
       McQueen.

       Short. 3 m. 2 f.

       In - Scholastic. 44: March 20,1944, 13-15.

1912. Let's Make Up by Esther E. Olson.

       Excerpt. 3 m. 3 f.

       In - Scholastic. 41: Nov.30,1942, 17-19.

1913. A Letter for Charlotte by Mary Malone.

       Short. 0 m. 3 f.

       In - Plays. 9: Jan.1950, 10-18.

1914. A Letter to Lincoln by Lindsey Barbee.

       Short. 0 m. 7 f.

       In - Plays. 5: Jan.1946, 45-50.

1915. Letter to Private Smith by Bernard J. Reines.

       Short. 5 m. 4 f.

       In - Plays. 3: Dec.1943, 62-69.

1916. Letters by Florence Ryerson.

       In - Drama. 16: April 1926, 253-254.

1917. Letters to Lucerne by Fritz Rotter and Allen
       Vincent. Ed. by Margaret Mayorga.

       Excerpt. 1 m. 7 f.

       In - Scholastic. 42: May 10,1943, 13-15.

1918. Liberty and Union by Dorothy Canfield Fisher
       and Sarah N. Cleghorn.

       Short. 17 m. 4 f. 1 b. 1 g. +X.

       In - Scholastic. 36: March 25 and April 1,1940,
            17-20, 23-25.

1919. The Library Circus by Helen Louise Miller.

       Short. 9 m. 16 un. +c.X.

       In - Plays. 20: Nov.1960, 65-70.

1920. Licha's Birthday Serenade by Paul T. Nolan.

       Short. 6 m. 8 f. +X.

       In - Plays. 20: Oct.1960, 77-82.

1921. Lies by Ferenc Molnar. Trans. by Benjamin F.
       Glazer.

       Short. 2 m. 2 f.

       In - Golden. 11: Feb.1930, 101-102.

1922. The Lieutenant Pays His Respects by Paul S. McCoy.

Short. 0 m. 6 f.

In - Plays. 3: March 1944, 57-67.

1923. The Life for Mother by Mildred Hark and Noel McQueen.

Short. 3 m. 3 f.

In - Plays. 22: May 1963, 43-52.

1924. Life is a Dream by Colin Campbell Clements.

In - Poet Lore. 31: June 1920, 204-209.

1925. Life of a Salesman by Thomas Meehan.

Short. 3 m. 1 f.

In - Sat. Evening. 239: June 18,1966, 20+.

1926. Life With Father by Howard Lindsay and Russel Crouse.

Excerpt. 2 m. 2 f.

In - Theatre. 24: Oct.1940. 754.

1927. Light Along the Rails by Zellah Macdonald.

Short. 4 m. 1 f.

In - Touchstone. 3: June 1918, 229-236.

1928. A Light in Darkness by Graham DuBois.

Short. 5 m. 3 f.

In - Plays. 10: Feb.1951, 23-33.

1929. The Light Of Other Days by Laura Spencer Portor.

Short. 3 m. 2 f.

In - Ladies' Home. 23: Dec.1905, 20.

1930. Light Up the Sky by Moss Hart.

Full. 9 m. 4 f.

In - Theatre. 33: Oct.1949, 59-88.

1931. Lightning in the Laboratory by Lewis W. Moyer.

Radio. 14 m. 0 f.

In - Scholastic. 33: Dec.10,1938, 17E-19E+.

1932. Like Father Like Son by Leila Weekes Wilson.

In - Drama. 13: Feb.1923, 188-191.

1933. Like Mother Used to Make by John Murray.

Short. 5 m. 5 f.

In - Plays. 24: Nov.1964, 23-35.

1934. Lilith by Remy De Gourmont. Trans. from the French by John Heard.

Full. 25 m. 15 f. +X.

In - Poet Lore. 51: Oct.1945, 298-344.

1935. A Lily in Little India by Donald Howarth.

Full. 6 m. 2 f.

In - Players. 13: May 1966, 31-43.

1936. Limpid River by Seamus de Burca.

Full. 6 m. 6 f.

In - First Stage. 5: March 1966, 30-55.

1937. The Lincoln Coat by Thelma W. Sealock.

Short. 4 m. 4 f. +X.

In - Plays. 4: Jan.1945, 36-43.

1938. The Lincoln Coat by Thelma W. Sealock.

Short. 4 m. 4 f. +X.

In - Plays. 12: Feb.1953, 27-34.

1939. The Lincoln Cupboard by Jane McGowan.

Short. 4 m. 2 f.

In - Plays. 15: Feb.1956, 31-41.

1940. The Lincoln Heart by Helen Louise Miller.

Short. 5 m. 3 f.

In - Plays. 7: Jan.1948, 1-10.

1941. Lincoln: Hero Unlimited by Leslie Hollings-worth.

Radio. 11 m. 0 f.

In - Plays. 4: Jan.1945, 80-85.

Lincoln In Illinois.

see

Lincoln Speaks For All Men.

and

The Election of Lincoln.

1942. The Lincoln Lady by Judith Seymour.

Short. 2 m. 6 f. +X.

In - Plays. 20: Feb.1961, 79-83.

1943. A Lincoln Museum by Helen Louise Miller.

Short. 4 m. 6 f. 11 un.

In - Plays. 13: Feb.1954, 65-70.

1944. Lincoln Reminders by Mildred Hark and Noel McQueen.

Short. 2 m. 0 f. 15 c.

In - Plays. 14: Feb.1955, 75-79.

1945. Lincoln Says Farewell by Graham DuBois.

Short. 1 m. 4 f.

In - Plays. 7: Jan.1948, 11-18.

1946. Lincoln Speaks For All Men by Robert E. Sherwood. From his Lincoln in Illinois.

Excerpt. 3 m. 0 f. +X.

In - Scholastic. 48: Feb.11,1946, 17-18+.

1947. The Lincoln Umbrella by Mildred Hark and Noel McQueen.

Short. 4 m. 4 f.

In - Plays. 9: Feb.1950, 40-47.

1948. The Lincoln Umbrella by Mildred Hark and Noel McQueen.

Short. 4 m. 4 f.

In - Plays. 23: Feb.1964, 55-63.

1949. Lincoln's Buckskin Breeches by Marjorie Ann York.

Short. 5 m. 4 f.

In - Plays. 11: Feb.1952, 74-78.

1950. Lincoln's Library Fine by Helen Louise Miller.

Short. 5 m. 5 f.

In - Plays. 21: Feb.1962, 53-58.

1951. A Link with Lincoln by Helen Louise Miller.

Short. 4 m. 4 f.

In - Plays. 25: Feb.1966, 1-14.

1952. Links by Herman Heijermans. Trans. by Howard Peacey and W.R. Brandt.

Full. 11 m. 7 f. 1 g.

In - Poet Lore. 38: March 1927, 1-76.

1953. The Lion by Amos Kenan. Trans. by Rosette Lamont.

Short. 2 m. 1 f.

In - First Stage. 4: March 1965, 8-13.

1954. The Lion and the Mouse by Rowena Bennett.

Short. 1 m. 1 f.

In - Plays. 5: Nov.1945, 53-55.

1955. The Lion and the Mouse adap. by June Barr.

Short. 7 un.

In - Plays. 10: Oct.1950, 64-66.

1956. Lion to Lamb by Claire Boiko.

Short. 11 b. 11 g.

In - Plays. 24: March 1965, 81-84.

1957. Listen to the People by Stephen Vincent Benét.

Radio. 7 m. 0 f.

In - Scholastic. 40: Feb.2,1942, 17-19+.

1958. Listening by John Redhead Froome, Jr.

Short. 0 m. 3 f.

In - Poet Lore. 28:no.4,1917, 422-431.

1959. The Little Bell by Claribel Spamer.

Short. 5 m. 4 un.

In - Plays. 7: Dec.1947, 67-69.

1960. Little Bird in the Tree by Eleanore Leuser.

Short. 8 m. 2 f.

In - Plays. 9: Jan.1950, 53-56.

1961. The Little Black Kettle by Claribel Spamer.

Short. 4 m. 2 f.

In - Plays. 6: Oct.1946, 64-66.

1962. The Little Blue Guinea-Hen by Gyp. Trans. from the French by Roy Temple House.

Short. 5 m. 4 f.

In - Poet Lore. 30:no.1,1919, 60-80.

1963. Little Chipmunk and the Old Woman by Elizabeth Renyi. From a Legend of the Okanagan Indians.

Short. 2 f. 2 un. 1 c.

In - Carolina. 13: Dec.1940, 155-158.

1964. Little Chip's Christmas Tree by Lucille M. Duvall.

Short. 10 m. 9 c.

In - Plays. 16: Dec.1956, 79-82.

1965. Little Christmas Guest by Karin Asbrand.

Short. 0 m. 8 f.

In - Plays. 5: Dec.1945, 53-54.

1966. The Little Christmas Tree by Claribel Spamer.

Short. 8 m. 6 f.

In - Plays. 7: Dec.1947, 61-63.

1967. The Little Circus Donkey by Helen Littler Howard.

Short. 10 m. 0 f.

In - Plays. 6: Feb.1947, 71-73.

1968. The Little Dream by John Galsworthy.

Short. 2 m. 1 f. +X.

In - Scribner's. 49: May 1911, 531-540.

1969. The Little Evergreen Tree by Anne Jennings.

Short. 4 m. 3 f. +g.X.

In - Plays. 28: Dec.1968, 77-82.

1970. **Little Father of the Wilderness** by Austin Strong and Lloyd Osbourne.

Short. 6 m. 1 f. +X.

In - Golden. 18: Oct.1933, 353-362.

1971. **Little February** by Claribel Spamer.

Short. 2 m. 1 f. 16 un.

In - Plays. 11: Feb.1952, 79-81.

1972. **The Little Fir Tree** adap. by Alice Very.

Short. 6 m. 2 f. +c.X.

In - Plays. 16: Dec.1956, 70-74.

1973. **Little Fish** by Hazel V. Gamble.

In - Drama. 14: Feb.1924, 185-187.

1974. **The Little Fool** by Adolph E. Meyer.

Short. 3 m. 1 f.

In - Drama. 17: Oct.1926, 13-14+.

1975. **Little Forget-Me-Not** by Claribel Spamer.

Short. 2 m. 6 f.

In - Plays. 4: Dec.1944, 63-65.

1976. **Little Friend** by Mary Peacock.

Short. 4 m. 2 f.

In - Plays. 18: Dec.1958, 81-85.

1977. **Little Friends** by Alice Very.

Short. 11 un.

In - Plays. 6: May 1947, 61-62.

1978. **The Little Hut** by Andre Roussin. Adap. by Nancy Mitford.

Full. 4 m. 1 f.

In - Theatre. 38: Oct.1954, 32-61.

1979. **Little Ida and the Flowers** by Edith Ormandy.

Short. 0 m. 10 f.

In - Plays. 11: May 1952, 60-63.

1980. **Little Jackie and the Beanstalk** by Harold Cable.

Short. 10 m. 9 f. + 1 cow.

In - Plays. 27: April 1968, 1-15.

1981. **Little Ki and the Serpent** by Hathaway Kale Melchior.

Short. 4 m. 4 f. 4 c.

In - Plays. 17: April 1958, 37-44.

1982. **The Little King** by Witter Bynner.

Short. 4 m. 1 f.

In - Forum. 51: April 1914, 605-632.

1983. **Little Known Louisa** by Marion Wefer.

Radio. 7 m. 7 f.

In - Plays. 5: May 1946, 75-80.

1984. **The Little Lion** by T. Morris Longstreth.

Short. 6 m. 3 f.

In - Plays. 3: March 1944, 21-27.

1985. **Little Malcolm and His Struggle Against the Eunuchs** by David Halliwell.

Full. 4 m. 1 f.

In - Players. 13: April 1966, 31-46+.

1986. **The Little Man Who Wasn't There** by Earl J. Dias.

Short. 2 m. 5 f.

In - Plays. 21: Jan.1962, 25-36.

1987. **Little Mary Sunshine** by Rick Besoyan.

Full (musical). 12 m. 8 f.

In - Theatre. 44: Dec.1960, 27-56.

1988. **Little Men** adap. by Elizabeth Lincoln Gould from story by Louisa May Alcott.

Short. 1 m. 1 f. 4 b. 4 g.

In - Ladies' Home. 18: Dec.1900, 3-4+.

1989. **The Little Miracle** by Zoe Akins.

Short. 0 m. 5 f. 1 g.

In - Ladies' Home. 53: April 1936, 30-31+.

1990. **Little Mortal Child** by Gladys La Due Evans.

In - Poet Lore. 32: Sept.1921, 409-415.

1991. **The Little Nut Tree** by Helen Louise Miller.

Short. 10 m. 7 f. +X.

In - Plays. 21: April 1962, 67-72.

1992. **The Little Patriot** by Lindsey Barbee.

Short. 2 m. 2 f.

In - Plays. 8: April 1949, 60-62.

1993. **The Little Pink Egg** by Claribel Spamer.

Short. 4 m. 5 un.

In - Plays. 7: March 1948, 55-58.

1994. <u>Little Polka Dot</u> by Karin Asbrand.

Short. 6 m. 5 f. +X.

In - Plays. 10: May 1951, 30-34.

1995. <u>The Little Princess</u> by Frances Hodgson Burnett. Adap. by Lewy Olfson.

Radio. 5 m. 5 f.

In - Plays. 17: Jan.1958, 87-96.

1996. <u>The Little Princess</u> by Frances Hodgson Burnett. Adap. by Adele Thane.

Short. 3 m. 9 f.

In - Plays. 22: Feb.1963, 33-44.

1997. <u>The Little Prop Boy</u> by Claribel Spamer.

Short. 5 m. 7 f.

In - Plays. 4: March 1945, 51-53.

1998. <u>The Little Red Hen</u> by June Barr.

Short. 4 un.

In - Plays. 8: Jan.1949, 46-50.

1999. <u>The Little Saint</u> by Roberto Bracco. English version by Victor Rietti.

Full. 7 m. 3 f.

In - Gambit. 2: no.6, 33-78.

2000. <u>Little Snow White</u> by Walter King.

Short. 8 m. 2 f.

In - Plays. 7: Jan.1948, 48-51.

2001. <u>Little Snow White</u> by Walter King.

Short. 8 m. 2 f.

In - Plays. 23: Jan.1964, 79-82.

2002. <u>The Little Whittler</u> by Karin Asbrand.

Short. 4 m. 2 f. 1 un. +X.

In - Plays. 13: Feb.1954, 41-45.

2003. <u>The Little Wild Things</u> (anon).

Excerpt. 5 m. 5 f. +X.

In - Scholastic. 30: May 22,1937, 10-14.

2004. <u>The Little Witch Who Forgot</u> by Claribel Spamer.

Short. 1 m. 4 f.

In - Plays. 4: Oct.1944, 55-57.

2005. <u>The Little Witch Who Tried</u> by Eleanore Leuser.

Short. 0 m. 8 f.

In - Plays. 9: Oct.1949, 59-62.

2006. <u>Little Women</u> by Louise May Alcott. Adap. by Elizabeth Lincoln Gould.

Short. 2 m. 6 f.

In - Ladies' Home. 18: Jan.1901, 3-4.

2007. <u>Little Women</u> by Louisa May Alcott. Adap. by Olive J. Morley.

Short. 0 m. 9 f.

In - Plays. 14: Dec.1954, 13-23.

2008. <u>Little Women</u> by Louisa May Alcott. Adap. by Lewy Olfson.

Radio. 2 m. 7 f.

In - Plays. 17: Oct.1957, 87-96.

2009. <u>Little Women</u> by Louisa May Alcott. Adap. by Lewy Olfson.

Short. 0 m. 6 f.

In - Plays. 21: April 1962, 85-96.

2010. <u>Little Women</u> by Louisa May Alcott. Adap. by Olive J. Morley.

Short. 0 m. 9 f.

In - Plays. 28: Dec.1968, 85-95.

2011. <u>The Littlest Fir</u> by Ella Stratton Colbo.

Short. 4 m. 1 f. 2 un.

In - Plays. 6: Dec.1946, 66-69.

2012. <u>The Littlest Month</u> by Dammally Faux.

Short. 9 m. 4 f.

In - Plays. 10: Feb.1951, 62-64.

2013. <u>The Littlest Month</u> by Dammally Faux.

Short. 9 m. 4 f.

In - Plays. 21: Feb.1962, 63-65.

2014. <u>The Living Dead</u> by Leo Tolstoy. Trans. by L. Maude and Aylmer Maude.

Full. 27 m. 8 f. +ch.

In - Golden. 1: March 1925, 395-419.

2015. <u>Living Hours</u> by Arthur Schnitzler. Trans. from the German by Helen Tracy Porter.

Short. 3 m. 0 f.

In - Poet Lore. 17:no.1,1906, 36-45.

2016. <u>Living Up To Lincoln</u> by Mildred Hark and Noel McQueen.

Short. 4 m. 3 f.

In - Plays. 7: Jan.1948, 28-36.

2017. <u>Living Up to Lincoln</u> by Mildred Hark and Noel McQueen.

Short. 4 m. 3 f.

In - Plays. 19: Feb.1960, 49-57.

2018. <u>Lock, Stock, and Barrel</u> by John Murray.

Short. 6 m. 6 f.

In - Plays. 16: Nov.1956, 11-24.

2019. <u>Lofty Motives</u> by Albert Weinberg.

Short. 2 m. 1 f.

In - Poet Lore. 38: Dec.1927, 603-606.

2020. <u>The Lonely Fir Tree</u> by Helen M. Roberts.

Short. 5 m. 5 f.

In - Plays. 4: Dec.1944, 52-56.

2021. <u>The Lonely Little Old Lady</u> by Peggy Cameron
King.

Short. 3 m. 4 f. 1 g.

In - Plays. 24: Dec.1964, 29-38.

2022. <u>Long Ago in Bethlehem</u> by Deborah Newman.

Short. 7 m. 10 f. +X.

In - Plays. 13: Dec.1953, 67-71.

2023. <u>Long Ago in Bethlehem</u> by Deborah Newman.

Short. 7 m. 10 f.

In - Plays. 26: Dec.1966, 44-48.

2024. <u>Long Box</u> by Zellah Macdonald.

In - Drama. 14: Feb.1924, 180-182.

2025. <u>Long Duel</u> by Lucy L. Clifford.

In - Fortnightly. 76 sup: Sept.1901, 1-50.

2026. <u>Long Line Christmas</u> by Islay Benson.

Short. 13 m. 6 f. 13 un. +X.

In - Plays. 21: Dec.1961, 57-66.

2027. <u>Look On Tempests</u> by Joan Henry.

Full. 3 m. 4 f.

In - Players. 7: July & Aug.1960, 25-31,
24-30.

2028. <u>Look to a New Day</u> by Aileen Fisher.

Short. 11 m. 13 f. +X.

In - Plays. 20: May 1961, 83-96.

2029. <u>Looking for Lincoln</u> by Deborah Newman.

Short. 7 m. 7 f.

In - Plays. 21: Feb.1962, 41-45.

2030. <u>The Looking-Glass</u> by Oscar W. Firkins.

Short. 3 m. 2 f.

In - Drama. 16: Feb.1926, 171-173.

2031. <u>Looking Glass Murder</u> by John Murray.

Short. 4 m. 5 f. 1 g.

In - Plays. 27: Jan.1968, 11-25.

2032. <u>The Lord's Will</u> by Paul Greene.

Short. 1 m. 2 f.

In - Poet Lore. 33: Sept.1922, 366-384.

2033. <u>Lorna Doone</u> by Richard Doddridge Blackmore.
Adap. by Jane McGowan.

Radio. 8 m. 3 f. 1 g.

In - Plays. 12: Oct.1952, 82-93.

2034. <u>The Lost Cherub</u> by Adele Thane.

Short. 5 m. 5 f. +X.

In - Plays. 20: Dec.1960, 61-65.

2035. <u>The Lost Christmas Cards</u> by Helen Louise
Miller.

Short. 7 m. 6 f. 8 un.

In - Plays. 18: Dec.1958, 71-75.

2036. <u>The Lost Colony of Roanoke</u> by Esther Frances
Royster.

Excerpts. 10 m. 5 f.

In - Scholastic. 31: Oct.2,1937,4-6+.

2037. <u>Lost in the Stars</u> by Maxwell Anderson and
Kurt Weill. Based on Alan Paton's novel
<u>Cry, the Beloved Country.</u>

Full (musical). 26 m. 9 f. +X +ch.(white &
Negro).

In - Theatre. 34: Dec.1950, 59-88.

2038. <u>De Lost John</u> by Walter Carroll.

Short. 1 m. 3 f. 1 b.

In - Carolina. 15: Sept.1942, 71-75.

2039. <u>The Lost Note</u> by Janice Auritt Oser.

Short. 2 m. 5 f. 7 un.

In - Plays. 17: May 1958, 54-58.

2040. <u>The Lost Princess</u> by Dan W. Totheroh.

Short. 10 m. 4 f. +X.

In - Drama. 19: Jan.1929, 107-109+.

2041. <u>The Lost Silk Hat</u> by Lord Dunsany.

Short. 5 m. 0 f.

In - Golden. 10: Aug.1929, 89-91.

2042. <u>The Loud-Speaker</u> by Morton K. Schwartz.

Short. 3 m. 1 f.

In - Plays. 10: Nov.1950, 43-47.

2043. Love of One's Neighbor by Leonid Andreyev.
Trans. by Thomas Seltzer.

Short. Indef.un. m. f. & c.

In - Golden. 4: Aug.1926, 181-190.

2044. The Loveliest Thing by Roland Pertwee.

Full. 3 m. 3 f. 1 g. +ch.

In - Ladies' Home. 39: Dec.1927, 10-11+.

2045. Lover's Knot by Marguerite Merington.

In - Harper's B. 44: June 1910, 384-386.

2046. Love's in Fashion by John Murray.

Short. 7 m. 7 f.

In - Plays. 22: May 1963, 29-41.

2047. The Loving Cup by Alice Brown.

Short. 4 m. 9 f. +X.

In - Woman's Home. 40: May 1913, 11-12+.

2048. The Loyal Venture by Wilkeson O'Connell.

Short. 7 m. 1 f.

In - Carolina. 5: March 1932, 11-25.

2049. Luck Takes a Holiday by Aileen Fisher.

Short. 9 m. 3 f. 3 un.

In - Plays. 12: May 1953, 40-48.

2050. Lucullus's Dinner - Party by Maurice Baring.

Short. 3 m. 3 f.

In - Golden. 5: June 1927, 778-780.

2051. Luigi Steps Aside by Walter Hackett.

Short. 4 m. 2 f.

In - Plays. 16: May 1957, 12-20.

2052. Lullaby Land by Karin Asbrand.

Short. 8 m. 9 f.

In - Plays. 7: Feb.1948, 61-63.

2053. Luncheon for Three by Paul S. McCoy.

Short. 2 m. 3 f.

In - Plays. 15: March 1956, 31-42.

2054. Lunchtime Concert by Olwen Wymark.

Short. 2 m. 1 f.

In - Gambit. 3: no.10, 67-88.

2055. Luther by John Osborne.

Excerpt. 4 m. 0 f.

In - Vogue. 139: March 1,1962, 112-115+.

2056. Macaire by Robert Louis Stevenson and
William Ernest Henley.

Full. 10 m. 2 f. +X.

In - Golden. 6: Dec.1927, 796-810.

2057. Macbeth by William Shakespeare. Adap. by
Levy Olfson.

Radio. 12 m. 5 f.

In - Plays. 14: April 1955, 87-95.

2058. Macbeth by William Shakespeare. Adap. by
Levy Olfson.

Radio. 13 m. 5 f. +X.

In - Plays. 25: Jan.1966, 79-90.

2059. MacDaragh's Wife by Lady Augusta Gregory.

Short. 1 m. 2 f. +X.

In - Outlook. 99: Dec.16,1911, 920-925.

2060. Mad About Art by John Murray.

Short. 6 m. 3 f.

In - Plays. 27: Feb.1968, 13-28.

2061. The Mad Dog by V. Kedrov. Trans. from the
Russian by Moshe Spiegel.

Short. 2 m. 1 f.

In - Poet Lore. 58: March 1963, 55-64.

2062. The Mad Dutchman's Magic Eye by R.E. Williams.

Short. 6 m. 2 f. +X.

In - Plays. 5: April 1946, 19-32.

2063. A Mad Tea Party adap. by Natalie S. Worcester.
From Lewis Carroll's Alice in Wonderland.

Short. 3 m. 1 f.

In - Plays. 12: Nov.1952, 66-69.

2064. Madam Takes a Bath by José Maria Bellido.
English version by Adrienne S. Mandel.

Full. 7 m. 10 f.

In - First Stage. 5: Dec.1966, 244-265.

2065. Madam, Will You Walk? by Sidney Howard.

Full. 11 m. 4 f.

In - Theatre. 41: Feb.1957, 33-60.

2066. Madame Major by Ippolit Vasilievich
Shpazhinsky. Trans. from the Russian
by Francis Haffkine Snow and Beatrice
M. Mekota.

Full. 8 m. 4 f.

In - Poet Lore. 28:no.3,1917, 257-324.

2067. Madelon; a Little Shepherdess at Bethlehem
by Alice Isabel Hazeltine.

Short. 7 m. 1 f.

In - Horn Book. 21: Nov.1945, 420-422.

2068. Mademoiselle Mystic by Anna Steese Richardson.

Short. 4 m. 6 f. +X.

In - Woman's Home. 37: Aug.1910, 8+.

2069. Madison Avenue Merry-Go-Round by Earl J. Dias.

Short. 4 m. 5 f.

In - Plays. 21: Nov.1961, 13-24.

2070. A Madison Square Arabian Night by Addison
Gerry Smith. From the story by O. Henry.

Short. 4 m. 0 f.

In - Scholastic. 49: Sept.16,1946, 19-21.

2071. The Madman and the Nun by Stanislav Ignacy
Witkiewicz. Trans. by C.S. Durer and
Daniel C. Gerould.

Short. 6 m. 2 f.

In - First Stage. 4: Dec.1965, 212-221.

2072. The Madman Divine by José Echégaray. Trans.
from the Spanish by Elizabeth Howard
West.

Full. 14 m. 5 f.

In - Poet Lore. 19:no.1.1908. 3-86.

2073. The Madonna and the Scarecrow by DeWitte
Kaplan.

Short. 16 m. 5 f. +X.

In - Poet Lore. 34: June 1923, 254-270.

2074. The Madwoman of Chaillot by Jean Giraudoux.
Adap. by Maurice Valency.

Full. 30 m. 11 f.

In - Theatre. 33: Nov.1949, 59-92.

2075. The Magic Bookshelf by Patricia Clapp.

Short. 5 m. 5 f. +X.

In - Plays. 19: Nov.1959, 35-42.

2076. The Magic Box by William H. Moore.

Short. 7 m. 4 f. +X.

In - Plays. 22: Nov.1962, 59-63.

2077. The Magic Bread by Evva Brinker.

Short. 5 m. 4 f.

In - Plays. 17: Jan.1958, 63-66.

2078. The Magic Carpet by Ida Lublenski Ehrlich.

Short. 12 m. 2 f. +X.

In - Poet Lore. 62: Dec.1967, 412-434.

2079. The Magic Carpet Sweeper by Helen Louise
Miller.

Short. 3 m. 3 f.

In - Plays. 16: May 1957, 69-76.

2080. The Magic Cloak adap. by Virginia Payne
Whitworth.

Short. 7 m. 6 f. 1 b. +X.

In - Plays. 27: April 1968, 37-43.

2081. Magic Cookie Jar by Helen Louise Miller.

Short. 2 m. 2 f.

In - Plays. 15: Oct.1955, 49-57.

2082. The Magic Egg by Mildred Hark and Noel
McQueen.

Short. 8 m. 9 f.

In - Plays. 4: March 1945, 29-36.

2083. The Magic Fishbone by Charles Dickens. Adap.
by Mary Nygaard Peterson.

Short. 4 m. 4 f. +c.X.

In - Plays. 20: Oct.1960, 51-56.

2084. The Magic Flowers by Karin Asbrand.

Short. 7 m. 6 f.

In - Plays. 21: March 1962, 73-76.

2085. The Magic Formula by Aileen Fisher.

Short. 4 m. 3 f.

In - Plays. 13: Oct.1953, 49-54.

2086. The Magic Goose by Deborah Newman.

Short. 8 m. 5 f. +X.

In - Plays. 10: Jan.1951, 68-71.

2087. The Magic Grapes by Eleanor Leuser.

Short. 6 m. 1 f. 2 c.

In - Plays. 12: Oct.1952, 57-61.

2088. Magic in the Deep Woods by Elsa DeBra.

Short. 5 m. 3 f.

In - Plays. 20: Oct.1960, 73-76.

2089. The Magic Jack-O-Lantern by Helen Littler
Howard.

Short. 6 un. +X.

In - Plays. 5: Oct.1945, 51-53.

2090. The Magic Mirror by Alice Very.

Short. 0 m. 3 f. 1 dog.

In - Plays. 12: April 1953, 74-76.

2091. The Magic Nutmeg-Grater by Adele Thane.

Short. 4 m. 5 f. +X.

In - Plays. 19: April 1960, 37-46.

2092. The Magic of Salamanca by Paul T. Nolan.
Short. 4 m. 2 f.
In - Plays. 21: Jan.1962, 48-54.

2093. The Magic Pencils by Helen Louise Miller.
Short. 9 m. 7 f. +X.
In - Plays. 22: May 1963, 79-84.

2094. The Magic Pumpkin Patch by Elsie M. Thomas.
Short. 1 m. 3 f. 7 un.
In - Plays. 25: Oct.1965, 73-78.

2095. The Magic Sea Shell by John Farrar.
Short. 1 m. 0 f. +c.X.
In - Bookman. 57: July 1923, 511-520.

2096. The Magic Shoes by Lucia Turnbull.
Short. 2 m. 5 f.
In - Plays. 15: March 1956, 67-73.

2097. The Magic Spell by Esther Cooper.
Short. 1 m. 5 f.
In - Plays. 3: Oct.1943. 56-58.

2098. The Magic Telephone by Helen Louise Miller.
Short. 3 m. 2 f. +20X.
In - Plays. 23: Feb.1924, 65-69.

2099. Magic Theatre. Trans. from El Retablo de las
Maravillas of Cervantes by Edith Fahnstock
and Florence Donnell White.
In - Poet Lore. 32: June 1921, 234-243.

2100. The Magic Tree by Dixie Willson.
Short. 0 m. 0 f. 7 b. 5 g.
In - Delineator. 127: Dec.1935, 8-9+.

2101. The Magic Weaver by Rowena Bennett.
Short. 2 m. 4 f. 10 or more c.X.
In - Plays. 20: April 1961, 71-74.

2102. The Magic Well by Eleanore Leuser.
Short. 12 m. 7 f. +X.
In - Plays. 12: March 1953, 62-66.

2103. The Magic Well by Eleanore Leuser.
Short. 12 m. 7 f. +f.X.
In - Plays. 22: May 1963, 91-95.

2104. The Magic Wishing Ring by Gwen Chaloner.
Short. 4 m. 5 f. 8 un.
In - Plays. 23: Oct.1963, 49-60.

2105. The Magical City by Zoe Akins.
Short. 11 m. 3 f.
In - Forum. 55: May 1916, 507-550.

2106. The Magnolia Tree by H.W.D. Manson.
Full. 6 m. 1 f.
In - Gambit. 2: no.8, 69-130.

2107. Magnus the Magnificent by Jean Robbins.
Short. 7 m. 0 f.
In - Plays. 21: Jan.1962, 74-78.

2108. Mail Call by Ralph Nelson.
Short. 7 m. 0 f.
In - Theatre. 27: Sept.1943, 515-523.

2109. The Mail Goes Through by Aileen Fisher.
Short. 3 m. 3 f.
In - Plays. 10: Jan.1951, 53-58.

2110. A Majority of One by Leonard Spigelgass.
Full. 8 m. 6 f. (some Japanese).
In - Theatre. 44: Sept.1960, 28-56.

2111. Make a Million by Norman Barasch and Carroll
Moore.
Full. 15 m. 4 f.
In - Theatre. 43: June 1959, 25-48.

2112. Make Him Smile! by E.W. Arnold.
Short. 4 m. 5 f.
In - Plays. 4: May 1945, 48-54.

2113. Make Him Smile! by E. W. Arnold.
Short. 4 m. 5 f.
In - Plays. 21: April 1962, 61-66.

2114. Making Room for the Little King by Helen
Boyd Higgins.
Short. 4 m. 1 f.
In - Plays. 5: Dec.1945, 29-33.

2115. The Male Animal by James Thurber and Elliott
Nugent.
Excerpt. 2 m. 2 f.
In - Theatre. 24: Oct.1940, 753-754.

Mama's Bank Account.
see
I Remember Mama.

2116. Man and His Wife by Colin Campbell Clements.
In - Poet Lore. 31: June 1930; 197.

2117. Man and Superman.

    see

    Don Juan in Hell.

2118. The Man and the Satyr by Rowena Bennett.
Short. 2 m. 0 f.
In - Plays. 5: April 1946, 67-69.

2119. A Man For All Seasons by Robert Bolt.
Full. 11 m. 3 f.
In - Players. 8: May & June 1961, 23-31,
25-34.

2120. A Man For All Seasons by Robert Bolt.
Full. 11 m. 3 f.
In - Theatre. 47: May 1963, 33-66.

2121. The Man from Cemetery Ridge by D.H. Johnson.
Radio. 4 m. 0 f.
In - Scholastic. 40: Feb.9,1942, 17-18+.

2122. The Man From Kiriot by Gustav Davidson.
Short. 9 m. 0 f. +X.
In - Poet Lore. 59: June 1964, 139-148.

2123. The Man in the Bowler Hat by A.A. Milne.
Short. 5 m. 2 f.
In - Ladies' Home. 40: April 1923, 5+.

2124. The Man in the Glass Booth by Robert Shaw.
Full. 13 m. 3 f. +X.
In - Players. 15: Nov.1967, 23-34.

2125. The Man in the Moon by Claribel Spamer.
Short. 6 m. 4 f.
In - Plays. 5: March 1946, 56-57.

2126. Man in the Red Suit by Bill Messenger.
Short. 9 m. 5 f. 5 c. +X.
In - Plays. 26: Dec.1966, 81-87.

2127. A Man Like Lincoln by Helen Louise Miller.
Short. 5 m. 4 f.
In - Plays. 23: Feb.1964, 1-12.

2128. The Man Masterful by George Middleton.
Short. 0 m. 2 f.
In - Forum. 42: Oct.1909, 369-382.

2129. Man-Trap for Mother by Helen Louise Miller.
Short. 2 m. 2 f.
In - Plays. 7: May 1948, 1-10.

2130. The Man Who Came to Dinner by George S.
Kaufman and Moss Hart.
Excerpt. 4 m. 1 f.
In - Theatre. 24: Oct.1940, 752.

2131. The Man Who Couldn't Talk by August von
Kotzebue. Trans. by Beatrice B. Beebe.
Short. 4 m. 2 f.
In - Poet Lore. 40: June 1929, 223-236.

2132. The Man Who Didn't Believe in Christmas by
Mary Hunter Austin
Short. 8 m. 3 f. 3 b. 2 g.
In - St. Nicholas. 45: Dec.1917, 156-162

2133. The Man Who Discovered the Sun by Gladys L.
Schmitt.
Radio. 5 m. 1 f.
In - Scholastic. 27: Oct.5,1935, 7-8+.

2134. The Man Who Found the King by Graham DuBois.
Short. 7 m. 3 f.
In - Plays. 13: Dec.1953, 11-22.

2135 The Man Who Married a Dumb Wife by Anatole
France.
Short. 8 m. 2 f.
In - Golden. 1: Jan.1925, 41-53.

2136. The Man Who Stayed at Home by Graham DuBois.
Short. 4 m. 3 f. +X.
In - Plays. 14: Dec.1954, 33-42.

2137. The Man With the Flower in His Mouth by
Luigi Pirandello.
Short. 2 m. 0 f.
In - Dial. 75: Oct.1923, 313-322.

2138. The Man With the Green Necktie by Averchenko
Arkadyl. Trans. by Bernard G. Guerney.
Short. 3 m. 1 f.
In - Golden. 17: May 1933, 449-453.

2139. The Man Without a Country by Ann Barley.
Based on the story by Edward Everett Hale.
Radio. 10 m. 1 f.
In - Scholastic. 38: Feb.17,1941, 17-18+.

2140. The Man Without A Country by Edward Everett
       Hale. Adap. by Walter Hackett.

       Radio. 23 m. 1 f.

       In - Plays. 7: March 1948, 67-77.

2141. The Mandarin Coat by Alice C.D. Riley.

       In - Drama. 13: Jan.1923, 132-135.

2142. Manny by Walter J. Vail.

       Short. 2 m. 0 f.

       In - First Stage. 4: March 1965, 14-25.

2143. A Man's a Man for a' That by Gladys L. Schmitt.

       Radio. 4 m. 3 f.

       In - Scholastic. 32: Feb.12,1938, 17E-18E.

2144. The Mantle by Earl J. Dias.

       Short. 9 m. 4 f.

       In - Plays. 19: May 1960, 23-34.

2145. Many a Slip by Aileen Fisher.

       Short. 1 m. 2 f. 6 un.

       In - Plays. 10: Feb.1951, 50-54.

2146. Many Loves by William Carlos Williams.

       Full. 13 m. 11 f. 1 g.

       In - Theatre. 46: Feb.1962, 25-56.

2147. Many Thanks by Mildred Hark and Noel
       McQueen.

       Short. 10 m. 9 f.

       In - Plays. 14: Nov.1954, 53-61.

2148. The March of Dimes by Dorothy Deming.

       Radio. 4 m. 3 f.

       In - Plays. 6: Jan.1947, 66-68.

2149. A Marine for Mother by Helen Louise Miller.

       Short. 2 m. 4 f.

       In - Plays. 3: May 1944, 61-69.

2150. Marjorie Daw by Thomas Bailey Aldrich.
       Adap. by Walter Hackett.

       Radio. 8 m. 2 f.

       In - Plays. 7: April 1948, 72-81.

2151. Marjorie Daw by Thomas Bailey Aldrich.
       Adap. by Levy Olfson.

       Radio. 4 m. 5 f.

       In - Plays. 21: Feb.1962, 67-78.

2152. Mark Twain by Leslie Hollingsworth.

       Radio. 7 m. 0 f.

       In - Plays. 4: Nov.1944, 72-76.

2153. Mark Twain Digs for Gold by Gladys L. Schmitt.

       Radio. 5 m. 0 f.

       In - Scholastic. 27: Nov.23,1935, 9-10.

2154. Mark Twain Digs for Gold by Gladys L. Schmitt.

       Radio. 4 m. 0 f.

       In - Scholastic. 52: May 10,1948, 23-25.

2155. The Marmalade Overture by Claire Boiko.

       Short. 2 m. 1 f. +X.

       In - Plays. 24: Nov.1964, 79-81.

2156. The Marriage by Douglas Hyde.

       Short. 2 m. 1 f. +X.

       In - Poet Lore. 20:no.2,1909, 135-145.

2157. The Marriage by Douglas Hyde. Trans. from the
       Gaelic by Lady Gregory.

       Short. 2 m. 1 f. +X.

       In - Golden. 6: Sept.1927, 327-332.

2158. A Marriage Has Been Arranged by Alfred Sutro.

       Short. 1 m. 1 f.

       In - Golden. 12: July 1930, 98-101.

2159. Marriage Is So Difficult by Lillian Harris.

       Short. 2 m. 2 f.

       In - Poet Lore. 38: Sept.1927, 452-463.

2160. Married Man by David Herbert Lawrence.

       Full. 5 m. 8 f.

       In - Virginia. 16: Oct.1940, 523-547.

2161. Martha Washington's Spy by Earl J. Dias.

       Short. 5 m. 2 f.

       In - Plays. 12: Feb.1953, 41-49.

2162. Martha Washington's Spy by Earl J. Dias.

       Short. 5 m. 2 f.

       In - Plays. 26: Feb.1967, 59-67.

2163. Martin Chuzzlewit by Charles Dickens. Adap.
       by Levy Olfson.

       Radio. 4 m. 5 f.

       In - Plays. 20: May 1961, 97-107.

2164   The Marvelous Romance of Wen Chun-Chin by
       Cheng-Chin Hsiung.

       Short. 6 m. 3 f. +m.X.

       In - Poet Lore. 35: June 1924, 298-313.

2165. The Marvelous Time Machine by Claire Boiko.

       Short. 6 m. 4 f.

       In - Plays. 18: May 1959, 35-41.

2166. Mary Elizabeth's Wonderful Dream by Miriam
      E. Mason.

      Short. 0 m. 6 f. 5 c.

      In - Plays. 9: Nov.1949, 33-40.

2167. Mary of Scotland by Maxwell Anderson.
      Ed. by Margaret Mayorga.

      Short. 21 m. 6 f. 1 b.

      In - Scholastic. 31: Jan.15,1938, 17E-20E+.

2168. Mary's Cake by Claribel Spamer.

      Short. 2 m. 5 f.

      In - Plays. 10: Nov.1950, 51-53.

2169. Mary's Garden by Claribel Spamer.

      Short. 5 m. 3 f.

      In - Plays. 5: May 1946, 55-58.

2170. Mary's Invitation by Helen Louise Miller.

      Short. 3 m. 6 f. +ch.

      In - Plays. 19: Nov.1959, 69-75.

2171. The Masque of the Red Death by Edgar Allan
      Poe.

      Radio. 9 m. 4 f. +X.

      In - Plays. 15: Jan.1956, 90-94.

2172. The Masque of Tomes or Boy Gets Book by
      Frances W. Binkley.

      Short. indef. un.

      In - Wilson. 23: Sept.1948, 66-67.

2173. The Master In the House by Betty Fitzgerald.

      Short. 2 m. 4 f.

      In - Scholastic. 24: April 28,1934, 11-13.

2174. Master of All Masters adap. by Virginia
      Payne Whitworth from a folk tale.

      Short. 1 m. 2 f. 1 "cat".

      In - Plays. 27: May 1968, 74-76.

2175. A Matter of Business by Elizabeth Wilkes.

      Short. 4 m. 1 f.

      In - Plays. 9: April 1950, 37-43.

2176. The Master of Palmyra by Adolf Wilbrandt.
      Trans. by Harriott S. Olive.

      Full. 12 m. 7 f.

      In - Poet Lore. 13:no.2,1901, 161-248.

2177. Master Patelin, the Lawyer trans. by Moritz
      Adolf Jagendorf.

      Short. 4 m. 1 f.

      In - Golden. 13: March 1931, 74-79.

2178. The Master of the Strait by Helen E. Waite
      and E.M. Hoppenstedt.

      Short. 4 m. 3 f.

      In - Plays. 5: Dec.1945, 12-18.

2179. The Master Salesman by William Hazlett Upson.

      Short. 2 m. 1 f.

      In - Scholastic. 51: Jan.12,1948, 18-21.

2180. Master Zacharius by Jules Verne. Adap. by
      Adele Thane.

      Short. 7 m. 5 f. +X.

      In - Plays. 28: Nov.1968, 97-106.

2181. The Matchmaker by Thornton Wilder.

      Full. 10 m. 6 f.

      In - Theatre. 42: April 1958, 32-58.

2182. A Matter of Conscience by Rollin W. Coyle.

      Short. 2 m. 3 f.

      In - Plays. 17: Jan.1958, 51-56.

2183. A Matter of Health by Jane McGowan.

      Short. 6 m. 9 f.

      In - Plays. 24: April 1965, 70-76.

2184. A Matter of Opinion by George Hibbard.

      Short. 1 m. 2 f.

      In - Scribner's. 45: Aug.1900, 233-245.

2185. Maudie's Diary by Albert G. Miller.

      Radio. 3 m. 3 f.

      In - Scholastic. 39: Nov.3,1941, 17-20.

2186. Maurine and the Bach Invention by Mildred
      T. Pettit.

      Short. 1 m. 1 f. 1 g.

      In - Etude. 54: Oct.1936, 672-673.

2187. May Basket by Mildred Hark and Noel McQueen.

      Short. 7 m. 6 f.

      In - Plays. 7: May 1948, 61-64.

2188. May Baskets New by Emma Mauritz Larson.

      In - Woman's Home. 45: May 1918, 39.

2189. May Day for Mother by Helen Louise Miller.

      Short. 10 m. 10 f. +g.X.

      In - Plays. 19: May 1960, 63-67.

2190. <u>May Night</u> by Priscilla Flowers.

Short. 2 m. 4 f.

In - Poet Lore. 37: Dec.1926, 551-564.

2191. <u>May Witch</u> by Margaret Wylie Brydon and Esther
  E. Ziegler.

Short. 0 m. 8 f.

In - Plays. 22: May 1963, 69-78.

2192. <u>The Mayflower</u> by Alice Very.

Short. 0 m. 18 f. +c.X.

In - Plays. 15: May 1956, 59-62.

2193. <u>The Mayor of Burgville</u> by Claribel Spamer.

Short. 5 m. 3 f. +f.X.

In - Plays. 18: Oct.1958, 54-58.

2194. <u>The Mayor's New Bridge</u> by Hy Radin and Ted
  Kaufman.

Radio. 10 m. 0 f.

In - Plays. 6: Dec.1946, 83-88.

2195. <u>Maze</u> by Arthur Corning White.

In - Poet Lore. 36: March 1925, 147-153.

2196. <u>The Meanest Witch</u> by Doris McBride.

Short. 4 m. 3 f.

In - Plays. 20: Oct.1960, 68-72.

2197. <u>The Meaning of Art</u> by Lucille Sylvester.

Short. 15 m. 5 f.

In - Plays. 7: Nov.1947, 30-37.

2198. <u>The Meaning of Thanksgiving Day</u> by Carolyn
  Wells.

Short. 4 m. 8 f.

In - Ladies' Home. 38: Nov.1921, 304.

2199. <u>The Mechanical Maid</u> by Virginia Payne
  Whitworth.

Short. 0 m. 7 f.

In - Plays. 20: May 1961, 24-32.

2200. <u>The Mechanical Man</u> by John Murray.

Short. 6 m. 6 f.

In - Plays. 13: Nov.1953, 41-48.

2201. <u>The Mechanical Man</u> by John Murray.

Short. 6 m. 6 f.

In - Plays. 28: Nov.1968, 89-96.

2202. <u>Medea</u> adap. by Robinson Jeffers from the
  play by Euripedes.

Full. 5 m. 2 f. 2 b. +X. +f.ch.

In - Theatre. 32: Fall 1948, 71-97.

2203. <u>Meet Mr. Muffin</u> by Helen Louise Miller.

Short. 10 m. 9 f.

In - Plays. 21: Jan.1962, 69-73.

2204. <u>Meet Mr. Murchinson</u> by Betty Tracy Huff.

Short. 3 m. 8 f.

In - Plays. 20: May 1961, 1-10.

2205. <u>Meet Mr. Witch</u> by Mildred Hark and Noel
  McQueen.

Short. 7 m. 7 f. +X.

In - Plays. 6: Oct.1947, 51-60.

2206. <u>Meet the Pilgrims!</u> by Claire Boiko.

Short. 6 b. 4 g.

In - Plays. 25: Nov.1965, 74-78.

2207. <u>The Meeting: a Mirror for Americans</u> by
  J.M. Linebarger.

Short. 12 m. 1 f.

In - Cimarron. 1: March 1968, 38+.

2208. <u>Meeting at the Well</u>.

see

<u>Three Chinese Folk Dramas</u>.

2209. <u>Melissa's Muffins</u> by Lindsey Barbee.

Short. 4 m. 4 f.

In - Plays. 10: Jan.1951, 48-52.

2210. <u>Melody for Lincoln</u> by Helen Louise Miller.

Short. 2 m. 6 f.

In - Plays. 17: Feb.1958, 43-50.

2211. <u>Mementos of Our Ancestors</u> by Mildred Hark
  and Noel McQueen.

Short. 5 m. 6 f.

In - Plays. 17: Nov.1957, 1-15.

2212. <u>Memorial Day for the Blue and Gray</u> by
  Deborah Newman.

Short. 3 m. 7 f.

In - Plays. 11: May 1952, 48-51.

2213. <u>Memorial Day for the Blue and Gray</u> by Deborah
  Newman.

Short. 3 m. 7 f.

In - Plays. 18: May 1959, 67-70.

2214. <u>A Memory of Two Mondays</u>.

see

<u>A View From the Bridge</u>.

2215. <u>A Merry Christmas</u> by Louisa May Alcott.
Adap. by Walter Hackett.

Radio. 3 m. 6 f.

In - Plays. 8: Dec.1948, 72-80.

2216. <u>A Merry Christmas</u> adap. by Walter Hackett.
Based on Louisa May Alcott's <u>Little</u>
<u>Women.</u>

Radio. 3 m. 7 f. 1 b.

In - Plays. 26: Dec.1966, 88-96.

2217. <u>Merry Christmas, Crawford's</u> by Mildred
Hark and Noel McQueen.

Short. 8 m. 7 f. +X.

In - Plays. 16: Dec.1956, 15-29.

2218. <u>Merry Christmas Customs</u> by Mildred Hark and
Noel McQueen.

Short. 8 m. 2 f. +X.

In - Plays. 17: Dec.1957, 63-66.

2219. <u>The Merry Christmas Elf</u> by Aileen Fisher.

Short. 6 m. 5 f. +X.

In - Plays. 10: Dec.1950, 36-42.

2220. <u>Merry-Go-Round</u> by D.H. Lawrence.

Full. 6 m. 5 f.

In - Virginia. 17: Jan.1941, 1-44.

2221. <u>Merry-Go-Round for Mother</u> by Helen Louise
Miller.

Short. 4 m. 11 f.

In - Plays. 20: May 1961, 45-52.

2222. <u>The Merry Mix-Up</u> by Frances B. Watts.

Short. 5 m. 6 f.

In - Plays. 26: May 1967, 73-77.

2223. <u>Merry Tyll and the Three Rogues</u> adap. by
Adele Thane from a German folk tale.

Short. 13 m. 4 f. 4 c. 1 "cow" +X.

In - Plays. 27: Dec.1967, 33-41.

2224. <u>Merton of the Movies</u> by George S. Kaufman and
Mark Connelly. Based on the novel by
Harry L. Wilson. Ed. by Margaret Mayorga.

Excerpt. 11 m. 5 f.

In - Scholastic. 34: March 18,1939, 19E-21E.

2225. <u>The Message</u> by Vernon Howard.

Short. 5 m. 0 f.

In - Plays. 13: March 1954, 75-77.

2226. <u>A Message from Robin Hood</u> by J.G. Colson.

Short. 11 m. 0 f. +m.X.

In - Plays. 12: Oct.1952, 39-47.

2227. <u>The Message of Lazarus</u> by C.E. Lawrence.

Short. 1 m. 2 f.

In - 19th C. 91: Jan.1922, 170-176.

2228. <u>The Message of the Hearts</u> by Deborah Newman.

Short. 2 m. 3 f. +X.

In - Plays. 11: Feb.1952, 70-73.

2229. <u>A Message to Garcia</u> by Elbert Hubbard.
Adap. by Walter Hackett.

Radio. 18 m. 0 f. 2 b. 2 g.

In - Plays. 7: Oct.1948, 83-92.

2230. <u>Metal of the Moon</u> by Irve Tunick.

Radio. 5 m. 4 f.

In - Scholastic. 62: March 18,1953, 20-23.

2231. <u>Mexico for Mexicans</u> by Samuel S. Ullman.

Short. 14 m. 3 f.

In - Plays. 6: Jan.1947, 29-35.

2232. <u>Mick and Mick</u> by Hugh Leonard.

Full. 8 m. 6 f.

In - Players. 14: Dec.1966, 31-46.

2233. <u>Midge Minds Her Sister's Business</u> by
Marjorie B. Paradis.

Short. 2 m. 8 f.

In - Plays. 7: March 1948, 1-8.

2234. <u>Midge Rings the Bell</u> by Marjorie B. Paradis.

Short. 0 m. 11 f.

In - Plays. 3: May 1944, 1-10.

2235. <u>Midnight Burial</u> by Kay Hill.

Short. 0 m. 8 f.

In - Plays. 7: March 1948, 30-32.

2236. <u>Midnight Burial</u> by Kay Hill.

Short. 0 m. 8 f.

In - Plays. 16: April 1957, 53-72.

2237. <u>Midnight Crossing</u> by John Murray.

Short. 4 m. 5 f.

In - Plays. 17: May 1958, 15-26.

2238. <u>A Midsummer Night's Dream</u> by William
    Shakespeare. Adap. by Levy Olfson.

    Radio. 7 m. 2 f.

    In - Plays. 18: Feb.1959, 87-96.

2239. <u>Midwinter Eve Fire</u> by Phillips Endicott
    Osgood.

    Short. 4 b. 3 g. +g.X.

    In - Horn Book. 15: Nov.1939, 359-367.

2240. Midwinter Eve Fire by Phillips Endicott
    Osgood.

    Short. 4 b. 3 g. +g.X.

    In - Scholastic. 35: Dec.18,1939, 17E-19E.

2241. <u>The Mighty Reservoy</u> by Peter Terson.

    Full. 2 m. 0 f.

    In - Players. 14: Aug.1967, 19-32.

2242. <u>Miguel Manara</u> by O.W. Milosz. Trans. from
    the French by Edward J. O'Brien.

    Full. 12 m. 0 f. +X.

    In - Poet Lore. 30:no.2,1919, 224-264.

2243. <u>Mila Whendle</u> by N.H. Musselman.

    Full. 3 m. 3 f.

    In - Poet Lore. 13:no.1,1901, 22-53.

2244. <u>The Milkmaid and Her Pail</u> by Valeska Joy.

    Short. 0 m. 3 f. +c.X.

    In - Plays. 7: Oct.1948, 73-74.

2245. <u>The Milky Way Conference</u> by Marshall Gray.

    Short. 5 m. 0 f.

    In - Sat. Review. 30: Aug.2,1947, 18-19.

2246. <u>Million Dollar Recipe</u> by Vernon Howard.

    Short. 5 m. 0 f.

    In - Plays. 13: April 1954, 66-69.

2247. <u>The Million-Pound Bank Note</u> by Mark Twain.
    Adap. by Walter Hackett.

    Radio. 13 m. 2 f.

    In - Plays. 9: Nov.1949, 80-92.

2248. <u>Mind Over Matter</u> by Jessie Nicholson.

    Short. 14 m. 4 f.

    In - Plays. 20: March 1961, 17-26.

2249. <u>Mind Your Manners</u> by Karin Asbrand.

    Short. 5 m. 6 f.

    In - Plays. 7: May 1948, 67-68.

2250. <u>Mind Your P's and Q's</u> by Mildred Hark and
    Noel McQueen.

    Short. 11 m. 6 f.

    In - Plays. 12: March 1953, 51-57.

2251. <u>Mind Your P's and Q's</u> by Mildred Hark and
    Noel McQueen.

    Short. 11 m. 6 f.

    In - Plays. 22: March 1963, 44-50.

2252. <u>Minick</u> by Edna Ferber and George S. Kaufman.
    Ed. by Margaret Mayorga.

    Short. 6 m. 9 f.

    In - Scholastic. 31: Dec.4,1937, 17E-19E.

2253. <u>The Minister's Dream</u> by Katherine Lord.

    Short. 6 m. 3 f. 2 b. 2 g. +X.

    In - Delineator. 80: Nov.1912, 358-359.

2254. <u>The Minister's First "At Home"</u> by John
    Kendrick Bangs.

    Short. 2 m. 3 f.

    In - Ladies' Home. 26: March 1909, 16+.

2255. <u>A Mink Coat's Only Skin Deep</u> by Marjorie B.
    Paradis.

    Short. 5 m. 7 f. +3m.X.

    In - Plays. 6: April 1947, 13-20.

2256. <u>Minor Developments</u> by W.E. Huntsberry.

    Short. 10 m. 3 f.

    In - Plays. 6: Oct.1947, 19-27.

2257. <u>Minority of Millions</u> by Mildred Hark and
    Noel McQueen.

    Short. 11 m. 18 f. +X.

    In - Plays. 17: Feb.1958, 1-12.

2258. <u>A Minuet</u> by Louis Napoleon Parker.

    Short. 2 m. 1 f.

    In - Century. 89: Jan.1915, 370-376.

2259. <u>The Minyana's Daughter</u> by Ralph Treitel.

    Short. 2 m. 2 f.

    In - First Stage. 7: Dec.1968, 150-158.

2260. <u>The Miracle Flower</u> by Elsa DeBra.

    Short. 3 m. 4 f. +ch.

    In - Plays. 20: Dec.1960, 67-70.

2261. <u>Miracle in Louisiana</u> by Gladys L. Schmitt.

    Radio. 4 m. 1 f.

    In - Scholastic. 35: Oct.23,1939, 21E-23E.

2262. Miracle Merchant by Hector Munro.
Short. 3 m. 2 f.
In - Scholastic. 30: April 17,1937, 9-10+.

2263. The Miracle of Paper by Peter J. Harkins.
Radio. 24 m. 1 f. 1 b.
In - Plays. 3: March 1944, 68-78.

2264. The Miracle of Spring by Helen Hanna.
Short. 12 m. 6 f. +X.
In - Plays. 23: March 1964, 71-76.

2265. The Miracle of the Corn by Padraic Colum.
Short. 3 m. 4 f. 1 c.
In - Theatre. 5: Nov.1921, 323-332.

2266. The Miraculous Tea Party by Jane McGowan.
Short. 7 m. 8 f.
In - Plays. 16: Nov.1956, 53-60.

2267. The Mirror Children by Claribel Spamer.
Short. 0 m. 6 f.
In - Plays. 4: April 1945, 50-52.

2268. A Mirror For Librarians by Marye D. Benjamin.
Short. 0 m. 11 f.
In - Wilson. 27: May 1953, 728-732.

2269. Mirthful Marionettes by Dan W. Totheroh.
Short. 1 m. 0 f. 3 b. 5 g.
In - Drama. 21: April 1931, 19-20+.

2270. Misalliance by George Bernard Shaw.
Full. 6 m. 3 f.
In - Theatre. 37: Sept.1953, 35-63.

2271. The Mish-Mosh Bird by John Murray.
Short. 9 m. 5 f. +X.
In - Plays. 16: Jan.1957, 15-26.

2272. Miss Barton is Needed by Jeanette Covert Nolan.
Short. 7 m. 2 f. +m.X.
In - Plays. 10: March 1951, 19-32.

2273. Miss Barton's in Charge by Marion Wefer.
Radio. 4 m. 1 f.
In - Scholastic. 49: Dec.2,1946, 17-18+.

2274. Miss Fix-It by Paul S. McCoy.
Short. 3 m. 4 f.
In - Plays. 15: April 1956, 31-42.

2275. Miss Fix-It by Paul S. McCoy.
Short. 3 m. 4 f.
In - Plays. 26: April 1967, 37-48.

2276. Miss Forsythe is Missing by John Murray.
Short. 3 m. 3 f.
In - Plays. 23: Jan.1964, 15-26.

2277. Miss Frankenstein by Helen Louise Miller.
Short. 8 m. 11 f. 1 b. 2 g. +X.
In - Plays. 25: Oct.1965, 13-22.

2278. Miss Hepplewhite Takes Over by John Murray.
Short. 4 m. 4 f.
In - Plays. 23: Nov.1963, 15-28.

2279. Miss Liberty Goes to Town by Norman Rosten.
Radio. 14 m. 8 f.
In - Scholastic. 43: Jan.17,1944, 13-15.

2280. Miss Lonelyheart by Helen Louise Miller.
Short. 5 m. 3 f.
In - Plays. 9: Feb.1950, 83-95.

2281. Miss Louisa and the Outlaws by Frances B. Watts.
Short. 6 m. 4 f. +c.X.
In - Plays. 23: Oct.1963, 55-60.

2282. Miss Manda by Gladys Bagg Taber.
Short. 3 m. 4 f.
In - Poet Lore. 38: Sept.1927, 412-421.

2283. Miss Robin's School by Claribel Spamer.
Short. 5 m. 2 f.
In - Plays. 9: March 1950, 71-73.

2284. The Missing Easter Eggs by June Barr.
Short. 5 m. 2 f.
In - Plays. 8: April 1949, 65-68.

2285. The Missing Gift by Robert Ronan.
Short. 5 m. 4 f. +X.
In - Plays. 20: March 1961, 71-74.

2286. The Missing "Linc" by Helen Louise Miller.
Short. 4 m. 3 f.
In - Plays. 5: Jan.1946, 1-10.

2287. The Missing Linc (sic.) by Helen Louise
      Miller.

      Short. 4 m. 3 f.

      In - Plays. 26: Feb.1967, 13-22.

2288. Mississippi, Father of Waters by George
      Jennings.

      Radio. 6 m. 2 f.

      In - Scholastic. 38: May 5,1941, 17-19.

2289. Mister A. Lincoln by Marjorie B. Paradis.

      Short. 0 m. 8 f.

      In - Plays. 15: Feb.1956, 13-20.

2290. Mister Antonio by Booth Tarkington.

      Full. 8 m. 6 f.

      In - Harper's M. 134: Jan.& Feb.1917,
      187-203, 374-387.

2291. Mr. Bates Goes to the Polls by Nina Butler
      Reay.

      Short. 3 m. 1 f. +c.X.

      In - Plays. 10: Nov.1950, 48-50.

2292. Mr. Bates Goes to the Polls by Nina Butler
      Reay.

      Short. 3 m. 1 f. +c.X.

      In - Plays. 24: Nov.1964, 76-78.

2293. Mister Bosphorus and the Muses by Ford Madox
      Ford.

      Full. many un. +ch.

      In - Poet Lore. 34: Dec.1923, 532-613.

2294. Mister Catchy Cold by Dorothy Deming.

      Short. 5 un. 10 c.

      In - Plays. 10: March 1951, 63-65.

2295. Mr. Elliot's Crazy Notion by Gladys L. Schmitt.

      Radio. 4 m. 2 f. 3 b.

      In - Scholastic. 26: May 18,1935, 8-9+.

2296. Mr. Enright Entertains by Avery Abbott.

      Short. 5 m. 2 f. 1 g.

      In - Poet Lore. 34: March 1923, 127-138.

2297. Mr. Filbert's Claim to Fame by John Murray.

      Short. 9 m. 5 f. +X.

      In - Plays. 18: Jan.1959, 13-26.

2298. Mr. Fix-It and Do-It-Now by Catherine Urban.

      Short. 7 m. 1 f.

      In - Plays. 6: May 1947, 55-57.

2299. Mr. Jay Does Some Thinking by Louise E.
      Alexander.

      Short. 4 m. 3 f.

      In - Plays. 3: Jan.1944, 48-50.

2300. Mr. Lazy Man's Family by Muriel Ward.

      Short. 3 m. 3 f.

      In - Plays. 10: April 1951, 41-52.

2301. Mr. Lazy Man's Family by Muriel Ward.

      Short. 3 m. 3 f.

      In - Plays. 26: Jan.1967, 45-56.

2302. Mr. Lincoln's Beard by Deborah Newman.

      Short. 5 m. 4 f. +X.

      In - Plays. 16: Feb.1957, 53-56.

2303. Mr. Lincoln's Grave by Thomas Edward
      O'Connell.

      Radio. 7 m. 0 f. +m.X.

      In - Plays. 3: Jan.1944, 67-75.

2304. Mr. Lincoln's Wife by Victor Wolfson. Based
      on the book by Anne Colver.

      Radio. 5 m. 5 f. 2 b.

      In - Scholastic. 44: Feb.7,1944, 17-19.

2305. Mr. Longfellow Observes Book Week by Edna
      G. Moore.

      Short. 6 m. 5 f.

      In - Plays. 3: Nov.1943, 53-57.

2306. Mr. Man by L. Miller. Trans. from the
      Yiddish by S.K. Padover and Chasye
      Cooperman.

      Full. 14 m. 7 f. +X.

      In - Poet Lore. 40: Dec.1929, 475-543.

2307. Mr. Mergenthwirker's Lobblies by Nelson Bond
      and David Kent.

      Full. 10 m. 1 f.

      In - Theatre. 35: July 1951, 62-79.

2308. Mr. Moore and Mr. Chew by Samuel C. Chew.

      Short. 2 m. 1 f.

      In - American Merc. 1: Jan.1924, 39-47.

2309. Mister Owl by Claribel Spamer.

      Short. 4 m. 2 f. +c.X.

      In - Plays. 9: Nov.1949, 68-71.

2310. Mr. Owl's Advice by Mildred Hark and Noel
      McQueen.

      Short. 7 un.

      In - Plays. 17: April 1958, 69-71.

2311. <u>Mister Roberts</u> by Thomas Heggen and Joshua Logan.

Full. 19 m. 1 f.

In - Theatre. 34: March 1950, 57-104.

2312. <u>Mr. Scrooge Finds Christmas</u> adap. by Aileen Fisher from Charles Dickens' <u>A Christmas Carol</u>.

Short. 14 m. 4 f. +m.X.

In - Plays. 20: Dec.1960, 75-85.

2313. <u>Mr. Smooch's Trap</u> by Sally Werner.

Short. 2 m. 0 f. 8 c.

In - Plays. 14: Feb.1955, 80-84.

2314. <u>Mr. Snow White's Thanksgiving</u> by Helen Louise Miller.

Short. 3 m. 4 f.

In - Plays. 15: Nov.1955, 31-40.

2315. <u>Mr. Thanks Has His Day</u> by Lee Kingman.

Short. 7 m. 4 f.

In - Plays. 3: Nov.1943, 37-42.

2316. <u>Mister Twister</u> by John Murray.

Short. 5 m. 4 f.

In - Plays. 22: Jan.1963, 13-26.

2317. <u>The Mistletoe Mystery</u> by Helen Louise Miller.

Short. 5 m. 4 f.

In - Plays. 21: Dec.1961, 1-11.

2318. <u>Mrs. Gibbs Advertises</u> by Mary Thurman Pyle.

Short. 5 m. 5 f. +X.

In - Plays. 10: Nov.1950, 36-43.

2319. <u>Mrs. Middleman's Descent</u> by Martin Halpern.

Short. 2 m. 3 f. 1 bulldog.

In - First Stage. 5: Sept.1966, 158-171.

2320. <u>Mrs. Mouse, Are You Within?</u> by Frank Marcus.

Full. 3 m. 2 f.

In - Players. 15: July 1968, 29-44+.

2321. <u>Mrs. Murgatroyd's Dime</u> by John Treville Latouche.

Radio. 1 m. 0 f.

In - Scholastic. 42: March 29,1943, 15+.

2322. <u>Mrs. Pipp's Waterloo</u> by Ellis O. Jones.

In - Woman's Home. 41: April 1914, 23-24.

2323. <u>Mrs. Santa's Christmas Gift</u> by Deborah Newman.

Short. 1 m. 1 f. 10 c.

In - Plays. 9: Dec.1949, 67-70.

2324. <u>Mrs. Sniffit's Christmas</u> by Alice V. Brown.

Short. 1 m. 3 f. +X.

In - Plays. 10: Dec.1950, 62-64.

2325. <u>Mrs. Tubbs's Telegram</u> by Katharine Rice.

In - St. Nicholas. 32: Feb.1905, 344-351.

2326. <u>The Mixing Stick</u> by Eleanore Leuser.

Short. 6 m. 5 f.

In - Plays. 8: Dec.1948, 51-54.

2327. <u>Models for Health</u> by Celia Gordon.

Short. 3 m. 7 f.

In - Plays. 11: Jan.1952, 67-70.

2328. <u>A Modern Cinderella</u> by Leslie Hollingsworth.

Short. 0 m. 5 f.

In - Plays. 15: Feb.1956, 21-30.

2329. <u>Modern Harlequinade in Three Plays</u> by Colin Campbell Clements.

In - Poet Lore. 31: Dec.1920, 579-603.

2330. <u>The Modern School Girl</u>.

see

<u>Snow White</u>.

2331. <u>Mollusk or Suffragette?</u> by Elizabeth Overstreet Cuppy.

Short. 3 m. 3 f.

In - Putnam's. 7(n.s.): Nov.1909, 172-181.

2332. <u>Mom's a Grandma Now</u> by Mildred Hark and Noel McQueen.

Short. 4 m. 3 f.

In - Plays. 9: May 1950, 1-14.

2333. <u>Mom's Perfect Day</u> by Edrie Pendleton.

Short. 5 m. 4 f.

In - Plays. 11: May 1952, 1-10.

2334. <u>The Money-Question</u> by Alexander Dumas, Fils.

Full. 5 m. 4 f. +X.

In - Poet Lore. 26:no.2,1915, 129-227.

2335. <u>The Money Tree</u> by Juliet Garver.

Short. 7 m. 10 f.

In - Plays. 20: April 1961, 1-11.

2336. The Monk Who Wouldn't by Oscar Mandel.

Short. 5 m. 1 f.

In - First Stage. 1: June 1962, 27-40.

2337. The Monkey's Paw by W.W. Jacobs. Adap. by
Louis N. Parker.

Short. 4 m. 1 f.

In - Golden. 5: April 1927, 511-519.

2338. Monna Vanna by Maurice Maeterlinck. Trans.
from the French by Charlotte Porter.

Full. 7 m. 1 f. +X.

In - Poet Lore. 15:no.3,1904, 1-52.

2339. Monsieur Beaucaire by Booth Tarkington.
Adap. by Levy Olfson.

Radio. 6 m. 1 f. 6 un. +X.

In - Plays. 15: May 1956, 63-72.

2340. Monsieur Beaucaire by Booth Tarkington.
Adap. by Levy Olfson.

Short. 7 m. 4 f. +X.

In - Plays. 23: Nov.1963, 83-94.

2341. Monsieur Santa Claus by Helen Louise Miller.

Short. 9 m. 7 f.

In - Plays. 17: Dec.1957, 1-10.

2342. The Monster by T.G. Schwartz.

Short. 2 m. 2 f.

In - Poet Lore. 37: Dec.1926, 597-606.

2343. The Moon is Blue by F. Hugh Herbert.

Full. 3 m. 1 f.

In - Theatre. 36: Jan.1952, 50-74.

2344. The Moon Keeps Shining by Mildred Hark and
Noel McQueen.

Short. 3 m. 2 f.

In - Plays. 10: May 1951, 1-10.

2345. Moon Miracle by Margaret Haley Carpenter.

Short. 6 m. 3 f. +g.X.

In - Plays. 3: May 1944, 36-42.

2346. Moonbeam Dares by Sylvia Lee.

Short. 4 m. 5 f.

In - Plays. 16: April 1957, 67-71.

2347. Moonlight is When by Kay Arthur.

Short. 3 m. 3 f.

In - Plays. 24: March 1965, 3-16.

2348. Moonlight Sonata by Victor Perez Petit.
Trans. by Willis Knapp Jones and
Carlos Escudero.

Short. 4 m. 2 f. 1 g.

In - Poet Lore. 51: Oct.1945, 353-368.

2349. The Moon's Up There by Paul T. Nolan.

Short. 6 m. 4 f.

In - Plays. 22: April 1963, 1-10.

2350. Moonshine by Arthur Hopkins.

Short. 2 m. 0 f.

In - Theatre. 3: Jan.1919, 51-62.

2351. Moonshine by Arthur Hopkins.

Short. 2 m. 0 f.

In - Golden. 10: Nov.1929, 102-105.

2352. A Morality Play For the Leisure Class by John
Lloyd Balderston.

Short. 2 m. 0 f.

In - Harper's M. 141: Sept.1920, 491-497.

2353. A Morality Play for the Leisure Class by John
Lloyd Balderston.

Short. 2 m. 0 f.

In - Golden. 10: Sept.1929, 87-90.

2354. More About Apples by A.H. Phipps.

Short. 0 m. 3 f.

In - Poet Lore. 40: March 1929, 144-149.

2355. More Ado About Nothing by St.John Hankin.

Short. 2 m. 1 f.

In - Golden. 11: June 1930, 99-101.

2356. More Than a Million by Mollie Kelly.

Short. 4 m. 3 f.

In - Scholastic. 25: Nov.24,1934, 5-7+.

2357. More Than Courage by Esther MacLellan and
Catherine V. Schroll.

Short. 13 m. 0 f.

In - Plays. 17: Oct.1957, 51-58.

2358. The Morning-Maker by Camilla Campbell.

Short. 4 m. 0 f. +m.X.

In - Plays. 9: Jan.1950, 64-66.

2359. A Morning's Work by Gerald Maxwell.

Short. 2 m. 1 f.

In - 19th C. 52: July 1902, 167-176.

2360. The Most Happy Fella by Frank Loesser.
Full (musical). 18 m. 10 f. +ch. +X.
In - Theatre. 42: Oct.1958, 26-53.

2361. The Most Important Guests by Graham DuBois.
Short. 7 m. 5 f. +m.X.
In - Plays. 20: Dec.1960, 15-24.

2362. Most Memorable Voyage by Katherine Little Bakeless.
Short. 10 m. 0 f. +m.X.
In - Plays. 15: Oct.1955, 32-42.

2363. A Most Special Dragon by David Ferguson.
Short. 4 m. 0 f. 1 b. 1 g. 1 "dragon".
In - Plays. 27: Jan.1968, 50-54.

2364. The Most Unusual Ghost by Gerry Lynn Haugh.
Short. 1 m. 1 f. 4 c.
In - Plays. 28: Oct.1968, 77-81.

2365. Mother by F.M. Mueffer.
In - Fortnightly. 75: April 1901, 741-746.

2366. Mother Beats the Band by Helen Louise Miller.
Short. 5 m. 10 f. +f.X.
In - Plays. 14: May 1955, 1-11.

2367. Mother Beats the Band by Helen Louise Miller.
Short. 5 m. 10 f. +f.X.
In - Plays. 27: May 1968, 23-33.

2368. Mother Earth's New Dress by Mildred Hark and Noel McQueen.
Short. 5 m. 11 f. +X.
In - Plays. 5: March 1946, 34-42.

2369. Mother for Mayor by Helen Louise Miller.
Short. 4 m. 4 f.
In - Plays. 12: May 1953, 1-13.

2370. Mother for Mayor by Helen Louise Miller.
Short. 4 m. 3 f. 1 g.
In - Plays. 24: May 1965, 31-43.

2371. Mother Goes Modern by Kay Arthur.
Short. 4 m. 4 f.
In - Plays. 25: May 1966, 1-14.

2372. The Mother Goose Bakeshop by Helen Louise Miller.
Short. 8 m. 6 f. 1 c. +X.
In - Plays. 19: Jan.1960, 69-74.

2373. A Mother Goose Christmas by S. Decatur Smith, Jr.
Short. 0 m. 1 f. + many c.
In - Ladies' Home. 25: Dec.1907, 19+.

2374. Mother Goose Gives a Dinner by J. Lilian Vandevere.
Short. 6 m. 6 f.
In - Plays. 5: April 1946, 73-75.

2375. Mother Goose's Christmas Surprise by Claire Boiko.
Short. 7 m. 6 f.
In - Plays. 25: Dec.1965, 77-82.

2376. Mother Goose's Magic Cookies by Betty Gray Blaine.
Short. 3 m. 5 f. +c.X.
In - Plays. 22: Jan.1963, 77-83.

2377. Mother Goose's Party by Aileen Fisher.
Short. 4 m. 6 f.
In - Plays. 21: Dec.1961, 80-84.

2378. Mother Library's Tea Party by Elizabeth Hamilton.
Short. 1 m. 1 f. 6 b. 2 g. 1 un.
In - Wilson. 3: Jan.1929, 427-433.

2379. Mother Makes a Choice by Helene Whittaker.
Short. 5 m. 9 f.
In - Plays. 25: May 1966, 73-78.

2380. Mother Saves Her Day by Edrie Pendleton.
Short. 3 m. 3 f.
In - Plays. 7: May 1948, 41-48.

2381. Mother's Admirers by Mildred Hark and Noel McQueen.
Short. 3 m. 3 f.
In - Plays. 5: May 1946, 33-42.

2382. Mother's Admirers by Mildred Hark and Noel McQueen.
Short. 1 m. 1 f. 2 b. 2 g.
In - Plays. 27: May 1968, 43-52.

2383. Mother's Apron Strings by Helen Louise Miller.
Short. 5 m. 3 f.
In - Plays. 10: May 1951, 21-29.

2384. Mother's Big Day by Helen Louise Miller.
Short. 2 m. 6 f.
In - Plays. 5: May 1946, 1-11.

2385. Mother's Choice by Mildred Hark and Noel McQueen.

Short. 2 m. 3 f.

In - Plays. 20: May 1961, 61-68.

2386. Mother's Day for Susan by June Barr.

Short. 0 m. 8 f.

In - Plays. 13: May 1954, 75-78.

2387. Mother's Fairy Godmother by Helen Louise Miller.

Short. 2 m. 4 f.

In - Plays. 16: May 1957, 31-36.

2388. Mother's Gift by Helen Littler Howard.

Short. 3 m. 4 f.

In - Plays. 3: May 1944, 34-36.

2389. Mother's Hidden Talent by Helen Louise Miller.

Short. 8 m. 3 f.

In - Plays. 13: May 1954, 1-12.

2390. Mother's V.I.P.'s by Mildred Hark and Noel McQueen.

Short. 4 m. 5 f.

In - Plays. 15: May 1956, 11-22.

2391. Mountain Madness by Earl J. Dias.

Short. 7 m. 7 f.

In - Plays. 24: Feb.1965, 17-27.

2392. The Mountain She-Devil trans. from the Noh drama by Yone Noguchi.

Short. 0 m. 3 f. +ch.

In - Poet Lore. 29:no.4,1918, 447-451.

2393. The Mouse That Soared by Helen Louise Miller.

Short. 5 m. 1 f. 12 c.

In - Plays. 23: Oct.1963, 61-66.

2394. Moving Day by Elaine Klein.

Short. 2 m. 4 f.

In - Plays. 23: May 1964, 37-44.

2395. Moving On Tomorrow by Marguerite Kreger Phillips.

Short. 0 m. 8 f.

In - Plays. 16: March 1957, 15-24.

2396. Mozart and Solieri by Aleksandr S. Pushkin. Trans. by Vladimir Nabokov.

Short. 3 m. 0 f.

In - New Republic. 104: April 21,1941, 559-560+.

2397. Mozart and the Gray Steward by Thornton Wilder.

Short. 2 m. 1 f.

In - Harper's M. 157: Oct.1928, 565-567.

2398. Mozart and the Princess by Louise Findlay.

Short. 1 m. 2 f. 2 b. 1 g.

In - Etude. 53: Oct.1935, 628-629.

2399. Much Ado About Ants by Anna Lenington Heath.

Short. 4 m. 3 f.

In - Plays. 24: Dec.1964, 61-66.

2400. Much Ado About Nothing by William Shakespeare. Adap. by Lewy Olfson.

Radio. 7 m. 2 f.

In - Plays. 17: April 1958, 87-96.

2401. Mud by Isabel McKinney.

Short. 3 m. 1 f.

In - Poet Lore. 30:no.3,1919, 417-427.

2402. Mud Pack Madness by Dawn and Marshall French.

Short. 0 m. 5 f.

In - Plays. 18: Jan.1959, 27-34.

2403. Mulvaney's First Case by John Murray.

Short. 4 m. 4 f.

In - Plays. 17: Jan.1958, 23-33.

2404. The Mummers' Play adap. by J. Kinchin Smith.

Short. 9 m. 0 f.

In - Theatre. 7: Jan.1923, 58-68.

2405. Murder in the Kitchen by Aileen Fisher.

Short. 2 m. 4 f. +X.

In - Plays. 9: March 1950, 46-52.

2406. The Murder of Marat by Patrick Kearney.

In - Drama. 18: April 1928, 208-210.

2407. The Murderer by Clarendon Ross.

Short. 2 m. 0 f.

In - Poet Lore. 30:no.4,1919, 596-600.

2408. Music Hath Charms by Mildred Hark and Noel McQueen.

Short. 3 m. 2 f.

In - Plays. 12: March 1953, 1-8.

2409. Music of the Woodland by D.V. Benedict.

Short. 0 m. 0 f. 2 b. 8 g. +c.X.

In - Etude. 57: Aug.1939, 493+.

2410. The Musicians of Bremen Town adap. by
      Walter Roberts from Grimms' Fairy Tales.

      Short. 4 m. 1 f. 5 c.

      In - Plays. 27: Jan.1968, 71-74.

2411. Mutilated by Tennessee Williams.

      Short. 7 m. 3 f.

      In - Esquire. 64: Aug.1965, 96-101.

2412. My Darlin' Aida by Charles Friedman. Based
      on opera Aida by Giuseppe Verdi.

      Full (musical). 16 m. 25 f.

      In - Theatre. 37: June 1953, 35-61.

2413. My Dear! by Patricia O'Connor.

      Short. 3 m. 4 f. 1 b.

      In - Drama. 14: Feb.1924, 188-189.

2414. My Fair Linda by Juliet Garver.

      Short. 4 m. 3 f.

      In - Plays. 22: May 1963, 1-13.

2415. My Fair Monster by Earl J. Dias.

      Short. 5 m. 8 f.

      In - Plays. 26: Feb.1967, 1-11.

2416. My Heart's In the Highlands by William
      Saroyan. Ed. by Margaret Mayorga.

      Excerpts. 8 m. 2 f. 1 dog +X.

      In - Scholastic. 37: Jan.6,1941, 17-19+.

2417. My Host - The Ghost by John Murray.

      Short. 4 m. 3 f.

      In - Plays. 24: Jan.1965, 25-36.

2418. My Own Self by A.V. Brown.

      Short. 0 m. 2 f. 1 b. +c.X.

      In - Plays. 4: Dec.1944, 61-62.

2419. My Patriot Mother by Katherine Little Bakeless.

      Short. 16 m. 2 f.

      In - Plays. 18: Feb.1959, 21-34.

2420. My Swinging Swain by Anne Coulter Martens.

      Short. 4 m. 4 f.

      In - Plays. 25: Oct.1965, 1-12.

2421. My Three Angels by Sam and Bella Spewack.
      Based on Albert Husson's La Cuisine
      des Anges.

      Full. 7 m. 3 f.

      In - Theatre. 38: June 1954, 34-61.

2422. My Unfinished Portrait by Ferdinand Voteur.

      Full. 8 m. 6 f.

      In - Poet Lore. 56: Jan.1951, 3-75.

2423. Myrrha by Olga Petrova.

      Full. 4 m. 4 f.

      In - Poet Lore. 60: Dec.1965, 291-344.

2424. The Mysterious Stranger by Jessie Nicholson.

      Short. 4 m. 3 f.

      In - Plays. 11: May 1952, 32-41.

2425. The Mysterious Stranger by Jessie Nicholson.

      Short. 4 m. 3 f.

      In - Plays. 18: April 1959, 47-56.

2426. Mystery at Knob Creek Farm by Helen Louise
      Miller.

      Short. 6 m. 5 f.

      In - Plays. 18: Feb.1959, 55-61.

2427. The Mystery in the Lab by John Murray.

      Short. 4 m. 3 f.

      In - Plays. 12: Jan.1953, 20-32.

2428. Mystery Manor by John Murray.

      Short. 3 m. 4 f.

      In - Plays. 28: Oct.1968, 33-46.

2429. The Mystery of Patriot Inn by Jessie Nicholson.

      Short. 5 m. 3 f.

      In - Plays. 17: Feb.1958, 35-42.

2430. The Mystery of the Gumdrop Dragon by Gerry
      Lynn Burtle.

      Short. 8 m. 6 f. 5 un.

      In - Plays. 19: May 1960, 35-46.

2431. The Mystery of Turkey-Lurkey by Helen
      Louise Miller.

      Short. 4 m. 2 f. 1 un. +X.

      In - Plays. 17: Nov.1957, 55-60.

2432. The Mystery Ring by Nathalie F. Gross.

      Short. 0 m. 8 f.

      In - Plays. 16: Jan.1957, 77-81.

2433. Mystic Land of Magic Music by Elva Numma.

      Short. 0 m. 1 f. 4 g.

      In - Etude. 52: Oct.1934, 581-582.

2434. "N" for Nuisance by Helen Louise Miller.
       Short. 3 m. 3 f.
       In - Plays. 12: Jan.1953, 1-12.

2435. Names of Note by Marjorie Mueller Freer.
       Radio. 5 m. 1 f.
       In - Plays. 5: April 1946, 82-86.

2436. The Names He Loved to Hear by Graham DuBois.
       Short. 3 m. 3 f.
       In - Plays. 13: Jan.1954, 27-37.

2437. Names to Remember by Helen Ramsey.
       Short. 1 m. 1 f. 10 un.
       In - Plays. 16: Nov.1956, 67-68.

2438. The Naming of the Flowers by Marjorie Ann
              York.
       Short. 12 m. 10 f.
       In - Plays. 11: March 1952, 73-77.

2439. Naomi-of-the-Inn by Helen E. Waite and Elbert
              M. Hoppenstedt.
       Short. 8 m. 7 f. +ch.
       In - Plays. 8: Dec.1948, 29-36.

2440. Napoleon Crossing the Rockies by Percy MacKaye.
       Short. 3 m. 1 f.
       In - Century. 107: April 1924, 867-882.

2441. Narcissus by Laurent Lourson. Trans. from
              the French by Donald Watson.
       Short. 3 m. 2 f.
       In - Gambit. 1: no.2, 72-97.

2442. Narrow Man by Anne Howard Bailey.
       Short. 4 m. 1 f. +c.X.
       In - Writer. 70: April 1957, 22-28.

2443. Narrow Road to the Deep North by Edward Bond.
       Full. 9 m. 1 f. +X.
       In - Players. 15: Sept.1968, 27-42.

2444. A Narrow Squeak by Dorothy Deming.
       Short. 1 m. 4 f.
       In - Plays. 9: April 1950, 21-25.

2445. The Narrowest Street by Richard M. Morse.
       Short. 6 m. 3 f. +X.
       In - Theatre. 29: Sept.1945, 523-531.

2446. Nathan Hale by Riley Hughes.
       Short. 4 m. 0 f.
       In - Plays. 3: Oct.1943, 33-37.

2447. Nathaniel Hawthorne and the Curse of the
              Pyncheons by Marion A. Taylor.
       Short. 7 m. 4 f.
       In - Plays. 19: March 1960, 84-96.

2448. The National Everything by John Murray.
       Short. 9 m. 6 f.
       In - Plays. 28: Nov.1968, 1-12.

2449. National Notes by Helen O. Bates.
       Short. 0 m. 10 f. +f.X.
       In - Etude. 54: March 1936, 192.

2450. A Nation's Song Is Born by Katherine Little
              Bakeless.
       Radio. 9 m. 1 f.
       In - Plays. 3: Dec.1943, 70-77.

2451. The Natives are Restless Tonight by Earl J.
              Dias.
       Short. 10 m. 3 f.
       In - Plays. 17: Jan.1958, 1-14.

2452. Nativity by Charles L. O'Donnell.
       In - Lippincott's. 82: Dec.1908, 713-716.

2453. Naughty Susan by Mary O. Slingluff.
       Short. 3 m. 4 f.
       In - Plays. 8: Jan.1949, 38-41.

2454. The Nautical Sheep by Jessie Nicholson.
       Short. 0 m. 0 f. 1 b. 1 g. 5 c.
       In - Plays. 10: Jan.1951, 59-63.

2455. The Navy and the Pirates by Eleanora Bowling
              Kane.
       Radio. 14 m. 1 f.
       In - Plays. 7: May 1948, 77-81.

2456. The Necklace adap. by Dean Charel. Based
              on the story by Guy deMaupassant.
       Short. 3 m. 3 f.
       In - Scholastic. 32: Jan.7,1939, 21E-23E+.

2457. The Necklace by Guy de Maupassant. Adap.
              by Walter Hackett.
       Radio. 11 m. 3 f.
       In - Plays. 9: Jan.1950, 76-87.

2458. A Needle Fights for Freedom by Esther MacLellan and Catherine V. Schroll.

Short. 3 m. 6 f.

In - Plays. 10: Feb.1951, 59-61.

2459. Neighbours by James Saunders.

Short. 1 m. 1 f.

In - Players. 14: Sept.1967, 19-27.

2460. Neighbors to the North by Mildred Hark McQueen.

Short. 17 m. 8 f. +X.

In - Plays. 22: Nov.1962, 79-88.

2461. Nemesis by Augustus Thomas.

Short. 7 m. 4 f.

In - Everybody's. 45: July 1921, 106-112.

2462. The Nerve of Napoleon by Juliet Garver.

Short. 4 m. 6 f.

In - Plays. 16: Oct.1956, 1-10.

2463. Nervous Prostration by Marie Manning.

Short. 3 m. 8 f. 1 c.

In - Harper's M. 125: Sept.1912, 641-644.

2464. Never Any Excuse by Graham DuBois.

Short. 10 m. 2 f.

In - Plays. 7: Feb.1948, 11-22.

2465. Never the Twain by Lydia Glover Deseo.

Short. 3 m. 3 f.

In - Poet Lore. 41: April 1930, 272-292.

2466. The New Broom by Mildred Hark and Noel McQueen.

Short. 3 m. 7 f.

In - Plays. 6: Oct.1946, 39-44.

2467. A New Compass by May Emery Hall.

Short. 5 m. 0 f. +m.X.

In - Plays. 4: April 1945, 29-36.

2468. New-Fangled Thanksgiving by Mildred Hark and Noel McQueen.

Short. 4 m. 3 f.

In - Plays. 8: Nov.1948, 25-31.

2469. New Hearts for Old by Aileen Fisher.

Short. 3 m. 3 f.

In - Plays. 10: Feb.1951, 34-40.

2470. A New Home for Mice by Sally Werner.

Short. 6 un. +X.

In - Plays. 15: Nov.1955, 65-67.

2471. The New New Year by Ada M. Skinner.

Short. 1 m. 1 f. 2 g. 2 b. 13 c.

In - St.Nicholas. 45: Jan.1918, 257-262.

2472. New Nigger by Fred Howard.

Short. 6 m. 2 f.

In - Carolina. 9: Sept.1936, 69-86.

2473. The New-Old Christmas by Doris L. Edwards.

Short. 7 m. 6 f.

In - Plays. 14: Dec.1954, 75-80.

2474. New Shoes by Helen Louise Miller.

Short. 3 m. 2 f. 13 un. +ch. +X.

In - Plays. 13: May 1954, 79-83.

2475. New Shoes by Helen Louise Miller.

Short. 3 m. 1 f. +X.

In - Plays. 26: May 1967, 85-89.

2476. The New Washington by Deborah Newman.

Short. 4 m. 6 f. +X.

In - Plays. 14: Feb.1955, 67-70.

2477. The New Wing At Elsinore by St. John Hankin.

Short. 5 m. 0 f.

In - Golden. 16: Oct.1932, 361-364.

2478. New Worlds by Jean Gould.

Short. 9 m. 1 f. +m.X.

In - Plays. 10: Oct.1950, 45-52.

2479. New Worlds by Jean Gould.

Short. 9 m. 1 f.

In - Plays. 28: Oct.1968, 55-61.

2480. New Year's Day by Helen M. Palmer.

In - Harper's B. 35: May 1901, 43-48.

Nicholas Nickleby.

see

Over the Garden Wall.

2481. A Night At an Inn by Lord Dunsany.

Short. y m. 0 f.

In - Golden. 4: Sept.1926, 377-381.

2482. The Night Before Christmas by William Dean Howells.

Short. 4 m. 4 f.

In - Harper's M. 120: Jan.1910, 207-216.

2483. Night Before Christmas by Margaret Freeman Turner.

Short. 0 m. 1 f. 3 b. 8 g.

In - Etude. 57: Dec.1939, 771-772.

2484. Night Brings a Counselor by Lilian Saunders.

Short. 1 m. 1 f.

In - Drama. 13: April 1923, 251-253.

2485. Night of Decision by Graham DuBois.

Short. 3 m. 3 f.

In - Plays. 21: Feb.1962, 1-10.

2486. Night of the Iguana by Tennessee Williams.

In - Esquire. 57: Feb.1962, 47-62+.

2487. The Night of the Iguana by Tennessee Williams.

Full. 8 m. 6 f.

In - Players. 12: May & June 1965, 23-30, & 23-30+.

2488. Night Train by Herbert Reinecker. Trans. from the German by Martha A. Fisher.

Full. 11 m. 2 f.

In - Mod. Drama. 1: Sept.1967, 65-102.

2489. The Nightcap of the Prophet Elias by August von Kotzebue. Trans. by Beatrice B. Beebe.

Short. 7 m. 1 f.

In - Poet Lore. 40: Sept.1929, 391-406.

2490. Nightingale; an Arabian Night's Fantasy by Alice Henson Ernst.

Short. 9 m. 2 f. +X.

In - Poet Lore. 37: June 1926, 293-314.

2491. A Night's Lodging by Maxim Gorki. Trans. from the Russian by Edwin Hopkins.

Full. 13 m. 4 f. +X.

In - Poet Lore. 16:no.4,1905, 3-64.

2492. Nine Times Christmas by Lewy Olfson.

Short. 7 m. 4 f.

In - Plays. 19: Dec.1959, 37-46.

2493. The Ninth Night by Victor Dyk. Trans. from the Bohemian by Cyril Jeffrey Arbek.

Short. 2 m. 2 f.

In - Poet Lore. 29:no.1,1918, 90-101.

2494. The No 'Count Boy by Paul Green.

Short. 2 m. 2 f.

In - Theatre. 8: Nov.1924, 773-784.

2495. No Garden This Year by Paul S. McCoy.

Short. 2 m. 1 f.

In - Plays. 17: April 1958, 81-85.

2496. No Hats, No Banquets by Ruth Brodsky.

Full. 15 m. 5 f. +X.

In - First Stage. 2: March 1963, 133-157.

2497. No Picnic by Marjorie B. Paradis.

Short. 3 m. 3 f.

In - Plays. 6: May 1947, 16-24.

2498. No Room at the Inn by Emma L. Patterson.

Short. 15 m. 1 f. +X.

In - Plays. 9: Dec.1949, 19-25.

2499. No Room in the Hotel by Dorothy Clarke Wilson.

Short. 5 m. 4 f.

In - Scholastic. 39: Dec.15,1941, 17-19+.

2500. No Treat for Gilbert by Paul S. McCoy.

Short. 2 m. 3 f.

In - Plays. 18: Oct.1958, 13-24.

2501. Nobody Believes in Witches! by Martha Swintz Watkins.

Short. 3 m. 3 f. +X.

In - Plays. 25: Oct.1965, 48-54.

2502. Noctes Ambrosiae by Kenneth Roberts.

Short. 4 m. 4 f. 1 parrot.

In - Sat. Evening. 201: Aug.11,1928, 33+.

2503. Non-Fiction Party by Ruth Dean.

Short. 4 m. 6 f. 1 b.

In - Wilson. 10: Nov.1935, 200-204+.

2504. Non-Fiction Party by Ruth Dean. (Abr.)

Short. 4 m. 6 f. 1 b.

In - Scholastic. 33: Nov.12,1938, 5-7.

2505. None But the Fair by Marjorie B. Paradis.

Short. 3 m. 3 f. +ch.

In - Plays. 14: Dec.1954, 24-32.

2506. None So Blind by Graham DuBois.

Short. 4 m. 4 f.

In - Plays. 9: March 1950, 31-40.

2507. The Noose by Tracy Dickinson Mygatt.

Short. 4 m. 2 f. +X.

In - Drama. 20: Nov.1929, 42-48.

2508. Nor Long Remember by Anne Coulter Martens.

Short. 5 m. 5 f.

In - Plays. 22: May 1963, 15-28.

2509. North Pole Confidential by Stanley C. Jensen.

Short. 5 m. 4 f.

In - Plays. 14: Dec.1954, 81-86.

2510. The North Wind and the Sun by Rowena Bennett.

Short. 1 m. 6 un.

In - Plays. 7: Dec.1947, 54-56.

2511. Northwest Passage. From the movie scenario based on the novel by Kenneth Roberts.

Short. 9 m. 0 f.

In - Scholastic. 36: Feb.26,1940, 19-22.

2512. The Nose by John A. Stone. Inspired by Gogol's short story.

Full. 16 m. 4 f. 2 life-size dog marionettes.

In - First Stage. 3: June 1964, 179-219.

2513. Not At Home by Henri Lavedan. Trans. from the French of Les Beaux Dimanches by by Sibyl Collar Holbrook.

Short. 2 m. 3 f.

In - Poet Lore. 28:no.4,1917, 407-413.

2514. Not Enough Rope by Elaine May.

Short. 1 m. 2 f.

In - Mlle. 66: Nov.1967, 152-153+.

2515. Not Fit for Man or Beast by Mildred Hark and Noel McQueen.

Short. 4 m. 3 f.

In - Plays. 13: Jan.1954, 47-56.

2516. Not Fit for Man or Beast by Mildred Hark and Noel McQueen.

Short. 4 m. 3 f.

In - Plays. 23: Jan.1964, 59-67.

2517. Not for Girls by Helen Louise Miller.

Short. 4 m. 5 f.

In - Plays. 14: May 1955, 44-52.

2518. Not For Ladies by Gladys L. Schmitt.

Radio. 4 m. 2 f.

In - Scholastic. 30: May 15,1937, 8-9.

2519. Not for Publication by Earl J. Dias.

Short. 5 m. 4 f.

In - Plays. 22: Oct.1962, 15-25.

2520. Not so Old as Some. Anon.

Short. 2 m. 2 f.

In - Survey. 72: July 1936, 203.

2521. Not So Simple Simon by Claribel Spamer.

Short. 4 m. 3 f.

In - Plays. 4: Nov.1944, 45-46.

2522. Not Worth a Continental by Marion L. Miller.

Short. 4 m. 2 f.

In - Plays. 12: Jan.1953, 12-20.

2523. Nothing To Be Thankful For by Edrie Pendleton.

Short. 3 m. 2 f.

In - Plays. 10: Nov.1950, 27-35.

2524. Nothing to be Thankful For by Mildred Hark and Noel McQueen.

Short. 3 m. 2 f.

In - Plays. 26: Nov.1966, 53-62.

2525. Nothing To Wear by Helen Louise Miller.

Short. 2 m. 4 f.

In - Plays. 5: March 1946, 1-11.

2526. Nothing Very Much Thank You by Patrick O'Connor.

Full. 10 m. 6 f. +X.

In - First Stage. 6: Dec.1967, 230-248.

2527. Now I Lay Me Down to Sleep by Elaine Ryan.

Full. 24 m. 12 f.

In - Theatre. 34: July 1950, 57-88.

2528. Nude with Violin by Noel Coward.

Full. 8 m. 6 f.

In - Players. 4: Dec.1956 & Jan.1957, 23-32, 23-30.

2529. Number One Apple Tree Lane by Claire Boiko.

Short. 4 m. 2 f. 11 un.

In - Plays. 27: May 1968, 69-73.

2530. Nursery Rhyme Diet by Mildred Hark and Noel McQueen.

Short. 7 m. 7 f.

In - Plays. 11: Oct.1951, 50-54.

2531. Nursing in the Mountains by Dorothy Deming.

Short. 1 m. 4 f.

In - Plays. 8: March 1949, 62-66.

2532. Odd Man In by Claude Magnier. Adap. by
Robin Maugham.

Full. 2 m. 1 f.

In - Players. 5: Dec.1957 & Jan.1958, 23-28,
23-28.

2533. An Ode to Spring by Mildred Hark and Noel
McQueen.

Short. 5 m. 6 f.

In - Plays. 12: April 1953, 1-14.

2534. An Ode to Spring by Mildred Hark and
Noel McQueen.

Short. 5 m. 6 f.

In - Plays. 25: May 1966, 41-53.

2535. The Odyssey by Homer. Adap. by Levy Olfson.

Radio. 13 m. 4 f.

In - Plays. 20: Oct.1960, 83-93.

2536. O'Fallon's Cup by Roy Marz.

Full. 5 m. 3 f.

In - First Stage. 5: June 1966, 90-119.

2537. Off the Road by Pauline Rodgers Young.

In - Poet Lore. 36: June 1925, 300-305.

2538. Off the Shelf by Mildred Hark and Noel
McQueen.

Short. 5 m. 3 f.

In - Plays. 4: Nov.1944, 29-35.

2539. Oft In the Stilly Night by Marian Spencer
Smith.

In - Drama. 15: Jan.1925, 75.

2540. The Ogre Who Built a Bridge adap. by Frances
Mapp from a Japanese Folk Tale.

Short. 3 m. 2 f. 5 c.

In - Plays. 28: Nov.1968, 77-82.

2541. Oh Dad, Poor Dad, Mama's Hung You in the
Closet and I'm Feelin' So Sad by
Arthur Kopit.

Full. 9 m. 2 f.

In - Players. 13: Nov.&Dec.1965, 24-30,
23-30+.

2542. Old Four-Legs by Mary Nygaard Peterson.

Short. 4 m. 2 f.

In - Plays. 17: May 1958, 65-68.

2543. Old Ghosts at Home by John Murray.

Short. 4 m. 5 f.

In - Plays. 19: Oct.1959, 1-15.

2544. Old Glory Grows Up by Helen Louise Miller.

Short. 5 m. 4 f. +10 X.

In - Plays. 19: Feb.1960, 83-87.

2545. Old King Cole's Christmas by Marguerite
Atherton.

Short. 7 m. 4 f. +X.

In - Plays. 17: Dec.1957, 70-74.

2546. The Old Love Affair by August Von Kotzebue.
Trans. from the German by Beatrice B.
Beebe.

Short. 1 m. 2 f.

In - Poet Lore. 38: June 1927, 220-239.

2547. Old Mother Hubbard adap. by June Barr.

Short. 5 m. 3 f. +c.X.

In - Plays. 9: Jan.1950, 57-62.

2548. Old Order by Evelyn Emig.

In - Poet Lore. 32: Dec.1921, 586-595.

2549. Old Peabody Pew by Kate Douglas Wiggin.

Full. 1 m. 8 f.

In - Ladies' Home. 34: Feb.1917, 214.

2550. Old Pipes and the Dryad by Frank R. Stockton.
Adap. by Adele Thane.

Short. 4 m. 3 f. +c.X.

In - Plays. 23: Jan.1964, 49-58.

2551. Old Wash Lucas by Paul Green.

Short. 3 m. 1 f.

In - Poet Lore. 35: June 1924, 254-270.

2552. The Old Woman and Her Pig by Alice Very.

Short. 1 m. 1 f. 10 c.

In - Plays. 3: March 1944, 53-55.

2553. The Oldest Trick in the World by Jay
Thompson.

Short (musical). 0 m. 1 f.(white) 2 f.(Negro).

In - Theatre. 45: July 1961, 40-52.

2554. Oliver Bean by Burgess Meredith.

Radio. 4 m. 1 f.

In - Scholastic. 31: Jan.22,1938, 21E-22E+.

2555. <u>Oliver Twist</u> by Charles Dickens. Adap. by Sarah Agnes Wallace.

Excerpts. 11 m. 4 f. 7 b.

In - Education. 50: April 1930, 499-506.

2556. <u>Oliver Twist</u> by Charles Dickens. Adap. by Levy Olfson.

Radio. 5 m. 4 f. 2 b.

In - Plays. 20: Jan.1961, 90-96.

2557. <u>Oliver Twist</u> by Charles Dickens. Adap. by Ronald K. Side.

Short. 9 m. 5 f. 15 b. +X.

In - Plays. 24: May 1965, 87-98.

<u>Oliver Twist.</u>

see

<u>Scenes from Oliver Twist.</u>

2559. <u>Olives</u> by Lope de Rueda. Trans. by W.K. Jones.

In - Poet Lore. 39: June 1928, 310-313.

2560. <u>Ollantay</u> by Padre Mossi. Trans. from the Spanish by Nuria Halty and Howard Richardson.

Full. 9 m. 5 f. +X.

In - First Stage. 6: March 1967, 12-36.

2561. <u>Olympus, Farewell</u> by Jefferson Bayley.

Full. 14 m. 4 f. +X.

In - First Stage. 2: Sept.1963, 336-362.

2562. <u>Omega's Ninth</u> by Ramon Delgado.

Short. 1 m. 1 f. 1 cat.

In - First Stage. 3: Dec.1963, 7-12.

2563. <u>On a Bicycle Built for One</u> by Samuel S. Richmond.

Short. 3 m. 3 f.

In - Plays. 8: March 1949, 31-35.

2564. <u>On Bayou La Batre</u> by Bessie Collins Moore.

Short. 1 m. 2 f.

In - Poet Lore. 37: Dec.1926, 576-582.

2565. <u>On Being a Goop</u> by Azile M. Wofford.

Short. 0 m. 0 f. 4 b. 1 g.

In - Wilson. 5: June 1931, 635.

2566. <u>On Probation</u> by Max Dreyer. Trans. by Mary Harned.

Full. 11 m. 4 f. 1 b.

In - Poet Lore. 14:no.2,1903, 40-113.

2567. <u>On Strike</u> by Aileen Fisher.

Short. 8 un.

In - Plays. 10: May 1951, 35-42.

2568. <u>On Such a Night</u> by Aileen Fisher.

Short. 4 m. 1 f. +X.

In - Plays. 12: Dec.1952, 50-53.

2569. <u>On the Air</u> by Leslie Hollingsworth.

Radio. 5 m. 3 f. 2 b. 1 g. +X.

In - Plays. 4: Dec.1944, 79-84.

2570. <u>On the Air</u> by Samuel S. Richmond.

Short. 4 m. 4 f.

In - Plays. 7: Oct.1948, 75-82.

2571. <u>On the Fence</u> by Marcia Moray Beach.

Short. 4 m. 3 f.

In - Plays. 10: March 1951, 33-41.

2572. <u>On the Fence</u> by Marcia Moray Beach.

Short. 4 m. 3 f.

In - Plays. 21: May 1962, 45-53.

2573. <u>On the Hire System</u> by L. Lockhart Lang.

Full. 2 m. 3 f.

In - Blackwood's. 170: Nov.1901, 591-612.

2574. <u>On the Lot</u> by Florence Ryerson and Colin Campbell Clements.

Short. 2 m. 1 f.

In - Drama. 19: Nov.1928, 46-47.

2575. <u>On the Racecourse</u> by Lady Gregory.

Short. 2 m. 1 f. +X.

In - Golden. 8: Sept.1928, 364-368.

2576. <u>On the Razor Edge</u> by Rupert Hughes.

In - Lippincott's. 85: Jan.1910, 73-82.

2577. <u>On the Shelf</u> by Christopher Morley.

In - Lit. Review. 4: Dec.22,1923, 385-386.

2578. <u>On the Terrace</u> by Ivo Vojnovich. Trans. from the Croatian by John J. Batistich and George Rapall Noyes.

Full. 10 m. 12 f.

In - Poet Lore. 56:no.4,1951, 291-340.

2579. <u>On Trial</u> by Samuel S. Richmond.

Short. 2 m. 1 f.

In - Plays. 5: Feb.1946, 67-71.

2580. Once Around the Block by William Saroyan.

Short. 3 m. 1 f.

In - American Merc. 69: Dec.1949, 663-675.

2581. Once in a Lifetime by Moss Hart and George S. Kaufman.

Excerpt. 0 m. 4 f.

In - Theatre. 22: Sept.1938, 692.

2582. Once Upon a Christmastime by Carolyn Wells.

Short. many c.

In - Ladies' Home. 31: Nov.1914, 75.

2583. Once Upon a Mattress by Jay Thompson, Marshall Barer and Dean Fuller. Music by Mary Rodgers.

Full (musical). 15 m. 14 f.

In - Theatre. 44: July 1960, 26-50.

2584. Once Upon A Time by Aileen Fisher.

Short. 11 m. 5 f. +c.X.

In - Plays. 10: Nov.1950, 70-78.

2585. Ondine by Jean Giraudoux. Adap. by Maurice Valency.

Full. 17 m. 12 f.

In - Theatre. 38: Dec.1954, 32-63.

2586. One Life to Lose by Anne Coulter Martens.

Short. 6 m. 6 f. 4 un.

In - Plays. 27: May 1968, 13-22.

2587. One May Spin a Thread Too Finely by Ivan Tourguenieff. Trans. by Margaret Gough.

Short. 5 m. 4 f.

In - Fortnightly. 85: April 1909, 786-804.

2588. One More River by Beverley Cross.

Full. 12 m. 0 f.

In - Players. 7: Nov. & Dec.1959, 24-30, 28-30.

2589. One Night in Bethlehem by Deborah Newman.

Short. 3 m. 5 f. +X.

In - Plays. 20: Dec.1960, 47-51.

2590. One-Ring Circus by Aileen Fisher.

Short. 6 m. 3 f.

In - Plays. 7: March 1948, 33-38.

2591. One to Grow On by Helen Louise Miller.

Short. 10 m. 9 f. 6 c.

In - Plays. 24: April 1965, 35-44.

2592. One Way Pendulum by N.F. Simpson.

Full. 10 m. 4 f.

In - Players. 17: March & April 1960, 27-31+, 25-30.

2593. The Onward Path by Edward Golden.

Radio. 2 m. 4 f.

In - Plays. 13: March 1954, 83-94.

2594. Open House by Anne Coulter Martens.

Short. 0 m. 23 f. +X.

In - Plays. 24: Oct.1964, 17-28.

2595. Open Twenty-Four Hours by Roger N. Cornish.

Short. 5 m. 2 f.

In - First Stage. 7: Sept.1968, 39-55.

2596. Operation Litterbug by Claire Boiko.

Short. 8 m. 2 f.

In - Plays. 20: April 1961, 65-69.

2597. Orange Soufflé by Saul Bellow.

Short. 1 m. 1 f.

In - Esquire. 64: Oct.1965, 130-131+.

2598. Orchids for Margaret by Pearl and Thatcher Allred.

Short. 2 m. 3 f.

In - Plays. 4: April 1945, 1-17.

2599. Orchids for Margaret by Pearl and Thatcher Allred.

Short. 2 m. 3 f.

In - Plays. 14: Jan.1955, 1-17.

2600. Orchids for Margaret by Pearl & Thatcher Allred.

Short. 2 m. 3 f.

In - Plays. 27: March 1968, 23-39.

2601. The Order of Release by Laurence Housman.

Short. 1 m. 2 f.

In - Fortnightly. 126: Sept.1926, 289-297.

2602. Orpheus and Eurydice by T. Sturge Moore.

In - Fortnightly. 92 sup: Dec.1909, 1-26.

2603. Orpheus Descending by Tennessee Williams.

Full. 10 m. 9 f.

In - Theatre. 42: Sept.1958, 26-55.

2604. <u>Orthodoxy</u> by Nina Wilcox Putnam.

Short. 18 m. 11 f. +ch.

In - Forum. 51: June 1914, 801-820.

2605. <u>The Other Room</u> by Harry Major Paull.

Short. 3 m. 2 f.

In - 19th C. 90: Nov.1921, 807-818.

2606. <u>The Other Room</u> by Frances Witherspoon.

Short. 3 m. 2 f.

In - Poet Lore. 38: June 1927, 269-290.

2607. <u>The Other Side of the Door</u> by Roland English Hartley.

Short. 2 m. 2 f.

In - Poet Lore. 41: April 1930, 223-238.

2608. <u>The Other Side of the Wall</u> by Patricia Clapp.

Short. 4 m. 3 f. +X.

In - Plays. 22: Feb.1963, 45-52.

2609. <u>An Ounce of Safety</u> by Louis Quentin Moss.

Short. 7 m. 0 f.

In - Indus. Educa. 37: Nov.1935, 242-247.

2610. <u>Our Book Hospital</u> by Ira Lois Brown.

Short. 1 m. 1 f.

In - Wilson. 29: April 1955, 640-641.

2611. <u>Our Famous Ancestors</u> by Mildred Hark and Noel McQueen.

Short. 2 m. 3 f.

In - Plays. 13: Nov.1953, 1-11.

2612. <u>Our Famous Ancestors</u> by Mildred Hark and Noel McQueen.

Short. 2 m. 3 f.

In - Plays. 25: Nov.1965, 27-36.

2613. <u>Our 49th State</u> by Aileen Fisher.

Short. 13 m. 4 f. 5 un.

In - Plays. 23: Jan.1964, 83-95.

2614. <u>Our Frank</u> by August von Kotzebue. Trans. from the German by Beatrice B. Beebe.

Short. 2 m. 2 f. 1 b.

In - Poet Lore. 38: June 1927, 206-219.

2615. <u>Our Library</u> by Alice F. Gilmore.

Short. 1 un. many c.

In - Wilson. 5: Nov.1930, 186-191.

2616. <u>Our Own Four Walls</u> by Mildred Hark and Noel McQueen.

Short. 3 m. 3 f.

In - Plays. 5: April 1946, 40-46.

2617. <u>Our Sister, Sitya</u> by Paul T. Nolan.

Short. 6 m. 2 f.

In - Plays. 19: Feb.1960, 91-96.

2618. <u>Out from Under</u> by Olive Rabe and Charles Baker.

Short. 8 m. 0 f.

In - Plays. 6: Feb.1947, 27-39.

2619. <u>Out of the Clock</u> by Rowena Bennett.

Short. 0 m. 0 f. 3 c.

In - Plays. 4: Jan.1945, 54-56.

2620. <u>Out of the Past</u> by Charles Gordon Rogers.

In - Canadian M. 30: Dec.1907, 102-109.

2621. <u>Out of This World</u> by Earl J. Dias.

Short. 2 m. 4 f.

In - Plays. 7: Feb.1948, 32-40.

2622. <u>Out of This World</u> by Earl J. Dias.

Short. 2 m. 4 f.

In - Plays. 22: Feb.1963, 13-21.

2623. <u>The Outcast</u> by August Strindberg. Trans. from the German of Emil Schering by Mary Harned.

Short. 2 m. 0 f.

In - Poet Lore. 17:no.3,1906, 8-21.

2624. <u>Outcasts</u> by Edward R. Sammis.

In - Poet Lore. 36: June 1925, 306-310.

2625. <u>The Outgoing Tide</u> by Walter Hackett.

Short. 4 m. 3 f.

In - Plays. 9: May 1950, 79-90.

2626. <u>Outside the Gate</u> by Dora Greenwell McChesney.

In - Fortnightly. 80: Dec.1903, 1035-1040.

2627. <u>Over the Garden Wall</u> by Daisy Melville Vance. From Charles Dickens' <u>Nicholas Nickleby</u>.

Short. 2 m. 2 f.

In - Scholastic. 29: Jan.30,1937, 6-7+.

2628. <u>Over the River</u> by Anne Coulter Martens.

Short. 8 m. 6 f.

In - Plays. 25: Nov.1965, 1-14.

2629. Overruled by George Bernard Shaw.

Short. 1 m. 2 f.

In - Hearst's. 23: May 1913, 680-696.

2630. The Owl Answers by Adrienne Kennedy.

Short. 5 m. 2 f. 1 un.

In - Poet Lore. 60: Sept.1965, 195-211.

2631. The Owl's Answer by Loleta Hagy.

Short. 2 m. 1 f.

In - Plays. 3: Oct.1943, 59-61.

2632. The Pageant of the Shearmen and Tailors
        adap. by John Mason Brown.

Short. 11 m. 1 f. 1 baby.

In - Theatre. 9: Dec.1925, 824-835.

2633. The Pageant of the Triads by Helen O. Bates.

Short. 9 un. +X.

In - Etude. 52: Dec.1934, 760-761.

2634. Paint Your Wagon by Alan Jay Lerner.

Full (musical). 19 m. 5 f. +ch.

In - Theatre. 36: Dec.1952, 36-60.

2635. The Painter and the Millionaire by Harry
        Major Paull.

Full. 12 characters +X.

In - Fortnightly. 86: Dec.1909, 1115-1136.

2636. The Pajama Game by George Abbott and
        Richard Bissell. Music and lyrics by
        Richard Adler and Jerry Ross.

Full (musical). 13 m. 5 f. +X & ch.

In - Theatre. 39: Sept.1955, 34-61.

2637. Paloma, Princess of Pluto by Vernon Howard.

Short. 2 m. 2 f.

In - Plays. 13: Jan.1954, 82-85.

2638. Pam Wilson, Night Nurse by Dorothy Deming.

Short. 1 m. 4 f.

In - Plays. 6: Oct.1946, 68-72.

2639. The Pamperers by Mina Loy.

Short. Miscellaneous characters, not all
        human.

In - Dial. 69: July 1920, 65-78.

2640. Pandora's Box by Karin Asbrand.

Short. 4 m. 6 f. +X.

In - Plays. 15: Jan.1956, 79-82.

2641. Panic in the Palace by Martha Swintz.

Short. 8 m. 5 f. +X.

In - Plays. 11: Jan.1952, 33-42.

2642. Pansy's Surprise by Sylvia Lee.

Short. 1 f. 11 un.

In - Plays. 13: Jan.1954, 75-77.

2643. Pantagleize by Michel de Ghelderode.
        Trans. by George Hauger.

Full. 15 m. 1 f. +X.

In - Theatre. 46: Aug.1962, 28-56.

2644. Papa and Mama by Eduardo Barrios. Trans.
        from the Spanish by Willis Knapp Jones.

Short. 1 m. 1 f.

In - Poet Lore. 33: June 1922, 286-290.

2645. Papá Juan or The Centenarian by Serafín
        and Joaquín Alvarez Quintero. Trans.
        from the Spanish by Thomas Walsh.

Full. 6 m. 6 f.

In - Poet Lore. 29:no.3,1918, 253-318.

2646. Papa Pepper's Bombshell by Helen Louise
        Miller.

Short. 3 m. 3 f.

In - Plays. 12: March 1953, 9-17.

2647. The Paper Bag Mystery by Helen Louise Miller.

Short. 6 m. 1 f. 6 g.

In - Plays. 25: Nov.1965, 47-55.

2648. The Paper Princess by Cena Christopher
        Draper.

Short. 1 m. 2 f.

In - Plays. 10: Feb.1951, 46-49.

2649. Paris and Oenone by Laurence Binyon.

In - Fortnightly. 83: June 1905, 1137-1146.

2650. Paris and Oenone by W.G. Hale.

Short. 2 m. 2 f.

In - Contemporary. 94 Lit.Sup.: Nov.1908, 1-5.

2651. Paris Impromptu by Jean Giraudoux.

Short. 12 m. 2 f.

In - Theatre. 22: March 1938, 218-230.

2652. Paris Interlude by Morris Brennan.

Short. 4 m. 0 f. +X.

In - Scholastic. 28: March 28,1936, 11-12.

2653. The Parrot and the Pirates by Helen Louise
Miller.

Short. 7 m. 0 f. +m.X.

In - Plays. 23: Nov.1963, 51-56.

2654. The Parrot Who Would Not Talk by Rita
Whitman Steingold.

Short. 2 m. 1 f. 4 un. +X.

In - Plays. 28: Nov.1968, 73-76.

2655. Part-Time Hero by Helen Louise Miller.

Short. 2 m. 3 f.

In - Plays. 6: May 1947, 25-31.

The Part You Can't Get in Your Mouth.

see

The Inheritors.

2657. Parting Friends by William Dean Howells.

Short. 2 m. 4 f.

In - Harper's M. 121: Oct.1910, 670-677.

2658. Partners in Velvet by Louise Jay Hazam.

Radio. 11 m. 4 f.

In - Scholastic. 58: March 21,1951, 12-13+.

2659. Party Dress by Marjorie B. Paradis.

Short. 4 m. 4 f.

In - Plays. 5: Feb.1946, 16-23.

2660. Party Line by Helen Louise Miller.

Short. 3 m. 4 f.

In - Plays. 17: March 1958, 29-38.

2661. Party of the Third Part by Clara Stow.

Short. 1 m. 2 f.

In - Drama. 15: Feb.1925, 110-111.

2662. Pascualina by Antonio Souza.

Short. 0 m. 4 f.

In - Américas. 9: Dec.1957, 22-25.

2663. The Pasculas by Isidora Aguirre. Trans. by
Willis Knapp Jones.

Full. 2 m. 6 f.

In - Poet Lore. 59: Dec.1964, 291-336.

2664. Pasque Flower by Gwendolyn Pharis.

Short. 2 m. 1 f.

In - Carolina. 12: March 1939, 7-20.

2665. A Passage to India by Santha Rama Rau.
From the novel by E.M. Forster.

Full. 13 m. 6 f. +X.

In - Theatre. 46: April 1962, 25-56.

2666. The Passer-By by Coppée. Trans. from the
French by Lucile Dora.

Short. 1 m. 1 f.

In - Poet Lore. 34: Sept.1923, 461-470.

2667. The Passing of Dena's People by Anne Abbott
Craig.

Short. 5 m. 4 f. +ch. +X.

In - Poet Lore. 35: Dec.1924, 605-611.

2668. Passion's Furnace by Josip Kosor. Trans.
from the Serbo-Croatian by F.S. Copeland.

Full. 21 m. 7 f. 1 g. +X.

In - Poet Lore. 41: Oct.1930, 459-516.

2669. The Pastrybaker by Lope de Vega. Trans. from
the Spanish by M. Jagendorf.

Short. 5 m. 0 f.

In - Theatre. 19: Sept.1935, 713-721.

2670. The Patchwork Princess by Margaret E. Slattery.

Short. 3 m. 4 f.

In - Plays. 11: April 1952, 30-36.

2671. Pathetic Prologue by Alfonso Sastre. Trans.
from the Spanish by Leonard Pronko.

Short. 11 m. 4 f.

In - Mod. Drama. 1: March 1968, 196-215.

2672. Patrick Pumpkin by Claribel Spamer.

Short. 3 m. 2 f.

In - Plays. 7: Nov.1947, 54-56.

2673. The Patriots by Sydney Kingsley.

Excerpt. 2 m. 2 f.

In - Scholastic. 42: April 12,1943, 15-17.

2674. Paul Bunyan and His Blue Ox adap. by Molly
Cone from an American folk tale.

Short. 2 m. 2 f. 1 "ox".

In - Plays. 26: Jan.1967, 69-74.

2675. Paul Revere Rides Again by Helen Louise
Miller.

Short. 22 m. 9 f.

In - Plays. 14: April 1955, 49-57.

2676. Paul Revere's Cloak by Gertrude Robinson.

Short. 8 m. 0 f. +m.X.

In - Plays. 3: April 1944, 15-24.

2677. <u>Peace at Home</u> by Georges Courteline.

Short. 1 m. 1 f.

In - Poet Lore. 29:no.3,1918, 331-345.

2678. <u>Peace on Earth</u> by Ada Mixon.

Short. 9 m. 4 f. +c.&m.X.

In - Poet Lore. 28:no.1,1917, 65-77.

2679. <u>Peace, Pilgrim</u> by Harold Cable.

Short. 8 m. 7 f. +X.

In - Plays. 26: Nov.1966, 1-14.

2680. <u>The Peach Tree Kingdom</u> by Rosemary Gabbert Musil.

Short. 3 m. 4 f.

In - Plays. 23: Jan.1964, 39-48.

2681. <u>The Pear Tree</u> by Ethel McFarlan.

Short. 3 m. 3 f. +X.

In - Plays. 22: April 1963, 71-73.

2682. <u>Pearls</u> by Dan W. Totheroh. Ed. by Margaret Mayorga.

Excerpt. 1 m. 2 f.

In - Scholastic. 31: Oct.9,1937, 17E-19E.

2683. <u>Pedro and the Burro</u> by Mary Nygaard Peterson.

Short. 4 m. 4 f. 1 "burro". (2 c.)

In - Plays. 18: April 1959, 39-46.

2684. <u>Peggy</u> by Rachel Crothers.

Short. 3 m. 4 f.

In - Scribner's. 76: Aug.1924, 175-183.

2685. <u>Penelope, Pride of the Pickle Factory</u> by Betty Tracy Huff.

Short. 6 m. 6 f.

In - Plays. 25: Feb.1966, 39-49.

2686. <u>The Pennsylvania Parakeet</u> by Helen Louise Miller.

Short. 5 m. 8 f. +X.

In - Plays. 15: Feb.1956, 42-46.

2687. <u>Penny Wise</u> by Claire Boiko.

Short. 3 m. 1 f. 13 c.

In - Plays. 24: Jan.1965, 78-82.

2688. <u>People With Light Coming Out of Them</u> by William Soroyan.

Radio. 9 m. 3 f.

In - Scholastic. 38: March 24, 1941, 17-19+.

2689. <u>The Peppermint Easter Egg</u> by Margaret E. Slattery.

Short. 5 m. 5 f.

In - Plays. 22, April 1963, 35-42.

2690. <u>The Perambulating Pie</u> by Mary Thurman Pyle.

Short. 5 m. 5 f.

In - Plays. 9: Dec.1949, 1-9.

2691. <u>The Perfect Couple</u> by John Murray.

Short. 5 m. 5 f. 1 un. +X.

In - Plays. 19: April 1960, 24-36.

2692. <u>The Perfect Gentleman</u> by W. Somerset Maugham. Adap. from Molière's <u>Le Bourgeois Gentilhomme.</u>

Full. 12 m. 3 f. +X & ch.

In - Theatre. 39: Nov.1955, 49-64.

2693. <u>The Perfect Gift</u> by Graham DuBois.

Short. 10 m. 2 f.

In - Plays. 3: Dec.1943, 12-19.

2694. <u>The Perfect Gift</u> by Graham DuBois.

Short. 9 m. 2 f. 1 b.

In - Plays. 28: Dec.1968, 11-18.

2695. <u>Perfect Tribute</u> by Alice M. Reilly.

Short. 4 m. 1 f. 1 b.

In - Education. 42: Oct.1921, 90-97.

2696. <u>Period of Adjustment</u> by Tennessee Williams.

Full. 4 m. 5 f.

In - Players. 9: August 1962, 25-42.

2697. <u>Perplexing Pirandello</u> by Carla L. Palm.

In - Drama. 15: Feb.1925, 102-104.

2698. <u>Persephone in Eden</u> by S. Foster Damon.

Short. Indefinite un.

In - Dial. 78: June 1925, 445-464.

2699. <u>The Persimmon Thief</u> by Ken Nakazawa.

Short. 3 m. 0 f.

In - Drama. 16: Dec.1925, 97-98.

2700. <u>Peter Gink</u> by Arthur H. Nethercot.

Short. 5 m. 3 f. +X.

In - Poet Lore. 35: March 1924, 118-126.

2701. <u>Peter, Peter, Peter!</u> by Claire Boiko.

Short. 8 m. 4 f.

In - Plays. 23: Feb.1964, 45-54.

2702. **Peter Rabbit Volunteers** by Helen Louise Miller.

Short. 2 m. 1 f. 9 c.

In - Plays. 27: April 1968, 59-64.

2703. **Peter Tomorrow** by Bernard Hirshberg.

Short. 1 m. 0 f. +ch.

In - Plays. 4: March 1945, 54-55.

2704. **Peter's Easter Basket Company** by Betty Gray Blaine.

Short. 5 m. 2 f. 4 c. +X.

In - Plays. 16: April 1957, 35-40.

2705. **Petr Vok Rozmberk** by Frantisek Adolf Subert. Trans. from the Bohemian.

In - Poet Lore. 31: March 1920, 1-68.

2706. **The Petrified Prince** by Helen Louise Miller.

Short. 6 m. 8 f.

In - Plays. 14: Jan.1955, 39-48.

2707. **The Petrified Prince** by Helen Louise Miller.

Short. 6 m. 8 f.

In - Plays. 27: Feb.1968, 47-56.

2708. **The Petticoat Brigade** by Gladys L. Schmitt and Pauline Gibson.

Radio. 8 m. 1 f. +X.

In - Scholastic. 29: Oct.10,1936, 15-16+.

2709. **Phantasms** by Roberto Bracco. Trans. by Dirce St. Cyr.

Full. 9 m. 9 f. +X.

In - Poet Lore. 19: no.3,1908, 241-292.

2710. **Pharaoh's Daughter** by August von Kotzebue. Trans. by Beatrice B. Beebe.

Short. 4 m. 1 f.

In - Golden. 8: July 1928, 53-59.

2711. **Pharaoh's Daughter** by Jon Trausti. Trans. from the Icelandic by Frederic T. Wood.

Full. 5 m. 2 f. 2 b. +X.

In - Poet Lore. 57: March 1952, 3-56.

2712. **Philadelphia Interlude** by Marcus Konick.

Radio. 4 m. 3 f. +X.

In - Plays. 6: Jan.1947, 60-65.

2713. **Phillip Hotz's Fury** by Max Frisch.

Short. 10 m. 3 f.

In - Esquire. 58: Oct.1962, 109-110+.

2714. **Philipp Hotz's Fury** by Max Frisch. Trans. from the German by Michael Bullock.

Short. 10 m. 3 f.

In - Gambit. 1: no.4, 75-98.

2715. **Philosopher in Grain: Michael Faraday** by Riley Hughes.

Short. 6 m. 2 f.

In - Plays. 4: Nov.1944, 16-20.

2716. **The Philosopher of Butterbiggins** by Harold Chapin.

Short. 2 m. 1 f. 1 b.

In - Golden. 9: Jan.1929, 87-90.

2717. **Philosophy of the Tooth Brush** by Anita Weinberg and Albert Weinberg.

In - Poet Lore. 36: Dec.1925, 615-623.

2718. **Piccola** adap. by Rowena Bennett from a French Christmas story.

Short. 2 m. 3 f.

In - Plays. 28: Dec.1968, 68-73.

2719. **The Pickwick Papers** by Charles Dickens. Adap. by Lewy Olfson.

Radio. 13 m. 2 f.

In - Plays. 16: Nov.1956, 89-95.

2720. **Picnic** by William Inge.

Full. 4 m. 7 f.

In - Theatre. 38: April 1954, 34-61.

2721. **The Pied Piper** by Lena Ruth Towles.

Short. 2 m. 0 f. 21 c.

In - Wilson. 11: Oct.1936, 135+.

2722. **The Pied Piper of Hamlin.** Adap. from the story by Robert Browning.

Short. 2 m. 0 f. +X.

In - Delineator. 94: June 1919, 46.

2723. **The Pied Piper of Hamelin** by Lucy Kennedy.

Short. 5 m. 1 f. 12 c. +f.X.

In - Plays. 12: April 1953, 47-56.

2724. **The Pied Piper of Hamelin** by Robert Browning. Adap. by Adele Thane.

Short. 4 m. 1 f. +X.

In - Plays. 21: Nov.1961, 37-47.

2725. **The Pied Piper of Hamelin** by Robert Browning. Adap. by Michael T. Leech.

Short. 6 m. 3 f. +X.

In - Plays. 27: April 1968, 79-86.

2726. Pierre Patelin adap. by Helene Koon.

Short. 4 m. 1 f.

In - Plays. 24: Jan.1965, 37-48.

2727. Piffle! It's Only a Sniffle! by Ted Kaufman.

Short. 7 m. 3 f. +X.

In - Plays. 7: Dec.1947, 57-60.

2728. The Pigeon by Robert Wilson McKnight.

Short. 3 m. 3 f. 3 b. 1 c.

In - Poet Lore. 30:no.4,1919, 579-587.

2729. The Pilgrim Painting by James Rawls.

Short. 5 m. 3 f.

In - Plays. 18: Nov.1958, 47-53.

2730. Pilgrim Parting by Helen Louise Miller.

Short. 8 m. 5 f. +X.

In - Plays. 14: Nov.1954, 45-52.

2731. The Pilgrim Spirit by Esther MacLellan and
Catherine V. Schroll.

Short. 10 m. 10 f.

In - Plays. 17: Nov.1957, 48-54.

2732. Pilot Lights of the Apocalypse by Louis
Nicot Ridenour.

Short. 12 m. 0 f.

In - Fortune. 33: Jan.1946, 116-117+.

2733. Pilot Lights of the Apocalypse by Louis
Nicot Ridenour.

Excerpt. 7 m. 0 f.

In - Scholastic. 48: April 29,1946, 17-19+.

2734. Pilot Lights of the Apocalypse by Louis Nicot
Ridenour.

Excerpt. 6 m. 0 f.

In - Scholastic. 52: April 12,1948, 18-20

2735. Pin Up Pals by Helen Louise Miller.

Short. 0 m. 5 f. +f.X.

In - Plays. 6: Feb.1947, 1-8.

2736. Piñata by Esther MacLellan and Catherine V.
Schroll.

Short. 2 m. 4 f.

In - Plays. 9: Dec.1949, 54-62.

2737. The Pinch-Hitter by Marjorie B. Paradis.

Short. 2 m. 4 f. +X.

In - Plays. 9: Dec.1949, 26-32.

2738. The Pinedus Affair by Paolo Levi. English
version by Robert Rietty.

Full. 15 m. 4 f.

In - Gambit. 1: no.2, 5-56.

2739. The Pink Parasol by Helen Louise Miller.

Short. 3 m. 6 f.

In - Plays. 3: May 1944, 11-20.

2740. Pink Roses for Christmas by Josephine E.
Campbell.

Short. 2 m. 2 f.

In - Plays. 4: Dec.1944, 14-19.

2741. Pinkie and the Robins by John F. Lehman.

Short. 2 m. 4 f.

In - Plays. 3: March 1944, 55-56.

2742. Pinocchio Goes to School by Carlo Collodi.
Adap. by Adele Thane.

Short. 6 m. 3 f. +m.X.

In - Plays. 20: Jan.1961, 63-70.

2743. The Pioneer Valentine by Esther Cooper.

Short. 1 m. 2 f.

In - Plays. 7: Feb.1948, 49-52.

2744. Pip Visits Miss Havisham adap. by Adele
Thane from Charles Dickens' Great
Expectations.

Short. 5 m. 5 f.

In - Plays. 28: Oct.1968, 87-95.

2745. The Pistol of the Beg by Karel M. Capek.
Trans. from the Czech by E.D. Schonberger.

Full. 7 m. 4 f. +X.

In - Poet Lore. 34: Dec.1923, 475-523.

2746. The Pitiless Policeman by Georges Courteline.
Trans. from the French by H. Isabelle
Williams.

Short. 4 m. 0 f.

In - Poet Lore. 28:no.2,1917, 217-230.

2747. Pixie in a Trap by Rowena Bennett.

Short. 7 un.

In - Plays. 22: Oct.1962, 72-74.

2748. The Pixy Jester's Joke by Helen Littler
Howard.

Short. 6 m. 0 f.

In - Plays. 3: Oct.1943, 45-50.

2749.   Plagiarized by Nishan Parlakian.

Full. 7 m. 4 f.

In - First Stage. 1: June 1962, 5-26.

2750.   Plain and Fancy by Joseph Stein and Will
Glickman. Lyrics by Arnold B. Horwitt;
music by Albert Hague.

Full (musical). 20 m. 10 f. +ch.

In - Theatre. 40: July 1956, 33-57.

2751.   Planting Time by Alice Very.

Short. 3 m. 3 f. +c.X.

In - Plays. 14: April 1955, 83-85.

2752.   A Play Without a Name by Aileen Fisher.

Short. 16 m. 5 f.

In - Plays. 10: Oct.1950, 12-19.

2753.   The Playboy of the Western World by John
Millington Synge.

Full. 7 m. 5 f. +X.

In - Golden. 4: Oct.1926, 513-537.

2754.   The Player Queen by William Butler Yeats.

Short. 7 m. 2 f. +X.

In - Dial. 73: Nov.1922, 486-506.

2755.   The Players' Dressing Room by Ashley Dukes.

Short. 7 m. 0 f.

In - Theatre. 20: June 1936, 473-480.

2756.   The Play's the Thing by Ferenc Molnar.
Adap. from the Hungarian by P.G.
Wodehouse.

Full. 8 m. 1 f.

In - Theatre. 33: March 1949, 67-90.

2757.   The Playwright and the Public by William
Saroyan.

Short. 2 m. 0 f.

In - Atlantic. 211: April 1963, 50.

2758.   Pleasant Dreams by Mildred Hark and Noel
McQueen.

Short. 2 m. 0 f. 7 c.

In - Plays. 4: Jan.1945, 50-53.

2759.   Please, No Flowers by Joel A. Ensana.

Short. 3 m. 6 f.

In - First Stage. 5: March 1966, 17-22.

2760.   The Pleasure of His Company by Samuel Taylor
with Cornelia Otis Skinner.

Full. 5 m. 2 f.

In - Players. 6 & 7: Sept.& Oct.1959, 27-31,
26-32.

2761.   The Pleasure of His Company by Samuel
Taylor with Cornelia Otis Skinner.

Full. 5 m. 2 f.

In - Theatre. 44: April 1960, 22-52.

2762.   A Plot in the Palace by Robert Watson.

Full. 9 m. 4 f. +X.

In - First Stage. 3: March 1964, 65-91.

2763.   The Plot Thickens by Aileen Fisher.

Short. 2 m. 3 f.

In - Plays. 9: April 1950, 44-50.

2764.   The Plot to Overthrow Christmas by Norman
Corwin.

Radio. 12 m. 2 f.

In - Scholastic. 43: Dec.13,1943, 17-20+.

2765.   Plum Blossom and the Dragon by Deborah
Newman.

Short. 2 m. 7 f. 1 "dragon" + ch.

In - Plays. 22: Jan.1963, 49-54.

2766.   Pluto by Cora Burlingame.

Short. 6 m. 3 f.

In - Plays. 6: April 1947, 21-31.

2767.   The Poacher by J.O. Francis.

Short. 3 m. 1 f.

In - Theatre. 9: May 1925, 327-337.

2768.   Poet's Nightmare by Elbert M. Hoppenstedt.

Short. 4 m. 4 f.

In - Plays. 9: Jan.1950, 37-44.

2769.   Poet's Paradise by Edward R. Sammis.

In - Poet Lore. 36: Dec.1925, 569-576.

2770.   Point of No Return by Paul Osborn. Based
on novel by John P. Marquand.

Full. 15 m. 8 f. +X.

In - Theatre. 37: March 1953, 34-64.

2771.   The Pointed Stick by Lee Devin.

Short. 1 m. 1 f.

In - Poet Lore. 59: June 1964, 174-182.

2772.   Poison Ivy by Graham DuBois.

Short. 5 m. 3 f.

In - Plays. 6: April 1947, 1-12.

2773. Poison Ivy by Graham Du Bois.

Short. 5 m. 3 f.

In - Plays. 22: April 1963, 23-34.

2774. The Poker Session by Hugh Leonard.

Full. 3 m. 3 f.

In - Players. 11: April & May 1964, 23-30+,
23-28.

2775. The Polka Dot Pup by Helen Louise Miller.

Short. 10 m. 6 f.

In - Plays. 14: Oct.1954, 55-61.

2776. Poof by Armand Salacrou. Trans. from the
French by Felicia Liss.

Full. 12 m. 4 f.

In - Mod. Drama. 1: Sept.1967, 105-131.

2777. The Pool of Bethesda by Hermann Hagedorn.

Short. 8 m. 0 f.

In - Outlook. 108: Dec.2,1914, 782-785.

2778. Poor Bitos by Jean Anouilh. Trans. by
Lucienne Hill.

Full. 10 m. 2 f. 1 b.

In - Players. 11: Feb.& March 1964, 23-30,
23-30+.

2779. Pop's Place by Samuel S. Richmond.

Short. 11 m. 3 f. +X.

In - Plays. 6: April 1947, 62-70.

2780. Porgy by Dubose and Dorothy Heyward. From
the novel by Dubose Heyward.

Full. 15 m. 6 f. (all Negro).

In - Theatre. 39: Oct.1955, 33-64.

2781. The Portal by Herbert Edward Mierow.

Short. 8 m. 4 f.

In - Poet Lore. 56: Sept.1951, 238-249.

2782. Portrait of an American by Mildred Hark and
Noel McQueen.

Short. 4 m. 4 f.

In - Plays. 12: May 1953, 14-22.

2783. Portrait of an American by Mildred Hark and
Noel McQueen.

Short. 4 m. 4 f.

In - Plays. 23: May 1964, 13-22.

2784. The Portrait of Tiero by Zoe Akins.

Short. 3 m. 2 f. +X.

In - Theatre. 4: Oct.1920, 316-337.

2785. Posies for the Potentate by Martha Swintz.

Short. 5 m. 2 f. +X.

In - Plays. 13: Jan.1954, 38-46.

2786. Posies for the Potentate by Martha Swintz.

Short. 5 m. 2 f. +X.

In - Plays. 25: Jan.1966, 45-53.

2787. The Post Office by Rabindranath Tagore.

Full. 8 m. 2 f.

In - Forum. 51: March 1914, 455-471.

2788. Pot Luck by Katherine Arthur.

3Short. 3 m. 2 f.

In - Plays. 21: April 1962, 1-17.

2789. The Pot of Gold by Claribel Spamer.

Short. 1 m. 8 f.

In - Plays. 5: March 1946, 58-60.

2790. Pot of Gold for Mother by Karin Asbrand.

Short. 1 m. 12 f. 1 un.

In - Plays. 21: May 1962, 65-68.

2791. Pottery Lane by Karin Asbrand.

Short. 3 m. 5 f.

In - Plays. 11: Jan.1952, 42-48.

2792. Pottery Lane by Karin Asbrand.

Short. 3 m. 5 f.

In - Plays. 20: April 1961, 75-81.

2793. The Potting Shed by Graham Greene.

Full. 6 m. 5 f.

In - Theatre. 42: March 1958, 24-48.

Power and Glory.

see

The White Scourge.

2795. The Prayer-Meeting by Paul Green.

Short. 6 m. 6 f.

In - Poet Lore. 35: June 1924, 232-253.

2796. Precedence: a Near Tragedy by Kenneth Lewis
Roberts.

Short. 5 m. 3 f.

In - Sat. Evening. 202: July 20,1929, 14-15.

2797. A Precedent in Pastries by Elsi Rowland.

Short. 14 m. 5 f. +X.

In - Plays. 4: March 1945, 37-41.

2798. Prelude to Victory by Graham DuBois.

Short. 5 m. 3 f.

In - Plays. 6: Feb.1947, 9-17.

2799. A Present for Mother by June Barr.

Short. 2 m. 1 f. 4 un.

In - Plays. 7: May 1948, 58-60.

2800. A Present from Abe by Deborah Newman.

Short. 5 m. 4 f. +X.

In - Plays. 10: Feb.1951, 55-58.

2801. A Present from Abe by Deborah Newman.

Short. 5 m. 4 f. +X.

In - Plays. 24: Feb.1965, 75-78.

2802. Present Laughter by Noel Coward.

Full. 5 m. 5 f.

In - Theatre. 33: Aug.1949, 59-96.

2803. The President's Bride by Mary Malone.

Short. 0 m. 7 f.

In - Plays. 17: May 1958, 27-34.

2804. Press Photographer by Samuel S. Richmond.

Short. 4 m. 1 f.

In - Plays. 7: March 1948, 59-66.

2805. Pretties by Dorothy Donnell Calhoun.

Short. 2 m. 1 f.

In - Touchstone. 6: Oct.1919, 26-31.

2806. The Price by Arthur Miller.

Excerpts. 3 m. 1 f.

In - Sat. Evening. 241: Feb.10,1968, 40-45+.

2807. The Price of Eggs by Mary Ann Nicholson.

Short. 2 m. 2 f.

In - Plays. 14: Feb.1955, 71-74.

2808. The Price of Love by Aurania Rouverol.

Short. 2 m. 1 f.

In - Drama. 16: March 1926, 219-220+.

2809. Pride and Prejudice adap. by Helen Jerome. From the novel by Jane Austen.

In - Scholastic. 31: Sept.18,1937, 21-23.

2810. Pride and Prejudice by Jane Austen. Adap. by Deborah Newman.

Radio. 5 m. 9 f.

In - Plays. 10: March 1951, 66-79.

2811. Pride and Prejudice by Jane Austin. Adap. by Olive J. Morley.

Short. 0 m. 8 f.

In - Plays. 16: Jan.1957, 37-48.

2812. Pride and Prejudice by Jane Austen. Adap. by Deborah Newman.

Radio. 5 m. 9 f.

In - Plays. 26: April 1967, 83-96.

2813. Primary Day by Viola Oliver.

Short. 12 m. 4 f.

In - Scholastic. 60: March 12,1952, 22-23+.

2814. Primrose Lane by Cornelia Meigs.

Short (musical). 3 m. 3 f. +c.X.

In - St. Nicholas. 46: May 1919, 641-647.

2815. The Prince and the Pauper by Mark Twain. Adap. by Celia Gordon.

Radio. 19 m. 8 f.

In - Plays. 12: Feb.1953, 62-76.

2816. The Prince and the Pauper by Mark Twain. Adap. by Elizabeth Brenner.

Short. 19 m. 2 f. +X.

In - Plays. 19: Jan.1960, 47-56.

2817. The Prince and the Pauper by Mark Twain. Adap. by Deborah Newman.

Radio. 26 m. 11 f. +X.

In - Plays. 26: Oct.1966, 81-95.

2818. The Prince and the Peddlers by Rowena Bennett.

Short. 7 m. 1 f.

In - Plays. 22: Nov.1962, 75-78.

2819. Prince Charming Smiles Again by Catherine Urban.

Short. 3 m. 2 f.

In - Plays. 7: Nov.1947, 49-52.

2820. Prince Charming's Fate by Caroline C. Lovell.

In - St. Nicholas. 30: Feb.1903, 350-359.

2821. A Prince is Where You Find Him by James R. Chisholm.

Short. 7 m. 6 f.

In - Plays. 19: Nov.1959, 49-53.

2822. The Prince of Semberia by Branislov Nooshich. Trans. by Luka Djurichich and Bertha W. Clark.

Short. 11 m. 0 f. +X.

In - Poet Lore. 33: March 1922, 85-96.

2823. The Prince, the Wolf and the Firebird by
      Jackson Lacey.

      Full. 16 m. 5 f.

      In - Gambit. 4: no.14, 5-107.

2824. The Prince Who Learned Everything Out of
      Books by Jacinto Benavente. Trans.
      from the Spanish by John Garrett
      Underhill.

      Short. 8 m. 6 f. 3 b. +X.

      In - Poet Lore. 29:no.4,1918, 505-530.

2825. The Prince With No Crown by Claribel Spamer.

      Short. 8 m. 1 f.

      In - Plays. 8: Nov.1948, 45-48.

      Princely Fortune.

             see

      Three Chinese Folk Dramas.

2827. The Princess Aline by S. Decatur Smith, Jr.

      Full. 4 m. 4 f. +X.

      In - Ladies' Home. 18: April 1901, 3-4+.

2828. The Princess and the Crystal Pipe by Beulah
      Folmsbee.

      Short. 4 m. 6 f. 1 b.

      In - St. Nicholas. 48: Nov.1920, 61-65.

2829. The Princess and the Horse by Ursula
      Hourihane.

      Short. 2 m. 3 f. +X.

      In - Plays. 7: March 1948, 50-55.

2830. The Princess and the Pea by Hans Christian
      Andersen. Adap. by Helen Louise Miller.

      Short. 2 m. 7 f. +X.

      In - Plays. 18: Jan.1959, 45-50.

2831. The Princess and the Pumpkin by Lucille
      Streacker.

      Short. 3 m. 2 f.

      In - Plays. 7: Oct.1948, 59-62.

2832. The Princess and the Rose Colored-Glasses
      by Mildred Hark and Noel McQueen.

      Short. 4 m. 4 f.

      In - Plays. 13: May 1954, 59-66.

2833. The Princess and the Rose-Colored Glasses by
      Mildred Hark and Noel McQueen.

      Short. 4 m. 7 f.

      In - Plays. 26: April 1967, 75-82.

2834. The Princess' Choice by Margaret Rahe.

      Short. 9 m. 5 f. 4 b. +X.

      In - Speech Educ. 5: May 1919, 279-286.

2835. The Princess from Norway by Esther MacLellan
      and Catherine V. Schroll.

      Short. 3 m. 7 f. +X.

      In - Plays. 17: May 1958, 59-64.

2836. Princess Lonely Heart by Helen Louise Miller.

      Short. 8 m. 11 f. +X.

      In - Plays. 22: Feb.1963, 81-86.

2837. Princess Nimble-Wit by Mary Ann Nicholson.

      Short. 5 m. 4 f.

      In - Plays. 15: Jan.1956, 45-48.

2838. Princess of Hearts by Mildred Hark and Noel
      McQueen.

      Short. 6 m. 5 f. 2 un.

      In - Plays. 20: Feb.1961, 73-78.

2839. The Princess of Virginia by Kate Tucker Goode.

      In - Lippincott's. 79: June 1907, 817-848.

2840. A Princess Too Little by Mary Ann Nicholson.

      Short. 4 m. 3 f.

      In - Plays. 22: April 1963, 79-82.

2841. Princess Weaver of the Skies by Ysabel De
      Witte Kaplan.

      In - Poet Lore. 32: June 1921, 267-278.

2842. The Princess Who Couldn't Dance by Lindsey
      Barbee.

      Short. 0 m. 6 f. +3X.

      In - Plays. 6: April 1947, 56-59.

2843. Printer's Devil by Earl J. Dias.

      Short. 3 m. 3 f.

      In - Plays. 16: Jan.1957, 27-36.

2844. The Prisoner by Clarendon Ross.

      Short. 2 m. 1 f.

      In - Poet Lore. 29:no.4,1918, 590-595.

2845. The Prisoner by Bruce P. Woodford.

      Short. 13 m. 2 f.

      In - Poet Lore. 57: June 1953, 195-217.

      Prisoner and Escort.

             see

      Cockade 1.

2847. The Prisoner of Zenda by Anthony Hope.
       Adap. by Levy Olfson.

       Radio. 6 m. 1 f. 1 b. +X.

       In - Plays. 22: Oct.1962, 85-95.

2848. Prisoners by Charles L. Atkins.

       Short. 4 m. 0 f.

       In - Christian. 53: Oct.21,1936, 1388-1390.

2849. The Private Life of the Master Race by
       Bertolt Brecht. Trans. by Eric Bentley.

       Full. 10 m. 8 f. 3 b.

       In - Theatre. 28: Sept.1944, 512-520.

2850. The Private Lives of Elizabeth and Essex.
       From the movie scenario.

       Excerpt. 4 m. 1 f.

       In - Scholastic. 35: Dec.4,1939, 21E-23E.

2851. A Prize for Mother by Mildred Hark and Noel
       McQueen.

       Short. 5 m. 3 f.

       In - Plays. 6: May 1947, 32-40.

2852. The Prize Shamrock by Deborah Newman.

       Short. 7 m. 5 f. +X.

       In - Plays. 12: March 1953, 58-61.

2853. The Prize Shamrock by Deborah Newman.

       Short. 7 m. 5 f. +X.

       In - Plays. 18: March 1959, 75-78.

2854. The Prodigies by Jean Vauthier. Trans. by
       Bettina L. Knapp.

       Full. 1 m. 2 f.

       In - First Stage. 4: Dec.1965, 237-259.

2855. The Professional Attitude by U. Harold Males.

       Full. 8 m. 1 f.

       In - First Stage. 1: Sept.1962, 8-34.

2856. Professor Countdown Takes Off by Polly Lewis
       Bradley.

       Short. 2 m. 2 f. +f.X.

       In - Plays. 20: April 1961, 83-87.

2857. Professor Hobo by Betty Tracy Huff.

       Short. 6 m. 4 f.

       In - Plays. 23: Nov.1963, 1-14.

2858. Professor Snaffle's Polypon by Oscar Mandel.

       Full. 16 m. 7 f.

       In - First Stage. 5: June 1966, 65-89.

2859. Professor Willy's Wisher-Switcher by Janice
       Auritt Oser.

       Short. 4 m. 4 f.

       In - Plays. 12: April 1953, 56-60.

2860. Progress by St.John Ervine.

       Short. 1 m. 2 f.

       In - Sat. Evening. 194: Feb.11,1922, p.10-11+.

2861. The Progress of Mrs. Alexander by Louise
       Rogers Stanwood.

       In - New England. 43(n.s.): Feb.1911,
       529-560.

2862. Progress To the Park by Alun Owen.

       Full. 18 m. 4 f.

       In - Players. 8: July & Aug.1961, 25-33,
       25-31.

2863. Prologue by Carl Glick.

       Short. 3 m. 0 f.

       In - Poet Lore. 33: Dec.1922, 553-562.

2864. Prologue by Hugo Von Hofmannsthal.

       Short. 4 m. 1 f. +X.

       In - Living Age. 322: July 5,1924, 33-37.

2865. Prologue to Balloon by Padraic Colum.

       Short. 9 m. 3 f. +X.

       In - Dial. 85: Dec.1928, 490-500.

2866. Prologue to Glory by Ellsworth Prouty Conkle.
       Ed. by Margaret Mayorga.

       Short. 11 m. 4 f. +X.

       In - Scholastic. 34: Feb.11,1939, 21E-24E.

2867. Prometheus Bound by Aeschylus. Trans. by
       Edith Hamilton.

       Short. 5 m. 2 f. +f.ch.

       In - Theatre. 11: July 1927, 545-562.

2868. Prometheus Rebound by Lawrence Wunderlich.

       Short. 5 m. 2 f.

       In - First Stage. 3: March 1964, 92-109.

2869. The Promise by Aleksei Arbuzov. Trans. by
       Ariadne Nicolaeff.

       Full. 2 m. 1 f.

       In - Players. 14: March 1967, 31-46+.

2870. A Proposal by George Duncan.

       Short. 1 m. 1 f.

       In - Harper's M. 108: April 1904, 796-801.

2871. The Proposal by Anton Chekhov.

Short. 2 m. 1 f.

In - Golden. 13: Feb.1931, 70-75.

2872. Protectors of the Poor by Kenneth Lewis
Roberts.

Short. 6 m. 0 f.

In - Sat. Evening. 202: Sep.21,1929, 44-47.

2873. Publicity by Lillian Harris.

Short. 4 m. 2 f.

In - Poet Lore. 38: Dec.1927, 590-602.

2874. The Pumpkineaters' Pumpkin by Deborah
Newman.

Short. 4 m. 4 f.

In - Plays. 10: Oct.1950, 53-56.

2875. Punch and Judy by Michael T. Leech.

Short. 4 m. 0 f. 10 c.

In - Plays. 26: Nov. 1966, 91-98.

2876. The Punctuation Proclamation by Claire
Boiko.

Short. 9 m. 3 f. +X.

In - Plays. 23: April 1964, 65-68.

2877. Puppy Love by Helen Louise Miller.

Short. 3 m. 4 f.

In - Plays. 9: Dec.1949, 10-18.

2878. Puppy Love by Helen Louise Miller.

Short. 3 m. 4 f.

In - Plays. 13: Dec.1953, 87-95.

2879. Puppy Love by Helen Louise Miller.

Short. 3 m. 4 f.

In - Plays. 26: Dec.1966, 11-19.

2880. Purloined by Leonard Casper.

Short. 6 m. 1 f.

In - Plays. 5: Oct.1945, 24-34.

2881. The Purloined Portrait by Earl J. Dias.

Short. 7 m. 3 f.

In - Plays. 27: Nov.1967, 23-34.

2882. Puss-in-Boots adap. by Josef A. Elfenbein.

Short. 4 m. 2 f.

In - Plays. 13: Feb.1954, 46-52.

2883. Puss In Boots by Charles Perrault. Adap.
by Adele Thane.

Short. 6 m. 2 f. 3 c.

In - Plays. 23: May 1964, 59-69.

2884. Pussy Pleases by Claribel Spamer.

Short. 5 m. 2 f.

In - Plays. 9: Jan.1950, 62-64.

2885. Putting Pop in His Place by Mildred Hark and
Noel McQueen.

Short. 3 m. 4 f.

In - Plays. 20: Jan.1961, 35-45.

2886. The Putty Club by Franz Molnár. Trans. by
Benjamin Glazer.

Short. 1 m. 0 f. 6 b.

In - Theatre. 7: July 1923, 251-256.

2887. Pygmalion by George Bernard Shaw.

Full. 4 m. 3 f.

In - Everybody's. 31: Nov.1914, 577-612.

2888. Pyramus and Thisbe by Erik Barnouw.

Radio. 7 m. 2 f.

In - Scholastic. 36: April 15,1940, 17-19.

2889. Pyramus and Thisbe by Erik Barnouw.

Short. 8 m. 2 f.

In - Education. 62: March 1942, 407-411.

2890. Pyramus and Thisbe by Erik Barnouw.

Radio. 8 m. 1 f.

In - Education. 62: March 1942, 411-414.

2891. Pythagoras and the Scales by Mary Finch
Harvey.

Short. 2 m. 10 un.

In - Etude. 50: April 1932, 306-307.

2892. The Quakers by August Von Kotzebue. Trans.
from the German by Beatrice B. Beebe.

Short. 5 m. 1 f.

In - Poet Lore. 38: June 1927, 177-191.

2893. Quality Street by James M. Barrie. Adap.
by Levy Olfson.

Radio. 2 m. 4 f. 3 g.

In - Plays. 18: March 1959, 87-96.

2894. Queen Christmas by Carolyn Wells.

Short. Large cast of c.

In - Ladies' Home. 37: Dec.1920, 32+.

2895. The Queen Comes to Pray by John Francis McDermott, Jr.

In - Poet Lore. 36: Sept.1925, 450-456.

2896. Queen Jezebel by Edith Lombard Squires.

Short. 8 m. 2 f. +m.X.

In - Poet Lore. 40: Dec.1929, 615-626.

2897. The Queen of Sew-and-Sew by Corinne Morse.

Short. 3 m. 5 f. +f.X.

In - Plays. 15: May 1956, 41-46.

2898. The Queen of Sheba by Stark Young.

Short. 3 m. 2 f.

In - Theatre. 6: April 1922, 152-164.

2899. The Queen with the Broken Heart by Catherine Urban.

Short. 2 m. 4 f.

In - Plays. 5: Feb.1946, 58-60.

2900. The Queen's Christmas Cake by Frances B. Watts.

Short. 6 m. 3 f. 6 c.

In - Plays. 25: Dec.1965, 69-75.

2901. The Queen's Enemies by Lord Dunsany.

Short. 9 m. 2 f. +X.

In - Golden. 6: Aug.1927, 258-263.

2902. The Queen's Mirror by Margaret E. Slattery.

Short. 6 m. 4 f.

In - Plays. 20: April 1961, 45-52.

2903. The Queens of France by Thornton Wilder.

Short. 1 m. 3 f.

In - Yale Review. 21(n.s.): Sept.1931,72-85.

2904. Quentin Durward by Sir Walter Scott. Adap. by Levy Olfson.

Radio. 8 m. 2 f. 4 un.

In - Plays. 15: Feb.1956, 89-96.

2905. Questions by Carol Sax and Christie Morris.

Short. 0 m. 3 f.

In - Touchstone. 5: May 1919, 111-114.

2906. A Quiet Christmas by Mildred Hark and Noel McQueen.

Short. 4 m. 5 f.

In - Plays. 10: Dec.1950, 1-14.

2907. A Quiet Christmas by Mildred Hark and Noel McQueen.

Short. 4 m. 4 f. 1 g.

In - Plays. 24: Dec.1964, 15-28.

2908. Quintila by Andrew Jolly.

Full. 6 m. 3 f.

In - First Stage. 1: Sept.1962, 53-79.

2909. Quitting Business by Mariano Jose de Larra. Trans. from the Spanish by Kenneth C. Kaufman.

Full. 8 m. 2 f.

In - Poet Lore. 35: June 1924, 159-209.

2910. Quiz Biz by John Murray.

Short. 8 m. 4 f. +X.

In - Plays. 18: March 1959, 1-15.

2911. R.U.R. by Karel Capek. Trans. by Paul Selver and Nigel Playfair. Ed. by Margaret Mayorga.

Short. 13 m. 4 f.

In - Scholastic. 33: Nov.5,1938, 17E-20E.

2912. Rabbit Foot by Helen Louise Miller.

Short. 4 m. 5 f.

In - Plays. 9: April 1950, 1-11.

2913. Rabbit Foot by Helen Louise Miller.

Short. 4 m. 5 f.

In - Plays. 17: April 1958, 13-22.

2914. The Rabbit Who Refused to Run by Helen Louise Miller.

Short. 2 m. 1 f. 1 b. +c.X.

In - Plays. 25: April 1966, 75-80.

2915. Rabbits, Rabbits, Rabbits by Deborah Newman.

Short. 12 m. 7 f.

In - Plays. 20: March 1961, 79-83.

2916. The Rabbits Who Changed Their Minds by Helen Louise Miller.

Short. 3 m. 1 f. +X.

In - Plays. 18: March 1959, 69-73.

2917. Raduz and Mahulena by Julius Zeyer. Trans. from the Bohemian by Zdenka Buben and George Rapall Noyes. Songs by Dorothea Prall.

Full. 5 m. 5 f.

In - Poet Lore. 34: March 1923, 1-62.

2918. The Raft of the Medusa by Georg Kaiser.
          Trans. from the German by Ulrich
          Weisstein.

      Short. 2 m. 1 f. 6 b. 5 g.

      In - First Stage. 1: March 1962, 35-48.

2919. A Railway Tragedy - Perhaps by Philip G.
          Hubert, Jr.

      Short. 7 m. 3 f. +X.

      In - Bookman. 24: Dec.1906, 340-343.

2920. Rain by Dana Burnet.

      In - Drama. 14: Oct.1923, 20-23.

2921. Rain and Rebellion by Graham DuBois.

      Short. 6 m. 2 f. +m.X.

      In - Plays. 10: Nov.1950, 18-26.

2922. Rain-in-the-Face by Helen Louise Miller.

      Short. 5 m. 2 f.

      In - Plays. 13: Jan.1954, 71-74.

2923. Rainbow Colors by Mildred Hark and Noel
          McQueen.

      Short. 2 m. 2 f. +c.X.

      In - Plays. 9: Jan.1950, 66-69.

2924. Rainbow Palace by Margaret E. Slattery.

      Short. 4 m. 4 f.

      In - Plays. 19: Jan.1960, 57-64.

2925. The Rainmaker by N. Richard Nash.

      Full. 6 m. 1 f.

      In - Theatre. 40: March 1956, 33-55.

2926. A Raisin in the Sun by Lorraine Hansberry.

      Full. 8 m. 3 f. (mostly Negro)

      In - Theatre. 44: Oct.1960, 27-58.

2927. Raising the Devil by Evelyn Elizabeth Gardner.

      In - Poet Lore. 39: March 1928, 134-152.

2928. The Rape of the Belt by Benn W. Levy.

      Full. 3 m. 7 f.

      In - Players. 5: April & May 1958, 27-32,
          25-32.

2929. The Rape of the Belt by Benn W. Levy.

      Full. 3 m. 7 f.

      In - Theatre. 45: March 1961, 25-56.

2930. Rapunzel by Alter Brody.

      Short. 1 m. 1 f. 1 g.

      In - Theatre. 9: April 1925, 257-266.

2931. Rapunzel by June Barr.

      Short. 2 m. 3 f.

      In - Plays. 9: Oct.1949, 49-53.

2932. Rapunzel adap. by Adele Thane from Grimms'
          Fairy Tales.

      Short. 2 m. 3 f. 1 b. 4 g.

      In - Plays. 26: Feb.1967, 79-88.

2933. Rats by M. Joseph Fruchter.

      Short. 2 m. 2 f.

      In - Poet Lore. 37: March 1926, 154-157.

2934. The Raven's First Flight by Gladys L. Schmitt.

      Radio. 4 m. 2 f.

      In - Scholastic. 26: Feb.2,1935, 7-8.

2935. Reaching For the Moon by M.C. Richmond.

      Short. 7 m. 0 f. +m.X.

      In - Indus. Arts. 18: June 1929, 210-214.

2936. A Real April Fool's Day by Marguerite Kreger
          Phillips.

      Short. 3 m. 3 f.

      In - Plays. 17: April 1958, 51-55.

2937. The Real Princess by Hans Christian
          Andersen. Adap. by Deborah Newman.

      Short. 4 m. 9 f.

      In - Plays. 14: April 1955, 71-76.

2938. The Real Thing by John Kendrick Bangs.

      In - Harper's B. 43: Feb.1909, 134-143.

2939. Really, My Dear . . . by Christopher Morley.

      Short. 2 un. 5 f. 4 c.

      In - Forum. 79: May 1928, 723-735.

2940. Rebel Poet adap. by Joseph Auslander and
          F.E. Hill from Winged Horse.

      Radio. 6 m. 5 f.

      In - Education. 67: May 1947, 578-589.

2941. The Rebellious Robots by Deborah Newman.

      Short. 5 m. 5 f. 6 c.

      In - Plays. 21: Nov.1961, 59-65.

2942. Rebirth in Barrows Inlet by Joseph Liss.

      Radio. 11 m. 6 f.

      In - Theatre. 30: Aug.1946, 465-471.

2943. Recipe for Rain by Betty Tracy Huff.

Short. 5 m. 6 f.

In - Plays. 25: Nov.1965, 15-25.

2944. The Reclining Figure by Harry Kurnitz.

Full. 9 m. 1 f.

In - Theatre. 40: June 1956, 33-55.

2945. Recoil by E. Llewellyn Hughes.

In - Canadian M. 54: Dec.1919, 125-136.

2946. The Reconciliation by Gerhardt Hauptmann. Trans. from the German by Roy Temple House.

Full. 4 m. 3 f. 1 un.

In - Poet Lore. 21: no.5,1910, 337-390.

2947. The Records Show by Gladys L. Schmitt.

Radio. 5 m. 3 f. +X.

In - Scholastic. 31: Oct.30,1937, 21E-23E.

2948. Red Carpet Christmas by Helen Louise Miller.

Short. 5 m. 7 f.

In - Plays. 22: Dec.1962, 1-13.

2949. The Red Flannel Suit by Helen Louise Miller.

Short. 6 m. 6 f.

In - Plays. 20: Dec.1960, 1-13.

2950. The Red Flower by Eleanore Leuser.

Short. 7 m. 4 f.

In - Plays. 13: Oct.1953, 59-63.

2951. Red Magic by Helen L. Howard.

Short. 4 m. 1 f.

In - Plays. 6: Oct.1946, 62-63.

2952. The Red 'n' Green Treasure Hunt by Dorothy Deming.

Short. 1 m. 2 f. +X.

In - Plays. 12: Nov.1952, 49-52.

2953. Red Riding Hood and the Wolf adap. by Carolyn F. Nutter.

Short. 6 m. 3 f. +X.

In - Plays. 11: April 1952, 62-66.

2954. The Red Slippers by Antoinette Panella.

Short. 2 m. 2 f.

In - Drama. 16: Dec.1925, 94-95.

2955. The Red, the Pink, and the True Blue by Paul Vincent Miller.

Short. 3 m. 1 f.

In - First Stage. 5: March 1966, 8-16.

2956. The Red Wagon by Marjorie B. Paradis.

Short. 3 m. 3 f.

In - Plays. 7: Dec.1947, 20-28.

2957. Red, White and Blue by James M. Cain.

Short. 3 m. 0 f.

In - American Merc. 12: Oct.1927, 129-134.

2958. Red, White, and Blue by Marjorie B. Paradis.

Short. 5 m. 5 f.

In - Plays. 7: Oct.1948, 13-19.

2959. Reference by Oscar W. Firkins.

In - Drama. 14: March 1924, 215-216.

2960. Refuge by Olga Petrova. From play originally entitled This Living Business.

Full. 6 m. 3 f.

In - Poet Lore. 58: Sept.1963, 195-257.

2961. The Refusal by Mario Fratti.

Short. 1 m. (white). 1 f. (Negro).

In - Poet Lore. 61: Dec.1966, 368-380.

2962. Reggie the Ghost by Margaret C. Hall.

Short. 7 m. 8 f.

In - Plays. 24: Oct.1964, 65-68.

2963. The Regulars Are Out by Graham DuBois.

Short. 5 m. 3 f.

In - Plays. 7: April 1948, 25-33.

2964. The Rehearsal by Maurice Baring.

Short. 7 m. 0 f.

In - Golden. 9: March 1929, 104-106.

2965. Reindeer on the Roof by Mildred Hark and Noel McQueen.

Short. 5 m. 5 f.

In - Plays. 12: Dec.1952, 13-26.

2966. Release by Helen R. Hull.

Short. 1 m. 1 f.

In - Touchstone. 6: Dec.1919, 122-127.

2967. The Reluctant Debutante by William Douglas
Home.

Full. 3 m. 5 f.

In - Players. 3: Aug.& Sept.1956, 21-29,
21-25.

2968. The Reluctant Debutante by William Douglas
Home.

Full. 3 m. 5 f.

In - Theatre. 41: May 1957, 34-63.

2969. The Reluctant Dragon by Kenneth Grahame.
Adap. by Adele Thane.

Short. 3 m. 1 f. +X.

In - Plays. 22: March 1963, 51-60.

2970. The Reluctant Ghost by Margaret Wylie Brydon
and Esther Ziegler.

Short. 0 m. 10 f.

In - Plays. 11: May 1952, 42-48.

2971. The Reluctant Ghost by Margaret Wylie Brydon
and Esther Ziegler.

Short. 0 m. 10 f.

In - Plays. 17: Oct.1957, 59-65.

2972. The Reluctant New Year by Janice Auritt Oser.

Short. 4 m. 2 f. 4 un.

In - Plays. 13: Jan.1954, 79-81.

2973. The Remarkable Mr. Pennypacker by Liam
O'Brien.

Full. 13 m. 7 f.

In - Theatre. 39: April 1955, 35-65.

2974. Rembrandt - Master Painter of Holland by Anna
Curtis Chandler.

Short. 11 m. 1 f.

In - Plays. 7: Oct.1948, 30-39.

2975. Remember the Alamo by Gladys L. Schmitt.

Radio. 5 m. 2 f.

In - Scholastic. 28: May 16,1936, 6-7+.

2976. Renaissance by Holger Drachmann. Trans.
from the Danish by Lee M. Hollander.

Full. 6 m. 2 f. +ch.

In - Poet Lore. 19:no.4,1908, 369-419.

2977. A Rent in the Universe by Bert O. States.

Short. 7 m. 1 f.

In - First Stage. 6: June 1967, 103-111.

2978. The Rented Tux by John Murray.

Short. 4 m. 4 f.

In - Plays. 13: May 1954, 28-38.

2979. Reprise by John Wheatcroft.

Short. 8 m. 6 f.

In - Poet Lore. 63: March 1968, 60-81.

2980. Reservations by Martin Halpern.

Short. 2 m. 1 f.

In - First Stage. 5: Dec.1966, 221-237.

2981. A Rest for Mr. Winkle by Vernon Howard.

Short. 4 m. 0 f.

In - Plays. 14: Oct.1954, 74-76.

2982. Resurrection by Daniel Corkery.

Short. 5 m. 2 f.

In - Theatre. 8: April 1924, 259-272.

2983. The Resurrection of Lazarus by Ivo Vojnovich.
Trans. from the Croatian by John J.
Batistich and George Rapall Noyes.

Full. Several un. several c. +X.

In - Poet Lore. 37: Sept.1926, 317-395.

2984. The Reticent Convict by Oscar W. Firkins.

Short. 3 m. 1 f.

In - Drama. 18: Feb.1928, 141-143+.

2985. The Return of Bobby Shafto by Helen Louise
Miller.

Short. 5 m. 4 f.

In - Plays. 27: Oct.1967, 69-76.

2986. Return of Columbus by Alice Very.

Short. 7 m. 4 f. +X.

In - Plays. 19: Oct.1959, 72-74.

2987. Return of the Nina by Esther MacLellan and
Catherine V. Schroll.

Short. 7 m. 4 f. +X.

In - Plays. 10: Oct.1950, 56-59.

2988. The Revellers by Laurence Housman.

Short. 7 m. 1 f. +X.

In - 19th C. 90: Oct.1921, 616-628.

2989. The Revolt of 'Mama' by Charles May.

Short. 3 m. 3 f.

In - Plays. 6: May 1947, 1-10.

2990. The Revolt of Santa Claus by Ednah Procter
      Clarke.

      Short. 1 m. 1 f. 8 b. 6 g. 1 c.

      In - Ladies' Home. 19: Dec.1901, 190.

2991. The Revolt of the Vegetables by Marion Carrie
      Crichton.

      Short. 5 m. 5 f.

      In - Plays. 24: Oct.1964, 69-72.

2992. Rhapsody in Blue. (Anon.)

      Radio. 13 m. 1 f. 1 b.

      In - Scholastic. 52: April 26,1948, 14-16.

2993. Rhapsody in Blue by Walter Hackett.

      Radio. 6 m. 3 f.

      In - Plays. 4: Oct.1944, 74-79.

2994. Rhetoric and Rhymes by Anna Lenington Heath.

      Short. 3 m. 2 f.

      In - Plays. 4: Nov.1944, 21-28.

2995. Rhinoceros by Eugene Ionesco. Trans. by
      Derek Prouse.

      Full. 6 m. 4 f.

      In - Theatre. 46: July 1962, 25-61.

2996. The Ribs and the Cover trans. from the
      Japanese by S. Sakanishi.

      Short. 5 m. 0 f.

      In - Golden. 15: March 1932, 263-265.

2997. Ricky and the Eggs by Estelle Ritchie.

      Short. 2 m. 1 f. 1 un. +X.

      In - Plays. 15: March 1956, 75-78.

2998. Ride Your Hobby by Robert Fontaine.

      Short. 6 m. 0 f.

      In - Plays. 25: Oct.1965, 83-86.

2999. Riders to the Sea by John Millington Synge.

      Short. 1 m. 3 f. +X.

      In - Poet Lore. 16:no.1,1905, 1-11.

3000. Riders to the Sea by John Millington Synge.

      Short. 1 m. 3 f. +X.

      In - Golden. 13: June 1931, 80-84.

3001. Right About Face by Delia Van Deusen.
      Ed. by Margaret Mayorga.

      Short. 3 m. 4 f.

      In - Scholastic. 36: May 13,1940, 17-19+.

3002. Right of Adoption by Helen Louise Miller.

      Short. 2 m. 10 f.

      In - Plays. 15: Jan.1956, 59-66.

3003. The Ring of Truth by Wynyard Browne.

      Full. 8 m. 6 f.

      In - Players. 7: Jan.& Feb.1960, 27-32, 27-32.

3004. Ring On Her Finger by Charles H. Hoffman.

      Short. 2 m. 2 f.

      In - American. 125: June 1938, 24-25+.

3005. Rip Van Winkle adap. by Walter F. Kerr.
      Based on the Story by Washington
      Irving. Ed. by Margaret Mayorga.

      Excerpt. 7 m. 2 f. 3 b. +X.

      In - Scholastic. 32: April 23,1938, 17E-19E.

3006. Rip Van Winkle by Washington Irving. Adap.
      by Walter Hackett.

      Radio. 7 m. 2 f. 2 b. 2 g. +X.

      In - Plays. 9: April 1950, 72-82.

3007. Rip Van Winkle by Washington Irving. Adap.
      by Lewy Olfson.

      Short. 13 m. 6 f.

      In - Plays. 19: Feb.1960, 13-23.

3008. Rip Van Winkle by Washington Irving. Adap.
      by Adele Thane.

      Short. 8 m. 2 f. 3 b. 3 g. +X.

      In - Plays. 25: April 1966, 53-61.

3009. Rip's Wrinkle by Roma Greth.

      Short. 2 m. 4 f.

      In - Plays. 27: May 1968, 1-12.

3010. A Rival for Dad by Mildred Hark and Noel
      McQueen.

      Short. 3 m. 2 f.

      In - Plays. 3: Dec.1943, 20-26.

3011. The Rivals by Richard Brinsley Sheridan.
      Adap. by Lewy Olfson.

      Radio. 4 m. 4 f.

      In - Plays. 15: March 1956, 87-95.

3012. The Rivals by Richard Brinsley Sheridan.
      Adap. by Lewy Olfson.

      Short. 4 m. 4 f.

      In - Plays. 22: March 1963, 87-96.

3013. **Rizal of the Philippines** by Bernard J.
Reines.

Short. 18 m. 2 f.

In - Plays. 3: Oct.1943, 1-14.

3014. **The Road** by Wole Soyinka.

Full. 8 m. 0 f. +X.

In - Gambit. 1: no.4, 5-69.

3015. **The Road Ahead** by Anne Coulter Martens.

Short. 4 m. 4 f.

In - Plays. 27: Feb.1968, 57-64.

3016. **The Road to Bethlehem** by Graham DuBois.

Short. 4 m. 3 f.

In - Plays. 11: Dec.1951, 11-19.

3017. **The Road to Bethlehem** by Graham DuBois.

Short. 5 m. 5 f. +X.

In - Plays. 23: Dec.1963, 27-35.

3018. **The Road to Connaught** by Daniel A. Lord.

In - Cath. World. 110: Dec.1919, 382-394.

3019. **Roamin' Jo and Juli** or **How the West was Lost**
by Claire Boiko.

Short. 13 m. 7 f. +X.

In - Plays. 26: April 1967, 1-13.

3020. **The Roaring March Lion** by Lucille Streacker.

Short. 3 m. 1 f.

In - Plays. 11: March 1952, 78-79.

Robert Burns.

see

Scenes in the Life of Robert Burns.

3022. **Robin Hood in Sherwood Forest** by J.G. Colson.

Short. 13 m. 0 f. +m.X.

In - Plays. 15: Jan.1956, 49-58.

3023. **Robin Hood Outwits the Sheriff** by Constance
Whitman Baher.

Short. 13 m. 6 f.

In - Plays. 25: Feb.1966, 51-60.

3024. **Robin Hood Tricks the Sheriff** by Eva Jacob.

Short. 15 m. 4 f. +m.X.

In - Plays. 16: Oct.1956, 77-81.

3025. **The Robin that Wouldn't Fly** by Claribel
Spamer.

Short. 5 m. 1 f. 4 un.

In - Plays. 7: May 1948, 65-67.

3026. **The Rock** by Shirley Simon.

Short. 6 m. 7 f.

In - Plays. 19: Jan.1960, 42-46.

3027. **The Rock** by Clayton Long.

Full. 25 m. 4 f. 4 b. 1 g.

In - Poet Lore. 61: June-Sept.1966,
117-164, 241-277.

3028. **Rocket to Freedom** by Aileen Fisher and
Olive Rabe.

Short. 4 m. 3 f. +X.

In - Plays. 23: May 1964, 53-58.

3029. **Roddy's Candy Bar** by June Barr.

Short. 6 m. 5 f.

In - Plays. 11: May 1952, 63-66.

3030. **Rollo's Wild Oat** by Clare R. Kummer. Ed. by
Margaret Mayorga.

Short. 4 m. 4 f.

In - Scholastic. 33: Dec.3,1938, 17E-19E+.

3031. **Roly-Poly Freckle-Face** by Sara Sloane McCarty.

Short. 1 m. 2 f.

In - Plays. 18: March 1959, 16-26.

3032. **The Romance of the Willow Pattern Plate** by
Betsy Scoville Provost.

Short. 5 m. 1 f.

In - School Arts. 27: June 1928, 616-620.

3033. **The Romancers** by Edmund Rostand.

In - Poet Lore. 32: Dec.1921, 520-561.

3034. **Romanoff and Juliet** by Peter Ustinov.

Full. 9 m. 4 f.

In - Theatre. 43: May 1959, 25-50.

3035. **The Romantic Ladies** by Moliere.

In - Golden. 11: April 1930, 103-108+.

3036. **Romeo and Juliet** by Dorothy Speare.

Short. 3 m. 2 f.

In - Bookman. 57: March 1923, 7-17.

3037. **Romeo and Juliet** by William Shakespeare.
Adap. by Levy Olfson.

Radio. 10 m. 2 f.

In - Plays. 16: May 1957, 79-90.

3038. **Romeo and Juliet** by William Shakespeare.
Adap. by Levy Olfson.

Radio. 10 m. 2 f.

In - Plays. 23: May 1964, 87-98.

3039. <u>Romulus</u> by Gore Vidal.

Full. 12 m. 2 f.

In - Esquire. 57: Jan.1962, 47-54.

3040. <u>Rondo Capriccioso</u> by Katharine Kester.

Short. 2 m. 2 f.

In - Poet Lore. 37: Sept.1926, 458-467.

3041. <u>Ronny, Donny, and Susy</u> by Helen Littler Howard.

Short. 6 m. 2 f.

In - Plays. 4: April 1945, 53-58.

3042. <u>A Room for a King</u> by Graham DuBois.

Short. 5 m. 5 f.

In - Plays. 12: Dec.1952, 27-37.

3043. <u>Room for Mary</u> by Muriel B. Thurston.

Short. 0 m. 6 f.

In - Plays. 13: Dec.1953, 33-39.

3044. <u>Room 226</u> by Mary Fagin.

In - Poet Lore. 36: Dec.1925, 610-614.

3045. <u>The Room With the Black Door</u> by Hinson Stiles.

In - Poet Lore. 39: March 1928, 101-116.

3046. <u>Roots</u> by Arnold Wesker.

Full. 5 m. 4 f.

In - Players. 7: May & June 1960, 25-31, 25-30.

3047. <u>Rope Dancers</u> by Morton Wishengrad.

Full. 5 m. 4 f.

In - Theatre. 44: Jan.1960, 33-64.

3048. <u>Ropes</u> by Wilbur Daniel Steele.

Short. 2 m. 2 f.

In - Harper's M. 142: Jan.1921, 193-208.

3049. <u>Rosamund At the Tracks</u> by Anita Ryttenberg and Albert Weinberg.

In - Poet Lore. 39: Sept.1928, 436-448.

3050. <u>Roscoe the Robot</u> by Anne Coulter Martens.

Short. 4 m. 4 f.

In - Plays. 28: Oct.1968, 1-10.

3051. <u>The Rose Tattoo</u> by Tennessee Williams.

Full. 9 m. 13 f.

In - Theatre. 39: May 1955, 34-64.

3052. <u>Rose Windows</u> by Stark Young.

Short. 2 m. 2 f.

In - Theatre. 9: Oct.1925, 682-693.

3053. <u>Rosemary for Remembrance</u> by Anne Coulter Martens.

Short. 0 m. 17 f. +f.X.

In - Plays. 23: April 1964, 27-36.

3054. <u>The Rosenhagens</u> by Max Halbe. Trans. by Paul H. Grummann.

Full. 13 m. 3 f.

In - Poet Lore. 21:no.1,1910, 1-87.

3055. <u>Roses for Mother</u> by Deborah Newman.

Short. 3 m. 4 f. +f.X.

In - Plays. 10: May 1951, 55-58.

3056. <u>Ross</u> by Terence Rattigan.

Full. 22 m. 0 f.

In - Theatre. 47: April 1963, 25-58.

3057. <u>The Rosy-Cheeked Ghost</u> by Betty Gray Blaine.

Short. 7 m. 5 f. +X.

In - Plays. 17: Oct.1957, 45-49.

3058. <u>The Royal Cloth of China</u> by Irma Fitz Adcock.

Short. 6 m. 6 f. +X.

In - Plays. 20: Feb.1961, 49-55.

3059. <u>The Royal Family</u> by George S. Kaufman and Edna Ferber. Ed. by Margaret Mayorga.

Excerpt. 9 m. 7 f.

In - Scholastic. 34: April 15,1939, 21E-23E+.

3060. <u>Royal Gambit</u> by Hermann Gressieker. Trans. and adap. by George White.

Full. 1 m. 6 f.

In - Theatre. 43: July 1959, 27-50.

3061. <u>The Royal Hunt of the Sun</u> by Peter Shaffer.

Full. 19 m. 2 f. 2 b.

In - Players. 12: Oct.& Nov.1964, 24-30, 24-32.

3062. <u>Royal Magic</u> by Margaret E. Slattery.

Short. 4 m. 3 f.

In - Plays. 12: May 1953, 54-60.

3063. <u>Rubber</u> by Cora Burlingame.

Short. 4 m. 3 f.

In - Plays. 5: Nov.1945, 11-19.

3064. Rubber Won't Stretch. (anon.)

Short. 3 m. 2 f.

In - Plays. 3: Nov.1943, 73-76.

3065. Rufus Robin's Day in Court by Rose Kacherian
Rybak.

Short. 7 m. 6 f. +X.

In - Plays. 22: April 1963, 74-78.

3066. The Rules of the Game by Luigi Pirandello.
Adap. by William Murray.

Full. 12 m. 3 f.

In - Theatre. 4?: April 1961, 27-52.

3067. The Ruling Class by Mary Winter.

Short. 1 m. 3 f.

In - Drama. 15: April 1925, 150-152.

3068. Ruling Powers by Laurence Housman.

Short. 3 m. 2 f.

In - Yale Review. 29(n.s.): June 1940,
689-705.

3069. Rummage for Victory by Helen Louise Miller.

Short. 1 m. 7 f.

In - Plays. 4: March 1945, 56-66.

3070. Rumplestiltskin by Helen Cotts Bennett.

Short. 7 m. 2 f.

In - Plays. 5: Nov.1945, 47-52.

3071. Rumpelstiltskin adap. by Rowena Bennett.

Short. 3 m. 3 f. +X.

In - Plays. 14: Jan. 1955, 79-83.

3072. Rumpelstiltskin adap. by Adele Thane.

Short. 4 m. 7 f.

In - Plays. 22: April 1963, 53-63.

3073. The Runaway Bookmobile by Claire Boiko.

Short. 4 m. 3 f. 15 c.

In - Plays. 25: Nov.1965, 60-66.

3074. The Runaway Genie by Frances B. Watts.

Short. 4 m. 2 f.

In - Plays. 23: Oct.1963, 43-48.

3075. The Runaway Pirate by Rowena Bennett.

Short. 4 m. 0 f. +m.X.

In - Plays. 10: Nov.1950, 54-56.

3076. The Runaway Toys by Helen Louise Miller.

Short. 6 m. 8 f.

In - Plays. 22: Dec.1962, 71-76.

3077. The Runaway Unicorn by Helen Louise Miller.

Short. 18 m. 5 f.

In - Plays. 21: Nov.1961, 67-72.

3078. Running the Country by Janice Auritt Oser.

Short. 6 m. 5 f.

In - Plays. 13: Nov.1953, 65-68.

3079. S.O.S. from Santa by Helen Louise Miller.

Short. 7 m. 5 f. 5 c.

In - Plays. 28: Dec.1968, 31-39.

3080. Sabrina Fair by Samuel Taylor.

Full. 7 m. 7 f.

In - Theatre. 38: Nov.1954, 34-70.

3081. The Sacrifice of Helen by Wolfgang Hildesheimer. Trans. from the German by
Jacques-Leon Rose.

Short. 2 m. 2 f.

In - Mod. Drama. 2: Sept.1968, 7-29.

3082. Sadco by Byron Pumphrey. Adap. from the
short story by Curtis Zahn.

Short. 3 m. 2 f.

In - First Stage. 6: Sept.1967, 187-194.

3083. Safe for Today by Fonrose Wainwright.

Short. 3 m. 2 f.

In - Survey. 68: July 1,1932, 309-311+.

3084. Safety First, Safety Last, Safety Always by
Edith Larson.

Short. 6 m. 1 f. 5 b. 8 c.

In - Plays. 27: May 1968, 35-41.

3085. The Safety Parade by Aileen Fisher.

Short. 7 m. 6 f. 3 un.

In - Plays. 26: April 1967, 62-64.

3086. Safety Patrol by Lindsey Barbee.

Short. 6 m. 5 f.

In - Plays. 7: Feb.1948, 68-69.

3087. The Safety Pup by Claire Pink.

Short. 7 m. 0 f.

In - Plays. 19: April 1960, 71-74.

3088. Saga of Little Fritjof by Karih Asbrand.

Short. 4 m. 7 f.

In - Plays. 7: Jan.1948, 53-55.

3089. Saint John's Fire by Hermann Sudermann.
Trans. from the German by Charlotte
Porter and H.C. Porter.

Full. 4 m. 6 f.

In - Poet Lore. 15:no.4,1904, 1-71.

3090. St. Nicholas by Katherine L. Oldmeadow.

Short. 1 m. 1 f. 3 g.

In - St. Nicholas. 65: Dec.1937, 14-17+.

3091. St. Patrick Saves the Day by Graham DuBois.

Short. 6 m. 5 f.

In - Plays. 11: March 1952, 38-47.

3092. St. Patrick's Day or The Scheming Lieutenant
by Richard Brinsley Sheridan.

Full. 5 m. 2 f. +X.

In - Golden. 7: March 1928, 351-360.

3093. St. Patrick's Eve by Josephine E. Campbell.

Short. 3 m. 3 f.

In - Plays. 4: March 1945, 15-20.

3094. Salesmanship by Dorothy Deming.

Short. 2 m. 3 f. +X.

In - Plays. 11: Oct.1951, 62-68.

3095. Salome by Oscar Wilde. Trans. from the
French.

Short. 11 m. 2 f. +X.

In - Poet Lore. 18:no.2,1907, 199-223.

3096. Salome by Oscar Wilde.

Short. 11 m. 2 f. +X.

In - Golden. 1: Feb.1925, 207-220.

3097. Salt Water by Benjamin William Newman.

In - Poet Lore. 36: June 1925, 232-242.

3098. Salted Almonds by Thomas Anstey Guthrie.

In - Golden. 14: Nov.1931, 372-375.

3099. Saltimbank by Herman Heijermans. Trans.
from the Dutch by Lilian Saunders and
Caroline Heijermans-Houwink.

In - Drama. 13: Aug.1923, 363-367.

3100. Salvage by Doris K. Thompson and Jane Assur.

Short. 4 m. 2 f.

In - Drama. 21: May 1931, 17-18+.

3101. Sam Tucker by Paul Green.

Short. 1 m. 2 f. 1 b. (all Negro).

In - Poet Lore. 34: June 1923, 220-246.

3102. Samson by Norman Corwin.

Radio. 8 m. 1 f. 1 b.

In - Theatre. 26: Sept.1942, 548-564.

3103. The Sand Dune Hillbillies by Earl J. Dias.

Short. 6 m. 5 f.

In - Plays. 26: May 1967, 15-26.

3104. Sand is My Uniform by Daniel Mauroc.

Short. 6 m. 0 f.

In - First Stage. 3: June 1964, 174-178.

3105. The Sands of Fate: Berlin, July 24 to 31,1914
by Thomas Barclay.

Full. 11 m. 2 f. +X.

In - 19th C. 78: Aug.1915, 444-476.

3106. The Sands of Time by Earl J. Dias.

Short. 3 m. 3 f.

In - Plays. 15: March 1956, 1-10.

3107. Santa and Priorities by Catherine Urban.

Short. 5 m. 1 f.

In - Plays. 4: Dec.1944, 45-47.

3108. Santa and the Efficiency Expert by Frances
B. Watts.

Short. 2 m. 2 f. 6 c.

In - Plays. 27: Dec.1967, 59-64.

3109. Santa and the Spacemen by Catherine Urban.

Short. 5 m. 1 f.

In - Plays. 22: Dec.1962, 67-70.

3110. Santa Calls a Conference by Helen Louise
Miller.

Short. 14 m. 6 f. 18 c.

In - Plays. 26: Dec.1966, 49-58.

3111. Santa Claus and the Three Polar Bears by
Rowena Bennett.

Short. 5 m. 1 f.

In - Plays. 23: Dec.1963, 81-85.

3112. Santa Claus for President by Helen Louise
Miller.

Short. 6 m. 1 f. +11 X.

In - Plays. 11: Dec.1951, 66-69.

3113. Santa Claus for President by Helen Louise
        Miller.
      Short. 6 m. 1 f. 11 un.
      In - Plays. 20: Dec.1960, 71-74.

3114. Santa Claus Is Born by Leslie Hollingsworth.
      Short. 14 m. 3 f. +X.
      In - Plays. 6: Dec.1946, 40-45.

3115. The Santa Claus Parade by Edrie Pendleton.
      Short. 2 m. 0 f. +X.
      In - Plays. 11: Dec.1951, 70-72.

3116. Santa Claus' Surprise Party by Mabell C.
        Flint.
      Short. 1 m. 1 f. +c.X.
      In - Etude. 52: Dec.1934, 705-706.

3117. The Santa Claus Twins by Helen Louise Miller.
      Short. 9 m. 4 f. 2 un. +X.
      In - Plays. 13: Dec.1953, 63-66.

3118. Santa Goes to Town by Marjorie B. Paradis.
      Short. 0 m. 10 f.
      In - Plays. 5: Dec.1945, 18-28.

3119. Santa's Lost Sack by Bartlett B. James.
      Short. 2 m. 2 f. +X.
      In - Ladies' Home. 22: Dec.1904, 28.

3120. Santa's Robbers by Catherine Blanton.
      Short. 4 m. 2 f.
      In - Plays. 8: Dec.1948, 64-65.

3121. Saturday Night by Jacinto Benavente. Trans.
        from the Spanish by John Garrett Under-
        hill.
      Full. 24 m. 20 f. +X.
      In - Poet Lore. 29:no.2,1918, 127-193.

3122. Saturday Night by Paul Green.
      Short. 5 m. 2 f.
      In - Scholastic. 30: Feb.13,1937, 5-7+.

3123. Saturday Night by Paul Green.
      Short. 5 m. 2 f.
      In - Scholastic. 45: Jan.22,1945, 13-14+.

3124. The Saucy Scarecrow by Adele Thane.
      Short. 3 m. 8 f. 6 un. +f.X.
      In - Plays. 20: Oct.1960, 37-44.

3125. Save the Wild Flowers by Frances Duncan and
        Elsie D. Yale.
      In - Woman's Home. 54: May 1927, 49.

3126. Saved by William Dean Howells.
      Short. 5 m. 2 f. 1 g.
      In - Harper's M. 52: Dec.26,1908, 22-24.

3127. Saved by Edward Bond.
      Full. 7 m. 3 f.
      In - Players. 13: Jan.1966, 29-44+.

3128. Saving the Old Homstead by Maxine Fay.
      Short. 7 m. 3 f.
      In - Plays1 12: Feb.1953, 19-26.

3129. Say It with Flowers by Helen Louise Miller.
      Short. 4 m. 5 f.
      In - Plays. 5: Feb.1946, 1-8.

3130. Say It With Flowers by Helen Louise Miller.
      Short. 4 m. 5 f.
      In - Plays. 11: Feb.1952, 85-92.

3131. Say Nothing by James Hanley.
      Full. 2 m. 2 f.
      In - Players. 10: Jan.1963, 27-48.

3132. The Scabs by Paul Mulet.
      Short. 16 m. (6 Negro) 3 f.
      In - First Stage. 1: Sept.1962, 35-49.

3133. The Scarecrow and the Witch by Rowena Bennett.
      Short. 3 m. 4 f. +X.
      In - Plays. 20: Oct.1960, 57-62.

3134. The Scarecrow Party by Vernon Howard.
      Short. 8 m. 0 f.
      In - Plays. 16: Oct.1956, 75-76.

3135. The Scarecrow's Eat by Catherine Urban.
      Short. 8 m. 3 un. +X.
      In - Plays. 23: Oct.1963, 67-72.

3136. Scaredy Cat by John Murray.
      Short. 4 m. 4 f.
      In - Plays. 17: April 1958, 1-12.

3137. Scaredy Cat by Claire Boiko.
      Short. 6 m. 3 f. 1 c.
      In - Plays. 26: Oct.1966, 41-46.

3138. The Scarlet Pimpernel by Baroness Orczy. Adap. by Michael T. Leech.

Short. 11 m. 3 f. 1 b. 1 g. 1 un. +X.

In - Plays. 26: May 1967, 93-108.

3139. Scenes From the Childhood of Franz Schubert by James Francis Cooke.

Short. 4 m. 1 f. 2 b. 1 g. +c.X.

In - Etude. 46: Aug.1928, 589+.

3140. Scenes From the Life of Franz Joseph Haydn by James Francis Cooke.

Short. 2 m. 2 f. 2 b. +ch.

In - Etude. 50: May 1932, 319-320+.

3141. Scenes in the Life of Robert Burns by Sarah Agnes Wallace.

Short. 4 m. 2 f. 5 c.

In - Education. 50: May & June 1930, 565-567, 627-632.

3142. A Scent of Flowers by James Saunders.

Full. 6 m. 3 f.

In - Players. 12: Dec.1964 & Jan.1965, 23-28, 23-30+.

3143. Scheherazade by May Lynch.

Short. 4 m. 6 f. +X.

In - Plays. 18: March 1959, 59-63.

The Scheming Lieutenant.

see

St. Patrick's Day.

3145. Schnitzleresque by Carla L. Palm.

Short. 2 m. 3 f.

In - Drama. 14: March 1924, 210-212.

3146. School for Jesters by Constance Whitman.

Short. 7 m. 3 f. +X.

In - Plays. 23: May 1964, 45-52.

3147. School for Scamperers by Rowena Bennett.

Short. 3 m. 2 f.

In - Plays. 20: May 1961, 69-72.

3148. A School for Scaring by Helen Louise Miller.

Short. 9 m. 8 f.

In - Plays. 17: Oct.1957, 69-74.

3149. Science In a Democracy by Bernard Jaffe.

Short. 6 m. 1 f.

In - Scholastic. 36: March 11,1940, 17-19+.

3150. Screen Test by Burgess Meredith.

Radio. 4 m. 1 f. +X.

In - Scholastic. 52: March 22,1948, 17-19.

3151. Scribe to General Washington by Gertrude Robinson.

Short. 12 m. 0 f. +m.X.

In - Plays. 3: Jan.1944, 12-23.

3152. The Sea People by Betty Tracy Huff.

Short. 5 m. 3 f. +X.

In - Plays. 19: Jan.1960, 75-78.

3153. The Search for Happiness by Marie Barlow Buckman.

Short. 6 m. 3 un. +X.

In - Plays. 13: Oct.1953, 55-57.

3154. The Search-Light by Lucy Clifford.

Short. 2 m. 5 f.

In - 19th C. 53: Jan.1903, 159-176.

3155. Season in the Sun by Wolcott Gibbs.

Full. 9 m. 6 f.

In - Theatre. 35: June 1951, 60-85.

3156. Season's Greetings by Helen Louise Miller.

Short. 8 m. 3 f.

In - Plays. 16: Dec.1956, 1-13.

3157. Second Life by Georg Hirschfeld. Adap. from the German by Mary L. Stephenson.

In - Poet Lore. 39: Dec.1928, 475-528.

3158. Second Marriage of Santa Claus by John A. Kirkpatrick. Ed. by Margaret Mayorga.

Short. 3 m. 4 f.

In - Scholastic. 33: Dec.17,1938, 15E-17E.

3159. The Second Sunday in May by Robert Downing.

Short. 0 m. 6 f.

In - Plays. 16: May 1957, 1-11.

3160. Second Threshold by Philip Barry. With revisions by Robert E. Sherwood.

Full. 4 m. 2 f.

In - Theatre. 35: Dec.1951, 50-70.

3161. The Secret Hiding Place by Sadye B. Wein.

Short. 4 m. 5 f.

In - Plays. 20: April 1961, 53-58.

3162. The Secret of Pinchpenny Manor by Herbert
      Ravetch.

      Short. 5 m. 3 f. +X.

      In - Plays. 17: March 1958, 39-45.

3163. The Secret of the Church Mouse by Karin
      Asbrand.

      Short. 5 m. 4 f.

      In - Plays. 18: April 1959, 81-85.

3164. The Secret of the Princess by Esther MacLellan
      and Catherine V. Schroll.

      Short. 0 m. 6 f.

      In - Plays. 15: March 1956, 61-66.

3165. Secret of the Roman Stairs by Leota B.
      Heshmati.

      Short. 3 m. 2 b. 2 g.

      In - Plays. 25: April 1966, 37-42.

3166. The Secret of the Windmill by Esther MacLellan
      and Catherine V. Schroll.

      Short. 4 m. 5 f.

      In - Plays. 21: May 1962, 39-44.

3167. Secret Session by Olive Rabe.

      Radio. 13 m. 0 f.

      In - Plays. 6: May 1947, 69-77.

3168. The Secret Weapon by Gladys L. Schmitt.

      Radio. 9 m. 2 f. +X.

      In - Scholastic. 37: Nov.4,1940, 17-20+.

3169. See the Jaguar by N. Richard Nash.

      Full. 12 m. 3 f. +X.

      In - Theatre. 37: Aug.1953, 33-64.

3170. See the Parade by Mildred Hark and Noel
      McQueen.

      Short. 5 m. 2 f.

      In - Plays. 6: May 1947, 44-50.

3171. See You in the Funnies by Earl J. Dias.

      Short. 4 m. 3 f. +c.X.

      In - Plays. 26: Jan.1967, 1-12.

3172. Seeing the Elephant (abr.) by Dan W. Totheroh.

      Short. 4 m. 1 f.

      In - Scholastic. 36: April 29, 1940, 17-19.

3173. Seeking Peace on Earth by Anna P. Shoemaker.

      Short. 3 m. 2 f. 1 b. +X.

      In - Jl., N.E.A. 28: Dec.1939, 261-262.

3174. Seize on Tragic Time by Ruth Forbes Sherry.

      Short. 3 m. 1 f. +ch. +c.X.

      In - Poet Lore. 58: June 1963, 99-117.

3175. Self Respect by Cahir Healy.

      In - Cath. World. 128: Oct.1928, 43-51.

3176. Self-Sacrifice: a Farce-Tragedy by William
      Dean Howells.

      Short. 1 m. 3 f.

      In - Harper's M. 122: April 1911, 748-757.

3177. The Selfish Giant by Cynthia Brown.

      Short. 6 m. 0 f. +c.X.

      In - Plays. 3: April 1944, 58-60.

3178. Send Me No Flowers by Norman Barasch and
      Carroll Moore.

      Full. 8 m. 4 f.

      In - Theatre. 45: June 1961, 33-57.

3179. Separate Tables by Terence Rattigan.

      2 "plays". 3 m. 8 f. in each.

      In - Theatre. 42: May 1958, 34-63.

3180. Sergeant Santa Claus by Helen Louise Miller.

      Short. 9 m. 3 f.

      In - Plays. 4: Dec.1944, 1-13.

3181. Serjeant Musgrave's Dance by John Arden.

      Full. 13 m. 2 f.

      In - Players. 8 & 9: Sept.& Oct.1961,
           25-32+, 25-33.

3182. The Servant In the House by Charles Rann
      Kennedy.

      Full. 4 m. 2 f. 1 b.

      In - Golden. 2: Dec.1925, 795-815.

3183. Servants of the People by James M. Cain.

      Short. 4 m. 0 f.

      In - American Merc. 4: April 1925, 393-398.

3184. Service for Hubert by Samuel S. Richmond.

      Short. 3 m. 1 f.

      In - Plays. 4: Oct.1944, 67-73.

3185. The Set Up by Eugene Weiger.

      Full. 7 m. 2 f.

      In - First Stage. 3: March 1964, 110-137.

3186. Setness of Abijah by Lucy Lane Clifford.

In - Harper's B. .: March 1903, 204-210.

3187. Setting Santa St right by Aileen Fisher.

Short. 10 m. 6 f.

In - Plays. 18: Dec.1958, 55-61.

3188. The Seven Little Seeds by Jean Gould.

Short. 3 m. 7 f.

In - Plays. 11: March 1952, 69-72.

3189. The Seven Year Itch by George Axelrod.

Full. 5 m. 6 f.

In - Theatre. 38: Jan.1954, 34-61.

3190. The Seventeenth Day by William E. Taylor.

Short. 3 m. 1 f.

In - Poet Lore. 61: March 1966, 39-57.

3191. Seventy-Three Voted Yes adap. by Tracy D.
Mygatt from an article by Maud Johnson
Elmore.

Short. 0 m. 7 f.

In - World Out. 4: Sept.1918, 18-19.

3192. Shades of Ransom by James R. Chisholm.

Short. 6 m. 3 f.

In - Plays. 18: Oct.1958, 35-43.

3193. Shades of Shakespeare by Earl J. Dias.

Short. 3 m. 4 f.

In - Plays. 25: April 1966, 1-12.

3194. The Shadowy Waters by William Butler Yeates.

Short. 2 m. 1 f. +X.

In - North Amer. 170: May 1900, 711-729.

3195. Shakespeare On the Razor's Edge by Ruth
Amelia Feley.

Short. 4 m. 0 f.

In - Education. 53: May 1933, 559-562.

3196. The Shakespearian Touch by Helen Louise
Miller.

Short. 10 m. 6 f.

In - Plays. 14: Nov.1954, 1-12.

3197. Sharing the Circus by Camilla Campbell.

Short. 4 m. 3 f.

In - Plays. 9: May 1950, 64-65.

3198. Shatter the Day by George Abbe.

Full. 4 m. 2 f. 5 un.

In - Poet Lore. 63: Dec.1968, 447-495.

3199. She Also Serves by Marjorie B. Paradis.

Short. 5 m. 7 f.

In - Plays. 10: April 1951, 1-6.

3200. She Borrowed Her Own Husband by Rupert Hughes.

In - Lippincott's. 77: May 1906, 541-554.

3201. She Laughs Last by Marjorie B. Paradis.

Short. 0 m. 10 f.

In - Plays. 10: May 1951, 10-21.

3202. She Laughs Last by Marjorie B. Paradis.

Short. 0 m. 10 f.

In - Plays. 13: March 1954, 1-11.

3203. She Laughs Last by Marjorie B. Paradis.

Short. 0 m. 10 f.

In - Plays. 22: March 1963, 25-35.

3204. She Stoops to Conquer by Oliver Goldsmith.
Adap. by Edward Golden.

Radio. 7 m. 3 f.

In - Plays. 16: March 1957, 83-94.

3205. She Was No Lady by St.John Ervine.

Short. 2 m. 2 f.

In - Golden. 13: July 1931, 81-85.

3206. She Who Was Fished. Trans. from the ancient
Japanese farce Tsuri Onna by Michio Itow
and Louis V. Ledoux.

Short. 2 m. 2 f.

In - Outlook. 133: Jan.31,1923, 218-219.

3207. Shee Shih, The Aching Heart by T'ang Wen
Shun.

Short. 8 m. 3 f.

In - Carolina. 15: Dec.1942, 100-109.

3208. Sheep Skin Po by Genevieve Wimsatt.

Short. 9 m. 5 f. +X.

In - Plays. 12: Jan.1953, 51-58.

3209. Shelter for the Night by Graham DuBois.

Short. 7 m. 5 f. +m.X.

In - Plays. 17: Dec.1957, 23-32.

The Shepherd's Chameleon.

see

Improvisation.

3211. Sherlock Holmes and the Gorgon's Head by
       Margaret Paulus.

       Short. 2 m. 0 f. 6 b.

       In - Scholastic. 41: Nov.9,1942, 17-19.

3212. Sherlock Holmes and the Red-Headed League
       by A. Conan Doyle. Adap. by Lewy Olfson.

       Radio. 6 m. 0 f.

       In - Plays. 19: Oct.1959, 87-96.

3213. Sherlock Holmes and the Stockbroker's Clerk
       by A. Conan Doyle. Adap. by Lewy Olfson.

       Radio. 6 m. 0 f.

       In - Plays. 23: Oct.1963, 85-95.

3214. She's Not Talking by Paul S. McCoy.

       Short. 2 m. 3 f.

       In - Plays. 17: April 1958, 23-36.

3215. Ship Forever Sailing by Stanley Young.

       Short. 13 m. 2 f. +X.

       In - Scholastic. 35: Nov.20,1939, 19E-22E.

3216. Ship's Boy to the Indies by Esther MacLellan
       and Catherine V. Schvoll.

       Short. 7 m. 3 f.

       In - Plays. 11: Oct.1951, 35-39.

3217. The Shipwrecked King by Margaret E. Slattery.

       Short. 6 m. 3 f.

       In - Plays. 25: May 1966, 55-61.

3218. Shirley Holmes and the FBI by Helen Louise
       Miller.

       Short. 9 m. 5 f.

       In - Plays. 24: April 1965, 45-53.

3219. Shiver My Timbers by John Murray.

       Short. 5 m. 3 f.

       In - Plays. 22: Oct.1962, 1-13.

3220. The Shoemaker and the Elves by Alice Very.

       Short. 6 m. 2 f.

       In - Plays. 8: Dec.1948, 54-58.

3221. The Shoemaker and the Elves by Rowena Bennett.

       Short. 4 m. 1 f.

       In - Plays. 22: Dec.1962, 77-81.

3222. Shoes and Stockings and Solomon by Aileen
       Fisher.

       Short. 4 un.

       In - Plays. 20: Dec.1960, 59-60.

3223. Shoes For Washington by Kate Arnold and
       Eleanor Winslow Williams.

       Short. 2 m. 1 f. 1 b. 1 g.

       In - St. Nicholas. 67: Feb.1939, 24-25+.

3224. The Shop Girl's Revenge by Robert Downing.

       Short. 4 m. 3 f.

       In - Plays. 15: Jan.1956, 25-34.

3225. Shouting the Battle Cry of "Feed 'Em" by
       Edna Randolph Worrell.

       Short. Large cast of children.

       In - Ladies' Home. 34: Nov.1917, 40.

3226. The Show-Off by George Kelly.

       Excerpt. 2 m. 2 f.

       In - Theatre. 22: Sept.1938, 686-689.

3227. The Shower Hearts by Helen Louise Miller.

       Short. 12 m. 8 f. +X.

       In - Plays. 19: Feb.1960, 67-72.

3228. The Shower: the Moon trans. from the Noh
       drama by Yone Noguchi.

       Short. 2 m. 1 f. +ch.

       In - Poet Lore. 29:no.4,1918, 455-458.

3229. Shrimp! by Elizabeth Lou Knight.

       Radio. 11 m. 4 f.

       In - Plays. 3: Nov.1943, 81-85.

3230. Shroud My Body Down by Paul Green.

       Excerpt. 9 m. 1 f. +X.

       In - Carolina. 7: Dec.1934, 99-111.

3231. The Shy Prince by Claribel Spamer.

       Short. 4 m. 4 f.

       In - Plays. 3: Nov.1943, 65-69.

3232. Sicilian Limes by Luigi Pirandello. Trans.
       by Elizabeth Abbott.

       Short. 2 m. 2 f. +X.

       In - Theatre. 6: Oct.1922, 329-344.

3233. Sickle by Britton B. Cooke.

       In - Canadian M. 46: Dec.1915, 111-118.

3234. The Sidhe of Ben-Mor by Ruth Sawyer.

       Short. 1 m. 9 f. 1 b. 1 g.

       In - Poet Lore. 21:no.4,1910, 300-310.

3235. The Signpost by Patricia Clapp.

       Short. 4 m. 2 f.

       In - Plays. 22: May 1963, 53-59.

3236. Sigrid by Margaret Radcliff.

Short. 3 m. 2 f.

In - Carolina. 7: Sept.1934, 67-80.

3237. Silas Marner by George Eliot. Adap. by Lewy Olfson.

Radio. 4 m. 5 f. 6 un.

In - Plays. 13: April 1954, 70-78.

3238. Silent Night by Leslie Hollingsworth.

Short. 4 m. 5 f. +ch.

In - Plays. 13: Dec.1953, 49-54.

3239. Silent Night by Leslie Hollingsworth.

Short. 2 m. 2 f. 1 b. 2 g. +X.

In - Plays. 27: Dec.1967, 91-96.

3240. Silent Night, Lonely Night by Robert Anderson.

Full. 3 m. 3 f.

In - Theatre. 45: Dec.1961, 25-56.

3241. The Silent Prince by Margaret E. Slattery.

Short. 5 m. 4 f.

In - Plays. 18: April 1959, 57-64.

3242. The Silly Citizens of Happy Valley by Gladys Guilford Scott.

Short. 7 m. +X.

In - Plays. 19: May 1960, 53-62.

3243. The Silly Princesses by Margaret E. Slattery.

Short. 4 m. 5 f.

In - Plays. 20: March 1961, 57-64.

3244. The Silver Coffeepot by Karin Asbrand.

Short. 2 m. 2 f. 8 b. 13 g.

In - Plays. 6: Oct.1946, 49-54.

3245. The Silver Whistle by Robert E. McEnroe.

Full. 10 m. 5 f.

In - Theatre. 33: July 1949, 59-92.

3246. Simoom by August Strindberg. Trans. from the German of Emil Schering by Mary Harned.

Short. 2 m. 1 f.

In - Poet Lore. 17:no.3,1906, 21-28.

3247. Simple Sam by Mary Nygaard Peterson.

Short. 7 m. 0 f. +X.

In - Plays. 17: Jan.1958, 71-76.

3248. Simple Simon's Reward by Helen Louise Miller.

Short. 9 m. 4 f. 2 b. 3 g.

In - Plays. 27: Nov.1967, 65-77.

3249. Sing a Song of Christmas by Karin Asbrand.

Short. 13 m. 11 f.

In - Plays. 6: Dec.1946, 69-72.

3250. Sing a Song of Pioneers by Aileen Fisher.

Short. 20 m. 8 f. +X.

In - Plays. 22: Jan.1963, 35-47.

3251. Sing, America, Sing by Aileen Fisher and Olive Rabe.

Short. 9 m. 3 f. +z.ch. +X.

In - Plays. 15: May 1956, 73-82.

3252. Sing the Songs of Christmas by Aileen Fisher.

Short. 21 m. 4 f. 7 un. +X.

In - Plays. 17: Dec.1957, 75-86.

3253. Sing the Songs of Cowboys by Aileen Fisher.

Short. 11 m. 1 f. +X.

In - Plays. 22: Oct.1962, 51-57.

3254. Sing the Songs of Freedom by Aileen Fisher.

Short. 12 m. 8 f. 2 un. +X.

In - Plays. 19: May 1960, 85-98.

3255. Sing the Songs of Lincoln by Aileen Fisher.

Short. 10 m. 8 f. +X.

In - Plays. 21: Feb.1962, 79-95.

3256. Sing the Songs of Springtime by Aileen Fisher.

Short. 8 un. +X.

In - Plays. 19: April 1960, 75-80.

3257. Sing the Songs of Thanksgiving by Aileen Fisher.

Short. 5 m. 6 f. +ch.

In - Plays. 18: Nov.1958, 76-85.

3258. Sing the Songs of Travel by Aileen Fisher.

Short. 8 m. 3 f.

In - Plays. 21: April 1962, 54-60.

3259. Singing Heart's Christmas Eve. (Anon.)

Short. 0 m. 3 f. +ch.

In - Etude. 56: Dec.1938, 842-843.

3260. The Singing Lesson by Marion E. Thorpe Diller.

Short. 4 m. 2 f.

In - Plays. 5: May 1946, 61-63.

3261. The Singing Pool by Helen L. Mobert.

Short. 4 m. 2 f.

In - Poet Lore. 30:no.2,1919, 275-288.

3262. The Singing Shark by Vernon Howard.

Short. 1 m. 8 un.

In - Plays. 16: May 1957, 77-78.

3263. Singing Valley by Josephina Niggli.

Excerpt. 2 m. 2 f.

In - Carolina. 9: Dec.1936, 107-110.

3264. Sir David Wears a Crown by Stuart Walker.

Short. Large cast of children.

In - Ladies' Home. 38: June 1921, 6-7+.

3265. Sir Osbert and Lester by Don McGregor.

Short. 8 m. 2 f. 7c. +X.

In - Plays. 28: Oct.1968, 73-76.

3266. Sir Robin of Locksley by Pauline Gibson. Based on the motion picture The Adventures of Robin Hood.

Radio. 9 m. 1 f. +X.

In - Scholastic. 32: May 14,1938, 30-33.

3267. The Sire de Malétroit's Door by Robert Louis Stevenson. Adap. by Walter Hackett.

Radio. 12 m. 2 f.

In - Plays. 8: March 1949, 67-75.

3268. The Sire de Malétroit's Door by Robert Louis Stevenson. Adap. by Walter Hackett.

Radio. 12 m. 2 f.

In - Plays. 27: April 1968, 87-95.

3269. Sixteen by Betty Keppler. Adap. from the story by Maureen Daly.

Radio. 3 m. 2 f. +X.

In - Scholastic. 37: Oct.21,1940, 32-34+.

3270. Skelton by Mark Dunster.

Short. 11 m. 0 f. +X.

In - First Stage. 7: Dec.1968, 141-149.

3271. The Skill of Pericles by Paul T. Nolan.

Short. 7 m. 3 f. +X.

In - Plays. 21: May 1962, 54-60.

3272. Skin Deep by Karin Asbrand.

Short. 5 m. 5 f. +X.

In - Plays. 4: April 1945, 40-44.

3273. The Slaughter of the Innocents by William Saroyan.

Full. 23 m. 6 f. 1 b. +X.

In - Theatre. 36: Nov.1952, 33-56.

3274. Sleep On, Lemuel by John W. Parker.

Short. 3 m. 2 f.

In - Carolina. 5: Dec.1932, 108-118.

3275. Sleeping Beauty by Caroline Verhoeff.

In - St. Nicholas. 40: April 1913, 548-552.

3276. Sleeping Beauty by Helen Cotts Bennett.

Short. 6 m. 11 f.

In - Plays. 4: Nov.1944, 35-41.

3277. Sleeping Beauty by Helen Cotts Bennett.

Short. 6 m. 11 f.

In - Plays. 20: April 1961, 59-64.

3278. The Sleeping Beauty by Charles Perrault. Adap. by Adele Thane.

Short. 4 m. 11 f. 2 b. 1 g.

In - Plays. 25: March 1966, 67-73.

3279. The Sleeping Beauty in the Wood adap. by Alice Very.

Short. 4 m. 15 f. +X.

In - Plays. 7: April 1948, 61-64.

3280. The Sleeping Chinese Beauty by Kay Locke.

Short. 5 m. 8 f.

In - Plays. 26: May 1967, 81-84.

3281. The Sleeping Prince by Terence Rattigan.

Full. 7 m. 6 f.

In - Theatre. 41: Dec.1957, 34-65.

3282. The Sleepy Little Elf by O.J. Robertson.

Short. 3 m. 0 f. 14 c.

In - Plays. 27: Dec.1967, 70-72.

3283. Slippers by Anne Macfarlane.

In - Poet Lore. 32: Sept.1921, 425-430.

3284. The Slippers That Broke of Themselves by Marie Drennan.

Short. 5 m. 2 f.

In - Poet Lore. 37: June 1926, 258-273.

3285. Slow But Sure by Marian Spencer Smith.
Short. 2 m. 2 f.
In - Drama. 17: Feb.1927, 138-140.

3286. Small Crimson Parasol by Claire Boiko.
Short. 6 m. 4 f. 5 c.
In - Plays. 25: Jan.1966, 67-72.

3287. Small Shoes and Small Tulips by Esther
MacLellan and Catherine V. Schroll.
Short. 4 m. 3 f.
In - Plays. 12: May 1953, 61-65.

3288. Small War on Murray Hill by Robert E. Sherwood.
Full. 18 m. 9 f.
In - Theatre. 42: Aug.1958, 26-47.

3289. A Small World by Janice Auritt Oser.
Short. 3 m. 1 f. +X.
In - Plays. 14: March 1955, 67-71.

3290. The Smell of New Bread by Shirley Simon.
Short. 6 m. 2 f. +X.
In - Plays. 21: May 1962, 69-74.

3291. The Smiling Angel by Aileen Fisher.
Short. 4 m. 3 f. 3 b. 3 g. +c.ch. +X.
In - Jl., N.E.A. 35: Dec.1946, 568-571.

3292. Smokey Wins His Star by Jane McGowan.
Short. 14 m. 4 f.
In - Plays. 22: Oct.1962, 75-80.

3293. The Smug Citizen by Maxim Gorki. Trans. by
Edwin Hopkins.
Full. 6 m. 6 f.
In - Poet Lore. 17:no.4,1906, 1-74.

3294. Snipe Hunt by George Llyonel Williams.
Short. 2 m. 1 f.
In - First Stage. 2: June 1963, 194-201.

3295. Snoop's Scoop by Helen Louise Miller.
Short. 6 m. 2 f.
In - Plays. 3: Jan.1944, 23-32.

3296. The Snow Goose by Paul Gallico.
Radio. 6 m. 0 f. 1 g.
In - Scholastic. 42: March 8,1943, 15-17.

3297. The Snow Man Who Overstayed by Claire Boiko.
Short. 6 m. 5 f. +X.
In - Plays. 26: March 1967, 70-74.

3298. The Snow Queen by Hans Christian Andersen.
Adap. by Michael T. Leech.
Short. 2 m. 6 f. +X.
In - Plays. 26: Feb.1967, 69-74.

3299. Snow White by Anne Crowell.
Short. 1 m. 2 f. 7 b.
In - Delineator. 93: July 1918, 324.

3300. Snow White by Eva Jacob.
Short. 9 m. 6 f.
In - Plays. 17: March 1958, 72-78.

3301. Snow White: or The Modern School Girl by
Roberta M. Ryan.
Short. 1 m. 2 f.
In - Wilson. 13: April 1939, 554-555.

3302. Snow White and Friends by Val Cheatham.
Short. 4 m. 2 f. 1 un.
In - Plays. 27: Dec.1967, 42-48.

3303. Snow White and Rose Red adap. by Rowena
Bennett.
Short. 5 m. 3 f. +X.
In - Plays. 24: Oct.1964, 53-64.

3304. The Snow Witch by Constance D'Arcy Mackay.
Short. 3 m. 3 f. +X
In - Delineator. '.   911, 161.

3305. The Snowdrop by Claribel Spamer.
Short. 5 m. 5 f. 4 c. +c.X.
In - Plays. 13: April 1954, 60-62.

3306. So Long at the Fair by Helen Louise Miller.
Short. 9 m. 5 f. +X.
In - Plays. 22: May 1963, 85-90.

3307. So Long, Miss Jones by Lydia Caplan.
Short. 6 m. 1 f.
In - Jl., N.E.A. 33: Mar.1944, 67-68.

3308. So Much of Light by Harriet Plimpton.
Full. 9 m. 8 f.
In - Poet Lore. 51: Jan.1945, 3-41.

3309. So Proud to Serve by Lindsey Barbee.
Short. 6 m. 2 f.
In - Plays. 5: Dec.1945, 65-69.

3310. So Shines A Good Deed by Graham DuBois.
      Short. 2 m. 4 f.
      In - Plays. 5: May 1946, 24-32.

3311. So This Is China by Karin Asbrand.
      Short. 6 m. 14 f.
      In - Plays. 9: March 1950, 52-61.

3312. Social Success by Max Beerbohm.
      In - Golden. 20: July 1934, 112-122.

3313. The Social Worker and the Alcoholic by
      George Kauffman.
      Short. 1 m. 1 f.
      In - First Stage. 3: Dec.1963, 43-46.

3314. Society Page by Joan and Pearl Allred.
      Short. 2 m. 6 f.
      In - Plays. 11: March 1952, 1-17.

3315. Socrates Saves the Day by Marjorie B.
      Paradis.
      Short. 8 m. 3 f. 2 c.
      In - Plays. 16: Nov.1956, 45-52.

3316. The Soft Hearted Ghost by Helen Louise
      Miller.
      Short. 5 m.
      In - Plays.   945, 1-8.

3317. The Soft-Hearted Ghost by Helen Louise Miller.
      Short. 5 m. 3 f. +X.
      In - Plays. 11: Oct.1951, 10-17.

3318. Softy the Snow Man by Helen Louise Miller.
      Short. 9 m. 4 f.
      In - Plays. 12: Dec.1952, 38-44.

3319. Softy the Snow Man by Helen Louise Miller.
      Short. 9 m. 4 f.
      In - Plays. 16: Dec.1956, 63-69.

3320. Soldadera (Soldier-Woman) by Josephina
      Niggli.
      Short. 1 m. 7 f.
      In - Carolina. 9: March 1936, 8-30.

3321. Soldiers on the Home Front by Mildred Hark
      and Noel McQueen.
      Short. 5 m. 5 f.
      In - Plays. 3: May 1944, 70-73.

3322. The Solemn Communion by Fernando Arrabal.
      Trans. from the French by John Calder.
      Short. 3 m. 3 f.
      In - Gambit. 3: no.12, 5-13.

3323. The Solid Gold Cadillac by Howard Teichmann
      and George S. Kaufman.
      Full. 13 m. 5 f.
      In - Theatre. 40: April 1956, 34-57.

3324. Soloman by Grace Dorcas Hutchinson Ruthenburg.
      In - Poet Lore. 34: Dec.1925, 600-609.

3325. The Solstice by Karel Matej Capek. Trans.
      from the Czech by E.D. Schonberger.
      Full. 9 m. 3 f. 1 b. 1 g.
      In - Poet Lore. 35: Dec.1924, 475-521.

3326. Some Are Teachers by Luise DeMarco.
      Short. 3 m. 4 f.
      In - Plays. 7: Nov.1947, 67-75.

3327. Some Party by Kenneth Lewis Roberts.
      Short. 4 m. 4 f.
      In - Sat. Evening. 199: April 23,1927, 32-33+.

3328. Some Tricks Are Treats by Francis L. Kroll.
      Short. 2 m. 2 f.
      In - Plays. 14: Oct.1954, 62-66.

3329. Somebody's Valentine by Joan Lawrence.
      Short. 3 m. 6 f.
      In - Plays. 12: Feb.1953, 50-53.

3330. Somebody's Valentine by Deborah Newman.
      Short. 3 m. 6 f.
      In - Plays. 26: Feb.1967, 75-78.

3331. Something About Songs by Leonora Sill Ashton.
      Short. 2 b. 2 g. +c.X.
      In - Etude. 72: April 1954, 54.

3332. Something New for Halloween by Deborah
      Newman.
      Short. 5 m. 4 f. +X.
      In - Plays. 12: Oct.1952, 53-57.

3333. Something New for Halloween by Deborah
      Newman.
      Short. 5 m. 4 f. +X.
      In - Plays. 23: Oct.1963, 73-77.

3334. Somewhat Forgetful by Morton K. Schwartz.

Short. 4 m. 0 f.

In - Plays. 9: April 1950, 51-56.

3335. The Son Left in the Plantation of Mulberry
Trees by Chin Lin Chen.

Short. 3 m. 1 f.

In - Poet Lore. 33: Dec.1922, 595-600.

3336. The Son of a Tanner by Cora Burlingame.

Short. 6 m. 3 f.

In - Plays. 4: March 1945, 20-28.

3337. A Son of America by Graham DuBois.

Short. 2 m. 4 f.

In - Plays. 7: Nov.1947, 20-29.

3338. Son of Liberty by Esther Lipnick.

Short. 2 m. 5 f.

In - Plays. 3: April 1944, 34-40.

3339. The Son of William Tell by Paul T. Nolan.

Short. 8 m. 3 f.

In - Plays. 19: April 1960, 81-87.

3340. Song From Heaven by Claudia Stewart Bachman.

Short. 2 m. 1 f.

In - Etude. 72: Dec.1954, 54.

3341. A Song Goes Forth by Claire Boiko.

Short (musical). 3 m. 2 f. 4 un. +ch.

In - Plays. 28: Oct.1968, 83-86.

3342. A Song in the Night by Graham DuBois.

Short. 6 m. 5 f. +X.

In - Plays. 16: Dec.1956, 31-39.

The Song of Drums.

see

Tyl Ulenspiegel.

3344. Song of the Forest by Vernon Howard.

Short. 1 m. 0 f. 4 b. 4 g.

In - Plays. 15: March 1956, 84-86.

3345. Song of the New World by Rose Schneideman.

Radio. 8 m. 1 f.

In - Scholastic. 39: Dec.1,1941, 18-19+.

3346. Songs of America Growing by Aileen Fisher.

Short. 19 m. 8 f. +X.

In - Plays. 21: May 1962, 75-84.

3347. Sophia the Seamstress by Earl J. Dias.

Short. 4 m. 7 f.

In - Plays. 24: April 1965, 1-13.

3348. Souls Exchanged by Wilhelm von Scholz.
Trans. by Lee M. Hollander.

Full. 26 m. 5 f. +X.

In - Poet Lore. 52: July & Oct.1945,
202-255, 291-352.

3349. Sound on the Goose by Nicholas Biel.

Full. 7 m. 3 f.

In - First Stage. 3: Dec.1963, 13-41.

3350. Soup Stone by W.A. Stigler.

Short. 4 m. 6 f.

In - Poet Lore. 35: March 1924, 91-99.

3351. The Soup Stone by Mary Nygaard Peterson.

Short. 4 m. 4 f.

In - Plays. 16: March 1957, 67-71.

3352. Sour Grapes and Apples by Ann Steward.

Short. 1 m. 3 f.

In - Plays. 6: Oct.1946, 55-58.

3353. Sourdough Sally by Helen Louise Miller.

Short. 7 m. 6 f.

In - Plays. 22: Jan.1963, 61-67.

3354. South of the Border by Rose W. Shenker.

Short. 5 m. 5 f.

In - Plays. 8: March 1949, 49-53.

3355. Space Suit with Roses by Juliet Garver.

Short. 2 m. 11 f.

In - Plays. 20: Oct.1960, 27-36.

3356. Spaceship Santa Maria by Claire Boiko.

Short. 12 m. 3 f.

In - Plays. 25: Oct.1965, 61-67.

3357. Spadassin! a Comically Fantastic Tragedy by
Montgomery Major.

In - Poet Lore. 36: June 1925, 265-279.

3358. Spanish Love by Mary Roberts Rinehart and
Avery Hopwood.

Short. 5 m. 1 f.

In - Everybody's. 45: August 1921, 91-98.

Spare.

see

Cockade 3.

3360.   The Spark by Edouard Pailleron. Trans. from
        the French by Abbie Findlay Potts.
        Short. 1 m. 2 f.
        In - Poet Lore. 38: Sept.1927, 373-400.

3361.   The Sparrow Family by Mildred Hark and Noel
        McQueen.
        Short. 5 m. 5 f. +X.
        In - Plays. 18: Feb.1959, 83-86.

3362.   Spartan Dorothy and Her Fox by Lou Rodman
        Teeple.
        Short. 2 m. 4 f.
        In - Overland. 39: Jan.1902, 548-553.

3363.   Special Delivery by van Tassel Sutphen.
        Short. 0 m. 1 f.
        In - Harper's M. 108: Feb.1904, 458-462.

3364.   Special Delivery by Samuel S. Richmond.
        Short. 5 m. 0 f. +m.& f.X.
        In - Plays. 6: May 1947, 63-68.

3365.   Special Edition by Aileen Fisher.
        Short. 4 m. 4 f.
        In - Plays. 6: Oct.1947, 44-51.

3366.   Special Edition by Aileen Fisher.
        Short. 4 m. 4 f.
        In - Plays. 22: May 1963, 61-68.

3367.   The Spelling Match by Evelyn Ray Sickels.
        Short. 3 m. 5 f. +X.
        In - Plays. 3: Oct.1943, 51-55.

3368.   Spiced Wine by Willis Knapp Jones.
        In - Poet Lore. 36: March 1925, 84-95.

3369.   Spies and Dolls by John Murray.
        Short. 8 m. 4 f.
        In - Plays. 26: March 1967, 13-25.

3370.   The Spineless Drudge by Richard W. Harris.
        Short. 6 m. 3 f.
        In - First Stage. 2: Dec.1962, 42-45.

3371.   The Spirit of Christmas by Aileen Fisher.
        Short. 2 m. 4 f. 2 un.
        In - Plays. 9: Dec.1949, 75-77.

3372.   The Spirit of Christmas Joy by Constance
        D'Arcy Mackay.
        Short. Many c.
        In - Delineator. 78: Dec.1911, 514-516.

3373.   Spitting Image by Colin Spencer.
        Full. 5 m. 2 f.
        In - Players. 16: Nov.1968, 27-45.

3374.   A Splendid Offer by Grace Elizabeth King.
        Short. 0 m. 5 f.
        In - Drama. 16: March 1926, 213-215+.

3375.   Spooks in Books by Helen Louise Miller.
        Short. 5 m. 5 f. +X.
        In - Plays. 15: Oct.1955, 1-8.

3376.   Spooky Spectacles by Helen Louise Miller.
        Short. 5 m. 6 f.
        In - Plays. 14: Oct.1954, 1-12.

3377.   Spreading the News by Lady Gregory.
        Short. 7 m. 3 f.
        In - Golden. 2: Sept.1925, 355-362.

3378.   Spring Dance by Philip Barry. Adap. by Eleanor
        Golden and Eloise Barrangon.
        Short. 7 m. 6 f.
        In - Scholastic. 32: Feb.19,1938, 17E-19E+.

3379.   Spring Daze by Mildred Hark and Noel
        McQueen.
        Short. 2 m. 2 f.
        In - Plays. 10: March 1951, 1-9.

3380.   Spring Daze by Mildred Hark and Noel McQueen.
        Short. 2 m. 2 f.
        In - Plays. 18: March 1959, 27-35.

3381.   Spring Fever by Mildred Hark and Noel
        McQueen.
        Short. 3 m. 2 f.
        In - Plays. 9: March 1950, 1-12.

3382.   Spring Fever by Mildred Hark and Noel McQueen.
        Short. 3 m. 2 f.
        In - Plays. 24: April 1965, 45-56.

3383.   Spring is Here by Sally Werner.
        Short. 7 m. 7 f. +X.
        In - Plays. 13: April 1954, 57-59.

3384. Spring is Here! by Lucille Miller Duvall.
Short. 8 m. 3 f. +X.
In - Plays. 18: May 1959, 71-74.

3385. Spring Neighbors by Deborah Newman.
Short. 5 m. 11 f.
In - Plays. 10: April 1951, 59-62.

3386. Spring, 1943 by Geraldine E. McGaughan.
Short. 4 m. 2 f.
In - Scholastic. 42: Feb.22,1943, 15-16+.

3387. Spring Secrets by Sylvia Lee.
Short. 3 m. 7 f.
In - Plays. 11: March 1952, 80-84.

3388. Spring Sluicing by Alice Henson Ernst.
Short. 4 m. 0 f.
In - Theatre. 12: Feb.1928, 125-138.

3389. Spring to the Rescue by Deborah Newman.
Short. 5 m. 10 f.
In - Plays. 10: March 1951, 56-59.

3390. Spring Tonic by Mildred Hark McQueen.
Short. 7 m. 6 f. 31 c. +X.
In - Plays. 24: March 1965, 71-76.

3391. Spring Will Come by Graham DuBois.
Short 4 m. 3 f.
In - Plays. 4: Jan.1945, 10-18.

3392. Springtime for Dan by Anne Coulter Martens.
Short. 2 m. 5 f.
In - Plays. 20: March 1961, 39-49.

3393. Spunky Punky by Helen Louise Miller.
Short. 5 m. 4 f. 13 or more c.
In - Plays. 19: Oct.1959, 67-71.

3394. The Spy by James Fenimore Cooper. Adap.
by Walter Hackett.
Radio. 10 m. 1 f.
In - Plays. 9: March 1950, 83-95.

3395. Spy for a Day by Betty Tracy Huff.
Short. 7 m. 5 f. +X.
In - Plays. 27: March 1968, 13-22.

3396. The Squander Bug's Christmas Carol by Aileen
Fisher.
Short. 6 m. 1 f. +m.X.
In - Plays. 4: Dec.1944, 66-71.

3397. The Square Box by Mazie Hall.
Short. 4 m. 3 f.
In - Plays. 16: April 1957, 47-51.

3398. The Squaw-Man by Edwin Milton Royle.
Short. 7 m. 1 f.
In - Cosmopolitan. 37: August.1904, 411-418.

3399. Squesknibble's Christmas by Jane McGowan.
Short. 2 m. 3 f. 5 c.
In - Plays. 19: Dec.1959, 79-83.

Squire Jonathan.
see
The True History of Squire Jonathan and
His Unfortunate Treasure.

3401. Stage Bore by Earl J. Dias.
Short. 2 m. 5 f.
In - Plays. 18: May 1959, 1-12.

3402. Stage Set for Murder by John Murray.
Short. 5 m. 4 f.
In - Plays. 20: March 1961, 1-15.

3403. Stage-Struck by E.B. Perkins.
In - Harper's B. 36: Feb.1902, 108-113.

3404. Staircase by Charles Dyer.
Full. 2 m. 1 f.
In - Players. 14: Jan.1967, 31-46.

3405. Stalag 17 by Donald Bevan and Edmund
Trzcinski.
Full. 21 m. 0 f.
In - Theatre. 37: Feb.1953, 34-63.

3406. Standing Up for Santa by Aileen Fisher.
Short. 1 m. 1 f. 10 un. +X.
In - Plays. 13: Dec.1953, 72-74.

3407. Stanislaw and the Wolf by Paul T. Nolan.
Short. 6 m. 3 f.
In - Plays. 19: Jan.1960, 79-84.

3408. Star Bright by Claire Boiko.
Short. 8 m. 3 f. +c.ch.
In - Plays. 25: Dec.1965, 63-67.

3409. Star Dust Path by Colin Campbell Clements.
In - Poet Lore. 31: June 1920, 181-186.

3410. A Star for Old Glory by Aileen Fisher and
      Olive Rabe.

      Short. 3 m. 4 f.

      In – Plays. 24: April 1965, 57-61.

3411. The Star in the Window by Edrie Pendleton.

      Short. 4 m. 3 f.

      In – Plays. 10: Dec.1950, 15-25.

3412. The Star in the Window by Mildred Hark and
      Noel McQueen.

      Short. 4 m. 3 f.

      In – Plays. 21: Dec.1961, 33-43.

3413. Star Light and the Sandman by Gladys V.
      Smith.

      Short. 1 m. 1 f. 2 b. 6 g. 7 c.

      In – Plays. 7: March 1948, 47-50.

3414. Star of Bethlehem by Anne Coulter Martens.

      Short. 9 m. 16 f. +X.

      In – Plays. 24: Dec.1964, 1-14.

3415. Star Over Bethlehem by Graham DuBois.

      Short. 8 m. 4 f. +m.X.

      In – Plays. 19: Dec.1959, 15-24.

3416. Star-Spangled Midge by Marjorie B. Paradis.

      Short. 5 m. 2 f. +5f.X.

      In – Plays. 8: Dec.1948, 22-29.

3417. The Stars and Stripes by Deborah Newman.

      Short. 5 m. 9 f.

      In – Plays. 12: Feb.1953, 53-57.

3418. The Stars and Stripes by Deborah Newman.

      Short. 5 m. 9 f.

      In – Plays. 27: Feb.1968, 73-77.

3419. Stars and Stripes Forever by Leonora Sill
      Ashton.

      Short. 1 m. 1 f.

      In – Etude. 71: Feb.1953, 54.

3420. Stars for Sale by Janice Auritt Oser.

      Short. 6 m. 4 f.

      In – Plays. 13: Oct.1953, 30-34.

3421. A Start In Life by Paul Green. From his
      short story Fine Wagon.

      Radio. 4 m. 2 f. 1 b. 4 c.

      In – Carolina. 14: June 1941, 35-47.

3422. State of the Union by Howard Lindsay and
      Russell Crouse.

      Excerpt. 7 m. 5 f.

      In – Scholastic. 52: March 1,1948, 20-22.

3423. The State Versus Joe Miller (anon.)

      Radio. 3 m. 2 f.

      In – Scholastic. 29: Jan.9,1937, 9-10.

3424. Station YYYY by Booth Tarkington.

      Short. 3 m. 3 f.

      In – Ladies' Home. 43: May 1926, 6-7+.

3425. A Statue for Joey by Marion Volzer.

      Radio. 7 m. 2 f. 4 b. 1 g.

      In – Scholastic. 50: Feb.24,1947, 13-14.

3426. Steamer Tenacity by Charles Vildrac. Trans.
      from the French.

      In – Poet Lore. 32: Dec.1921, 463-496.

3427. A Steed in the Senate by Leonid Andreev.

      Short. 20 m. 0 f.

      In – Living Age. 322: Sept.6,1924, 498-507.

3428. Steinway Grand by Ferenc Karinthy. Trans.
      from the Hungarian by Mátyás Eszterhazy.
      Ed. by Bertha Gaster.

      Short. 1 m. 2 f.

      In – Mod. Drama. 1: March 1968, 138-152.

3429. The Sterling Silver Tree by Aileen Fisher
      and Olive Rabe.

      Short. 4 m. 2 f.

      In – Plays. 14: May 1955, 39-43.

3430. Sticks and Stones by Robert Downing.

      Short. 3 m. 5 f.

      In – Plays. 13: May 1954, 13-27.

3431. Sticks and Stones by Robert Downing.

      Short. 3 m. 5 f.

      In – Plays. 21: May 1962, 25-38.

3432. Still Fires by Jan Quackenbush.

      Short. 0 m. 0 f. 2 b.

      In – Gambit. 3: no.11, 111-116.

3433. Still Stands the House by Gwendolyn Pharis.

      Short. 2 m. 2 f.

      In – Carolina. 11: June 1938, 37-49.

3434. The Stolen Cook by Margaret E. Slattery.

Short. 6 m. 4 f.

In - Plays. 24: Nov.1964, 67-75.

3435. The Stolen Heart by Deborah Newman.

Short. 0 m. 9 f.

In - Plays. 9: Feb.1950, 79-82.

3436. The Stolen Heart by Deborah Newman.

Short. 0 m. 9 f.

In - Plays. 25: Feb.1966, 85-88.

3437. The Stolen Prince by Dan. W. Totheroh.

Short. 5 m. 2 f. 2 b. 1 g. +X.

In - Drama. 15: Nov.1924, 30-32.

3438. The Stolen Prince by Dan W. Totheroh.

Short. 5 m. 2 f. 2 b. 1 g. +X.

In - Delineator. 116: June 1930, 13-14+.

3439. The Stolen Pumpkin by Esther W. Arnold.

Short. 7 m. 2 f.

In - Plays. 12: Oct.1952, 65-69.

3440. The Stolen Tarts by Lida Lisle Molloy.

Short. 6 m. 1 f.

In - Plays. 7: Feb.1948, 52-56.

3441. The Stone Venus by Katharine Metcalf Roof.

Full. 4 m. 3 f. +X.

In - Poet Lore. 37: March 1926, 124-152.

3442. Stop the Presses! by Earl J. Dias.

Short. 6 m. 2 f.

In - Plays. 17: Nov.1957, 17-28.

3443. The Storm by John Drinkwater.

Short. 2 m. 3 f.

In - Theatre. 4: July 1920, 191-199.

3444. Storm Warning by John Murray.

Short. 4 m. 4 f.

In - Plays. 13: Jan.1954, 57-64.

3445. Story Books Before the Judge by Jeanette Willets.

Short. 1 un. many c.

In - Wilson. 6: Oct.1931, 127-130.

3446. The Story Machine by Isaac Asimov.

Short. 3 m. 3 f.

In - Plays. 17: Feb.1958, 13-23.

3447. The Story of Gilbert and Sullivan by Michael T. Leech.

Short. 6 m. 4 f. +X.

In - Plays. 27: Nov.1967, 83-96.

3448. Story Told in Indiana by Betty Smith.

Short. 4 m. 1 f.

In - Theatre. 28: Nov.1944, 677-680.

3449. The Storybook Revolt by Frances B. Watts.

Short. 7 m. 7 f.

In - Plays. 25: Nov.1965, 67-73.

3450. Straight From the Heart by Constance Whitman.

Short. 3 m. 6 f.

In - Plays. 23: Feb.1964, 35-43.

3451. The Strange Passenger by Tymoteusz Karpowicz. Trans. by Edward J. Czerwinski.

Full. 7 m. 2 f. 3 b. 4 g.

In - First Stage. 7: Dec.1968, 116-140.

3452. The Stranger's Choice by Helen Littler Howard.

Short. 5 m. 1 f.

In - Plays. 5: Dec.1945, 50-52.

3453. The Straw Boy by Paul T. Nolan.

Short. 7 m. 4 f.

In - Plays. 17: Nov.1957, 29-36.

3454. Street and Number by Ferenc Molnar.

In - Golden. 17: April 1933, 367-369.

3455. A Street in Samarkand by Betty Tracy Huff.

Short. 5 m. 7 f. +X.

In - Plays. 19: Oct.1959, 62-66.

3456. The Street Singer by Jose Echegaray y Eizaguirre. Trans. by John Garrett Underhill.

Short. 2 m. 3 f. +X.

In - Golden. 5: Feb.1927, 192-196.

3457. Stretch a Point by Mildred Hark and Noel McQueen.

Short. 6 m. 6 f.

In - Plays. 3: Jan.1944, 63-66.

3458. Strictly for Relatives by Marguerite Kreger Phillips.

Short. 3 m. 4 f.

In - Plays. 12: March 1953, 18-31.

3459. Strictly Puritan by Helen Louise Miller.
       Short. 3 m. 9 f.
       In - Plays. 12: Nov.1952, 32-39.

3460. Strictly Puritan by Helen Louise Miller.
       Short. 3 m. 9 f.
       In - Plays. 22: Nov.1962, 51-58.

3461. The String of Pearls by Claire Wallace Flynn.
       In - Woman's Home. 37: Feb.1910, 8.

3462. Stringing Beads by Lillian Sutton Pelee.
       In - Poet Lore. 39: June 1928, 295-305.

3463. Strong and Silent by Earl J. Dias.
       Short. 4 m. 3 f.
       In - Plays. 15: May 1956, 23-31.

3464. The Stronger by August Strindberg. Trans.
       by F.I. Ziegler.
       Short. 1 m. 1 f.
       In - Poet Lore. 17:no.1,1906, 47-50.

3465. Study in the Nude by June Etta Downey.
       In - Poet Lore. 31: June 1920, 253-260.

3466. The Stuff of Heroes by Edrie Pendleton.
       Short. 4 m. 1 f.
       In - Plays. 5: Nov.1945, 39-44.

3467. The Stupid Lady by Lope Felix de Vega Carpio.
       Trans. by Willis Knapp Jones.
       Full. 10 m. 4 f. +X.
       In - Poet Lore. 57: Sept.1962, 291-354.

3468. Such Things Only Happen in Books by Thornton
       Wilder.
       Short. 3 m. 1 f.
       In - Golden. 15: April 1932, 369-373.

3469. Sugar and Spice by Jessie Nicholson.
       Short. 2 m. 5 f. +cX.
       In - Plays. 11: Jan.1952, 48-55.

3470. Sugar and Spice by Jessie Nicholson.
       Short. 2 m. 5 f. 4 c. +X.
       In - Plays. 20: May 1961, 53-60.

3471. Summer Folk by Maxim Gorki. Trans. from the
       Russian by Aline Delano.
       Full. 14 m. 11 f.
       In - Poet Lore. 16:no.3,1905, 1-90.

3472. Summer of the Seventeenth Doll by Ray Lawler.
       Full. 3 m. 4 f.
       In - Theatre. 43: Aug.1959, 24-56.

3473. Summer Stock à la Carte by Earl J. Dias.
       Short. 5 m. 5 f.
       In - Plays. 21: May 1962, 1-12.

3474. The Sun by John Galsworthy.
       Short. 2 m. 1 f.
       In - Scribner's. 65: May 1919, 513-516.

3475. The Sun Bride by Robert St.Clair.
       Short. 6 m. 4 f.
       In - Plays. 17: March 1958, 13-27.

3476. The Sun Machine by Christopher Morley.
       Short. 3 m. 7 f. +f.X.
       In - Sat. Review. 5: Dec.8,1928, 461.

3477. Sun Up! by Claire Boiko.
       Short. 4 m. 1 f. +X.
       In - Plays. 23: April 1964, 73-76.

3478. Suncold by Carl Glick.
       In - Poet Lore. 36: June 1925, 280-293.

3479. A Sunny Morning by Serafin and Joaquin
       Alvarez Quintero. Trans. from the
       Spanish by Lucretia Xavier Floyd.
       Short. 2 m. 2 f.
       In - Golden. 12: Aug.1930, 106-109.

3480. Sunrise at Campobello by Dore Schary.
       Full. 18 m. 6 f.
       In - Theatre. 43: Nov.1959, 33-58.

3481. Super-Sleuths, Inc. by Marjorie B. Paradis.
       Short. 0 m. 10 f.
       In - Plays. 17: Jan. 1958, 15-21.

3482. The Supermarket Blues by Robert Fontaine.
       Short. 2 m. 3 f.
       In - Plays. 24: Dec.1964, 83-86.

3483. Surprise Guests by Mildred Hark and Noel
       McQueen.
       Short. 5 m. 5 f.
       In - Plays. 9: Nov.1949, 1-10.

3484. Surprise Guests by Mildred Hark and Noel
       McQueen.
       Short. 5 m. 5 f.
       In - Plays. 19: Nov.1959, 1-10.

3485.   The Surprise Package by Dorothy Deming.

Short. 2 m. 3 f.

In - Plays. 7: May 1948, 48-52.

3486.   Surprise Party by John Dorand.

Short. 3 m. 5 f.

In - Plays. 14: Jan.1955, 18-26.

3487.   Surprise Party by John Dorand.

Short. 1 m. 4 f. 2 b. 1 g.

In - Plays. 26: Jan.1967, 25-33.

3488.   Susan and Alladin's Lamp by Patricia Clapp.

Short. 0 m. 3 f.

In - Plays. 19: Oct.1959, 53-61.

3489.   Susan Goes Hollywood by Charles F. Wilde.

Radio. 4 n. 3 f.

In - Plays. 5: March 1946, 73-83.

3490.   Susannah by Carlisle Floyd.

Full (musical). 7 m. 5 f. +ch.

In - Theatre. 42: Jan.1958, 34-49.

3491.   The Suspected Truth by Juan Ruíz de Alarcón.
        English version by Sevilla Gross and
        Henry F. Salerno.

Full. 11 m. 3 f.

In - First Stage. 6: March & June 1967,
        37-50, 133-139.

3492.   Sutter's San Francisco by Ray Hamby.

Radio. 10 m. 2 f.

In - Plays. 3: Oct.1943, 78-84.

3493.   The Swamp by Robert Keith MacKaye.

Short. 2 m. 1 f.

In - Drama. 21: March 1931, 19-20+.

3494.   Swamp Outlaw by Clare Johnson Marley.

Short. 5 m. 1 f.

In - Carolina. 13: March 1940, 10-22.

3495.   The Sweeps of Ninety-Eight by John Masefield.

Short. 5 m. 1 f. +m.X.

In - Golden. 17: June 1933, 550-556.

3496.   Sweet Land of Liberty by Morton Wishengrad.
        From the story Anna Zenger: Mother of
        Freedom by Kent Cooper.

Radio. 8 m. 1 f. 10 un. +X.

In - Scholastic. 57: Dec.6,1950, 13-16.

3497.   Sweet Sixteen by Mildred Hark and Noel
        McQueen.

Short. 4 m. 2 f.

In - Plays. 3: April 1944, 8-15.

3498.   Sweethearts by William Schwenck Gilbert.

Short. 1 m. 3 f.

In - Golden. 4: Dec.1926, 763-772.

3499.   The Swineherd by Hans Christian Andersen.
        Adap. by Adele Thane.

Short. 3 m. 9 f. 2 b.

In - Plays. 26: March 1967, 75-81.

3500.   The Swiss Chalet Mystery by John Murray.

Short. 5 m. 4 f.

In - Plays. 14: Jan.1955, 27-38.

3501.   The Swiss Family Robinson by Johann Wyss.
        Adap. by Levy Olfson.

Radio. 9 m. 2 f.

In - Plays. 23: Feb.1964, 85-96.

3502.   Swiss Mystery by Esther MacLellan and
        Catherine V. Schroll.

Short. 3 m. 4 f.

In - Plays. 17: March 1958, 47-54.

3503.   The Switch - About Shopkeepers by Sara E.
        Sagoff.

Short. 8 m. 8 f.

In - Plays. 22: March 1963, 69-76.

3504.   Sword in Hand by Lindsey Barbee.

Short. 7 m. 4 f.

In - Plays. 5: Feb.1946, 23-32.

3505.   T for Turkey by Mildred Hark and Noel
        McQueen.

Short. 4 m. 4 f.

In - Plays. 13: Nov.1953, 61-64.

3506.   The "T" Party by Claire Boiko.

Short. 5 m. 6 f.

In - Plays. 23: Nov.1963, 78-82.

3507.   The Tables Turned by Joyce Brown.

Short. 5 m. +X.

In - Plays. 26: May 1967, 78-80.

3508.   Taffy and Sylvie by Shirley Simon.

Short. 2 m. 8 f.

In - Plays. 19: Oct.1959, 75-80.

3509. Take Care, Anne! by Paul S. McCoy.

Short. 4 m. 4 f.

In - Plays. 19: Jan.1960, 29-41.

3510. Take Her, She's Mine by Phoebe and Henry
          Ephron.

Full. 13 m. 6 f.

In - Theatre. 47: July 1963, 37-70.

3511. Take My Advice by John Murray.

Short. 4 m. 4 f.

In - Plays. 25: Oct.1965, 23-35.

3512. A Tale of Two Cities by Charles Dickens.
          Adap. by Walter Hackett.

Radio. 14 m. 4 f.

In - Plays. 10: Feb.1951, 65-77.

3513. A Tale of Two Cities by Charles Dickens.
          Adap. by Walter Hackett.

Radio. 15 m. 4 f.

In - Plays. 26: Nov.1966, 99-111.

3514. A Tale of Two Drummers by Claire Boiko.

Short. 8 m. 2 f. 1 b. 1 g.

In - Plays. 27: Feb.1968, 39-45.

3515. Talent Scouts by Dorothy Deming.

Short. 4 m. 3 f.

In - Plays. 7: April 1948, 20-25.

3516. Talk Their Language by Millard Lampell.

Radio. 10 m. 2 f.

In - Scholastic. 46: April 9,1945, 13-15.

3517. The Talking Christmas Tree by Margaret Georgia
          Fawcett.

Short. 2 m. 5 f.

In - Plays. 17: Dec.1957, 67-69.

3518. The Talking Flag by Jane McGowan.

Short. 9 m. 6 f. +X.

In - Plays. 17: Nov.1957, 37-40.

3519. The Talking Trees by Helen M. Roberts.

Short. 2 m. 3 f. +X.

In - Plays. 6: May 1947, 50-54.

3520. The Tall Stranger by Earl J. Dias.

Short. 9 m. 3 f.

In - Plays. 22: March 1963, 1-12.

3521. The Taming of the Shrew by William Shakespeare.
          Condensed by Erik Barnouw.

Radio. 7 m. 2 f.

In - Scholastic. 34: April 22,1939, 19E-22E.

3522. The Taming of the Shrew by William
          Shakespeare. Adap. by Lewy Olfson.

Radio. 8 m. 1 f.

In - Plays. 19: Jan.1960, 85-96.

3523. The Taper and the Torch by Dorothy Margaret
          Stuart.

Short. 0 m. 4 f.

In - 19th C. 140: Sept.1946, 140-146.

3524. Taps is Not Enough by Carl Carmer.

Radio. 2 m. 1 f.

In - Sat. Review. 28: May 19,1945, 6.

3525. Tarts for the King by Corinne Morse.

Short. 10 m. 5 f.

In - Plays. 19: Feb.1960, 45-48.

3526. A Taste of Honey by Shelagh Delaney.

Full. 3 m. (1 Negro) 2 f.

In - Players. 5: July & Aug.1958, 25-29,
          25-28.

3527. A Taste of Honey by Shelagh Delaney.

Full. 3 m. (1 Negro) 2 f.

In - Theatre. 47: Jan.1963, 25-56.

3528. Tavern Meeting by Robert C. Jones.

Short. 5 m. 5 f.

In - Plays. 10: Jan.1951, 23-34.

3529. Taxi by Alice C.D. Riley.

Short. 1 m. 1 f.

In - Drama. 16: Feb.1926, 177-178.

3530. Tea and Sympathy by Robert Anderson.

Full. 9 m. 2 f.

In - Theatre. 38: Sept.1954, 34-61.

3531. Tea for Six by Walton Butterfield.

Short. 3 m. 4 f.

In - Drama. 16: Jan.1926, 134-136+.

3532. The Teahouse of the August Moon by John
          Patrick.

Full. 13 m. 9 f. 3 c. +X (some Oriental).

In - Theatre. 39: June 1955, 34-61.

3533. <u>Teapot Trouble</u> by Jessie Nicholson.

Short. 3 m. 5 f.

In - Plays. 10: March 1951, 47-55.

3534. <u>Teapot Trouble</u> by Jessie Nicholson.

Short. 3 m. 5 f.

In - Plays. 24: March 1965, 61-69.

3535. <u>Tears of Dawn</u> by Faith Van Valkenburgh Vilas.

Short. 2 m. 2 f.

In - Poet Lore. 33:no.1,1922, 105-113.

3536. <u>The Tears of the Birds</u> trans. from the Noh drama by Yone Noguchi.

Short. 2 m. 1 f. 1 c. +ch.

In - Poet Lore. 29:no.4,1918, 451-455.

3537. <u>The Teddy Bear Hero</u> by Jane McGowan.

Short. 4 m. 3 f. 6 un. +m.X.

In - Plays. 19: May 1960, 68-72.

3538. <u>Teen and Twenty</u> by John Dorand.

Short. 4 m. 5 f.

In - Plays. 14: March 1955, 19-34.

3539. <u>Teen and Twenty</u> by John Dorand.

Short. 4 m. 5 f.

In - Plays. 18: Nov.1958, 13-28.

3540. <u>Teja</u> by Hermann Sudermann. Trans. by Archibald Alexander.

Short. 9 m. 2 f.

In - Golden. 6: Oct.1927, 493-503.

3541. <u>Television-itis</u> by Mildred Hark and Noel McQueen.

Short. 3 m. 2 f.

In - Plays. 9: May 1950, 24-34.

3542. <u>The Tempest</u> by William Shakespeare. Adap. by Levy Olfson.

Radio. 8 m. 1 f.

In - Plays. 20: Nov.1960, 87-96.

3543. <u>Tempest in a Teapot</u> by Mildred Hark and Noel McQueen.

Short. 3 m. 2 f.

In - Plays. 5: Nov.1945, 19-27.

3544. <u>The Ten Fingers of François</u> by Delle Houghton Oglesbee.

Short. 2 m. 1 f. 3 b. 3 g. +X.

In - Drama. 14: Nov.1923, 65-69.

3545. <u>Ten Pennies for Lincoln</u> by Helen Louise Miller.

Short. 3 m. 3 f. +X.

In - Plays. 18: Feb.1959, 79-82.

3546. <u>The Ten-Penny Tragedy</u> by Josef A. Elfenbein.

Short. 4 m. 4 f.

In - Plays. 16: Oct.1956, 37-46.

3547. <u>The Ten-Penny Tragedy</u> by Josef A. Elfenbein.

Short. 4 m. 4 f.

In - Plays. 26: May 1967, 27-35.

3548. <u>The Tender Trap</u> by Max Shulman and Robert Paul Smith.

Full. 5 m. 3 f.

In - Theatre. 40: Feb.1956. 36-61.

3549. <u>The Tenor</u> by Frank Wedekind. Trans. by André Tridon.

Short. 4 m. 3 f. 1 b.

In - Golden. 5: Jan.1927, 65-73.

3550. <u>The Tenth Circle</u> by L.W. Michaelson.

Short. 6 m. 3 f.

In - Poet Lore. 59: March 1964, 36-57.

3551. <u>The Tenth Man</u> by Elma Ehrlich Levinger.

Short. 10 m. 1 f.

In - Drama. 19: April 1929, 204-206.

3552. <u>The Tenth Man</u> by Paddy Chayefsky.

Full. 12 m. 1 f.

In - Theatre. 45: Jan.1961, 25-56.

3553. <u>Tents of the Arabs</u> by Lord Dunsany.

Short. 6 m. 0 f.

In - Golden. 1: June 1925, 849-855.

3554. <u>Terrible Terry's Surprise</u> by Claire Boiko.

Short. 4 m. 3 f. +X.

In - Plays. 22: April 1963, 65-70.

3555. <u>The Terrible Turkey</u> by Erva Loomis Merow.

Short. 2 m. 2 f.

In - Plays. 17: Nov.1957, 69-70.

3556. <u>Terrible Woman</u> by Wilbur Daniel Steele.

Short. 2 m. 2 f.

In - Pictorial. 26: Nov.1924, 6-7+.

3557. <u>Terror on the Island</u> by John Murray.

Short. 5 m. 4 f.

In - Plays. 22: Nov.1962, 13-24.

3558. <u>Test</u> by Pierre Chamberlain de Marivaux.
Trans. from the French by Willis Knapp
Jones.

Short. 3 m. 3 f.

In - Poet Lore. 35: Dec.1924, 533-561.

3559. <u>Test For A Witch</u> by Esther MacLellan and
Catherine V. Schroll.

Short. 4 m. 7 f. +X.

In - Plays. 15: Oct.1955, 43-48.

3560. <u>The Thankful Elf</u> by Gwen Chaloner.

Short. 9 m. 3 f.

In - Plays. 23: Nov.1963, 73-77.

3561. <u>Thankful Hearts</u> by Marjorie B. Paradis.

Short. 0 m. 7 f.

In - Plays. 13: Nov.1953, 12-20.

3562. <u>Thankful Indeed</u> by Helen Littler Howard.

Short. 6 m. 0 f.

In - Plays. 5: Nov.1945, 55-57.

3563. <u>Thankful's Pumpkin</u> by Karin Asbrand.

Short. 1 m. 2 f.

In - Plays. 3: Nov.1943, 63-65.

3564. <u>Thankful's Red Beads</u> by Helen Louise Miller.

Short. 7 m. 3 f.

In - Plays. 19: Nov.1959, 43-48.

3565. <u>Thankless Tate</u> by Cena Christopher Draper.

Short. 2 m. 2 f. 7 c.

In - Plays. 14: Nov.1954, 62-68.

3566. <u>Thanks for Thanksgiving</u> by Deborah Newman.

Short. 3 m. 9 f. +X.

In - Plays. 17: Nov.1957, 65-68.

3567. <u>Thanks to Billy</u> by Mildred Hark and Noel
McQueen.

Short. 3 m. 2 f.

In - Plays. 9: Nov.1949, 40-49.

3568. <u>Thanks to Butter-Fingers</u> by Helen Louise
Miller.

Short. 2 m. 3 f.

In - Plays. 13: Nov.1953, 31-40.

3569. <u>Thanks to Butter-Fingers</u> by Helen Louise
Miller.

Short. 2 m. 1 f. 2 g.

In - Plays. 27: Nov.1967, 35-44.

3570. <u>Thanks to George Washington</u> by Edrie Pendleton.

Short. 4 m. 3 f.

In - Plays. 10: Feb.1951, 11-23.

3571. <u>Thanks to George Washington</u> by Mildred
Hark and Noel McQueen.

Short. 4 m. 3 f.

In - Plays. 16: Feb.1957, 23-35.

3572. <u>Thanks to Sammy Scarecrow</u> by Helen L. Howard.

Short. 3 m. 1 f.

In - Plays. 6: Nov.1946, 53-55.

3573. <u>Thanks to Sammy Scarecrow</u> by Helen S. Howard.

Short. 3 m. 1 f.

In - Plays. 19: Nov.1959, 65-67.

3574. <u>Thanksgiving</u> by Elsie Duncan Yale.

In - Woman's Home. 54: Nov.1927, 43.

3575. <u>Thanksgiving à la Carte</u> by Helen Louise
Miller.

Short. 9 m. 3 f.

In - Plays. 10: Nov.1950, 1-10.

3576. <u>Thanksgiving à la Carte</u> by Helen Louise Miller.

Short. 9 m. 3 f.

In - Plays. 20: Nov.1960, 25-34.

3577. <u>Thanksgiving Beats the Dutch</u> by Helen
Louise Miller.

Short. 3 m. 5 f.

In - Plays. 6: Nov.1946, 1-11.

3578. <u>Thanksgiving Dinner</u> by Tudor Jenks.

Short. 4 m. 3 f.

In - Independent. 61: Nov.29,1906, 1258-1260.

3579. <u>Thanksgiving Farm</u> by Deborah Newman.

Short. 5 m. 9 f.

In - Plays. 20: Nov.1960, 59-64.

3580. <u>Thanksgiving Feast</u> by Aileen Fisher.

Short. 4 m. 3 f.

In - Plays. 9: Nov.1949, 60-63.

3581. <u>Thanksgiving for Frieda</u> by Helen Louise
Miller.

Short. 9 m. 10 f.

In - Plays. 3: Nov.1943, 26-36.

3582. Thanksgiving Night by Alice Very.

Short. 0 m. 0 f. 10 c.

In - Plays. 4: Nov.1944, 49-50.

3583. Thanksgiving Night by Alice Very.

Short. 1 m. 1 f. +X.

In - Plays. 6: Nov.1946, 58-59.

3584. Thanksgiving Postscript by Mildred Hark and Noel McQueen.

Short. 3 m. 5 f.

In - Plays. 18: Nov.1958, 1-12.

3585. A Thanksgiving Riddle by Helen Louise Miller.

Short. 5 m. 6 f.

In - Plays. 18: Nov.1958, 71-75.

3586. The Thanksgiving Scarecrow by Eleanore Leuser.

Short. 5 m. 4 f.

In - Plays. 8: Nov.1948, 31-34.

3587. Thanksgiving Wishbone by Mildred Hark and Noel McQueen.

Short. 5 m. 6 f.

In - Plays. 16: Nov.1956, 61-63.

3588. Thar She Blows by Earl J. Dias.

Short. 8 m. 2 f.

In - Plays. 25: Nov.1965, 37-46.

3589. That Christmas Feeling by Mildred Hark and Noel McQueen.

Short. 6 m. 4 f. +ch.

In - Plays. 18: Dec.1958, 45-54.

3590. That Lady by Kate O'Brien.

Full. 12 m. 5 f.

In - Theatre. 34: June 1950, 60-88.

3591. That's the Spirit by John Murray.

Short. 4 m. 6 f.

In - Plays. 15: Oct.1955, 9-22.

3592. Their Very Own and Golden City by Arnold Wesker.

Full. 10 m. 2 f. +X.

In - Players. 13: Aug.1966, 31-46+.

3593. Then Came the Good Harvest by Christine E. Scott.

Short. 5 m. 3 f. +X.

In - Plays. 26: Nov.1966, 70-74.

3594. Theological Interlude by James M. Cain.

Short. 2 m. 1 f.

In - American Merc. 14: July 1928, 325-331.

3595. There is a Tide by Marcella Rawe.

Short. 10 m. 4 f.

In - Plays. 27: Feb.1968, 29-38.

3596. There is Room by Charles C. Noble.

Short. 1 m. 2 f.

In - Christian C. 47: Dec.10,1930, 1525-1526.

3597. There Shall Be No Night by Robert E. Sherwood.

Excerpt. 3 m. 0 f.

In - Theatre. 24: Oct.1940, 747-748.

3598. There's a Girl In My Soup by Terence Frisby.

Full. 5 m. 2 f.

In - Players. 13: Sept.1966, 31-46+.

3599. There's Some Milk in the Icebox by Bonnie Jo Henderson.

Short. 4 m. 2 f. 1 b.

In - Mlle. 62: Nov.1965, 176-177+.

3600. There's Something I Got to Tell You by William Saroyan.

Radio. 5 m. 0 f. 1 b. 1 g. +c.X.

In - Scholastic. 41: Dec.14,1942, 18-20.

3601. These Doggone Elections by Fred Koch, Jr.

Short. 4 m. 1 f. 1 dog.

In - Carolina. 12: Sept.1939, 80-90.

3602. They Banish Our Anger by Graham DuBois.

Short. 3 m. 4 f.

In - Plays. 4: May 1945, 11-20.

3603. They Burned the Books by Stephen Vincent Benét.

Radio. 6 m. 1 f.

In - Scholastic. 41: Sept.14,1942, 25-28.

3604. They Burned the Books by Stephen Vincent Benét.

Radio. 4 m. 0 f. +m.X.

In - Sat. Review. 26: May 8,1943, 3-5.

3605. They Burned the Books by Stephen Vincent Benét.

Radio. 12 m. 1 f. 1 b. +X.

In - Education. 65: Dec.1944, 208-217.

3606. They Burned the Books by Stephen Vincent
Benét.

Radio. 5 m. 1 f. 3 un.

In - Wilson. 19: May 1945, 603-606.

3607. They Dared to Teach by Eleanor C. Fishburn
and Mildred Sandison Fenner.

Short. 6 m. 2 f.

In - Jl., N.E.A. 29: April 1940, 123-124.

3608. A Thing of Beauty by Kay Arthur.

Short. 3 m. 2 f.

In - Plays. 22: Nov.1962, 1-12.

3609. The Third Daughter by Mario Fratti. Trans.
by Adrienne S. Mandel.

Full. 6 m. 7 f.

In - First Stage. 5: Sept.1966, 139-157.

3610. The Third Fourth of July by Countee Cullen
and Owen Dodson.

Short. 6 m. 4 f. few c. +X (white & Negro).

In - Theatre. 30: Aug.1946, 488-490+.

3611. The Third Night by Thomas Wolfe.

Short. 4 m. 0 f.

In - Carolina. 11: Sept.1938, 70-75.

3612. The Thirsty Flowers by June Barr.

Short. 2 m. 1 f. +X.

In - Plays. 8: April 1949, 72-74.

3613. Thirteen by Anne Coulter Martens.

Short. 0 m. 13 f.

In - Plays. 16: Oct.1956, 47-56.

3614. Thirteen and Hallowe'en by Lindsey Barbee.

Short. 0 m. 15 f.

In - Plays. 4: Oct.1944, 52-53.

3615. This I Believe by William Saroyan.

Short. 2 m. 0 f.

In - Atlantic. 211: April 1963, 52.

This Living Business.

see

Refuge.

3616. This New World of Peace. Abr. by Allan
Doyle Wilson.

Radio. 15 m. 4 f.

In - Scholastic. 37: Dec.9, 1940, 17-20.

3617. A Thousand Clowns by Herb Gardner.

Full. 4 m. 1 f. 1 b.

In - Theatre. 48: Jan.1964, 33-64.

3618. Three Against Death by John Henderson.

Short. 5 m. 1 f.

In - Plays. 19: April 1960, 1-11.

3619. Three and the Dragon by Aileen Fisher.

Short. 5 m. 5 f.

In - Plays. 8: April 1949, 20-27.

3620. Three and the Dragon by Aileen Fisher.

Short. 4 m. 3 f. 1 b. 2 g.

In - Plays. 25: May 1966, 87-94.

3621. The Three Aunts by Elsi Rowland.

Short. 5 m. 10 f. +X.

In - Plays. 3: March 1944, 37-43.

3622. The Three Aunts by Elsi Rowland.

Short. 5 m. 10 f. +X.

In - Plays. 27: May 1968, 77-84.

3623. Three Cheers for Mother by Helen Louise
Miller.

Short. 6 m. 8 f.

In - Plays. 4: May 1945, 1-10.

3624. Three Chinese Folk Dramas trans. by Kwei
Chen. 1: Princely Fortune; 2: Meeting
at the Well; 3: Woman-Song.

Full (3). 1 m. 1 f. each.

In - Theatre. 14: Nov.1930, 967-978.

3625. The Three Heron's Feathers by Hermann Sudermann. Trans. by Helen Tracy Porter.

Full. 10 m. 3 f. +X.

In - Poet Lore. 12:no.2,1900, 161-234.

3626. The Three Little Kittens by June Barr.

Short. 0 m. 1 f. 3 c.

In - Plays. 8: Jan.1949, 55-57.

3627. Three Little Kittens by Helen Louise Miller.

Short. 5 m. 3 f. +X.

In - Plays. 23: April 1964, 69-72.

3628. The Three Musketeers by Alexander Dumas.
Adap. by the Alameda School of the Air.

Radio. 7 m. 2 f.

In - Plays. 12: April 1953, 87-93.

3629. The Three Royal R's by Mary Thurman Pyle.

Short. 5 m. 1 f. 4 b. 4 g. +c.X.

In - Scholastic. 37, Nov.11,1940, 17-19+.

3630. The Three Royal R's by Mary Thurman Pyle.

Short. 8 m. 6 f. +X.

In - Plays. 16: Nov.1956, 69-78.

3631. Three Saturdays by Edward Daniel Covington.

Radio. 0 m. 0 f. 2 b.

In - Indus. Educa. 40: Nov.1938, 253-255.

3632. The Three Sillies by Alice Very.

Short. 6 m. 4 f. +X.

In - Plays. 4: April 1945, 37-40.

3633. Three Souls in Search of a Dramatist by Esther Dresden Schwartz.

In - Drama. 16: April 1926, 247-248.

3634. The Three Spinners by Florence Kiper Frank.

Short. 3 m. 9 f. +X.

In - Drama. 16: Feb.1926, 179-180+.

3635. Three Sundays a Week by Edgar Allan Poe. Adap. by Paul T. Nolan.

Short. 4 m. 2 f.

In - Plays. 22: Nov.1962, 89-95.

3636. The Three Wishes by Cora Burlingame.

Short. 5 m. 4 f.

In - Plays. 3: March 1944, 44-49.

3637. The Three Wishes by Ernestine Phillips.

Short. 4 m. 4 f.

In - Plays. 20: March 1961, 65-70.

3638. The Three Wishes adap. by Adele Thane from an English folk tale.

Short. 1 m. 2 f. 5 c.

In - Plays. 25: April 1966, 69-74.

3639. The Three Wishes by Cora Burlingame.

Short. 4 m. 2 f.

In - Plays. 27: March 1968, 75-79.

3640. Three Wishes for Mother by Mildred Hark and Noel McQueen.

Short. 4 m. 4 f.

In - Plays. 11: May 1952, 55-59.

3641. The Three Wishing Bags by Martha Swintz.

Short. 5 m. 4 f. +X.

In - Plays. 9: April 1950, 26-37.

3642. The Three Wishing Bags by Martha Swintz.

Short. 5 m. 4 f. +X.

In - Plays. 17: April 1958, 57-68.

3643. The Thrice Promised Bride by Cheng-Chin Hsiung.

Short. 8 m. 2 f. +X.

In - Theatre. 7: Oct.1923, 329-347.

3644. The Thrice Promised Bride by Cheng-Chin Hsiung.

Short. 8 m. 2 f. +X.

In - Golden. 2: Aug.1925, 230-236.

3645. Thrift by W. Lloyd Berridge.

Short. 3 m. 0 f. 1 b. 2 g.

In - Ladies' Home. 35: Nov.1918, 57.

3646. Through the Looking-Glass by Lewis Carroll. Adap. by Levy Olfson.

Short. 5 m. 3 f.

In - Plays. 25: May 1966, 95-105.

3647. Through the Picture Frame by Irma Sompayrac.

Short. 0 m. 0 f. 3 b. 17 g.

In - School Arts. 23: May 1924, 528-534.

3648. The Thumbscrew by Edith Lyttelton.

Short. 2 m. 4 f. 2 b. 1 g.

In - 19th C. 69: May 1911, 938-960.

3649. The Thump-ity Bump-ity Box by Irving A. Leitner.

Short. 2 m. 0 f. 6 b. 6 g. +X.

In - Plays. 27: Feb.1968, 65-68.

3650. Thy Kingdom Come by Florence Converse.

Short. 3 m. 0 f. 8 c. +X.

In - Atlantic. 127: March 1921, 353-362.

3651. Tick Tock by Karin Asbrand.

Short. 14 m. 12 f.

In - Plays. 12: Dec.1952, 57-60.

3652. Tick-Tock by Alice Very.

Short. 1 m. 2 f. 6 un.

In - Plays. 13: March 1954, 70-71.

3653. Ties of Blood by Lillian Sutton Pelée.

In - Poet Lore. 32: Dec.1921, 572-580.

3654. <u>Tiger</u> by Witter Bynner.

Short. 2 m. 3 f.

In - Forum. 49: May 1913, 522-547.

3655. <u>The Tiger and the Brahman</u> by Shirley Simon.

Short. 3 m. 0 f. 2 c.

In - Plays. 17: May 1958, 69-72.

3656. <u>The Tiger Catcher</u>. Adap. by Ethel McFarlan from a Chinese folk tale.

Short. 4 m. 2 f. 1 "tiger" +X.

In - Plays. 26: Jan.1967, 65-68.

3657. <u>The Tiger in the Rockery</u> by Richard Drain.

Short. 2 m. 2 f.

In - First Stage. 6: Dec.1967, 260-272.

3658. <u>The Tiger, the Brahman, and the Jackal</u> adap. by Gladys V. Smith from a folk tale of India.

Short. 0 m. 0 f. 9 c.

In - Plays. 26: Nov.1966, 75-78.

3659. <u>The Tiger Who Wanted a Boy</u> by Margaret G. Hall.

Short. 3 m. 3 f.

In - Plays. 16: March 1957, 72-76.

3660. <u>Time for Mom</u> by Aileen Fisher.

Short. 3 m. 5 f. +X.

In - Plays. 15: May 1956, 53-56.

3661. <u>A Time for Purpose</u> by Marcella Rawe.

Short. 9 m. 4 f. 1 b.

In - Plays. 25: Feb.1966, 27-38.

3662. <u>A Time from Now</u> by Lee Kingman.

Short. 7 m. 8 f.

In - Plays. 3: Dec.1943, 1-11.

3663. <u>Time Limit!</u> by Henry Denker and Ralph Berkey.

Full. 18 m. 1 f.

In - Theatre. 41: April 1957, 33-57.

3664. <u>The Time of the Cuckoo</u> by Arthur Laurents.

Full. 5 m. 5 f.

In - Theatre. 37: Nov.1953, 34-60.

3665. <u>The Time of Your Life</u> by William Saroyan.

Excerpt. 3 m. 0 f.

In - Theatre. 24: Oct.1940, 751-752.

3666. <u>Time Out for Christmas</u> by Aileen Fisher.

Short. 3 m. 1 f. 24 c.

In - Plays. 8: Dec.1948, 46-51.

3667. <u>Time Out for Ginger</u> by Ronald Alexander.

Full. 5 m. 5 f.

In - Theatre. 38: Feb.1954, 36-64.

3668. <u>Time Remembered</u> by Jean Anouilh. English version by Patricia Moyes.

Full. 15 m. 2 f.

In - Theatre. 43: Feb.1959, 25-46.

3669. <u>A Time to Reap</u> by Stephen Vincent Benét.

Radio. 12 un.

In - Scholastic. 42: May 3,1943, 15-18.

3670. <u>Time to Think</u> by Jesse Stuart.

Short. 2 m. 1 f.

In - Poet Lore. 62: June 1967, 172-181.

3671. <u>The Timid Little Witch</u> by Catherine Urban.

Short. 1 m. 2 f. 5 c.

In - Plays. 14: Oct.1954, 67-70.

3672. <u>The Tiniest Heart</u> by Frances B. Watts.

Short. 5 m. 1 f. +c.X.

In - Plays. 20: Feb.1961, 56-62.

3673. <u>The Tinker's Christmas</u> by Robert St. Clair.

Short. 3 m. 4 f.

In - Plays. 18: Dec.1958, 33-44.

3674. <u>The Tired Woman</u> by Max Michelson.

Short. 1 m. 1 f. +X.

In - Poetry. 11: Feb.1918, 255-259.

3675. <u>Tit-for-Tat</u> by Aileen Fisher.

Short. 2 m. 3 f.

In - Plays. 9: May 1950, 66-67.

3676. <u>To Be or Not To Be</u> by Mildred Hark and Noel McQueen.

Short. 3 m. 2 f.

In - Plays. 5: Jan.1946, 11-19.

3677. <u>To Bethlehem</u> by Laura Spencer Portor.

Short. 10 m. 0 f. +X.

In - Woman's Home. 58: Dec.1931, 21-22+.

3678. <u>To Live in Peace</u> by Giovacchino Forzano. English version by Victor Rietti.

Full. 12 m. 3 f. +X.

In - Gambit. 2: no.7, 3-57.

3679. <u>To Mother, With Love</u> by Edrie Pendleton.

Short. 2 m. 2 f.

In - Plays. 3: May 1944, 27-33.

3680. <u>To My Valentine</u> by Mildred Hark and Noel McQueen.

Short. 4 m. 2 f.

In - Plays. 13: Feb.1954, 19-28.

3681. <u>To the Moon</u> by Robert Fontaine.

Short. 4 m. 2 f.

In - Plays. 25: Feb.1966, 93-95.

3682. <u>To the Rescue</u> by Olive Rabe.

Short. 3 m. 3 f.

In - Plays. 4: Nov.1944, 57-65.

3683. <u>To the Stars</u> by Leonid Andreieff. Trans. from the Russian by A. Goudiss.

Full. 10 m. 5 f.

In - Poet Lore. 18: no.4,1907, 417-467.

3684. <u>To You the Torch</u> by Irving H. Marcus.

Short. 8 m. 2 f. +X.

In - Plays. 9: May 1950, 71-78.

3685. <u>To You the Torch</u> by Irving H. Marcus.

Short. 8 m. 2 f. +X.

In - Plays. 18: May 1959, 89-96.

3686. <u>The Tobacco Evil</u> by Anton Chekhov. Trans. from the Russian by Henry James Forman.

Short. 1 m. 0 f.

In - Theatre. 7: Jan.1923, 77-82.

3687. <u>Today?</u> by Joanna Gleed Strange.

Short. 1 m. 3 f. 1 b. 1 g.

In - Survey. 36: June 10,1916, 287-289.

3688. <u>Toinette and the Elves</u> by Susan Coolidge.

Short. 2 m. 4 f. 3 un.

In - Plays. 23: Dec.1963, 59-68.

3689. <u>Tom Paine</u> by Lucy Kennedy.

Short. 5 m. 0 f.

In - Plays. 4: March 1945, 10-14.

3690. <u>Tom Sawyer and Injun Joe</u> by Mark Twain. Adap. by Lewy Olfson.

Radio. 8 m. 3 f. 2 b. +X.

In - Plays. 18: April 1959, 87-95.

3691. <u>Tom Sawyer, Pirate</u> by Mark Twain. Adap. by Adele Thane.

Short. 6 m. 6 f.

In - Plays. 23: March 1964, 77-84.

3692. <u>The Tomboy and the Dragon</u> by Helen Louise Miller.

Short. 6 m. 2 f. 3 b. 1 "dragon".

In - Plays. 27: Dec.1967, 73-80.

3693. <u>The Tomboy Princess</u> by Helen M. Roberts.

Short. 7 m. 5 f. +X.

In - Plays. 4: March 1945, 42-46.

3694. <u>Tommy's Adventure</u> by Eleanore Leuser.

Short. 6 m. 5 f.

In - Plays. 7: Jan.1948, 56-59.

3695. <u>Tomorrow Is Easter</u> by Mildred Hark and Noel McQueen.

Short. 6 m. 1 f.

In - Plays. 8: April 1949, 10-19.

3696. <u>Tomorrow the World</u> by James Gow and Arnaud d'Usseau.

Excerpt. 1 m. 1 f. 1 b. 1 g.

In - Scholastic. 43: Oct.11,1943, 17-19.

3697. <u>The Tongue-Cut Sparrow</u> by Loretta Camp Capell.

Short. 11 m. 6 f. +X.

In - Plays. 6: April 1947, 48-53.

3698. <u>Tony Kytes, the Arch Deceiver</u> by Thomas Hardy. Adap. by Paul T. Nolan.

Short. 4 m. 3 f.

In - Plays. 22: Feb.1963, 87-94.

3699. <u>Too Many Cooks</u> by Betty Tracy Huff.

Short. 7 m. 8 f. 2 c. +X.

In - Plays. 23: May 1964, 1-12.

3700. <u>Too Many Kittens</u> by Mildred Hark and Noel McQueen.

Short. 2 m. 6 f.

In - Plays. 14: Jan.1955, 49-58.

3701. <u>Top of the Bill</u> by J.G. Colson.

Short. 5 m. 0 f.

In - Plays. 12: March 1953, 32-44.

3702. <u>Topsy-Turvy Weather</u> by Claribel Spamer.

Short. 2 m. 0 f. 5 un.

In - Plays. 20: Jan.1961, 81-83.

3703. A Touch of Brightness by Partap Sharma.
Full. 9 m. 1 f. +X.
In - Gambit. 3: no.9, 3-54.

3704. The Touch of Genius by Earl J. Dias.
Short. 8 m. 3 f.
In - Plays. 21: April 1962, 19-30.

3705. Touchstone by Helen V. Rummette.
Short. 28 un. +X.
In - Plays. 14: Dec.1954, 53-61.

3706. The Town Mouse and His Country Cousin by
Violet Muse.
Short. 4 m. 2 f. 2 c.
In - Plays. 3: Jan.1944, 42-48.

3707. The Town That Learned by Shirley Simon.
Short. 5 m. 5 f.
In - Plays. 18: Jan.1959, 77-82.

3708. The Toy Scout Jamboree by Helen Louise Miller.
Short. 10 m. 11 f. +c.X.
In - Plays. 24: Dec.1964, 67-72.

3709. Toys for Santa by O.J. Robertson.
Short. 1 m. 0 f. 10 b. 12 g.
In - Plays. 26: Dec.1966, 69-71.

3710. Toys in the Attic by Lillian Hellman.
Full. 7 m. 4 f.
In - Theatre. 45: Oct.1961, 25-56.

3711. The Toys on Strike by Phoebe Lou Adams.
Short. 2 m. 2 f.
In - Plays. 3: Jan.1944, 52-54.

3712. The Toys' Rebellion by Edna Randolph Worrell.
In - Ladies' Home. 20: Dec.1902, 16.

3713. The Tragedian in Spite of Himself by Anton
Chekhov. Trans. from the Russian by
Olive Frances Murphy.
Short. 2 m. 0 f.
In - Poet Lore. 33: June 1922, 268-273.

3714. The Tragic Song by Roberto Payro. Trans.
from the Spanish by Willis Knapp Jones
and Carlos Escudero.
Short. 3 m. 3 f. +X.
In - Poet Lore. 50: Jan.1944; 3-24.

3715. Train to H ... by José María Bellido Cor-
menzana. Trans. from the Spanish by
Ronald C. Flores.
Short. 8 m. 3 f. 1 c. +X.
In - Mod. Drama. 1: March 1968, 218-228.

3716. Trains by Evelyn Emig Mellon.
Short. 1 m. 2 f.
In - Poet Lore. 41: July 1930, 424-432.

3717. The Traitor's Wife by Doris Pitkin Buck.
Short. 0 m. 4 f.
In - Plays. 3: March 1944, 9-20.

3718. Transcontinental by A.M. Sullivan.
Radio. 6 un.
In - Scholastic. 40: May 18,1942, 17-18.

3719. The Transferred Ghost by Frank R. Stockton.
Adap. by Walter Hackett.
Radio. 3 m. 1 f.
In - Plays. 9: Oct.1949, 75-85.

3720. The Transferred Ghost by Frank R. Stockton.
Adap. by Levy Olfson.
Short. 3 m. 2 f.
In - Plays. 20: April 1961, 13-22.

3721. Translated by Grace Wilcox.
Short. 2 m. 3 f.
In - Poet Lore. 41: April 1930, 251-260.

3722. Trap Doors by Alfred Kreymborg.
Short. 8 m. 1 f. +X.
In - Theatre. 9: Nov.1925, 742-751.

3723. A Travel Game by Helen Louise Miller.
Short. 14 m. 15 f. 1 un.
In - Plays. 23: May 1964, 77-82.

3724. Travel is So Broadening by Kenneth Roberts.
Short. 4 m. 5 f. +X.
In - Sat. Evening. 200: Aug.6,1927, 20-21+.

3725. Travelers by Booth Tarkington.
Short. 6 m. 3 f.
In - Ladies' Home. 42: March 1926, 16-17+.

3726. Traveling Light by Leonard Kingston.
Full. 3 m. 2 f.
In - Players. 12: July& Aug.1965, 23-30+,
21-32.

3727. Traveling Man by Lady Gregory.
Short. 1 m. 1 f. 1 c.
In - Golden. 14: Oct.1931, 274-279.

3728. Traveling Man by Lady Gregory.
Short. 1 m. 1 f. 1 c.
In - Scholastic. 25: Dec.15,1934, 9-10+.

3729. The Traveling Man by Lady Gregory.
Short. 1 m. 1 f. 1 c.
In - Scholastic. 49: Dec.9,1946, 17-19.

3730. Treasure! by Sylvia Hunt.
Short. 1 un. many c.
In - Wilson. 8: Oct.1933, 107-110.

3731. Treasure at Bentley Inn by Earl J. Dias.
Short. 6 m. 5 f.
In - Plays. 21: March 1962, 1-14.

3732. The Treasure Chest by Virginia Bond.
Short. 8 m. 0 f.
In - Plays. 16: March 1957, 79-81.

3733. Treasure Hunt by Aileen Fisher.
Short. 13 m. 11 f.
In - Plays. 9: Nov.1949, 55-59.

3734. Treasure in the Smith House by Grace T. Barnett.
Short. 2 m. 3 f.
In - Plays. 9: May 1950, 43-52.

3735. Treasure in the Smith House by Grace T. Barnett.
Short. 2 m. 3 f.
In - Plays. 20: Feb.1961, 63-72.

3736. Treasure Island by Marjorie Ann York.
Radio. 10 m. 0 f. 1 b. +m.X.
In - Plays. 11: April 1952, 77-84.

3737. Treasure Island by Robert Louis Stevenson. Adap. by Marjorie Ann York.
Short. 10 m. 0 f. +X.
In - Plays. 25: March 1966, 87-94.

3738. The Tree Friends by Sara Sloane McCarty.
Short. 7 m. 12 f.
In - Plays. 20: May 1961, 73-76.

3739. The Tree of Hearts by Jane McGowan.
Short. 5 m. 3 f. +X.
In - Plays. 16: Feb.1957, 57-65.

3740. A Tree on the Plains, libretto by Paul Horgan. Music by Ernst Bacon.
Excerpt (musical). 5 m. 2 f. +ch.
In - Theatre. 27: Feb.1943, 120-126.

3741. Tree to the Sky by Paul T. Nolan.
Short. 4 m. 4 f.
In - Plays. 25: May 1966, 27-39.

3742. A Tree to Trim by Aileen Fisher.
Short. 3 m. 3 f.
In - Plays. 19: Dec.1959, 1-13.

3743. The Trees at School by Alice Very.
Short. 11 un. +X.
In - Plays. 17: May 1958, 73-75.

3744. The Trees Go to School by A.V. Brown.
Short. 11 un. +c.X.
In - Plays. 3: Dec.1943, 55-58.

3745. Trial by Fury by June Bingham.
Short. 4 m. 3 f.
In - Plays. 4: Nov.1944, 51-57.

3746. Trial by Jury by James M. Cain.
Short. 12 m. 0 f.
In - American Merc. 13: Jan.1928, 30-34.

3747. Trial by Jury by William Schwenk Gilbert.
Short. 6 m. 0 f. +X.
In - Golden. 9: April 1929, 102-106.

3748. Trial By Jury by Lindsey Barbee.
Short. 2 m. 4 f.
In - Plays. 8: Nov.1948, 35-37.

3749. The Trial of Manfred the Magician by Constance Whitman Baher.
Short. 11 m. 5 f. +X.
In - Plays. 26: Dec.1966, 59-68.

3750. The Trial of Mother Goose by Helen Louise Miller.
Short. 9 m. 6 f. 3 b. 1 g. 12 c.
In - Plays. 26: April 1967, 65-72.

3751. The Trial of Peter Zenger by Paul T. Nolan.

   Short. 10 m. 5 f. +12X.

   In - Plays. 25: April 1966, 13-25.

3752. Trifles by Susan Glaspell.

   Short. 3 m. 2 f.

   In - Golden. 11: March 1930, 97-102.

   A Trilogy of Dubrovnik.

      see

   Allons Enfants!

   On the Terrace.

      and

   The Twilight.

3754. Triumph for Two by Hazel W. Corson. From a Bohemian folk tale.

   Short. 15 m. 6 f. +X.

   In - Plays. 26: March 1967, 37-44.

3755. Triumph of Instinct by Rufus Learsi.

   In - Drama. 14: Oct.1923, 26-28.

3756. Trolls' Christmas by Georg Thorne-Thomsen.

   In - Elem. School. 38: Dec.1907, 210-215.

3757. Tropics by Clifford M. Montague.

   Short. 4 m. 0 f.

   In - Poet Lore. 40: Sept.1929, 414-419.

3758. A Troubadour's Dream by Claudine E. Clements.

   Short. 7 m. 2 f. 1 b. +X.

   In - Drama. 16: Nov.1925, 57-58.

3759. Trouble in Outer Space by Robert A. Anderson.

   Short. 4 m. 3 f.

   In - Plays. 26: Dec.1966, 1-9.

3760. Trouble in the Air by Aileen Fisher and Olive Rabe.

   Short. 14 m. 14 f. +X.

   In - Plays. 27: Feb.1968, 79-95.

3761. Trouble in Tick Tock Town by Helen Louise Miller.

   Short. 7 m. 6 f. +12X.

   In - Plays. 19: April 1960, 65-70.

3762. Trouble in Tree-Land by Claire Boiko.

   Short. 5 m. 1 f. 9 c.

   In - Plays. 23: May 1964, p.83-86.

3763. Truce by Donald Lindsay.

   Radio. 5 m. 0 f. +X.

   In - Scholastic. 29: Nov.7,1936, 16+.

3764. A True Hero by William Dean Howells.

   Short. 3 m. 1 f.

   In - Harper's M. 119: Nov.1909, 866-875.

3765. The True History of Squire Jonathan and His Unfortunate Treasure by John Arden.

   Short. 1 m. 1 f. +X.

   In - Players. 15: Aug.1968, 60-64.

3766. The True Story of Humpty Dumpty by Donald Pelz.

   Radio. 11 m. 1 f. 1 b. +X.

   In - Scholastic. 30: May 1,1937, 11-12.

3767. The Truth About Liars by Helene Mullins.

   Short. 2 m. 1 f.

   In - Poet Lore. 34: March 1923, 145-151.

3768. The Truth Suspected by D. Juan Ruiz de Alarcon. Trans. from the Spanish by Julio del Toro and Robert V. Finney.

   Full. 12 m. 3 f.

   In - Poet Lore. 38: Dec.1927, 475-530.

3769. Trying a Dramatist by Sir William S. Gilbert.

   Short. 12 m. 2 f. +X.

   In - Century. 83: Dec.1911, 179-189.

3770. The Trysting Place by Booth Tarkington.

   Short. 3 m. 3 f.

   In - Ladies' Home. 39: Sept.1922, 3-5+.

3771. Tugging by Nancy Burney Cox.

   In - Drama. 15: Feb.1925, 107-109.

3772. Tulips and Two Lips by Graham DuBois.

   Short. 2 m. 5 f.

   In - Plays. 12: April 1953, 15-26.

3773. The Tumbler by Everett Glass.

   Short. 4 m. 0 f. +X.

   In - Poet Lore. 37: Dec.1926, 516-536.

3774. Turkey, Anyone? by Juliet Garver.

   Short. 2 m. 6 f.

   In - Plays. 15: Nov.1955, 41-50.

3775. Turkey for All by Vernon Howard.

   Short. 6 un.

   In - Plays. 13: Nov.1953, 84-87.

3776. Turkey Gobblers by Mildred Hark and Noel McQueen.

Short. 3 m. 4 f.

In - Plays. 12: Nov.1952, 1-12.

3777. Turkey Gobblers by Mildred Hark and Noel McQueen.

Short. 3 m. 4 f.

In - Plays. 23: Nov.1963, 29-41.

3778. Turkey Turns the Tables by Helen Louise Miller.

Short. 2 m. 2 f.

In - Plays. 5: Nov.1945, 1-11.

3779. The Turkish Ambassador by August von Kotzebue. Trans. from the German by Beatrice B. Beebe.

Short. 4 m. 4 f. +X.

In - Poet Lore. 38: June 1927, 192-205.

3780. The Turn of a Hair by Phoebe Hoffman.

Short. 0 m. 4 f.

In - Drama. 15: Jan.1925, 85-87.

Turn of the Screw.

see

The Innocents.

3782. Turnabout in Time by Anne Coulter Martens.

Short. 5 m. 4 f.

In - Plays. 23: Jan.1964, 1-13.

3783. Turning the Tables by Aileen Fisher and Olive Rabe.

Short. 4 m. 3 f.

In - Plays. 14: Oct.1954, 77-86.

3784. Turning the Tables by Helen Louise Miller.

Short. 15 m. 10 f. +X.

In - Plays. 18: Nov.1958, 37-46.

3785. A Turtle, a Flute, and the General's Birthday by Lavinia R. Davis.

Short. 15 m. 1 f.

In - Plays. 21: Feb.1962, 35-40.

3786. 'Twas the Night Before Christmas by Mildred Hark and Noel McQueen.

Short. 3 m. 2 f.

In - Plays. 5: Dec.1945, 1-11.

3787. 'Twas Well Done and Quickly by John Francis McDermott, Jr.

In - Poet Lore. 39: Sept.1928, 415-430.

3788. The Twelve Dancing Princesses adap. by Adele Thane from Grimms' Fairy Tales.

Short. 4 m. 13 f. +X.

In - Plays. 24: Nov.1964, 37-46.

3789. The Twelve Days of Christmas by Doris Wright.

Short. 50 m. 28 f. +X.

In - Plays. 11: Dec.1951, 62-65.

3790. The Twelve Days of Christmas by Doris Wright.

Short. 50 m. 28 f. +ch.

In - Plays. 17: Dec.1957, 59-62.

3791. Twenty Thousand Leagues Under the Sea by Jules Verne. Adap. by Lewy Olfson.

Radio. 8 m. 1 f. 5 un.

In - Plays. 17: May 1958, 83-91.

3792. The Twilight by Ivo Vojnovich. Trans. from the Croatian by John J. Batistich and George Rapall Noyes.

Short. 4 m. 6 f.

In - Poet Lore. 56:no.3,1951, 195-218.

3793. The Twilight of the Gods by Josephine Daskam Bacon.

Short. Indef.un.

In - Forum. 53: Jan.1915, 7-20.

3794. Twin Cousins by Morton K. Schwartz.

Short. 3 m. 2 f.

In - Plays. 6: Nov.1946, 46-52.

3795. Twinkle by Claribel Spamer.

Short. 4 m. 3 f. +X.

In - Plays. 12: Dec.1952, 54-56.

3796. The Twisting of the Rope by Douglas Hyde.

Short. 2 m. 3 f.

In - Poet Lore. 16:no.1,1905, 12-22.

3797. Two Against Napoleon by Eleanora Bowling Kane.

Radio. 10 m. 1 f.

In - Plays. 5: Jan.1946, 72-76.

3798. Two Black Sheep by Arthur Corning White.

Short. 2 m. 2 f.

In - Poet Lore. 35: Sept.1924, 464-470.

3799. Two Blind Men and a Donkey by Mathurin M. Dondo.

In - Poet Lore. 32: Sept.1921, 391-402.

3800. Two Blind Mice by Samuel Spewack.

Full. 11 m. 4 f.

In - Theatre. 33: Dec.1949, 59-90.

3801. Two for the Money by John Murray.

Short. 5 m. 8 f.

In - Plays. 24: March 1965, 17-30.

3802. Two for the Show by Paul S. McCoy.

Short. 1 m. 1 f.

In - Plays. 18: Oct.1958, 79-84.

3803. Two Gentlemen of Soho by Alan P. Herbert.

Short. 5 m. 3 f.

In - Atlantic. 139: May 1927, 577-592.

3804. Two Husbands by Henri Lavedan. Trans. from
the French by R.T. House.

Short. 2 m. 0 f.

In - Poet Lore. 19:no.2,1908, 207-211.

3805. Two Masks by Roma Greth.

Short. 3 m. 4 f.

In - Plays. 25: Feb.1966, 15-25.

3806. Two Milords; or The Blow of Thunder by
Stephen Leacock.

Short. 3 m. 1 f.

In - Atlantic. 159: May 1937, 597-599.

3807. The Two of Them by Roland E. Hartley and
Caroline M. Power. From the story by
Sir James M. Barrie.

Short. 1 m. 1 f.

In - Golden. 21: April 1935, 355-358.

3808. Two Passengers for Chelsea by Oscar W.
Firkins.

Short. 8 m. 2 f.

In - Golden. 11: Jan.1930, 95-103.

3809. Two-Penny Show by John F. Lehman.

Short. 1 m. 1 f. +X.

In - Plays. 4: May 1945, 57-60.

3810. Two Slaps in the Face by Ferenc Molnar.

Short. 2 m. 0 f.

In - Golden. 2: July 1925, 65-67.

3811. Two Strangers from Nazareth by Graham DuBois.

Short. 5 m. 5 f.

In - Plays. 21: Dec.1961, 44-50.

3812. Two Travelers and a Bear by Rowena Bennett.

Short. 3 m. 0 f.

In - Plays. 6: Jan.1947, 43-45.

3813. Tyl Ulenspiegel or The Song of Drums by
Ashley Dukes.

Full. 12 m. 5 f. 2 c. +m.X.

In - Theatre. 10: April-July,1926, 240-253,
312-324, 385-395, 481-486.

3814. U.S.A. by John Dos Passos and Paul Shyre.

Full. 3 m. 3 f.

In - Theatre. 44: June 1960, 24-50.

3815. Unaccustomed As I Am . . . by Mildred Hark
and Noel McQueen.

Short. 3 m. 2 f.

In - Scholastic. 39: Oct.20,1941, 17-19.

3816. The Unbidden Guest by Oscar W. Firkins.

Short. 6 m. 1 f.

In - Poet Lore. 35: June 1924, 276-297.

3817. Umbrella Magic by Esther MacLellan and
Catherine V. Schroll.

Short. 7 m. 2 f.

In - Plays. 11: Jan.1952, 56-60.

3818. Uncle Jimmy by Zona Gale.

Short. 5 m. 4 f.

In - Ladies' Home. 38: Oct.1921, 18-19+.

3819. Uncle Tertius on the Home Front by Frederick
Lambeck.

Short. 1 m. 2 f.

In - Publish. W. 143: Jan.23,1943, 342-346.

3820. Uncle Tom's Cabin by Aileen Fisher and Olive
Rabe.

Short. 4 m. 5 f.

In - Plays. 15: March 1956, 24-30.

3821. Uncle Vania by Anton Chekhov. Trans. from the
Russian by Frances Arno Saphro.

Full. 5 m. 4 f.

In - Poet Lore. 33: Sept.1922, 317-361.

3822. The Uncolored Easter Eggs by Claribel Spamer.

Short. 5 m. 4 f. +X.

In - Plays. 10: March 1951, 60-62.

3823. Under Milk Wood by Dylan Thomas.

Full. Large cast of m. & f., many of which
may be doubled.

In - Mlle. 38: Feb.1954, 110-124+.

3824. <u>Under Milk Wood</u> by Dylan Thomas.

Full. See cast note above.

In - Players. 4: Feb.& March 1957, 23-34, 25-29.

3825. <u>Under the Harvest Moon</u> by Mildred Hark and Noel McQueen.

Short. 1 m. 1 f. 5 un.

In - Plays. 4: Oct.1944, 32-37.

3826. <u>Under the Skin</u> by Kenneth Ross.

Full. 4 m. 2 f.

In - Players. 15: Aug.1968, 27-46.

3827. <u>The Undercurrent</u> by Fay Ehlert.

Short. 2 m. 4 f.

In - Drama. 18: Jan.1928, 111-114.

3828. <u>Underground</u> by Benjamin W. Newman.

Short. 4 m. 0 f.

In - Poet Lore. 38: Dec.1927, 571-578.

3829. <u>The Undersea Visitor</u> by Dorothy Deming.

Short. 3 m. 1 f.

In - Plays. 6: May 1947, 41-44.

3830. <u>Undine</u> by William Leonard Courtney.

In - Fortnightly. 77: June 1902, 1092-1116.

3831. <u>Unexpected Guests</u> by Aileen Fisher.

Short. 6 m. 6 f.

In - Plays. 12: Nov.1952, 58-61.

3832. <u>Unforeseen</u> by Julio Jimenez Rueda.

Full. 4 m. 9 f.

In - Poet Lore. 35: March 1924, 1-42.

3833. <u>The Uninvited Guests</u> by Helen Louise Miller.

Short. 3 m. 3 f. +m.X.

In - Plays. 17: May 1958, 77-82.

3834. <u>United Spies</u> by Robert Fontaine.

Short. 4 m. 1 f.

In - Plays. 25: May 1966, 106-108.

3835. <u>The Unknown Star</u> by Harry Major Paull and Laurence Houseman.

Full. 12 m. 3 f. +X.

In - 19th C. 86: Dec.1919, 1065-1095.

3836. <u>Unpublished Story</u> by Paolo Levi. English version by Robert Rietty.

Full. 8 m. 6 f.

In - Gambit. 3: no.11, 3-91.

3837. <u>The Unsinkable Molly Brown</u> by Richard Morris. Music and lyrics by Meredith Wilson.

Full. 30 m. 12 f. +ch.

In - Theatre. 47: Feb. 1963, 25-56

3838. <u>Unsuspected Fruit</u> by Earl J. Dias.

Short. 4 m. 2 f.

In - Plays. 10: April 1951, 7-16.

3839. <u>Untitled</u> by Norman Corwin.

Radio. 8 m. 4 f.

In - Scholastic. 45: Sept.18,1944, 17-20.

3840. <u>Unto the Least of These</u> by Adelaide Rowell.

Short. 4 m. 6 f. 1 b.

In - Drama. 18: Nov.1927, 43-46+.

3841. <u>Up (a mime)</u> by R.L. Sassoon and D.H. Elliott.

Short. 2 m. 0 f.

In - First Stage. 2: Sept.1963, 363-364.

3842. <u>Up a Christmas Tree</u> by Aileen Fisher.

Short (Musical). 1 m. 1 f. 2 b. 2 g.

In - Plays. 28: Dec.1968, 83-84.

3843. <u>An Up-and-Doing Day</u> by Aileen Fisher.

Short. 10 m. 11 f. +X.

In - Plays. 14: April 1955, 81-82.

3844. <u>Up in the Air</u> by Marjorie B. Paradis.

Short. 0 m. 6 f.

In - Plays. 14: March 1955, 11-18.

3845. <u>Up to the Women</u> by John H. Werner.

Short. 1 m. 1 f.

In - Ladies' Home. 50: Sept.1933, 54.

3846. <u>Upon the Waters</u> by Tacie May Hanna.

In - Drama. 14: Nov.1923, 58-62.

3847. <u>Ups and Downs</u> by John Murray.

Short. 4 m. 2 f.

In - Plays. 13: March 1954, 27-37.

3848. <u>Upward, Upward</u> by George Hitchcock.

Full. 15 m. 4 f.

In - First Stage. 3: June 1964, 142-166.

3849. <u>The Useful Scarecrow</u> by Claribel Spamer.

Short. 5 m. 1 f.

In - Plays. 5: Nov.1945, 57-59.

3850. The Useless Little Wind by June Barr.
Short. 5 m. 6 f.
In - Plays. 8: March 1949, 54-57.

3851. The Valentine Box by Vernon Howard.
Short. 4 m. 2 f.
In - Plays. 13: Feb.1954, 71-73.

3852. A Valentine for Kate by Helen Louise Miller.
Short. 4 m. 5 f.
In - Plays. 24: Feb.1965, 29-39.

3853. A Valentine for Mary by Rowena Bennett.
Short. 0 m. 1 f. 4 un.
In - Plays. 27: Feb.1968, 69-71.

3854. Valentine Sale by Alice Very.
Short. 16 un.
In - Plays. 6: Feb.1947, 76-78.

3855. Valentine Stardust by Jessie Nicholson.
Short. 4 m. 5 f. 2 c.
In - Plays. 11: Feb.1952, 50-57.

3856. The Valentine Tree by Marjorie Barrows.
Short. 3 m. 2 f. 3 un. +X.
In - Plays. 17: Feb.1958, 67-71.

3857. Valentine's Day by Lucile M. Duvall.
Short. 6 m. 3 f. +c.X.
In - Plays. 15: Feb.1956, 71-77.

3858. Valerie's Valentine by Karin Asbrand.
Short. 9 m. 8 f. +X.
In - Plays. 5: Feb.1946, 46-49.

3859. The Valiant by Holworthy Hall and Robert Middlemass.
Short. 4 m. 1 f.
In - Scholastic. 52: Feb.16,1948, 16-18.

3860. The Valiant Villain by Robert Combs.
Short. 4 m. 4 f.
In - Plays. 18: April 1959, 1-12.

3861. Valley Forge Was Never Like This by Vernon Howard.
Short. 3 m. 2 f.
In - Plays. 13: Feb.1954, 74-76.

3862. The Valley of Gloom by Marie Drennan.
Short. 5 m. 1 f. +X.
In - Poet Lore. 34: Sept.1923, 449-457.

3863. The Valley of Lost Men by Alice Henson Ernst.
Short. 5 m. 0 f.
In - Theatre. 14: May 1930, 430-440.

3864. Vanessa and the Blue Dragon by Constance Whitman Baher.
Short. 6 m. 1 f. +X.
In - Plays. 28: Nov.1968, 53-60.

3865. The Vanishing Easter Egg by Helen Louise Miller.
Short. 4 m. 4 f.
In - Plays. 26: March 1967, 27-36.

3866. Varnishing Day by Frederick J. Pohl.
Short. 3 m. 4 f.
In - Poet Lore. 38: March 1927, 128-140.

3867. Vasco by Georges Schehade. Trans. from the French by Robert Baldick.
Full. 18 m. 3 f. +X.
In - Gambit. 1: no.1, 6-67.

3868. The Vast Domain by Arthur Schnitzler. Trans. from Das Weite Land by Edward Woticky and Alexander Caro.
Full. 15 m. 11 f. 2 c. +X.
In - Poet Lore. 34: Sept.1923, 317-407.

3869. Vegetable Salad by Vernon Howard.
Short. 1 m. 3 f. 19 c.
In - Plays. 15: Feb.1956, 78-80.

3870. Venice Preserved by Hugo von Hofmannsthal. Trans. from the German by Elizabeth Walter.
Full. 15 m. 6 f. +ch.
In - Poet Lore. 26: no.5,1915, 529-643.

3871. Very Crude Oil by Stella Dunaway Whipkey.
Short. 3 m. 2 f.
In - Drama. 20: May 1930, 236-239.

3872. Very Special Service by Virginia Church.
In - Drama. 15: Dec.1924, 54-56.

3873. A Veterinarian in Time by Samuel S. Richmond.
Short. 3 m. 2 f.
In - Plays. 7: Feb.1948, 70-74.

3874. The Vicar Saves the Day by Gladys L. Schmitt.
Radio. 4 m. 1 f. 1 b.
In - Scholastic. 27: Jan.11,1936, 7-8+.

3875. Vicky Gets the Vote by Helen Louise Miller.
Short. 8 m. 5 f.
In - Plays. 16: Nov.1956, 37-44.

3876. Victims of the Plague by Kenneth Lewis
Roberts.
Short. 5 m. 3 f.
In - Sat. Evening. 200: Jan.21,1928, 10-11+.

3877. Victoria by Jane Winsor Gale.
Short. 8 m. 7 f. 4 b.
In - Poet Lore. 26:no.1,1915, 78-110.

3878. The Victory Garden by Blanche Day.
Short. 5 m. 5 f.
In - Plays. 3: May 1944, 74-76.

3879. Victory Gardens by Alice Very.
Short. 5 m. 1 f. 5 c. +X.
In - Plays. 4: May 1945, 55-57.

3880. Video Christmas by Earl J. Dias.
Short. 3 m. 4 f. +X.
In - Plays. 18: Dec.1958, 1-12.

3881. A View of the Sea by Paul T. Nolan.
Short. 4 m. 5 f.
In - Plays. 24: March 1965, 31-41.

3882. The Violent Wedding by Robert Lowry.
Full. 11 m. 5 f. (Some Negro).
In - Poet Lore. 58: March 1963, 3-43.

3883. Violets for Christmas by Marguerite Kreger
Phillips.
Short. 1 m. 4 f.
In - Plays. 11: Dec.1951, 32-42.

3884. Virtue Is Her Own Reward by Michael Hervey.
Short. 6 m. 6 f.
In - Plays. 25: April 1966, 27-35.

3885. The Vision by Harry Major Paull.
Full. 8 m. 1 f. +m.X.
In - 19th C. 89: Jan.1921, 175-188.

3886. Vision of the Silver Bell by Winston Weathers.
Radio. 5 m. 5 f.
In - Plays. 5: Dec.1945, 70-75.

3887. A Vision of Youth by Eleanor Colby.
Short. 1 m. 1 f. +c.X.
In - Ladies' Home. 30: March 1913, 91+.

3888. Visions of Sugar Plums by Barry Pritchard.
Full. 4 m. 0 f.
In - First Stage. 4: Sept.1965, 176-195.

3889. Visions of Sugar Plums by Anne Coulter
Martens.
Short. 2 m. 3 f. 1 b. 1 g.
In - Plays. 26: Dec.1966, 33-43.

3890. The Visit by Friedrich Duerrenmatt. Adap. by
Maurice Valency.
Full. 24 m. 7 f.
In - Theatre. 43: Dec.1959, 33-64.

3891. Visit of Johnny Appleseed by Mildred Hark
and Noel McQueen.
Short. 3 m. 3 f.
In - Plays. 8: March 1949, 35-43.

3892. The Visit of the Touter by Mabel Ray
Goodlander.
Short. 0 m. 1 f. 4 c. +c.X.
In - Woman's Home. 41: Dec.1914, 66.

3893. Visit to a Small Planet by Gore Vidal.
In - Cosmopolitan. 143: Aug.1957, 58-64.

3894. Visit to a Small Planet by Gore Vidal.
Full. 9 m. 2 f.
In - Theatre. 42: Feb.1958, 32-56.

3895. A Visit to Goldilocks by Jane McGowan.
Short. 2 m. 3 f. 4 c.
In - Plays. 19: Nov.1959, 61-64.

3896. A Visit to the Library by Katherine Searcy,
et al.
Short. 0 m. 0 f. 9 b. 3 g. 2 c.
In - Wilson. 24: Oct.1949, 166-167.

3897. Visit to the Planets by Hathaway Kale
Melchior.
Short. 9 m. 7 f. 3 un.
In - Plays. 16: May 1957, 37-44.

3898. <u>A Visit to the White House</u> by Mildred Hark
and Noel McQueen.

Short. 29 m. 6 f. 6 b. 6 g. -c.X.

In - Plays. 24: Jan.1965, 83-95.

3899. <u>Visiting Mamma</u> by Myra Emmons.

In - Harper's B. 43: Sept.1909, 860-864.

3900. <u>Visitor from Outer Space</u> by John Murray.

Full. 7 m. 8 f.

In - Plays. 24: Oct.1964, 1-16.

3901. <u>Visitor of Gettysburg</u> by Earl J. Dias.

Short. 4 m. 3 f.

In - Plays. 11: Feb.1952, 30-38.

3902. <u>Visitor to Mount Vernon</u> by Helen Louise Miller.

Short. 12 m. 7 f.

In - Plays. 13: Feb.1954, 53-59.

3903. <u>Visitors for Nancy Hanks</u> by Rowena Bennett.

Short. 0 m. 4 f.

In - Plays. 4: Jan.1945, 18-27.

3904. <u>Vitamin "U"</u> by Southwest High School Students,
Minneapolis, Minn.

Radio. 2 m. 3 f.

In - Scholastic. 43: Nov.29,1943, 15-16.

3905. <u>Vittoria</u> by Margaret Sherwood.

Short. 2 m. 1 f.

In - Scribner's. 37: April 1905, 497-504.

3906. <u>The Voice of Liberty</u> by Aileen Fisher.

Short. 6 m. 4 f.

In - Plays. 8: March 1949, 19-26.

3907. <u>The Voice of Liberty</u> by Aileen Fisher.

Short. 5 m. 2 f. 3 c.

In - Plays. 23: April 1964, 57-64.

3908. <u>Voices of America</u> by Mildred Hark and
Noel McQueen.

Short. 12 m. 4 f.

In - Plays. 4: Nov.1944, 41-44.

3909. <u>Vote for Miss Checkout</u> by John Murray.

Short. 7 m. 7 f. +X.

In - Plays. 20: May 1961, 11-23.

3910. <u>Vote for Uncle Sam</u> by Mildred Hark and
Noel McQueen.

Short. 6 m. 3 f. +10X.

In - Plays. 10: Nov.1950, 11-18.

3911. <u>Vote for Your Hero</u> by Edrie Pendleton.

Short. 5 m. 3 f.

In - Plays. 12: Nov.1952, 22-31.

3912. <u>Vote for Your Hero</u> by Edrie Pendleton.

Short. 5 m. 3 f.

In - Plays. 20: Nov.1960, 77-86.

3913. <u>The Wages of War</u> by J. Wiegand and Wilhelm
Scharrelmann.

Short. 10 m. 4 f. +X.

In - Poet Lore. 19:no.2,1908, 129-164.

3914. <u>Wait and See</u> by Mary F. Smith.

Short. 2 m. 7 f.

In - Plays. 17: Jan.1958, 67-70.

3915. <u>Waiting</u> by Mario Fratti.

Short. 4 m. 3 f.

In - Poet Lore. 63: Sept.1968, 330-342.

3916. <u>Waiting for Godot</u> by Samuel Beckett.

Full. 5 m. 0 f.

In - Theatre. 40: Aug.1956, 36-61.

3917. <u>Waiting for Santa</u> by Chris Parsons.

Short. 6 m. 5 f.

In - Plays. 18: Dec.1958, 76-80.

3918. <u>Waiting Room</u> by George M.P. Baird.

In - Drama. 15: Oct.1924, 6-9.

3919. <u>Wake Up, Santa Claus!</u> by Helen Louise Miller.

Short. 6 m. 3 f. 7 c. +X.

In - Plays. 19: Dec.1959, 73-78.

3920. <u>Waking the Daffodil</u> by Rowena Bennett.

Short. 2 f. 3 un.

In - Plays. 26: April 1967, 73-74.

3921. <u>Walk Proudly Here - Americans</u> by Lyda M.
Ickler.

Radio. 3 m. 1 f. 1 g.

In - Plays. 5: Nov.1945, 71-75.

3922. <u>The Walled-Up Window</u> by August von Kotzebue.
Trans. from the German by Beatrice B.
Beebe.

Short. 4 m. 1 f.

In - Poet Lore. 38: June 1927, 246-263.

3923. <u>Walt</u> by Christopher Morley.

Short. 6 m. 1 f.

In - Bookman. 59: Aug.1924, 646-662.

3924. The Waltz of the Toreadors by Jean Anouilh.
Trans. by Lucienne Hill.

Full. 4 m. 7 f.

In - Players. 4: Oct.& Nov.1956, 23-31,
23-29.

3925. The Waltz of the Toreadors by Jean Anouilh.
Trans. by Lucienne Hill.

Full. 4 m. 7 f.

In - Theatre. 41: Sept.1957, 34-54.

3926. The Waltz That Was Lost by Leonora Sill
Ashton.

Short. 1 m. 2 f. 1 b. 2 g.

In - Etude. 70: June 1952, 54.

3927. The Wanderers by Josephine Dodge Daskam.

Short. 2 m. 1 f.

In - Century. 62: Aug.1901, 583-589.

3928. The Wandering Dragon by T'ang Wen Shun.

Short. 8 m. 4 f.

In - Carolina. 15: March 1942, 7-17.

3929. War Brides by Marion Craig Wentworth.

Short. 3 m. 3 f.

In - Century. 89: Feb.1915, 527-544.

3930. The War Indemnities by George Bernard Shaw.

Short. 7 m. 0 f.

In - American Merc. 35: Aug.1935, 395-397.

3931. Was Her Face Red by Marjorie B. Paradis.

Short. 2 m. 10 f.

In - Plays. 8: March 1949, 12-19.

3932. Was Her Face Red by Marjorie B. Paradis.

Short. 0 m. 12 f.

In - Plays. 26: April 1967, 29-36.

3933. Wash Carver's Mouse Trap by Fred Koch, Jr.

Short. 2 m. 2 f.

In - Carolina. 11: Dec.1938, 101-108.

3934. Washed in de Blood by Rietta Winn Bailey.

Short. 6 m. 7 f. +X.

In - Carolina. 11: March 1938, 9-19.

3935. Washington At Home by Esther Shenk.

Short. 5 m. 2 f.

In - Wilson. 6: May 1932, 611-615.

3936. Washington Marches On by Aileen Fisher.

Short. 26 m. 7 f. +X.

In - Plays. 13: Feb.1954, 29-40.

3937. The Washington Shilling by Helen Louise
Miller.

Short. 8 m. 6 f. +X.

In - Plays. 16: Feb.1957, 43-52.

3938. Washington Square by Henry James. Adap. by
Lewy Olfson.

Radio. 4 m. 4 f.

In - Plays. 24: March 1965, 85-94.

3939. Washington's Gold Button by Deborah Newman.

Short. 2 m. 6 f.

In - Plays. 9: Feb.1950, 71-75.

3940. Washington's Gold Button by Deborah Newman.

Short. 2 m. 6 f.

In - Plays. 20: Feb.1961, 84-88.

3941. Washington's Leading Lady by Helen Louise
Miller.

Short. 7 m. 13 f.

In - Plays. 16: Feb.1957, 81-87.

3942. Washington's Lucky Star by Helen Louise
Miller.

Short. 5 m. 4 f.

In - Plays. 22: Feb.1963, 75-80.

3943. Washington's Sacrifice by Helen M. Roberts.

Short. 4 m. 2 f.

In - Plays. 6: Jan.1947, 40-43.

3944. The Washingtons Slept Here by Helen Louise
Miller.

Short. 2 m. 4 f. +X.

In - Plays. 21: Feb.1962, 23-34.

3945. Wasted Lives by Antonio de Lezama and
Enrique de Meneses. Trans. by Hermann
Schnitzler; Adap. for the English stage
by Gustav Davidson.

Full. 8 m. 11 f.

In - Poet Lore. 41: April 1930, 159-203.

3946. The Watch and the Almond Tart by August
von Kotzebue. Trans. from the German
by Beatrice B. Beebe.

Short. 1 m. 2 f.

In - Poet Lore. 38: June 1927, 240-245.

3947. Watch on the Rhine by Lillian Hellman.
Excerpt. 4 m. 2 f. 1 b. 1 g.
In - Scholastic. 43: Sept.13,1943, 17-19.

3948. Watch Out for Aunt Hattie by Maxine Shore.
Short. 2 m. 2 f.
In - Plays. 11: March 1952, 28-38.

3949. Watching for Santa Claus by Horace Varney.
Short. 1 m. 1 f. 1 b. 4 g.
In - Ladies' Home. 21: Dec.1903, 19.

3950. The Water Hen by Stanislaw Ignacy Witkiewicz.
English version by C.S. Durer and Daniel C. Gerould.
Full. 13 m. 2 f. 1 b.
In - First Stage. 6: June 1967, 86-102.

3951. The Way-Out Cinderella by Harold Cable.
Short. 4 m. 5 f.
In - Plays. 23: May 1964, 23-35.

3952. The Way to Norwich by Aileen Fisher.
Short. 6 m. 4 f. 1 un.
In - Plays. 6: April 1947, 39-43.

3953. The Way to the Inn by Celia Gordon.
Short. 5 m. 5 f. +X.
In - Plays. 11: Dec.1951, 53-56.

3954. The Way to the Inn by Deborah Newman.
Short. 5 m. 5 f. +X.
In - Plays. 22: Dec.1962, 53-56.

3955. Way, Way Down East by Earl J. Dias.
Short. 5 m. 5 f.
In - Plays. 14: March 1955, 1-10.

3956. Way, Way Down East by Earl J. Dias.
Short. 6 m. 3 f.
In - Plays. 23: May 1964, 99-107.

3957. Way, Way Off Broadway by Betty Tracy Huff.
Short. 7 m. 6 f. +X.
In - Plays. 27: Oct.1967, 29-41.

3958. The Wayfarers by Louise A. Stinetorf.
Short. 7 m. 1 f.
In - Plays. 7: Dec.1947, 28-40.

3959. We Are Three by Evelyn Henderson Fife.
Short. 2 m. 1 f.
In - Drama. 16: Oct.1925, 17-18+.

3960. We But Teach by Samuel S. Richmond.
Short. 3 m. 4 f. +X.
In - Plays. 4: April 1945, 67-71.

3961. We Hold These Truths by Marguerite Fellows Melcher.
Short. 3 m. 5 f.
In - Plays. 6: Oct.1946, 1-12.

3962. We Pledge Ourselves by Minnie M. Rugg and Morton Sonnenfeld.
Short. Indef.un. +c.X.
In - Scholastic. 43: Nov.8,1943, 17-19.

3963. We, the People by Myriam Toles.
Short. 15 m. 6 f. 1 un. +m.X.
In - Plays. 22: Feb.1963, 23-32.

3964. We Want Mother by Mildred Hark and Noel McQueen.
Short. 2 m. 3 f.
In - Plays. 15: May 1956, 33-40.

3965. The Weatherman on Trial by Helen Louise Miller.
Short. 5 m. 2 f. 6 un. +X.
In - Plays. 19: May 1960, 73-78.

3966. The Weaver's Son by Aileen Fisher.
Short. 1 m. 1 f. 2 b. 1 g.
In - Plays. 12: Oct.1952, 33-39.

3967. We'd Never Be Happy Otherwise by Ellsworth P. Conkle. Ed. by Hermann Hagedorn.
Short. 10 m. 2 f.
In - Scholastic. 35: Oct.2,1939, 21E-23E+.

3968. Wedded, But No Wife by Katherine Dayton.
Short. 1 m. 1 f.
In - Sat. Evening. 204: Dec.12,1931, 11+.

3969. Wedded Husband by Shen Hung.
In - Poet Lore. 32: March 1921, 110-135.

3970. The Wedding Anniversary by Marian Spencer Smith.
Short. 1 m. 1 f.
In - Drama. 17: April 1927, 206-207.

3971. The Wedding Dress by Edna O'Brien.
Short. 1 m. 5 f.
In - Mlle. 58: Nov.1963, 134-135+.

3972. Wedding Guest by Arthur Bourchier.
In - Fortnightly. 74 sup: Dec.1900, 1-42.

3973. The Wedding Guest by Rosalee Kerley.
Short. 4 m. 4 f. +X.
In - Poet Lore. 33: June 1922, 232-238.

3974. The Week Before Christmas by Aileen Fisher.
Short. 0 m. 0 f. 10 b. 10 g.
In - Plays. 14: Dec.1954, 87.

3975. Weeping Willow's Happy Day by Janice Auritt Oser.
Short. 6 m. 4 f. 8 un.
In - Plays. 13: May 1954, 71-74.

3976. Welcome, Parents by Eva Cole.
Short. 1 m. 2 f. 3 b. 6 g.
In - Plays. 25: Nov.1965, 56-59.

3977. The Well of Hazels by Anne Throop Craig.
Short. 4 m. 1 f. +X.
In - Poet Lore. 34: Sept.1923, 429-444.

3978. A Wen by Saul Bellow.
Short. 1 m. 1 f.
In - Esquire. 63: Jan.1965, 72-74+.

3979. A West Point Regulation by Mary R.S. Andrews.
Short. 2 m. 1 f.
In - McClure's. 23: Aug.1904, 385-394.

3980. West Side Story by Arthur Laurents. Music by Leonard Bernstein; lyrics by Stephen Sondheim.
Full (musical). 25 m. 14 f. +ch.
In - Theatre. 43: Oct.1959, 33-55.

3981. West to the Indies by Aileen Fisher and Olive Rabe.
Short. 4 m. 3 f.
In - Plays. 17: Oct.1957, 14-22.

3982. What a Life by Clifford H. Goldsmith.
Excerpt. 4 m. 2 f.
In - Scholastic. 34: March 4,1939, 19E-21E.

3983. What Are They Fighting For? by Alice Duer Miller.
Short. 2 m. 2 f.
In - Sat. Evening. 192: Feb.21,1920, 10-11+.

3984. What Can I Do? by Carolyn Wilson.
Short. 8 m. 4 f. 1 g. +48 c.X.
In - St. Nicholas. 45: May 1918, 599-603.

3985. What Happened in Toyland by Aileen Fisher.
Short. 7 m. 2 f. +X.
In - Plays. 22: Dec.1962, 57-65.

3986. What Happened on Clutter Street by Aileen Fisher.
Short. 2 m. 2 un. +X.
In - Plays. 13: Oct.1953, 44-48.

3987. What Happened on Clutter Street by Aileen Fisher.
Short. 4 m. 0 f. +c.X.
In - Plays. 24: Oct.1964, 47-52.

3988. What Happened to the Tarts by Nora A. Smith.
Short. 2 m. 1 f. 1 un. +X.
In - St. Nicholas. 47: Aug.1920, 936-940.

3989. What He Deserves by Helen Littler Howard.
Short. 6 m. 1 f.
In - Plays. 7: Jan.1948, 42-45.

3990. What Ho! by Earl J. Dias.
Short. 6 m. 4 f.
In - Plays. 17: May 1958, 1-14.

3991. What is a Patriot by Aileen Fisher and Olive Rabe.
Short. 17 m. 12 f.
In - Plays. 15: April 1956, 23-30.

3992. What Makes It Tick by Helen Louise Miller.
Short. 5 m. 4 f.
In - Plays. 12: Nov.1952, 82-93.

3993. What Makes Thanksgiving? by Aileen Fisher.
Short. 0 m. 0 f. 14 c.
In - Plays. 14: Nov.1954, 72.

3994. What Mildred Found Out by Claribel Spamer.
Short. 2 m. 5 f. +X.
In - Plays. 8: March 1949, 26-30.

3995. What More Do You Want by Marguerite Fellows
Melcher.

Short. 3 m. 6 f.

In - Plays. 6: Nov.1946, 68-79.

3996. What Never Dies by Percival Wilde.

Short. 0 m. 3 f. 1 b.

In - Drama. 21: Jan.1931, 21-24+.

3997. What ... No Hearts? by Helen M. Roberts.

Short. 4 m. 5 f. +X.

In - Plays. 6: Feb.1947, 49-53.

3998. What, No Santa Claus? by Mildred Hark and
Noel McQueen.

Short. 8 m. 1 f.

In - Plays. 5: Dec.1945, 43-49.

3999. What, No Venison? by Mildred Hark and Noel
McQueen.

Short. 4 m. 4 f.

In - Plays. 15: Nov.1955, 1-13.

4000. What the Public Wants by Arnold Bennett.

Full. 9 m. 6 f. 1 b.

In - Living Age. 262 & 263: Sept.25-
Oct.16,1909, 801-820, 32-44, 104-117,
172-180.

4001. What the Public Wants by Arnold Bennett.

Full. 9 m. 6 f. 1 b.

In - McClure's. 34: Jan.- March 1910,
300-315, 419-429, 499-517.

4002. What They Think by Rachel Crothers.

Short. 2 m. 2 f.

In - Ladies' Home. 40: Feb.1923, 12-13+.

4003. What Will the Toys Say? by Rowena Bennett.

Short. 4 m. 3 f. +c.X.

In - Plays. 21: Dec.1961, 76-79.

4004. What's A Penny? by Karin Asbrand.

Short. 5 m. 4 f.

In - Plays. 7: Feb.1948, 63-65.

4005. What's Cooking? by Eelen Louise Miller.

Short. 5 m. 5 f. +X.

In - Plays. 5: Oct.1945, 65-75.

4006. What's Cookin'? by Helen Louise Miller.

Short. 5 m. 5 f. +X.

In - Plays. 11: April 1952, 67-76.

4007. What's in a Name? by Graham DuBois.

Short. 2 m. 6 f.

In - Plays. 14: Nov.1954, 13-23.

4008. Wheels Within Wheels by Aileen Fisher and
Olive Rabe.

Short. 9 m. 8 f. +X.

In - Plays. 24: Feb.1965, 61-64.

4009. When a Man Wanders by Hazel Harper Harris.

Short. 0 m. 5 f.

In - Poet Lore. 40: Dec.1929, 602-609.

4010. When Do We Eat? by Mildred Hark and Noel
McQueen.

Short. 2 m. 6 f.

In - Plays. 14: Oct.1954, 39-48.

4011. When Do We Eat? by Mildred Hark and Noel
McQueen.

Short. 1 m. 4 f. 1 b. 2 g.

In - Plays. 26: March 1967, 45-53.

4012. When It's Moonlight on Pike's Peak by
Vernon Howard.

Short. 7 m. 0 f.

In - Plays. 13: March 1954, 78-82.

4013. When Miss Brown Was Absent by M.F. Dinkins.

Short. 0 m. 2 f. +c.X.

In - Etude. 54: June 1936, 400-401.

4014. When Mozart Was Sixteen by Patricia James.

Short. 4 m. 4 f. +X.

In - Plays. 20: Jan.1961, 14-20.

4015. When Shakespeare's Ladies Meet by Charles
George.

Short. 0 m. 6 f.

In - Scholastic. 42: April 19,1943, 15-16.

4016. When the Cat's Away by Ethel McFarlan.

Short. 6 m. 7 f.

In - Plays. 15: May 1956, 47-52.

4017. When the Hurlyburly's Done by John Murray.

Short. 5 m. 6 f.

In - Plays. 13: Oct.1953, 17-29.

4018. When the Hurlyburly's Done by John Murray.

Short. 5 m. 6 f.

In - Plays. 20: Oct.1960, 13-25.

4019. When the Ship Goes Down by Harry McGuire.

Short. 10 m. 0 f.

In - Drama. 18: Dec.1927, 82-84+.

4020. Where Is Phronsie Pepper? adap. by Ruth Putnam Kimball from Margaret Sidney's Five Little Peppers Midway.

Short. 5 m. 4 f.

In - Plays. 24: March 1965, 51-59.

4021. Where Love Is by Iden Payne. From the story Where Love Is, There God Is Also by Leo Tolstoy.

Short. 3 m. 2 f. 1 b.

In - Poet Lore, 37: Dec.1926, 475-485.

4022. Where Shall We Go? by Henri Lavedan. Trans. from the French of Les Beaux Dimanches by Sibyl Collar Holbrook.

Short. 1 m. 6 f.

In - Poet Lore. 28:no.4,1917, 397-402.

4023. Which, 3 R's or 3 R's Plus Industrial Arts and Domestic Science? by Arthur Feuerstein.

Short. 8 m. 5 f.

In - Indus. Educa. 19: July 1930, 254-256.

4024. Which Way to Halloween? by Helen Louise Miller.

Short. 15 m. 16 f.

In - Plays. 22: Oct.1962, 65-71.

4025. While the Mushrooms Bubble by Dan W. Totheroh.

In - Poet Lore. 32: June 1921, 251-261.

4026. The Whirlwind Comes by Sylvia Lee.

Short. 12 um.

In - Plays. 11: Oct.1951, 58-61.

4027. The Whistle Blows by Philip L. Ketchum.

Short. 5 m. 0 f.

In - Survey. 67: Jan.1,1932, 361-363+.

4028. The Whistler by Lucile E. Langston.

Short. 2 m. 1 f. 8 um.

In - Plays. 17: April 1958, 75-77.

4029. A White Christmas by June Barr.

Short. 9 m. 6 f.

In - Plays. 8: Dec.1948, 61-63.

4030. The White House Rabbit by Helen Louise Miller.

Short. 8 m. 5 f.

In - Plays. 22: March 1963, 37-43.

4031. The White Liars by Peter Shaffer.

Short. 2 m. 1 f.

In - Players. 15: April 1968, 31-42.

4032. The White Scourge by Karel Capek. Trans. from Power and Glory by Paul Selver and Ralph Neale.

Excerpt. 4 m. 0 f.

In - Living Age. 356: March 1939, 17-25.

4033. White Water Man by Amanda Benjamin Hall.

Short. 2 m. 2 f. +c.X.

In - Poet Lore. 49: Jan.1943, 3-24.

4034. The White Whale by Marion A. Taylor.

Short. 11 m. 3 f. +X.

In - Plays. 19: Nov.1959, 84-96.

4035. The Whites of Their Eyes by Frank Willment.

Short. 9 m. 10 f.

In - Plays. 26: Feb.1967, 89-95.

4036. Whither by Alice Mary Matlock Griffith.

Short. 1 m. 2 f.

In - Poet Lore, 35: March 1924, 140-147.

4037. Who Goes Home? by Gerald Maxwell.

Short. 2 m. 1 f.

In - 19th C. 60: Sept.1906, 508-520.

4038. Who Scared Whom? by Marguerite Chapin.

Short. 4 m. 1 f.

In - Plays. 15: Oct.1955, 58-59.

4039. Who Started the Fire by Catherine Urban.

Short. 5 m. 3 f.

In - Plays. 7: Nov.1947, 56-58.

4040. The Whole City's Down Below by Paul T. Nolan.

Short. 5 m. 5 f.

In - Plays. 27: Dec.1967, 12-22.

4041. Who's Necessary? by Ella Williams Porter.

Short. 3 m. 4 f.

In - Plays. 9: March 1950, 41-46.

4042. Who's Old-Fashioned by Mildred Hark and Noel McQueen.

Short. 4 m. 3 f.

In - Plays. 11: May 1952, 21-31.

4043. Who's Old-Fashioned? by Mildred Hark and
      Noel McQueen.

      Short. 4 m. 3 f.

      In - Plays. 16: May 1957, 21-30.

4044. Who's the President? by Mildred Hark McQueen.

      Short. 15 m. 16 f.

      In - Plays. 20: Jan.1961, 47-55.

4045. Who's Who by Anna Lenington Heath.

      Short. 3 m. 4 f.

      In - Plays. 7: April 1948, 37-42.

4046. Who's Who at the Zoo by Helen Louise Miller.

      Short. 9 m. 9 f.

      In - Plays. 23: March 1964, 65-70.

4047. Whose Birthday Is It? by Dorothy F. Thompson.

      Short. 3 m. 3 f.

      In - Plays. 12: March 1953, 45-51.

4048. Why Marry? by Jesse Lynch Williams.

      Full. 7 m. 3 f.

      In - Golden. 3: June 1926, 789-826.

4049. Why Puss Washes After She Eats by Bertha
      Nathan.

      Short. 4 m. 1 f.

      In - Plays. 6: Oct.1946, 66-67.

4050. Why She Would Not by George Bernard Shaw.

      Short. 4 m. 2 f.

      In - Theatre. 40: Aug.1956, 24-27.

4051. Why the Ant's Waist is Small by Isabel
      Christie and Elizabeth Tenyi. From
      an Okanagan Indian folk tale.

      Short. 3 un. 1 c.

      In - Carolina. 12: Dec.1939, 111-112.

4052. Why the Chipmunk's Coat is Striped by
      Isabel Christie and Elizabeth Tenyi.
      From an Okanagan Indian folk tale.

      Short. 3 un. 1 c.

      In - Carolina. 12: Dec.1939, 109-110.

4053. Why the Indians Wear Moccasins by Ronald
      Lackmann.

      Short. 6 m. 0 f. +m.X.

      In - Plays. 17: Nov.1957, 61-64.

4054. Why the Sleepy Dormouse by Aileen Fisher.

      Short. 3 m. 3 f.

      In - Plays. 23: Feb.1964, 75-78.

4055. Widow's Eyes by Serafín and Joaquín Alvarez
      Quintero. Trans. by Ana Lee Utt.

      Short. 1 m. 2 f.

      In - Poet Lore. 40: Dec.1929, 552-566.

4056. The Wife by Arthur Schnitzler.

      Short. 2 m. 1 f.

      In - Current Lit. 39: Nov.1905, 553-556.

4057. The Wife of Usher's Well by John Joseph
      Martin.

      Short. 3 m. 3 f.

      In - Poet Lore. 30:no.1,1919, 94-111.

4058. The Wild Boar by Seumas O'Brien.

      Short. 6 m. 3 f. +X.

      In - Poet Lore. 38: Dec.1927, 536-550.

4059. The Wild Swans by Anne Crowell.

      Short. 11 m. 2 f. +X.

      In - Delineator. 93: Oct.1918, 26-27.

4060. Will-O'-Wisp by John Murray.

      Short. 3 m. 3 f.

      In - Plays. 11: Jan.1952, 8-20.

4061. The Will of the People by James M. Cain.

      Short. 3 m. 0 f.

      In - American Merc. 16: April 1929, 394-398.

4062. Will Somebody Please Say Something? by
      David Baxter.

      Full. 2 m. 1 f.

      In - Players. 14: April 1967, 27-42+.

4063. William Rob Attacks a Problem by Shirley
      Simon.

      Short. 2 m. 2 f. 3 un.

      In - Plays. 18: Oct.1958, 65-68.

4064. Wind by Agnes E. Peterson.

      In - Drama. 15: May 1925, 174-177.

4065. Wind in the Branches of the Sassafras by
      René de Obaldia. Trans. from the
      French by Joseph G. Foster.

      Full. 5 m. 3 f.

      In - Mod. Drama. 1: March 1968, 154-193.

4066. The Wind Ward by Alice Dennis.

      Short. 1 m. 1 f. 3 c.

      In - Plays. 4: April 1945, 44-48.

4067. Windblown by Edna M. Harris.

Short. 2 m. 2 f.

In - Poet Lore. 38: Sept.1927, 426-434.

4068. The Windows of Heaven by Shimon Wincelberg.
Based on the novella A Cat in the Ghetto
by Rachmil Bryks.

Full. 7 m. 4 f.

In - Gambit. 1: no.3, 19-84.

Winged Horse.

see

Rebel Poet.

4069. The Wings by Josephine Preston Peabody.

Short. 3 m. 1 f.

In - Harper's M. 110: May 1905, 947-956.

The Wings of the Dove.

see

A Late Spring.

4070. Wings Over Europe by Robert Nichols and
Maurice Browne.

Excerpt. 11 m. 0 f.

In - Scholastic. 47: Oct.8,1945, 17-19.

4071. The Winslow Boy by Terence Rattigan.

Full. 6 m. 4 f. 1 b.

In - Theatre. 32: Oct.1948, 63-89.

4072. Winter Bloom by Bridget T. Hayes.

Short. 2 m. 4 f.

In - Poet Lore. 30:no.3,1919, 385-411.

4073. The Winter Garden by Ethel McFarlan.

Short. 2 m. 4 f. +m.X.

In - Plays. 23: Jan.1964, 75-78.

4074. The Winter of Our Discontent by Graham DuBois.

Short. 7 m. 2 f.

In - Plays. 5: Feb.1946, 8-16.

4075. A Winter Thaw by June Barr.

Short. 0 m. 0 f. 5 b. 2 g. 8 c.

In - Plays. 10: Jan.1951, 64-68.

4076. The Winter Wizards by Rowena Bennett.

Short. 5 m. 2 f.

In - Plays. 22: Jan.1963, 69-72.

4077. The Wise and Clever Maiden by Helen A. Murphy.

Short. 8 m. 1 f. +X.

In - Plays. 6: Dec.1946, 56-65.

4078. Wise Child by Simon Gray.

Full. 2 m. 2 f.

In - Players. 15: Dec.1967, 23-38+.

4079. The Wise People of Gotham by Eleanor Leuser.

Short. 9 m. 6 f. 1 b.

In - Plays. 25: Feb.1966, 79-84.

4080. The Wise Wife by Mary Ann Nicholson.

Short. 4 m. 3 f.

In - Plays. 15: April 1956, 63-68.

4081. The Wishing Pot by Amy S. Grubb.

Short. 6 m. 2 f.

In - Plays. 6: Feb.1947, 65-68.

4082. The Wishing Stream by Helen Louise Miller.

Short. 4 m. 4 f. +ch.

In - Plays. 20: Jan.1961, 71-76.

4083. The Wishing-Well by May Emery Hall.

Short. 2 m. 2 f.

In - Plays. 3: March 1944, 28-31.

4084. The Wishing Well by May Emery Hall.

Short. 2 m. 2 f.

In - Plays. 21: March 1962, 47-50.

4085. Wispy by Claribel Spamer.

Short. 6 m. 3 f.

In - Plays. 14: Oct.1954, 71-73.

4086. The Witch Doctor by John F. Lehman.

Short. 2 m. 1 f. +8X.

In - Plays. 6: Oct.1947, 67-71.

4087. The Witch in the Golden Hat by Frances B.
Watts.

Short. 5 m. 5 f.

In - Plays. 25: Oct.1965, 68-72.

4088. The Witch Who Wasn't by Helen L. Howard.

Short. 2 m. 3 f.

In - Plays. 7: Oct.1948, 68-69.

4089. Witches' Delight by Esther MacLellan and
Catherine V. Schroll.

Short. 9 m. 9 f.

In - Plays. 14: Oct.1954, 49-54.

4090. The Witch's Pattern by John F. Lehman.

Short. 2 m. 3 f. +X.

In - Plays. 10: Oct.1950, 60-63.

4091. The Witch's Pumpkin by Esther Cooper.

Short. 0 m. 3 f.

In - Plays. 5: Oct.1945, 40-42.

4092. Witches' Sabbath by Harry Granick.

Full. 14 m. 2 f.

In - First Stage. 1: Dec.1961, 51-79.

4093. With Chains of Gold by José Andrés Vásquez.
Trans. by Willis Knapp Jones.

Short. 1 m. 1 f.

In - Poet Lore. 34: Sept.1923, 417-425.

4094. With Malice Toward None by Graham DuBois.

Short. 4 m. 3 f.

In - Plays. 14: Feb.1955, 1-12.

4095. Within the Gates by Elizabeth Stuart Phelps.

Full. 3 m. 3 f. 1 b.

In - McClure's. 17: May-July 1901, 35-43,
142-149, 236-250.

4096. The Wizard of Oz by L. Frank Baum. Adap.
by Lynne Sharon Schwartz.

Short. 6 m. 6 f. +X.

In - Plays. 22: April 1963, 83-96.

4097. The Wizard of the Wireless by Cora Burlingame.

Short. 8 m. 2 f.

In - Plays. 5: March 1946, 27-33.

4098. The Woes of Two Workers by Helen G. Van
Campen.

Full. 0 m. 2 f.

In - McClure's. 41 & 42: Aug.-Nov.1913,
190+, 198+, 216+, 65-68.

4099. Wohelo or A Day in Everygirl's Life by
Lucy Dickinson.

Short. 1 m. 19 f.

In - St. Nicholas. 51: May 1924, 730-734.

4100. The Wolf and the Kid by Rowena Bennett.

Short. 6 m. 1 f.

In - Plays. 7: Jan.1948, 45-47.

4101. Wolves and Sheep by Alexander Ostrovsky.
Trans. from the Russian by Inez Sachs
Colby and George Rapall Noyes.

Full. 13 m. 3 f. +X.

In - Poet Lore. 37: June 1926, 159-253.

4102. The Wolves and the Lamb by William Makepeace
Thackeray.

Full. 6 m. 7 f. 4 b. 1 g. +X.

In - Golden. 3: Feb.1926, 216-240.

4103. The Woman by Josip Kosor. Trans. from the
Serbo-Croation by P. Selver.

Full. 18 m. 6 f. +X.

In - Poet Lore. 41: July 1930, 317-369.

4104. A Woman Alone by Lucy Clifford.

Full. 9 m. 5 f. +X.

In - 19th C. 75: May 1914, 1144-1184.

4105. The Woman from Merry River by Chase Webb.

Short. 9 m. 4 f. +X.

In - Carolina. 14: March 1941, 7-22.

4106. Woman of No One by Cesare Lodovici.
Trans. from the Italian.

In - Poet Lore. 32: June 1921, 159-200.

Woman Song.

see

Three Chinese Folk Dramas.

4107. The Woman Who Didn't Want Christmas by
Marguerite Kreger Phillips.

Short. 0 m. 9 f.

In - Plays. 13: Dec.1953, 55-62.

4108. The Woman Who Never Gets Any Sympathy by
Dorothy Canfield.

In - Harper's B. 40: Nov.1906, 1002-1005.

4109. The Woman With the Dagger by Arthur
Schnitzler. Trans. from the German
by Horace B. Samuel.

Short. 2 m. 1 f.

In - Fortnightly. 85: June 1909, 1179-1191.

4110. Woman's Heart by Arthur L. Phelps.

In - Canadian M. 46: April 1916, 496-499.

4111. Women As Advocates by Grace Denio Litchfield.

Short. 0 m. 2 f.

In - Independent. 55: July 9,1903, 1627-1630.

4112. The Wonderful, Beautiful Day by Mary Nygaard
Peterson.

Short. 3 m. 4 f.

In - Plays. 20: Jan.1961, 57-62.

4113. The Wonderful Circus of Words by Claire
Boiko.

Short. 3 m. 1 f. +X.

In - Plays. 21: Nov.1961, 53-58.

4114. The Wonderful Halloween Cape by Deborah
       Newman.

       Short. 2 m. 8 f. 6 c.

       In - Plays. 20: Oct.1960, 45-50.

4115. The Wonderful Witchware Store by Elinor
       R. Alderman.

       Short. 2 m. 5 f. +f.X.

       In - Plays. 16: Oct.1956, 63-67.

4116. The Wonderful Wizard of Oz by L. Frank
       Baum. Adap. by Frances Mapp.

       Short. 0 m. 0 f. 5 b. 5 g. 1 "dog" +c.X.

       In - Plays. 25: March 1966, 49-58.

4117. The Wonderful World of Hans Christian
       Andersen by Deborah Newman.

       Short. 11 m. 7 f. +X.

       In - Plays. 21: Jan.1962, 55-61.

4118. Wonders of Storybook Land by Alice D'Arcy.

       Short. 7 m. 8 f.

       In - Plays. 3: April 1944, 47-54.

4119. The Wondership by Leon Cunningham.

       Short. 3 m. 3 f.

       In - Poet Lore. 30:no.3,1919, 363-376.

4120. The Wood Folk and the Litter Bugs by
       Catherine Urban.

       Short. 4 m. 3 f.

       In - Plays. 13: March 1954, 72-74.

4121. The Wooden Box by Patrick O'Connor.

       Short. 19 m. 4 f.

       In - First Stage. 4: March 1965, 26-32.

4122. The Woods of Ida by Olive Tilford Dargan.

       Short. 1 m. 4 f.

       In - Century. 74: Aug.1907, 590-604.

4123. A Word In Season by Jean Blewett.

       In - Canadian M. 36: Dec.1910, 182-184.

4124. Word of Honor by Paul S. McCoy.

       Short. 1 m. 2 f.

       In - Plays. 19: Nov.1959, 77-83.

4125. The Words We Live By by Herbert Ravetch.

       Short. 6 m. 1 f. +37X.

       In - Plays. 17: May 1958, 47-53.

4126. The Workhouse Donkey by John Arden.

       Full. 31 m. 20 f.

       In - Players. 10: Aug.& Sept.1963, 18-29,
            19-32.

4127. Workhouse Ward by Lady Gregory.

       Short. 2 m. 1 f.

       In - Golden. 9: June 1929, 100-103.

4128. The Work-Out by Albert Bermel.

       Short. 1 m. 1 f.

       In - Gambit. 1: no.3, 5-17.

4129. The World is In Your Hands by Elizabeth
       Sampson.

       Short. 6 m. 4 f.

       In - Scholastic. 34: April 29,1939, 27-29.

4130. The World's My Village by Cornel Lengyel.

       Short. 4 m. 2 f.

       In - Poet Lore. 52: July 1950, 195-229.

4131. The Worm Turns. (anon.)

       Short. 3 m. 3 f.

       In - Plays. 3: Jan.1944, 55-62.

4132. Worth His Salt by Lida Lisle Molloy.

       Short. 1 m. 3 f.

       In - Plays. 8: Jan.1949, 18-26.

4133. The Would-Be Gentleman. Trans. from Molière's
       Le Bourgeois Gentilhomme.

       Excerpts. 2 m. 2 f.

       In - Scholastic. 46: March 26,1945, 23-24+.

4134. The Would-Be Gentleman by Molière. Adap.
       by Lewy Olfson.

       Radio. 7 m. 2 f.

       In - Plays. 19: May 1960, 99-107.

4135. The Wrong Side of the Park by John Mortimer.

       Full. 3 m. 3 f.

       In - Players. 8: Jan.& Feb.1961, 23-32,
            23-29+.

4136. The Wrong Time by Vernon Howard.

       Short. 9 m. 0 f. 2 b. 2 g.

       In - Plays. 16: Jan.1957, 74-76.

4137. Wuthering Heights by Emily Brontë. Adap.
       by Lewy Olfson.

       Radio. 4 m. 2 f.

       In - Plays. 13: Jan.1954, 86-95.

4138. Wuthering Heights by Emily Brontë. Adap. by
       Lewy Olfson.

       Short. 3 m. 2 f.

       In - Plays. 24: Oct.1964, 83-95.

4139. Wuthering Heights by Emily Brontë. Adap. by
       Lewy Olfson.

       Radio. 4 m. 2 f.

       In - Plays. 27: Jan.1968, 87-96.

4140. Xantippe and Socrates by Maurice Baring.

       Short. 1 m. 1 f.

       In - Golden. 5: March 1927, 347-349.

4141. Yankee Doodle Dandy by Aileen Fisher.

       Short. 6 m. 2 f. +m.X.

       In - Plays. 25: Jan.1966, 61-62.

4142. The Yankee Doodle Kitten by Deborah Newman.

       Short. 7 m. 8 f. +X.

       In - Plays. 23: Nov.1963, 67-71.

4143. Ye Good Old Days by Helen M. Roberts.

       Short. 0 m. 6 f.

       In - Plays. 7: Nov.1947, 38-42.

4144. Ye Olde Book Shoppe by Samuel S. Richmond.

       Short. 4 m. 3 f.

       In - Plays. 8: Nov.1948, 59-67.

4145. Yes, I'm Going Away by Bertolt Brecht.
       Trans. by Ruth Norden.

       Short. 1 m. 1 f.

       In - Living Age. 356: May 1939, 238-242.

4146. Yes, M'Lord by William Douglas Home.

       Full. 4 m. 4 f.

       In - Theatre. 34: April 1950, 57-88.

4147. Yes, Virginia, There is a South Pole Santa
       Claus by Jerome Beatty, Jr.

       In - Colliers. 136: Dec.23,1955, 70+.

4148. Yes, Yes, a Thousand Times Yes! by Claire
       Boiko.

       Short. 4 m. 6 f.

       In - Plays. 28: Nov.1968, 35-44.

4149. Yet Not As One by Gertrude May Lutz.

       Short. 2 m. 1 f.

       In - Poet Lore. 60: March 1965, 77-86.

4150. The Yorktown Lass by Celia Gordon.

       Short. 3 m. 4 f.

       In - Plays. 10: Feb.1951, 40-45.

4151. You by Colin C. Clements.

       Short. 1 m. 1 f. 1 un.

       In - Poet Lore. 29:no.4,1918, 472-485.

4152. You Can't Fool With Love by Pedro E. Pico.
       Trans. by Willis Knapp Jones and Carlos
       Escudero.

       Short. 7 m. 1 f. +X.

       In - Poet Lore. 49: Jan.1943, 107-134.

4153. You Can't Live Just As You Please by
       Alexander Ostrovsky. Trans. from the
       Russian by Philip Winningstad, G.R.
       Noyes and John Heard.

       Full. 7 m. 5 f. +c.X.

       In - Poet Lore. 49: April 1943, 203-240.

4154. You Can't Run Away From It by Herbert
       Ravetch.

       Short. 9 m. 3 f.

       In - Plays. 18: Nov.1958, 29-36.

4155. You Don't Belong to Me by Paul S. McCoy.

       Short. 3 m. 4 f.

       In - Plays. 14: Oct.1954, 13-25.

4156. You Don't Belong to Me by Paul S. McCoy.

       Short. 3 m. 3 f. 1 g.

       In - Plays. 24: April 1965, 15-27.

4157. You'd Never Think It by Paul S. McCoy.

       Short. 1 m. 1 f.

       In - Plays. 18: May 1959, 75-80.

4158. You'll Come to Love Your Sperm Test by John
       Antrobus.

       Full. 7 m. 2 f.

       In - Players. 12: Feb.& March 1965, 24-30+,
       27-32+.

4159. Young Abe Lincoln by Aileen Fisher.

       Short. 8 m. 9 f. +X.

       In - Plays. 22: Feb.1963, 1-12.

4160. Young Abe's Destiny by Claire Boiko.

       Short. 2 m. 0 f. 3 b. 2 g.

       In - Plays. 26: Feb.1967, 43-48.

4161. The Young and Fair by N. Richard Nash.

       Full. 0 m. 21 f.

       In - Theatre. 33: May 1949, 58-88.

4162. Young D'Arcy by Jasmine Van Dresser.

Short. 3 m. 2 f.

In - Delineator. 99: Aug.1921, 24-25+.

4163. Young Forever by Harold Cable.

Short. 4 m. 4 f.

In - Plays. 26: Oct.1966, 1-14.

4164. Young Franklin Takes Over by Bernard J.
Reines.

Short. 8 m. 0 f.

In - Plays. 4: Oct.1944, 9-19.

4165. Young Irving by Marguerite Kreger Phillips.

Short. 6 m. 4 f.

In - Plays. 10: April 1951, 31-40.

4166. A Young Man of Considerable Value by Paul
T. Nolan.

Short. 6 m. 4 f.

In - Plays. 28: Nov.1968, 13-24.

4167. The Young Man with the Cream Tarts by Robert
Louis Stevenson. Adap. by Walter Hackett.

Radio. 7 m. 0 f.

In - Plays. 8: April 1949, 75-85.

4168. Young Tom Jefferson by Lindsey Barbee.

Short. 5 m. 7 f.

In - Plays. 6: Nov.1946, 36-41.

4169. The Youngest Witch by Helen Louise Miller.

Short. 1 m. 3 f. +X.

In - Plays. 3: Oct.1943, 15-24.

4170. The Youngster (Mocasita) by Armando Moock.
Trans. by Willis Knapp Jones.

Full. 4 m. 8 f.

In - Poet Lore. 62: Sept.1967, 266-317.

4171. Your Opportunity by G. Lewis Parsons.

Short. 8 m. 0 f.

In - Indus. Arts. 18: Feb.1929, 51-54.

4172. The Youth, Bolivar by Samuel S. Ullman.

Short. 3 m. 2 f.

In - Plays. 3: Dec.1943, 38-45.

4173. The Youth, Bolivar by Samuel S. Ullman.

Short. 1 m. 2 f. 2 b.

In - Plays. 25: March 1966, 59-65.

4174. Youth Day at the U. N. by Walter Hackett.

Short. 14 m. 4 f.

In - Plays. 9: May 1950, 34-42.

4175. Youth Goes West by Raymond Knister.

In - Poet Lore. 39: Dec.1928, 582-595.

4176. The Youth of Don Juan by Arthur J. Gorman.

Radio. 4 m. 2 f.

In - Scholastic. 24: March 3,1934, 7-8+.

4177. Youth Will Be Served by Harry Leon Wilson.

Full. 6 m. 3 f.

In - Sat. Evening. 194: Jan.7,1922, 3-4+.

4178. Zaragueta by Miguel Ramos Carrión and Vital
Aza. Trans. from the Spanish by Stephen
Scatori and Roy Temple House.

Full. 7 m. 4 f.

In - Poet Lore. 33: March 1922, 1-57.

4179. Zombi by Natalie Vivian Scott.

Short. 2 m. 2 f. +X.

In - Theatre. 13: Jan.1929, 53-61.

Author Index

Andes, Charles.
250.

Andrews, John William.
1446.

Andrews, Mary R.S.
3979.

Andreyev, Leonid.
1448, 2043, 3427, 3683.

Anglund, Bob.
563.

Angoff, Charles.
249.

Anouilh, Jean.
843, 1075, 1867, 2778, 3668, 3924, 3925.

Anstey, F. (pseud.)
see
Guthrie, Thomas. Anstey.

Antrobus, John.
4158.

Applegate, Allita.
547.

Arbuzov, Aleksei.
2869.

Archibald, William.
1665.

Arden, John.
3181, 3765, 4126.

Ardrey, Robert.
1284.

Arkadyl, Averchenko.
2138.

Arlen, Michael.
617.

Arlett, Vera I.
1207, 1871.

Arnold, Esther W.
2112, 2113, 3439.

Arnold, Kate.
3223.

Arrabal, Fernando.
3322.

Arrufat, Anton.
457.

Arthur, Kay.
2347, 2371, 2788, 3608.

Asbrand, Karin.
16, 109, 111, 118, 381, 536, 664, 696, 707,
752, 1042, 1180, 1199, 1289, 1461, 1478,
1584, 1965, 1994, 2002, 2052, 2084, 2249,
2640, 2790, 2791, 2792, 3088, 3163, 3244,
3249, 3272, 3311, 3563, 3651, 3858, 4004.

Asckenasy, Ysidor.
1627.

Ashman, Jane.
296.

Ashton, Leonora Sill.
3331, 3419, 3926.

Ashton, Recene.
1251.

Asimov, Isaac.
3446.

Assur, Jane.
3100.

Atherton, Marguerite.
2545.

Atkins, Charles L.
2848.

Auchincloss, Louis.
651.

Augenlicht, J.C.
1298.

Auslander, Joseph.
2940.

Austen, Jane.
2809, 2810, 2811, 2812.

Austin, Mary Hunter.
94, 2132.

Axelrod, George.
3189.

Aymar, Frances.
1851.

Ayme, Marcel.
641.

Aza, Vital.
4178.

Bach, Marcus.
1123, 1124.

Bachman, Claudia Stewart.
3340.

Bacon, Ernst.
3740.

Bacon, Josephine Daskam.
1105, 3793, 3927.

Bagdad, Anna Emilia.
314.

Bagnold, Enid.
510.

Baber, Constance Whitman.
618, 966, 3023, 3749, 3864.

Bailey, Anne Howard.
615, 2442.

Bailey, Carolyn Sherwin.
1147.

Bailey, Riecta Winn.
3934.

Bailey, Loretto Carroll.
647.

Baird, George M.P.
3918.

Bakeless, Katherine Little.
1320, 2362, 2419, 2450.

Baker, Charles.
2618.

Baker, Gretta.
1371.

Baker, Jane L.
511.

Baker, Nina Brown.
846.

Balderston, John Lloyd.
2352, 2353.

Baldick, Robert.
3867.

Ballesteros, Antonio Martínez.
255.

Bangs, John Kendrick.
2254, 2938.

Barasch, Norman.
2111, 3178.

Barbee, Lindsey.
354, 666, 871, 894, 980, 1094, 1099, 1100,
1101, 1167, 1176, 1423, 1511, 1580, 1693,
1914, 1992, 2209, 2842, 3086, 3309, 3504,
3614, 3748, 4168.

Barbour, Ralph Henry.
693.

Barclay, Sir Thomas.
1200, 1631, 3105.

Barer, Marshall.
2583.

Baring, Maurice.
35, 62, 874, 2050, 2964, 4140.

Bariteau, Maud S.
1142.

Barley, Ann.
2139.

Barnes, Eleanor.
648.

Barnett, Grace T.
3734, 3735.

Barnouw, Erik.
1889, 2888, 2889, 2890, 3521.

Barr, Betty.
1302.

Barr, Glenn.
17.

Barr, June.
120, 138, 411, 412, 493, 622, 917, 1892,
1955, 1998, 2284, 2386, 2547, 2799, 2931,
3029, 3612, 3626, 3850, 4029, 4075.

Barrangon, Eloise.
3378.

Barrie, James M.
2893, 3807.

Barrios, Eduardo.
2644.

Barrows, Marjorie.
3856.

Barry, Philip.
3160, 3378.

Bartholome, Virginia.
1427.

Barton, Lucy.
1216.

Basudeb, Sree.
179.

Bates, Arlo.
417, 3103, 1673.

Bates, Helen O.
2449, 2633.

Batistich, John J.
93, 2578, 2983, 3792.

Baukage, Hilmar.
347.

Baum, L. Frank.
4096, 4116.

Baunevji, Inar Prakas.
1321.

Baxter, David.
4062.

Bayley, Jefferson.
2561.

Benson, Stuart.
1152.

Bentley, Eric.
1077, 2849.

Bentley, Leverett D.G.
166.

Barkey, Ralph.
3663.

Bermel, Albert.
827, 4128.

Bernard, Tristan.
975.

Bernstein, Leonard.
3980.

Berridge, W. Lloyd.
3645.

Besoyan, Rick.
1987.

Best, Sasha.
667.

Bevan, Donald.
3405.

Biel, Nicholas.
1300, 3349.

Biggs, Louise.
1794.

Bingham, June.
3745.

Binkley, Frances W.
2172.

Binyon, Laurence.
2649.

Birnbaum, Perry.
101.

Bissell, Richard.
2636.

Bissell, Walter Lewis
1502.

Bjorkman, Edwin.
1379.

Bjornson, Bjornstjerne.
1847.

Blackman, Carrie Horton.
990.

Blackmore, Richard.
2033.

Beach, Marcia Moray.
2571, 2572.

Bealmear, J.H.
720, 860.

Beatty, Jerome, Jr.
4147.

Beatty, Jessica.
1004.

Beckett, Samuel.
1414, 3916.

Bédollierre, E. de la.
25.

Beebe, Beatrice B.
808, 1549, 2131, 2489, 2546, 2614, 2710,
2892, 3779, 3922, 3946.

Beer, Thomas.
398.

Beerbohm, Max.
3312.

Behan, Brendan.
1538, 1539.

Bellah, Melanie.
316.

Bellido Cormenzana, José María.
2064, 3715.

Bellow, Saul.
2597, 3978.

Benavente y Martinez, Jacinto.
1503, 2824, 3121.

Benedict, D.V.
2409.

Benét, Stephen Vincent.
522, 833, 1957, 3603, 3604, 3605, 3606,
3669.

Bengal, Ben.
72, 73.

Benjamin, Marye D.
2268.

Bennett, Arnold.
1524, 4000, 4001.

Bennett, Helen Cotts.
3070, 3276, 3277.

Bennett, Rowena.
153, 485, 525, 631, 1102, 1175, 1311, 1432,
1472, 1646, 1954, 2101, 2118, 2510, 2619,
2718, 2747, 2818, 3071, 3075, 3111, 3133,
3147, 3221, 3303, 3812, 3853, 3903, 3920,
4003, 4076, 4100.

Benson, Islay.
2026.

Blaine, Betty Gray.
719, 1248, 1908, 2376, 2704, 3057.

Blake, Robert.
1887, 1888.

Blanton, Catherine.
907, 908, 3120.

Blewett, Jean.
4123.

Bloch, Bertram.
1578.

Block, Jerry.
1088.

Bloomfield, Leonard.
237.

Boas, Frederick Samuel.
1474.

Boatright, Mody C.
46, 426.

Bobb, Ralph.
1880.

Boiko, Claire.
74, 80, 87, 129, 278, 331, 597, 619, 704,
735, 763, 1014, 1172, 1567, 1666, 1841, 1852,
1956, 2155, 2165, 2206, 2375, 2529, 2596,
2687, 2701, 2876, 3019, 3073, 3137, 3286,
3297, 3341, 3356, 3408, 3477, 3506, 3514,
3554, 3762, 4113, 4148, 4160.

Bolt, Robert.
1139, 2119, 2120.

Bolton, Guy.
106.

Bond, Edward.
2307, 2443, 3127.

Bond, Nelson.
2307.

Bond, Virginia.
3732.

Botrel, Theodore.
1373.

Bourchier, Arthur.
3972.

Bracco, Roberto.
1480, 1999, 2709.

Bradley, Polly Lewis.
2856.

Brady, Jack.
1823.

Brander, Edith V.
156.

Brandt, W.R.
1952.

Brecht, Bertolt.
1640, 1658, 2849, 4145.

Breckinridge, Beulah.
1719.

Breit, Harvey.
845.

Brenman, Morris.
2652.

Brenner, Elizabeth.
1057, 1168, 2816.

Bridgman, Betty.
212.

Brinker, Evva.
2077.

Britt, Janie Malloy.
1897.

Brodsky, Ruth.
2496.

Brody, Alter.
2930.

Brontë, Charlotte.
1715, 1716, 1717, 1718.

Brontë, Emily.
4137, 4138, 4139.

Brooke, Eleanor.
1817.

Brookman, Katherine Barron.
1671.

Brooks, Charlotte K.
1092, 1093.

Broun, May Heywood.
888.

Brown, Alice V.
1231, 2047, 2324, 2418, 3744.

Brown, Cynthia.
3177.

Brown, Ira Lois.
2610.

Brown, John Mason.
2632.

Brown, Joyce.
3507.

Brown, Laura Norton.
1839.

Brown, Ralph.
250.

Browne, Maurice.
4070.

Browne, Wynyard.
3003.

Browning, Robert.
    2722, 2724, 2725.

Bryan, G.S.
    154.

Brydon, Margaret Wylie.
    890, 891, 2191, 2970, 2971.

Bryks, Rachmil.
    4068.

Buben, Zdenka.
    2917.

Buck, Doris Pitkin.
    3717.

Buck, Pearl S.
    538.

Buckman, Marie Barlow.
    3153.

Bullock, Michael.
    2714.

Buntain, Ruth Jaeger.
    333.

Burea, Seamus de.
    1936.

Burgess, Jackson.
    913.

Burlingame, Cora.
    271, 1166, 1182, 1326, 2766, 3063, 3336,
    3636, 3639, 4097.

Burnet, Dana.
    1622, 2920.

Burnett, Frances Hodgson.
    1995, 1996.

Burtle, Gerry Lynn.
    2430.

Butterfield, Walton.
    3531.

Byers, Jean M.
    110.

Bynner, Witter.
    1982, 3654.

Cabell, James Branch.
    1729.

Cable, Harold.
    124, 256, 828, 1024, 1876, 1980, 2679, 3951,
    4163.

Cain, James M.
    629, 1468, 1473, 2957, 3183, 3594, 3746,
    4061.

Calder, John.
    3322.

Callanan, Cecelia C.
    757.

Cameron, Margaret.
    564.

Calhoun, Dorothy Donnell.
    2805.

Cameron, Margaret.
    680.

Campbell, Camilla.
    241, 2358, 3197.

Campbell, Jane Paxton.
    487.

Campbell, John A.
    472.

Campbell, Josephine E.
    1375, 2740, 3093.

Campbell, Lawton.
    1264.

Canfield, Dorothy.
    see
Fisher, Dorothy Canfield.

Cannan, Gilbert.
    1280.

Capek, Karel.
    2745, 2911, 3325, 4032.

Capell, Loretta Camp.
    1098, 3697.

Caplan, Lydia.
    3307.

Capote, Truman.
    1329.

Carmer, Carl.
    688, 3524.

Caro, Alexander.
    3868.

Carpenter, Margaret Haley.
    2345.

Carrion, Miguel Ramos.
    4178.

Carroll, John.
    959.

Carroll, Lewis.
    68, 69, 2063, 3646.

Carroll, Walter.
    2038.

Casper, Leonard.
    2880.

Cauman, Sarah.
    64.

Colette.
1257.

Collins, Bessie F.
1418.

Collodi, Carlos.
2742.

Colson, John G.
213, 307, 356, 924, 2226, 3022, 3701.

Colum, Padraic.
2265, 2865.

Colver, Anne.
2304.

Combs, Robert.
1801, 3860.

Comden, Betty.
244.

Compton, Dorothy M.
1390.

Conacher, W.M.
1628.

Conboy, Frank J.
507.

Cone, Molly.
2674.

Conkle, Ellsworth P.
1898. 2866, 3967.

Connelly, Marc.
557, 1359, 2224.

Converse, Florence.
3650.

Cook, Richard.
1661.

Cooke, Britton B.
1274, 3233.

Cooke, James Francis.
527, 3139, 3140.

Cooke, Nicilas.
779.

Coolidge, Susan.
3688.

Cooper, Esther.
2097, 2743, 4091.

Cooper, Giles.
1417.

Cooper, James Fenimore.
823, 3394.

Cooper, Kent.
3496.

Cooperman, Chasye.
2306.

Copeland, F.S.
2668.

Copeau, Jacques.
1552.

Coppée.
2666.

Corbett, Elizabeth F.
36, 1407.

Corey, Caroline H.
776.

Corkery, Daniel.
2982.

Cornell, Mary.
1591.

Cornish, Roger N.
2595.

Corson, Hazel W.
642, 771, 1112, 1356, 3754.

Corwin, Norman.
2764, 3102, 3839.

Courteline, Georges.
2677, 2746.

Courtney, William Leonard.
3830.

Covington, Edward Daniel.
3631.

Cowan, Sada.
176, 1642.

Coward, Noel.
312, 2528, 2802.

Cox, Nancy Burney.
3771.

Coxe, Louis O.
280.

Coyle, Rollin W.
2182.

Craig, Anne Abbott.
2667.

Craig, Anne Throop.
3977.

Craven, Eleanor.
1910.

Craven, Frank.
1111.

Creegan, George.
1411.

Creighton, Anthony.
987.

Crichton, Marion Carrie.
2991.

Crockett, Otway.
410.

Cross, Beverley.
2588.

Crothers, Rachel.
2684, 4002.

Crouse, Russell.
1347, 1926, 3422.

Crowell, Anne.
3299, 4059.

Crowell, Chester T.
42.

Culbertson, Ernest Howard.
15, 972.

Cullen, Countee.
3610.

Cummings, E.E.
1492.

Cummings, Parke.
1130.

Cunningham, Leon.
889, 4119.

Cuppy, Elizabeth Overstreet.
2331.

Curel, François de.
225.

Cutting, Mary Stewart.
1304.

Czerniowski, Adam.
1672.

Czerwinski, Edward J.
3451.

Dabney, Julia P.
534.

Daly, Maureen.
3269.

Damon, S. Foster.
1837, 2698.

Daniels, C.C.
1026.

D'Annunzio, Gabriele.
787, 895, 896.

DaPonte, Lorenzo.
708.

D'Arcy, Alice.
621, 4118.

Dargan, Olive Tilford.
4122.

Daskam, Josephine Dodge.
see
Bacon, Josephine Daskam.

Davidson, Gustav.
1273, 1334, 2122, 3945.

Davidson, Madeline.
1080.

Davis, Lavinia R.
1429, 3785.

Day, Blanche.
3878.

Dayton, Katherine.
3968.

Dean, Ruth.
2503, 2504.

DeBra, Elsa.
2088, 2260.

DeBritto, Edgardo R.
1727.

DeCamp, Rosemary Shirley.
686.

Deevy, Teresa.
1818.

DeJong, Modzy.
1905.

Delaney, Shelagh.
3526, 3527.

Delano, Aline.
3471.

Delgado, Ramon.
2562.

DeMarco, Luise.
1499, 3326.

DeMarco, Norman.
169, 1499.

Deming, Dorothy.
277, 731, 824, 1015, 1045, 1235, 1363, 1569,
1780, 2148, 2294, 2444, 2531, 2638, 2952,
3094, 3485, 3515, 3829.

Denker, Henry.
1039, 3663.

Dennis, Alice.
4066.

Dennis, Nigel.
177.

Dennis, Patrick.
180.

Dennler, Florence E.
437.

Denny, Norman.
641.

DePue, Elva.
1438.

Deseo, Lydia Glover.
2465.

Devin, Lee.
2771.

Dias, Earl J.
9, 204, 227, 230, 357, 473, 480, 605, 606,
639, 659, 811, 879, 1011, 1012, 1018, 1068,
1214, 1218, 1232, 1250, 1506, 1844, 1863,
1986, 2069, 2144, 2161, 2162, 2391, 2415,
2451, 2519, 2621, 2622, 2843, 2881, 3103,
3106, 3171, 3193, 3347, 3401, 3442, 3463,
3473, 3520, 3588, 3704, 3731, 3838, 3880,
3901, 3955, 3956, 3990.

Dickens, Charles.
186, 553, 558, 559, 560, 561, 562, 789, 1340,
1341, 1859, 2083, 2163, 2312, 2555, 2556,
2557, 2627, 2719, 2744, 3512, 3513.

Dickerman, Elizabeth S.
1373.

Dickinson, Lucy.
4099.

Dietz, Howard.
328.

Dinkins, M.F.
4013.

Djurichich, Luka.
2822.

Doan, Robert J.
1679.

Dobie, Charles Caldwell.
1616.

Dodson, Owen.
1003, 3610.

Dondo, Mathurin M.
3799.

Donleavy, J.P.
1258.

Dora, Lucile.
2666.

Dorand, John.
3486, 3487, 3538, 3539.

Dos Passos, John.
3814.

Downey, June Etta.
146, 3465.

Downing, Robert.
1734, 1735, 3159, 3224, 3430, 3431.

Doyle, A. Conan.
3212, 3213.

Doyle, Louis F.
782, 1171.

Drachmann, Holger.
2976.

Drain, Richard.
3657.

Draper, Cena Christopher.
951, 2648, 3565.

Drennan, Marie.
3284, 3862.

Dreyer, Max.
2566.

Drinkwater, John.
3443.

DuBois, Graham.
132, 173, 187, 285, 297, 330, 368, 405, 422,
496, 497, 523, 524, 705, 783, 788, 956, 957,
969, 1001, 1067, 1189, 1277, 1279, 1305, 1306,
1316, 1322, 1355, 1575, 1588, 1778, 1815,
1845, 1846, 1870, 1928, 1945, 2134, 2136,
2361, 2436, 2464, 2485, 2506, 2693, 2694,
2772, 2773, 2798, 2921, 2963, 3016, 3017,
3042, 3091, 3209, 3310, 3337, 3342, 3391,
3415, 3591, 3602, 3772, 3811, 4007, 4074,
4094.

Duerrenmatt, Friedrich.
3890.

Duggar, Frances.
821.

Duhamel, Georges.
667.

Dukes, Ashley.
2755.

Dumas, Alexander.
711, 3628.

Dumas, Alexander, Fils.
2334.

Dumas, André.
990.

Dunbar, Newell.
999.

Dunbar, Olivia Howard.
3 3.

Duncan, Frances.
3125.

Duncan, George.
2870.

Duncan, Kunigunde.
167.

Duncan, Ronald.
1244.

Duncan, Winifred.
635.

Dunsany, Edward Moreton Drax Plunkett, Baron.
see
Dunsany, Lord.

Dunsany, Lord.
1031. 1032, 1272, 1601, 1725, 1883, 2041,
2481, 2901, 3553.

Dunster, Mark.
3270.

Duras, Marguerite.
805.

Durer, C.S.
726, 2071, 3950.

Duvall, Lucille Miller.
139, 184, 550, 660, 1377, 1964, 3384, 3857.

Dyer, Charles.
3404.

Dyk, Victor.
2493.

Dyson, John P.
674.

Eastman, Fred.
1337.

Eberhart, Richard.
131.

Echégaray, José.
2072, 3456.

Edmond, Reby.
1374.

Edwards, Doris L.
2473.

Ehlert, Fay.
3827.

Ehrlich, Ida Lublenski.
2078.

Elfenbein, Josef A.
136, 1822, 2882, 3546, 3547.

Eliot, George.
3237.

Elliott, D.H.
3841.

Elmore, Maud Johnson.
3191.

Elton, Richard D.
1405.

Emig, Evelyn.
537, 2548.

Emmons, Myra.
3899.

Ensana, Joel A.
2759.

Ephron, Henry.
3510.

Ephron, Phoebe.
3510.

Ernst, Alice Henson.
2490, 3388, 3863.

Erskine, John.
1462.

Ervine, St. John.
2860, 3205.

Escudero, Carlos.
1760, 2348, 3714, 4152.

Eszterhazy, Mátyás.
3428.

Euripides.
937, 2202.

Evans, F. Cridland.
818.

Evans, Gladys LaDue.
1990.

Evans, Margaret.
1029.

Fagin, Mary.
3044.

Fahnstock, Edith.
2099.

Farrar, John.
1551, 2095.

Faux, Dammally.
2012, 2013.

Fawcett, Margaret Georgia.
3517.

Fay, Maxine.
3128.

Feiffer, Jules.
725.

Feinstein, Alan S.
217.

Feinstein, Joe.
698.

Feley, Ruth Amelia.
3195.

Felice, James De.
942.

Fenner, Mildred Sandison.
see
Sandison, Mildred.

Ferber, Edna.
2252, 3059.

Ferguson, David.
2363.

Ferrier, Paul.
658.

Feuerstein, Arthur.
4023.

Field, Eugene.
678.

Fields, Joseph.
122.

Field, Lauraine.
1579.

Field, Rachel (Lyman)
196, 1005.

Fife, Evelyn Henderson.
3959.

Filippo, Eduardo de.
1077.

Finch, Lucine.
423.

Findlay, Louise.
2398.

Finney, Robert V.
3768.

Firkins, Oscar W.
39, 2030, 2959, 2984, 3808, 3816.

Fishburn, Eleanor C.
3607.

Fisher, Aileen.
8, 67, 85, 114, 115, 294, 303, 383, 424,
436, 491, 494, 498, 499, 505, 556, 583,
608, 610, 637, 718, 796, 848, 1035, 1241,
1459, 1479, 1522, 1622, 1680, 1710, 1745,
1749, 1835, 2028, 2049, 2085, 2109, 2145,
2219, 2312, 2377, 2405, 2469, 2567, 2568,
2584, 2590, 2613, 2752, 2763, 3028, 3085,
3187, 3222, 3250, 3251, 3252, 3253, 3254,
3255, 3256, 3257, 3258, 3291, 3346, 3365,
3366, 3371, 3396, 3406, 3410, 3429, 3580,

3619, 3620, 3660, 3666, 3675, 3733, 3742,
3760, 3783, 3820, 3831, 3842, 3843, 3906,
3907, 3936, 3952, 3966, 3974, 3981, 3985,
3986, 3987, 3991, 3993, 4008, 4054, 4141,
4159.

Fisher, Dorothy Canfield.
1918, 4108.

Fisher, Martha A.
2488.

Fiske, Isabella Howe.
675.

Fitzgerald, Betty.
2173.

Flanagan, Hallie F.
767.

Flanders, Florence Reiter.
1132.

Flavin, Martin A.
430.

Fleming, Berry.
14.

Fletcher, Lucille.
1504.

Flint, Mabell C.
3116.

Flokos, N.G.
1494.

Flores, Ronald C.
3715.

Flower, Elliott.
1498.

Flowers, Priscilla.
2190.

Floyd, Carlisle.
3490.

Floyd, Lucretia Xavier.
3479.

Flynn, Claire Wallace.
3461.

Foley, Marie Agnes.
953.

Folmsbee, Beulah.
2828.

Fontaine, Robert.
123, 927, 1023, 1909, 2998, 3482, 3681, 3834.

Fontana, Ferdinando.
1557.

Foranzo, Giovacchino.
1378, 3678.

Forbes, Kathryn.
1589.

Ford, Ford Madox.
2293.

Forman, Henry James.
3686.

Forster, E.M.
2665.

Forsyth, James.
1464.

Foster, Joseph G.
4065.

France, Anatole.
669, 1769, 2135.

Francis, J.O.
2767.

Frank, Florence Kiper.
3634.

Frank, Grace.
1038.

Frank, Maude Morrison.
1178.

Fraser, Hermia Harris.
1793.

Fratti, Mario.
2961, 3609, 3915.

Freeman, Mary E. Wilkins.
928.

Freer, Marjorie Mueller.
2435.

French, Dawn.
2402.

French, Marshall.
2402.

Freyhe, C.E.
1629.

Friedman, Bruce Jay.
451.

Friedman, Charles.
2412.

Frink, Charles.
1576.

Frisby, Terence.
3598.

Frisch, Max.
541, 2713, 2714.

Frith, Walter.
394.

Froome, John Redhead, Jr.
1958.

Fruchter, M. Joseph.
2933.

Fulda, Ludwig.
314.

Fulham, William H.
834.

Fuller, Dean.
2583.

Fuller, John Grant.
690.

Furness, Edna Lue.
1345.

Fussler, Irene.
998.

Gabbert, Rosemary.
2680.

Gable, J. Harris.
975.

Gaines, Joysa.
663.

Galdós, Perez.
1327.

Gale, Jane Winsor.
3877.

Gale, Zona.
3818.

Gallico, Paul.
3296.

Galsworthy, John.
1389, 1968, 3474.

Gamble, Hazel V.
1973.

Gamble, Mary R.
178.

Gardner, Evelyn Elizabeth.
2927.

Gardner, Herb.
3617.

Garland, Robert.
885.

Garrigue, Frederick.
841.

Garver, Juliet.
503, 1048, 1049, 1051, 1430, 1570, 1571,
2335, 2414, 2462, 3355, 3774.

Gassner, John.
1659.

Gaster, Bertha.
3428.

Gavin, Mary.
768.

Gazzo, Michael Vincente.
1436.

Geijerstam, Gustaf of
728.

George, Charles.
4015.

Gerould, Daniel C.
441, 692, 726, 2071, 3950.

Gerould, Eleanor S.
441, 692.

Gerry, Margarita Spalding.
1674.

Gest, Elizabeth A.
458.

Getchell, Margaret Colby.
291.

Ghelderode, Michel de.
2643.

Gibbs, Wolcott.
3155.

Gibson, Pauline.
1076, 2708, 3266.

Gifford, Franklin Kent.
86.

Gilbert, Helen.
1317.

Gilbert, Sir William S.
3498, 3747, 3769.

Gilder, Rosamond.
1623.

Gilmore, Alice F.
2615.

Givens, Helen M.
400, 1624.

Giraudoux, Jean.
958, 1623, 2074, 2585, 2651.

Glaspell, Susan.
3752.

Glass, Everett.
3773.

Glazer, Benjamin F.
1073, 1921, 2886.

Glick, Carl.
1613, 2863, 3478.

Glickman, Will.
2750.

Glynn-Ward, H.
40.

Golden, Edward.
1340, 1341, 1376, 1426, 2593, 3204.

Golden, Eleanor.
3378.

Goldsmith, Clifford H.
61, 3982.

Goldsmith, Oliver.
3204.

Goode, Kate Tucker.
2839.

Goodell, Patricia.
224.

Goodlander, Mabel Ray.
3892.

Goodman, Kenneth S.
911.

Goodman, Paul.
501.

Gordon, Celia.
683, 2327, 2815, 3953, 4150.

Gordon, Homer King.
1639.

Gordon, Ruth.
1893.

Gorki, Maxim.
532, 2491, 3293, 3471.

Gorman, Arthur J.
4176.

Gorman, Herbert S.
817.

Goudiss, A.
3683.

Gough, A. Eulalia.
552.

Gough, Margaret.
2587.

Gould, Elizabeth Lincoln.
1988, 2006.

Gould, Jean.
171, 2478, 2479, 3188.

Gourmont, Remy de.
1934.

Gow, James.
3696.

Graham, Manta S.
18, 746.

Grahame, Kenneth.
2696.

Grahn, Mary.
1600.

Granick, Harry.
4092.

Gray, Marshall.
2245.

Gray, Simon.
4078.

Green, Adolph.
244.

Green, Carolyn.
1720.

Green, Paul.
247, 733, 970, 1135, 1484, 1540, 2494, 2551,
2795, 3101, 3122, 3123, 3230, 3421.

Greene, Graham.
2793.

Greene, Lida Lisle.
270, 389.

Greene, Paul.
2032.

Gregory, Isabella Augusta (Persse), Lady.
see
Gregory, Lady.

Gregory, Lady.
325, 326, 2059, 2157, 2575, 3377, 3727, 3728,
3729, 4127.

Gressieker, Hermann.
3060.

Greth, Roma.
3009, 3805.

Griffith, Alice Mary Matlock.
4036.

Gross, Nathalie F.
1653, 2432.

Gross, Sevilla.
255, 3491.

Grubb, Amy S.
4081.

Grummann, Paul H.
3054.

Gryphius, Andreas.
245.

Guerney, Bernard G.
2138.

Guiterman, Arthur.
607, 1755.

Gurney, A.R., Jr.
376.

Guthrie, Thomas Anstey.
1201, 3098.

Gutierrez, Eduardo.
1760.

Gutman, John.
142, 349.

Gwynn, S.L.
883.

Gyp.
1962.

Hackett, Walter.
445, 446, 558, 559, 561, 562, 1020, 1173,
1222, 1275, 1276, 1348, 1349, 1650, 1769,
1885, 1899, 2051, 2140, 2150, 2215, 2216,
2229, 2247, 2457, 2625, 2993, 3006, 3267,
3268, 3394, 3512, 3513, 3719, 4167, 4174.

Hagedorn, Hermann.
247, 1452, 1788, 2777, 3967.

Hague, Albert.
2750.

Hagy, Loleta.
1090, 2631.

Haines, Wister.
679.

Haitov, Nicolai.
321.

el-Hakim, Tawfiq.
816.

Halbe, Max.
3054.

Hale, Edward Everett.
2139, 2140.

Hale, W.G.
2650.

Hall, Amanda Benjamin.
4033.

Hall, Holworthy.
3859.

Hall, Margaret C.
71, 859, 1811, 2962, 3659.

Hall, May Emery.
1145, 2467, 4083, 4084.

Hall, Mazie.
1864, 1865, 3397.

Hall, Willis.
281, 282.

Halliwell, David.
1985.

Halpern, Martin.
2319, 2980.

Halty, Nuria.
2560.

Hamby, Ray.
3492.

Hazam, Louise Jay.
2658.

Hazeltine, Alice Isabel.
2067.

Head, Cloyd.
768.

Heal, Edith.
1676.

Healy, Cahir.
3175.

Heard, John.
748, 1537, 1577, 1760, 1934, 4153.

Heath, Anna Lenington.
1383, 2399, 2994, 4045.

Heath, James.
1513.

Hebbel, Frederick.
49.

Hecht, Ben.
1188.

Hedberg, Tor.
348, 1739.

Heggen, Thomas.
2311.

Heiberg, Gunnar.
203.

Heiderstadt, Dorothy.
1626, 1655.

Heijermens, Hermann.
50, 1762, 1952, 3099.

Heijermans-Hauwink, Caroline.
50, 3099.

Heller, M.M.
264.

Hellman, Lillian.
183, 535, 1867, 3710, 3947.

Hemingway, Ernest.
1073.

Henderson, Bonnie Jo.
3599.

Henderson, John.
3618.

Henley, William Ernest.
2056.

Hennefeld, Edmund B.
500.

Hennique, Leon.
818.

Henry, Alice.
787.

Henry, Joan.
2027.

Henry, O.
2070.

Herbert, Alan P.
3803.

Herbert, F. Hugh.
2343.

Herford, Beatrice.
377.

Herman, George.
1435.

Hervey, Michael.
3884.

Herrick, Gertrude.
1191.

Hervieu, Paul.
1627.

Heshmati, Leota B.
3165.

Heyward, Dorothy.
2780.

Heyward, Dubose.
2780.

Hibbard, George.
2184.

Higgins, Helen Boyd.
2114.

Hildesheimer, Wolfgang.
3081.

Hill, F.E.
2940.

Hill, Kay.
2235, 2236.

Hill, Lucienne.
1075, 2778, 3924, 3925.

Hill, Rochelle.
69.

Hilton, Charles.
387.

Hirshberg, Bernard.
367, 2703.

Hirschfeld, Georg.
3157.

Hitchcock, George.
421, 3848.

Hoffman, Charles H.
  3004.

Hoffman, E.T.A.
  588.

Hoffman, Phoebe.
  3780.

Hofmannsthal, Hugo von.
  142, 732, 1056, 1598, 2864, 3870.

Holbrook Sibyl Collar.
  43, 96, 1151, 2513, 4022.

Holdas, A.
  1447.

Hollander, Lee M.
  1728, 2976, 3348.

Holler, Rose M.
  369.

Hollingsworth, Leslie.
  100, 188, 1941, 2152, 2328, 2569, 3114, 3238,
  3239.

Holton, Jack.
  905.

Home, William Douglas.
  2967, 2968, 4146.

Homer.
  1605, 2535.

Hoover, Margaretta E.
  186.

Hope, Anthony.
  2847.

Hopkins, Arthur.
  2350, 2351.

Hopkins, Edwin.
  2491.

Hoppenstedt, Elbert M.
  581, 582, 2178, 2439, 2768.

Hopwood, Avery.
  3358.

Horvath, Ernestine.
  322, 1253.

Horvath, Florence.
  322, 1253.

Horwood, Ruth.
  662.

Horwitt, Arnold B.
  2750.

Hourihane, Ursula.
  2829.

House, Roy Temple.
  732, 1962, 2946, 3804, 4178.

Housman, Laurence.
  261, 393, 515, 2601, 2988, 3068, 3835.

Howard, Fred.
  2472.

Howard, Helen Littler.
  248, 263, 319, 327, 442, 570, 609, 858, 1198,
  1493, 1607, 1967, 2089, 2388, 2748, 2951,
  3041, 3452, 3562, 3572, 3573, 3989, 4088.

Howard, Mary Warner.
  157.

Howard, Sidney.
  1877, 1878, 2065.

Howard, Vernon.
  193, 286, 309, 315, 777, 1425, 1891, 2225,
  2246, 2637, 2981, 3134, 3262, 3344, 3775,
  3851, 3861, 3869, 4012, 4136.

Howarth, Donald.
  1935.

Howell, Corrie Crandall.
  1161.

Howell-Carter, Josephine.
  1480.

Howells, William Dean.
  38, 576, 577, 578, 1470, 1620, 2482, 2657,
  3126, 3176, 3764.

Hrbek, Cyril Jeffrey.
  2493.

Hrbkova, Sarka B.
  1714.

Hsiung, Cheng-Chin.
  2164, 3643, 3644.

Hubbard, Elbert.
  2229.

Huber, Mary B.
  898.

Hubert, Philip G., Jr.
  2919.

Huff, Betty Tracy.
  148, 226, 471, 699, 1059, 1136, 1230, 1261,
  1338, 1381, 1490, 1562, 2204, 2685, 2857,
  2943, 3152, 3395, 3455, 3699, 3957.

Hughes, E. Llewellyn.
  2945.

Hughes, Glen.
  203, 355.

Hughes, Richard.
  672.

Hughes, Riley.
  358, 2446, 2715.

Hughes, Rupert.
  2576, 3200.

Hugo, Victor.
299, 300, 579.

Hull, Helen R.
1595, 2966.

Hummell, Violet.
923.

Hung, Shen.
3969.

Hunt, Sylvia.
3730.

Huntsberry, W.E.
2256.

Husson, Albert.
2421.

Huston, John.
1648.

Hutchins, Will.
1722.

Huxley, Aldous.
1259.

Hyde, Douglas.
2156, 2157, 3796.

Ickler, Lyda M.
1842, 3921.

Inclan, Don Ramon del Valle.
888.

Indick, Benjamin P.
341.

Inge, William.
414, 668, 781, 2720.

Ionesco, Eugene.
509, 1625, 1904, 2995.

Ireland, Donna.
321.

Ireland, Kevin.
321.

Irving, Washington.
1899, 3005, 3006, 3007, 3008.

Isola, Pietro.
787.

Isom, Louise Metcalfe.
365.

Itow, Michio.
1169, 3206.

Jackson, Frederick.
298.

Jacob, Eva.
742, 3024, 3300.

Jacobs, M.G.
1677.

Jacobs, W.W.
2337.

Jaffe, Bernard.
3149.

Jagendorf, Mortiz Adolf.
1197, 2177, 2669.

Jakobi, Paula.
539.

James, Bartlett B.
3119.

James, Henry.
1880, 3938.

James, Patricia.
4014.

Janusch, Mildred June.
1445.

Jeffers, Robinson.
2202.

Jellicoe, Ann.
1843.

Jenks, Tudor.
3578.

Jennings, Anne.
1969.

Jennings, Edith.
1084.

Jennings, George.
941, 2288.

Jensen, Stanley C.
2509.

Jerome, Helen B.
1715, 2809.

Jirásek, Alois.
853, 1866.

Johnson, D.H.
1868, 2121.

Jolly, Andrew.
2908.

Jones, Don C.
1663.

Jones, Ellis O.
2322.

Jones, Henry Arthur.
872, 1283.

Jones, Howard Mumford.
1043.

Kingston, Leonard.
3726.

Kipling, Rudyard.
450.

Kirker, Katherine.
1849.

Kirkpatrick, John A.
3158.

Kishon, Ephraim.
310.

Klauber, Amy Josephine.
1009.

Klein, Elaine.
2394.

Knapp, Bettina L.
2854.

Knee, Allan.
983.

Knight, Elizabeth Lou.
3229.

Knight, Lee.
1128.

Knister, Raymond.
4175.

Knott, Fred.
836.

Knox, Alexander.
649.

Koch, Fred, Jr.
3601, 3933.

Koch, Howard.
1648.

Koestler, Arthur.
784.

Konick, Marcus.
168, 2712.

Koon, Helene.
2726.

Kopit, Arthur.
2541.

Korvin-Kroukovsky, E.
1874.

Kosor, Josip.
2668, 4103.

Kotzebue, August von.
808, 1549, 2131, 2489, 2546, 2614, 2710,
2892, 3779, 3922, 3946.

Kozlenko, William.
1690.

Kreymborg, Alfred.
392, 1467, 1609, 1610, 3722.

Kring, Hilda Adam.
287.

Kroll, Francis L.
1344, 1391, 1481, 1726, 3328.

Krumpelmann, John T.
245, 388.

Kummer, Clare R.
3030.

Kurnitz, Harry.
2944.

Kvapil, Jaroslav.
650.

Labiche, Eugene.
1901.

Labrenz, Theodore.
1330.

Lacey, Jackson.
2823.

Lackman, Ronald.
736, 4053.

Lahr, Georgiana Lieder.
960.

Lamb, Esther Hill.
1860.

Lambeck, Frederick.
3819.

Lamont, Rosette.
205, 1953.

Lampell, Millard.
360, 3516.

Lane, Burton.
1086.

Lane, Marion.
1686.

Lang, L. Lockhart.
2573.

Lang, V.R.
1592.

Langley, Noel.
926.

Langston, Lucile E.
1149, 4028.

Languirand, Jacques.
827.

Larra, Mariano Jose de.
2909.

Larson, Edith.
555, 3084.

Larson, Emma Mauritz.
2188.

Lathers, Helen Q.
332.

Latouche, John Treville.
2321.

Lauré, Katherine.
900, 1295.

Laurents, Arthur.
1382, 1684, 3664, 3980.

Lavedan, Henri.
43, 47, 96, 195, 850, 985, 1151, 1177, 1649,
2513, 3804, 4022.

Lavine, Eugene.
78.

Lawler, Ray.
3472.

Lawrence, C.E.
1545, 2227.

Lawrence, D.H.
786, 2160, 2220.

Lawrence, Jerome.
180, 1204, 1660, 1667.

Lawrence, Joan.
3329.

Lescock, Stephen.
3806.

Learsi, Rufus,
3755.

Ledoux, Louis V.
1169, 3206.

Lee, Emma.
164.

Lee, James.
453.

Lee, Melicent H.
1645.

Lee, Robert E.
180, 1204, 1660.

Lee, Sylvia.
723, 1360, 2346, 2642, 3387, 4026.

Leech, Michael T.
231, 948, 1196, 1565, 2725, 2875, 3138, 3298,
3447.

Lehman, John F.
1310, 2741, 3809, 4086, 4090.

Leitner, Irving A.
1008, 3649.

Leivick, H.
1298.

Lengyel, Cornel.
4130.

Leonard, Hugh.
174, 2232, 2774.

Lerner, Alan Jay.
380, 2634.

Leuser, Eleanore.
391, 396, 599, 714, 1116, 1228, 1526, 1832,
1900, 1960, 2005, 2087, 2102, 2103, 2326,
2950, 3586, 3694, 4079.

Levi, Paolo.
3836.

Levi, Shelley.
13, 2738.

Levinger, Elma Ehrlich.
3551.

Levitt, Saul.
112.

Levy, Benn W.
2928, 2929.

Lezama, Antonio de.
3945.

Lindsay, Howard.
1347, 1926, 3422, 3763.

Linebarger, J.M.
2207.

Lipnick, Esther.
116, 3338.

Liss, Felicia.
2776.

Liss, Florence.
26, 1758.

Liss, Joseph.
2942.

Litchfield, Grace Denio.
4111.

Locke, Kay.
3280.

Lodovici, Cesare.
989, 4106, 1597.

Loesser, Frank.
2360.

Loewe, Frederick.
380.

Masefield, John.
1309, 3495.

Mason, Miriam E.
2166.

Matto, Jose Maria Rivarola.
967.

Maude, Aylmer.
2014.

Maude, L.
2014.

Maugham, Robin.
2532.

Maugham, W. Somerset.
2692.

Maupassant, Guy de.
2456, 2457.

Maurette, Marcelle.
106.

Mauroc, Daniel.
3104.

Maxwell, Gerald.
2359, 4037.

May, Charles.
2989.

May, Elaine.
2514.

May, J. Lewis.
669.

Mayorga, Margaret.
176, 298, 700, 997, 1111, 1369, 1374, 1422,
1610, 1663, 1877, 1917, 2167, 2224, 2252,
2416, 2866, 2911, 3001, 3005, 3030, 3059,
3158.

Mazaud, Emile.
1509.

Meehan, Thomas.
1925.

Meeker, Arthur, Jr.
1431.

Meigs, Cornelia.
2814.

Mekota, Beatrice M.
185, 1342, 2066.

Melcher, Marguerite Fellows.
1263, 3961, 3995.

Melchior, Hathaway Kale.
1981, 3897.

Mellon, Evelyn Emig.
3716.

Melville, Herman.
280.

Mendel, Paula.
1755.

Meneses, Enrique de.
1273, 3945.

Mercer, David.
239, 1323.

Meredith, Burgess.
2554, 3150.

Mérimée, Prosper.
694.

Merington, Marguerite.
724, 1195, 1242, 1367, 2045.

Merow, Erva Loomis.
3555.

Merry, Ruth C.
1747.

Messenger, Bill.
2126.

Meyer, Adolph E.
1974.

Michaelson, L.W.
3550.

Michel, Marc.
1901.

Middleton, George.
2128.

Michelson, Max.
3674.

Middlemass, Robert.
3859.

Mierow, Herbert Edward.
893, 1489, 2781.

Miles, Josephine.
1546.

Milhous, John Philip.
790.

Millar, Ronald.
32.

Millay, Kathleen.
1127.

Miller, Agnes.
1083, 1110.

Miller, Albert G.
2185.

Miller, Alice Duer.
3983.

Miller, Arthur.
    37, 745, 813, 2806.

Miller, Helen Louise.
    2, 75, 172, 206, 207, 208, 215, 216, 218, 222,
    223, 258, 267, 288, 289, 334, 345, 346, 363,
    366, 373, 385, 390, 403, 404, 420, 433, 449,
    467, 468, 470, 475, 476, 569, 589, 591, 592,
    598, 627, 713, 760, 765, 803, 835, 839, 867,
    868, 1052, 1053, 1054, 1062, 1063, 1148,
    1162, 1205, 1210, 1220, 1233, 1234, 1255,
    1266, 1267, 1270, 1307, 1308, 1353, 1387,
    1441, 1442, 1443, 1444, 1453, 1456, 1463,
    1476, 1512, 1519, 1520, 1527, 1528, 1532,

    1534, 1535, 1541, 1543, 1606, 1732, 1764,
    1765, 1771, 1782, 1783, 1848, 1919, 1940,
    1943, 1950, 1951, 1991, 2035, 2079, 2081,
    2093, 2098, 2127, 2129, 2149, 2170, 2189,
    2203, 2210, 2221, 2277, 2280, 2286, 2287,
    2314, 2317, 2341, 2366, 2367, 2369, 2370,
    2372, 2383, 2384, 2387, 2389, 2393, 2426,
    2431, 2434, 2474, 2475, 2517, 2525, 2544,
    2591, 2646, 2647, 2653, 2655, 2660, 2675,
    2686, 2702, 2706, 2707, 2730, 2735, 2739,
    2775, 2830, 2836, 2877, 2878, 2879, 2912,

    2913, 2914, 2916, 2922, 2948, 2949, 2985,
    3002, 3069, 3076, 3077, 3079, 3110, 3112,
    3113, 3117, 3129, 3130, 3148, 3156, 3180,
    3196, 3218, 3227, 3248, 3295, 3306, 3316,
    3317, 3318, 3319, 3353, 3375, 3376, 3393,
    3459, 3460, 3545, 3564, 3568, 3569, 3575,
    3576, 3577, 3581, 3585, 3623, 3627, 3692,
    3708, 3723, 3750, 3761, 3778, 3784, 3833,
    3852, 3865, 3875, 3920, 3919, 3937, 3941,
    3942, 3944, 3965, 3992, 4005, 4006, 4024,
    4030, 4046, 4082, 4169.

Miller, L.
    2306.

Miller, Marion L.
    749, 750, 2522.

Miller, Paul Vincent.
    2955.

Miller, Stephanie.
    778.

Miller, William C.
    794.

Mills, Grace Evelyn.
    566.

Mills, Hugh.
    1548.

Milne, A.A.
    2123.

Milner, Roger.
    1572.

Milosz, O.W.
    2242.

Mitford, Nancy.
    1978.

Mixon, Ada.
    2678.

Miyameri, Asataro.
    1850.

Mobert, Helen L.
    3261.

Molière.
    857, 1143, 1223, 2692, 3035, 4133, 4134.

Molloy, Lida Lisle.
    484, 1165, 1536, 1723, 4132.

Molnar, Ferenc.
    1896, 1921, 2756, 2886, 3454, 3810.

Monroe, Harriet.
    33.

Montague, Clifford M.
    3757.

Montgomery, Major.
    3357.

Moock, Armando.
    4170.

Moore, Bessie Collins.
    2564.

Moore, Carroll.
    2111, 3178.

Moore, Edna G.
    2305.

Moore, George.
    130, 1224, 1225, 1226.

Moore, Jocelyn.
    1566.

Moore, T. Sturge.
    2602.

Moore, William H.
    2076.

Moran, Irene.
    1826.

Moratin, José.
    1037.

Morley, Christopher.
    3, 234, 916, 1318, 1319, 2577, 2939, 3476,
    3923.

Morley, Olive J.
    2007, 2010, 2811.

Morley, Robert.
    926.

Morris, Christie.
    2905.

Morris, Richard.
    3837.

Morse, Corinne.
    2897, 3525.

Morse, Richard M.
2445.

Mortimer, John.
4135.

Morwood, William.
19.

Mosel, Tad.
89.

Moss, Louis Quentin.
2609.

Mossi, Padre.
2560.

Motoyazu, Komparu Zembo.
915.

Mowatt, Anna Cora.
1044.

Mowery, William Byron.
936.

Mowrer, Paul Scott.
1158, 1626.

Moyer, Lewis W.
1931.

Moyes, Patricia.
3668.

Mozart, Wolfgang Amadeus.
708.

Mueffer, F.M.
2365.

Mulet, Paul.
3132.

Mullin, Elizabeth Lester.
658.

Mullins, Helene.
3767.

Muni, Ann.
520.

Munro, Hector H.
200, 2262.

Murdoch, Iris.
1691.

Murdoch, Marion.
754, 755.

Murphy, Elinor.
1608.

Murphy, Helen A.
4077.

Murphy, Olive Frances.
3713.

Murray, Gilbert.
937.

Murray, John.
198, 221, 243, 361, 462, 463, 464, 465, 474,
477, 632, 665, 809, 877, 881, 968, 1002,
1017, 1078, 1117, 1202, 1333, 1450, 1495,
1523, 1564, 1587, 1593, 1621, 1670, 1682,
1797, 1933, 2018, 2031, 2046, 2060, 2200,
2201, 2237, 2271, 2276, 2278, 2297, 2316,
2403, 2417, 2427, 2428, 2448, 2543, 2691,
2910, 2978, 3136, 3219, 3369, 3402, 3444,
3500, 3511, 3557, 3801, 3847, 3900, 3909,
4017, 4018, 4060.

Murray, William.
3066.

Muse, Violet.
3706.

Musil, Rosemary G.
1681.

Musselman, N.H.
2243.

Musset, Alfred de.
448, 883.

Mussorgsky, Modest.
349.

Myers, Mildred E.
186.

Mygatt, Tracy Dickinson.
51, 1501, 2507, 3191.

Nabokov, Vladimir.
2396.

Nadin, Marilyn C.
1707.

Nakazawa, Ken.
2699.

Nash, N. Richard.
2925, 3169, 4161.

Nash, Ogden.
1694.

Nathan, Bertha.
1602, 4049.

Neale, Ralph.
4032.

Neilson, Francis.
214.

Nellhaus, Gerhard.
1640.

Nelson, Ralph.
2108.

Nesbit, Edith.
620.

Nessenson, Elsa Behaim.
1644.

Nestrick, Nova G.
1758.

Nethercot, Arthur H.
1193, 1352, 2700.

Newman, Benjamin W.
3097, 3828.

Newman, Deborah.
53, 76, 257, 406, 553, 594, 611, 623, 684,
952, 963, 1109, 1246, 1358, 1396, 1421, 1633,
1784, 1795, 1796, 2022, 2023, 2029, 2086,
2212, 2213, 2228, 2302, 2323, 2476, 2589,
2765, 2810, 2812, 2817, 2852, 2853, 2874,
2915, 2937, 2941, 3055, 3330, 3332, 3333,
3385, 3389, 3417, 3418, 3435, 3436, 3566,
3579, 3939, 3940, 3954, 4114, 4117, 4142.

Niccodemi, Dario.
791.

Nichols, Dudley.
1659, 1689.

Nichols, Robert.
4070.

Nicholson, Jessie.
229, 481, 1237, 1238, 1439, 1440, 1510,
2248, 2424, 2425, 2429, 2454, 3469, 3470,
3533, 3534, 3855.

Nicholson, Mary Ann.
751, 1058, 1882, 2807, 2837, 2840, 4080.

Nicolaeff, Araidne.
2869.

Niggli, Josephina.
1022, 3263, 3320.

Nightingale, E.M.
144.

Noah, Robert.
30.

Noble, Charles C.
3596.

Noguchi, Yone.
826, 2392, 3228, 3536.

Nolan, Jeannette Covert.
1412, 1413, 2272.

Nolan, Paul T.
99, 107, 125, 293, 351, 716, 886, 1174, 1209,
1287, 1297, 1416, 1477, 1485, 1632, 1657,
1744, 1894, 1920, 2092, 2349, 2617, 3271,
3339, 3407, 3453, 3635, 3698, 3741, 3751,
3881, 4040, 4166.

Nooshich, Branislav.
2822.

Norden, Ruth.
1658, 4145.

Novak, David.
630.

Novo, Salvador.
930.

Noyes, George Rapall.
93, 487, 1026, 1874, 2578, 2917, 2983, 3792,
4101, 4153.

Nugent, Elliott.
2115.

Nuhardt, John G.
931.

Numma, Elva.
2433.

Nutter, Carolyn F.
2953.

Obaldia, René de.
925, 4065.

O'Brien, Edna.
3971.

O'Brien, Edward J.
158, 2242.

O'Brien, Kate.
3590.

O'Brien, Liam.
2973.

O'Brien, Seumas.
304, 4058.

O'Casey, Sean.
901.

O'Connell, Richard L.
1555.

O'Connell, Thomas Edward.
2303.

O'Connell, Wilkeson.
2048.

O'Connor, Frank.
165.

O'Connor, Patricia.
2413.

O'Connor, Patrick.
2526, 4121.

Odets, Clifford.
712.

O'Donnell, Charles L.
2452.

O'Flaherty, Liam.
1659.

Oglesbee, Della Houghton.
3544.

Okamoto, Kido.
219, 1850.

Paull, Harry Major.
  329, 2605, 2635, 3835, 3885.

Paulus, Margaret.
  3211.

Payne, Iden.
  4021.

Payro, Roberto.
  3714.

Peabody, Josephine Preston.
  4069.

Peacey, Howard.
  1952.

Peacock, Mary.
  1789, 1976.

Pearson, John.
  238.

Pedder, D.C.
  265.

Pelée, Lillian Sutton.
  160, 3462, 3653.

Pelz, Donald.
  3766.

Pendleton, Edrie.
  1, 323, 797, 1229, 1240, 1457, 1634, 1635,
  2333, 2380, 2523, 3115, 3411, 3466, 3570,
  3679, 3911, 3912.

Peple, Edward.
  1260.

Pérez, José Cid.
  674.

Perkins, E.B.
  3403.

Perlmutter, Ruth.
  1798.

Perrault, Charles.
  2883, 3278.

Pertwee, Roland.
  992, 2044.

Petersen, Ruth I.
  1879.

Peterson, Agnes Emelie.
  1641, 4064.

Peterson, Mary Nygaard.
  4, 24, 268, 939, 1027, 1254, 2083, 2542,
  2683, 3247, 3351, 4112.

Petit, Victor Perez.
  2348.

Petrova, Olga.
  2423, 2960.

Pettit, Mildred T.
  2186.

Pharis, Gwendolyn.
  2664, 3433.

Phelps, Arthur L.
  4110.

Phelps, Elizabeth Stuart.
  4095.

Phelps, Sydney K.
  1028.

Phillips, Charles.
  1146.

Phillips, Ernestine.
  31, 3637.

Phillips, Marguerite Kreger.
  77, 152, 730, 1126, 1146, 1361, 1433, 1434,
  1664, 1746, 2395, 2936, 3458, 3883, 4107,
  4165.

Phillips, Olive.
  452.

Phillips, Stephen
  28.

Phipps, A.H.
  2354.

Pico, Pedro E.
  4152.

Pink, Claire.
  3087.

Pinner, David.
  1036.

Pirandello, Luigi.
  2137, 3066, 3232.

Playfair, Nigel.
  2911.

Plimpton, Harriet.
  3308.

Podesta, Jose J.
  1760.

Poe, Edgar Allan.
  2171, 3635.

Pohl, Frederick J.
  3866.

Polk, William R.
  816.

Porras, Antonio.
  17.

Porter, Charlotte.
  48, 787, 2338, 3089.

Porter, Cole.
  1838.

Porter, Ella Williams.
435, 4041.

Porter, Ethel H.
1469.

Porter, H.C.
3089.

Porter, Helen Tracy.
1856, 2015, 3625.

Portor, Laura Spencer.
1929, 3677.

Potts, Abbie Findlay.
3360.

Power, Caroline M.
3807.

Prall, Dorothea.
2917.

Priestly, J.B.
1668.

Prins, Peter de.
914.

Pritchard, Barry.
3888.

Privacky, Augusta Hutson.
1364.

Prouse, Derek.
2995.

Provost, Betsy Scoville.
3032.

Puccini, Giacomo.
328.

Pumphrey, Byron.
3082.

Purcell, Margaret Barbrick.
971.

Purdy, James.
529.

Pushkin, Aleksandr S.
349, 2396.

Putnam, Nina Wilcox.
2604.

Pyle, Howard.
133.

Pyle, Mary Thurman.
382, 643, 802, 1392, 2318, 2690, 3629, 3630.

Quackenbush, Jan.
3432.

Rabe, Olive.
67, 294, 383, 498, 499, 637, 848, 1035, 1522, 1680, 1745, 1749, 2618, 3028, 3167, 3251, 3410, 3429, 3682, 3760, 3783, 3820, 3981, 3991, 4008.

Radcliff, Margaret.
3236.

Radin, Hy.
2194.

Rahe, Margaret.
2834.

Ramsey, Helen.
800, 1061, 1331, 1643, 2437.

Randolph, Edith.
1857.

Rattigan, Terence.
822, 3056, 3179, 3281, 4071.

Rau, Santha Rama.
2665.

Ravetch, Herbert.
10, 274, 3162, 4125, 4154.

Rawe, Marcella.
438, 3595, 3661.

Rawls, James.
2729.

Reay, Nina Butler.
1315, 2291, 2292.

Recht, Charles.
650.

Reely, Mary Katherine.
1133.

Regan, Sylvia.
1074.

Reilly, Alice M.
2695.

Reinecker, Herbert.
2488.

Reines, Bernard J.
1531, 1915, 3013, 4164.

Reitti, Victor.
1999, 3678.

Relonde, Maurice.
1040.

Renyi, Elizabeth.
1963.

Rice, Elmer.
1013.

Rice, Katharine.
2325.

Richardson, Anna Steese.
567, 2068.

Richardson, Howard.
2560.

Richardson, Margaret C.
    804.

Richmond, Grace S.
    1525.

Richmond, M.C.
    311, 1021, 2935.

Richmond, Samuel S.
    12, 155, 273, 276, 317, 350, 416, 419, 466,
    495, 652, 706, 753, 974, 1010, 1125, 1129,
    1144, 1150, 1156, 1269, 1487, 1491, 1496,
    1497, 1516, 1561, 2563, 2570, 2579, 2779,
    2804, 3184, 3364, 3873, 3960, 4144.

Ridenour, Louis Nicot.
    2732, 2733, 2734.

Rietty, Robert.
    791, 1378, 2738, 3826.

Riley, Alice C.D.
    2141, 3529.

Rinehart, Mary Roberts.
    3358.

Ringwood, Gwen Pharis.
    717.

Ritchie, Estelle.
    1141, 1372, 2997.

Rittenhouse, Charles.
    533, 1034.

Robbins, Jean.
    2107.

Roberts, Helen M.
    262, 359, 399, 1155, 2020, 3519, 3693, 3943,
    3997, 4143.

Roberts, Kenneth.
    995, 1402, 2502, 2511, 2796, 2872, 3327,
    3724, 3876.

Roberts, Marion A.
    844.

Roberts, Walter.
    2410.

Robertson, O.J.
    119, 3282, 3709.

Robinson, Christina.
    320.

Robinson, Gertrude.
    2676, 3151.

Robinson, Lennox.
    721.

Rodgers, Mary.
    2583.

Roeder, Ralph.
    1509, 1552.

Rogers, Charles Gordon.
    2620.

Rogers, John William, Jr.
    401.

Ronan, Robert.
    2285.

Roof, Katharine Metcalf.
    612, 3441.

Rose, Jacques-Leon.
    3081.

Rosenberg, James S.
    541.

Ross, Clarendon.
    829, 2407, 2844.

Ross, Fannie R.
    149, 1688.

Ross, Jerry.
    773, 2636.

Ross, Kenneth.
    3826.

Rostand, Edmond.
    766, 3033.

Rosten, Norman.
    2279.

Rotter, Fritz.
    1917.

Roussin, Andre.
    1978.

Rouverol, Aurania.
    1369, 2808.

Rowe, Marcella.
    1388.

Rowell, Adelaide C.
    246, 1482, 1869, 3840.

Rowland, Elsi.
    2979, 3621, 3622.

Roy, Jessie H.
    378.

Royle, Edwin Milton.
    3398.

Royster, Esther Frances.
    2036.

Rozewicz, Tadeusz.
    1672.

Rudd, Martin.
    1076.

Rueda, Julio Jimenez.
    3832.

Rueda, Lope de.
2559.

Rugg, Minnie M.
3962.

Ruibal, José.
238, 1711.

Ruiz, Raúl.
513.

Runnette, Helen V.
593, 3705.

Ruskin, John.
1819.

Rust, Mary Elizabeth.
211.

Ruthenburg, G. Hutchinson.
528, 3324.

Rutherford, Margery C.
58.

Ryan, Elaine.
2527.

Ryan, Roberta M.
3301.

Rybak, Rose Kacherian.
801, 934, 3065.

Ryerson, Florence.
997, 1775, 1916, 2574.

Ryttenberg, Anita.
see
Weinberg, Anita.

Saavedra, Miguel de Cervantes.
982.

Saavedra y Bessey, Rafael M.
543.

Sabath, Bernard.
1853.

Sachs, Hans.
388.

Sage, Selwin.
1043.

Sagoff, Sara E.
1401, 3503.

Saidy, Fred.
1086.

St.Clair, Robert.
415, 459, 823, 1211, 3475, 3673.

St.Cyr, Dirce.
1480, 2709.

Sakanishi, S.
2996.

Salacrou, Armand.
2776.

Salerno, Henry F.
3491.

Salerno, Henry F.
255.

Salt, Peter Sydney.
242.

Sammis, Edward R.
2624, 2769.

Sampson, Elizabeth.
4129.

Samuel, Horace B.
4109.

Sanchez, Florencio.
1157.

Sanders, Jean.
994.

Sandiford, Betti Primrose.
744.

Sandison, Mildred.
1910, 3607.

Sansom, Clive.
820.

Saphro, Frances Arno.
3821.

Sapinsley, Alvin.
641.

Saroyan, William.
502, 854, 1403, 2416, 2580, 2688, 2757, 3273, 3600, 3615, 3665.

Sassoon, R.L.
3841.

Sastre, Alfonso.
2671.

Saunders, Clerk.
657.

Saunders, James.
1691, 2459, 3142.

Saunders, Lilian.
235, 543, 2484, 3099.

Sawyer, Ruth.
3234.

Sax, Carol.
2905.

Sayre, George Wallace.
1079.

Scatori, Stephen.
4178.

Schaaf, Albert.
1772.

Scharrelmann, Wilhelm.
3913.

Schary, Dore.
3480.

Schehade, Georges.
3867.

Schenck, Anna.
895, 896.

Schering, Emil.
819, 2623, 3246.

Schlumberger, Jean.
508.

Schmidt, Godfrey P. Jr.
1586.

Schmitt, Gladys L.
830, 865, 910, 1071, 2133, 2143, 2153, 2154,
2261, 2295, 2518, 2708, 2934, 2947, 2975,
3168, 3874.

Schneideman, Rose.
3345.

Schnitzler, Arthur.
849, 906, 986, 1197, 1354, 1856, 2015, 3868,
4056, 4109.

Schnitzler, Hermann.
3945.

Schoenfeld, Bernard C.
1743.

Scholl, Ralph.
1016.

Scholz, Wilhelm von.
1728, 3348.

Schonberger, E.D.
2745, 3325.

Schroll, Catherine V.
253, 292, 407, 486, 626, 646, 739, 1137,
1465, 1550, 1858, 2357, 2458, 2731, 2736,
2835, 2987, 3164, 3166, 3216, 3287, 3502,
3559, 3817, 4089.

Schulberg, Budd.
845.

Schwartz, Esther Dresden.
3633.

Schwartz, Jerome L.
1667.

Schwartz, Lynne Sharon.
1809, 4096.

Schwartz, Morton K.
82, 175, 1890, 2042, 3334, 3794.

Schwartz, T.G.
2342.

Scott, Christine E.
3593.

Scott, Gladys Guilford.
3242.

Scott, Mariana.
1056.

Scott, Natalie Vivian.
4179.

Scott, Sir Walter.
1854, 2904.

Sealock, Thelma W.
1937, 1938.

Searcy, Katherine.
3896.

Sée, Edmond.
1179.

Sellers, Irma Peixotto.
25.

Selnick, Eugene.
1290.

Seltzer, Thomas.
2043.

Selver, Paul.
2911, 4032, 4103.

Seward, Thomas.
1711.

Sewell, Anna.
302.

Seymour, Judith.
1942.

Shaffer, Peter.
305, 1118, 1119, 3061, 4031.

Shakespeare, William.
127, 150, 1400, 1770, 1816, 2057, 2058, 2238,
2400, 3037, 3038, 3521, 3522, 3542.

Sharma, Pertap.
3703.

Sharp, H. Sutton.
1229.

Shaw, George Bernard.
113, 428, 873, 1336, 2270, 2629, 2887, 3930,
4050.

Shaw, Irwin.
413.

Shaw, Robert.
2124.

Shenk, Esther.
3935.

Shenker, Rose W.
3354.

Sheridan, Richard Brinsley.
3011, 3012, 3092.

Sherry, Ruth Forbes.
3174.

Sherwood, Margaret.
3905.

Sherwood, Robert E.
6, 935, 1946, 3160, 3288, 3597.

Shoemaker, Anna P.
3173.

Shore, Maxine.
490, 3948.

Shpezhinsky, Ippolit.
2066.

Shriner, Fleming.
20.

Shulman, Max.
3548.

Shun, T'ang Wen.
3207, 3928.

Sickels, Eleanor.
780, 3367.

Side, Ronald K.
2557.

Sidney, Margaret.
4020.

Sierra, Martinez.
1599.

Silberschlag, Eisig.
991.

Silverberg, William V.
47, 195, 850, 985, 1177, 1649.

Silverman, Stanley H.
1687.

Simmonds, Mattie Frances.
1370.

Simon, Shirley.
201, 764, 855, 3026, 3290, 3508, 3655, 3707, 4063.

Simonds, Natalie.
1408, 1409.

Simpson, N.F.
727, 1163, 1508, 2592.

Skinner, Ada M.
2471.

Skinner, Cornelia Otis.
2760.

Skrivanek, Camille.
546.

Slattery, Margaret E.
878, 1296, 1812, 1813, 2670, 2689, 2902, 2924, 3062, 3217, 3241, 3243, 3434.

Slingluff, Mary O.
2453.

Smith, Addison Gerry.
2070.

Smith, Alice Thornberry.
892.

Smith, Betty.
1107, 3448.

Smith, Gladys V.
492, 918, 3413, 3658.

Smith, Hyacinth Stoddart.
703.

Smith, J. Kinchin.
2404.

Smith, Marian Spencer.
103, 1314, 1399, 2539, 3285, 3970.

Smith, Marion.
670.

Smith, Mary F.
3914.

Smith, Nora A.
3988.

Smith, Peter J.
1208.

Smith, Robert Paul.
3548.

Smith, S. Decatur.
1703, 2373, 2827.

Snider, Charles Lee.
1751.

Snow, C.P.
32.

Snow, Francis Haffkine.
2066.

Sobel, Bernard.
1613.

Sombart, Petronelle.
989, 1597.

Sompayrac, Irma.
3647.

Sondheim, Stephen.
1382, 3980.

Sonnenfeld, Morton.
3962.

Sorabji, Cornelia.
1292.

Soyinka, Wole.
     3014.

Souza, Antonio.
     2662.

Spaeth, Claribel.
     140, 252, 318, 371, 386, 408, 409, 443, 734,
     912, 1095, 1185, 1395, 1529, 1708, 1709, 1713,
     1810, 1825, 1959, 1961, 1966, 1971, 1975,
     1993, 1997, 2004, 2125, 2168, 2169, 2193,
     2267, 2283, 2309, 2521, 2672, 2789, 2825,
     2884, 3025, 3231, 3305, 3702, 3795, 3822,
     3849, 3994, 4085.

Speare, Dorothy.
     3036.

Speare, Elizabeth George.
     1160.

Speirs, Russell F.
     512, 1257, 1332, 1505.

Spencer, Colin.
     3373.

Spewack, Bella.
     1838, 2421.

Spewack, Sam.
     1838, 2421, 3800.

Spiegel, Moshe.
     2061.

Spigelgass, Leonard.
     2110.

Spyri, Johanna.
     1460, 1461.

Squires, Edith Lombard.
     2896.

Stansbury, Mary.
     919.

Stanwood, Louise Rogers.
     2861.

Starling, Lynn.
     1153.

States, Bert.
     2977.

Steele, Wilbur Daniel.
     3048, 3556.

Stein, Gertrude.
     1637.

Stein, Joseph.
     2750.

Steiner, Barbara A.
     1106.

Steingold, Rita Whitman.
     2654.

Stephens, Nan Bagby.
     514.

Stephenson, Mary L.
     3157.

Sterling, George.
     904.

Stevens, Gould.
     1302.

Stettner, Louis.
     993.

Stevens, Caroline D.
     944.

Stevens, Wallace.
     456.

Stevenson, Robert Louis.
     1799, 2056, 3267, 3268, 3736, 3737, 4167.

Steward, Ann.
     3352.

Stigler, W.A.
     3350.

Stiles, Hinson.
     3045.

Stinehart, Esther.
     1397.

Stinetorf, Louise A.
     3958.

Stockton, Frank R.
     1855, 2550, 3719, 3720.

Stokes, Charles W.
     880.

Stone, John A.
     549, 2512.

Stoppard, Tom.
     59.

Storts, Adeline M.
     661.

Stow, Clara.
     2661.

Strachan, Edna Higgins.
     542.

Strange, Joanna Gleed.
     3687.

Stratton, Clarence.
     41, 1759.

Strauss, Richard.
     142.

Streacker, Lucille.
     324, 2831, 3020.

Street, Julia M.
     1800.

Strindberg, August.
819, 988, 1379, 2623, 3246, 3464.

Stringer, Arthur.
1557.

Strong, Austin.
902, 1970.

Stuart, Dorothy Margaret.
3523.

Stuart, Jesse.
3670.

Stump, Anna Louise.
264.

Sturgis, Julian.
740.

Styne, Jule.
244, 1382.

Subert, Francis Adolf.
185, 1342, 1714, 2705.

Subert, Frantisek Adolf.
see
Subert, Francis Adolf.

Sudermann, Hermann.
1038, 3089, 3540, 3625.

Suerken, Ernst H.
1741.

Sullivan, A.M.
3718.

Sullivan, Warren.
1122.

Sumner, John N.
1183.

Sutphen, William Gilbert Van Tassal.
1556, 3363.

Sutro, Alfred.
2158.

Swanson, Roy W.
728.

Swenson, May.
1134.

Swift, Jonathan.
1376.

Swintz, Martha.
1829, 1830, 1831, 2501, 2641, 2785, 2786,
3641, 3642.

Svortzell, Lowell.
929, 1113.

Sylvester, Lucille.
2197.

Symons, Arthur.
640.

Synge, John Millington.
825, 2753, 2999, 3000.

Szebenyei, J.
1536.

Taber, Gladys Bagg.
2282.

Tagore, Rabindranath.
2787.

Tarkington, Booth.
232, 284, 634, 1236, 1675, 2290, 2339, 2340,
3424, 3725, 3770.

Taylor, Cecil P.
372.

Taylor, L.M.
657.

Taylor, Marion A.
2447, 4034.

Taylor, Samuel.
1428, 2760, 2761, 3080.

Taylor, William E.
3190.

Teeple, Lou Rodman.
3362.

Teichmann, Howard.
3323.

Teitel, Irving.
799.

Tennyson, Alfred, Lord.
976, 1884.

Tenyi, Elizabeth.
4051, 4052.

Terson, Peter.
135, 2241.

Thackeray, William Makepeace.
4102.

Thane, Adele.
54, 370, 395, 432, 577, 588, 624, 840, 909,
946, 954, 1245, 1410, 1460, 1705, 1806, 1821,
1895, 1996, 2034, 2091, 2080, 2223, 2550,
2724, 2742, 2744, 2883, 2932, 2969, 3008,
3072, 3124, 3278, 3499, 3638, 3691, 3788.

Thomas, Augustus.
700, 2461.

Thomas, Dylan.
3823, 3824.

Thomas, Elsie M.
2094.

Thomas, Gwyn.
1712, 1786.

Thompson, Doris K.
3100.

Thompson, Dorothy.
4047.

Thompson, Jay.
272, 2553, 2583.

Thorne-Thomsen, Georg.
3756.

Thorpe, Heather G.
1566.

Thorpe, Marion E.
3260.

Thurber, James.
2115.

Thurston, Muriel B.
3043.

Tilden, Freeman.
977.

Toles, Myriam.
3963.

Tolstoy, Leo.
1565, 2014, 4021.

Toro, Julio del.
3768.

Totheroh, Dan W.
1339, 2040, 2269, 2682, 3172, 3437, 3438,
4025.

Tourguenief, Ivan.
2587.

Towles, Lena Ruth.
2721.

Towne, Charles Hanson.
70.

Trausti, Jan.
2711.

Tridon, André.
3549.

Treitel, Ralph.
2259.

Trumbo, Dalton.
279.

Trzcinski, Edmund.
3405.

Tunberg, Karl A.
1406.

Tunick, Irve.
2230.

Turnbull, Lucia.
1313, 2096.

Turner, Geneva C.
378.

Turner, Margaret Freeman.
2483.

Twain, Mark.
27, 690, 691, 1275, 1276, 1575, 2247, 2815,
2816, 2817, 3690, 3691.

Ullman, Samuel S.
875, 2231, 4172, 4173.

Underhill, John Garrett.
1503, 1820, 2824, 3121, 3456.

Upson, William Hazlett.
2179.

Urban, Catherine.
65, 869, 1706, 2298, 2819, 2899, 3107, 3109,
3135, 3671, 4039, 4120.

Usigli, Rudolfo.
1345.

Usseau, Arnaud d'
3696.

Ustinov, Peter.
3034.

Utt, Ana Lee.
1365, 4055.

Vahl, Rod.
628, 1652.

Vail, Laurence.
1651.

Vail, Walter J.
815, 2142.

Valency, Maurice.
958, 2074, 2585, 3890.

Vallejo, Antonio Buero.
685.

Van Campen, Helen G.
4098.

Vance, Daisy Melville.
2627.

Van Delden, Egbert H.
66, 1380.

Van Deusen, Delia.
3001.

Vandevere, J. Lillian.
2374.

Van Dresser, Jasmine S.
932, 4162.

Van Druten, John.
240, 1582, 1583, 1589.

Van Dyke, Henry.
1558.

Van Kaathoven, Alice.
225.

Van Tassell, Mabel S.
965.

Varney, Horace.
1206, 3949.

Vásquez, José Andrés.
4093.

Vauthier, Jean.
2854.

Vega Carpio, Lope Felix de.
1820, 2669, 3467.

Verdi, Giuseppe.
2412.

Verhoeff, Caroline.
3275.

Verne, Jules.
145, 306, 1121, 2180, 3791.

Very, Alice.
7, 362, 434, 489, 584, 587, 653, 775, 864,
920, 1006, 1138, 1184, 1215, 1252, 1293,
1486, 1704, 1733, 1742, 1972, 1977, 2090,
2192, 2552, 2751, 2986, 3220, 3279, 3582,
3583, 3632, 3652, 3743, 3854, 3879.

Vian, Boris.
955.

Vickner, Edwin Johan.
203.

Vidal, Gore.
254, 3039, 3893, 3894.

Vilas, Faith Van Valkenburgh.
3535.

Vildrac, Charles.
3426.

Vincent, Allen.
1917.

Vojnovich, Ivo.
93, 2578, 2983, 3792.

Volzer, Marion.
3425.

Voteur, Ferdinand.
2422.

Wainwright, Fonrose.
3083.

Waite, Helen E.
506, 581, 582, 2178, 2439.

Waley, Arthur.
915.

Walker, Stuart.
3264.

Wallace, Elizabeth.
1327.

Wallace, Ruth.
469.

Wallace, Sarah Agnes.
2555, 3141.

Wallop, Douglas.
773.

Walsh, Thomas.
1324, 2645.

Walter, Elizabeth.
3870.

Walter, Otto F.
482.

Walters, Anne B.
1449.

Wangenheim, Alice.
504.

Ward, Elizabeth Stuart Phelps.
1756.

Ward, Muriel.
1033, 1697, 1698, 2300, 2301.

Ward, Winifred Duncan.
189.

Waterhouse, Keith.
281, 282.

Watkins, Martha Swintz.
see
Swintz, Martha.

Watson, Donald.
925, 1904, 2441.

Watson, Robert.
2762.

Watts, Frances B.
147, 210, 571, 729, 1581, 1731, 1902, 1903,
2222, 2281, 2900, 3074, 3108, 3449, 3672, 4087.

Weathers, Winston.
3886.

Webb, Chase.
4105.

Webber, C.E.
220.

Wedekind, Frank.
3549.

Wefer, Marion.
137, 1630, 1983, 2273.

Weidman, Jerome.
1088.

Weiger, Eugene.
3185.

Weill, Kurt.
2037.

Wein, Sadye B.
3161.

Weinberg, Albert.
2019, 2717, 3049.

Weinberg, Anita.
2717, 3049.

Weinberger, Mildred.
933.

Weisburd, Melvin Irving.
134.

Weisstein, Ulrich.
2918.

Welburn, Vivienne C.
1750.

Wells, Carolyn.
141, 551, 580, 793, 1025, 1350, 1351, 1685,
2198, 2582, 2894.

Wells, H.G.
1657, 1683.

Welsh, Robert Gilbert.
1730.

Wentworth, Marion Craig.
3929.

Werner, John H.
3845.

Werner, Sally.
548, 1065, 1827, 2313, 2470, 3383.

Wesker, Arnold.
519, 544, 545, 1611, 1840, 3046, 3592.

West, Elizabeth Howard.
2072.

Wexley, John.
676.

Weysz, Hans.
906.

Wharton, Edith.
701, 702.

Wheatcroft, John.
2979.

Wheeler, Hugh.
275.

Whipkey, Stella Dunway.
882, 3871.

White, Amelia D.
1108, 3798.

White, Florence Donnell.
2099.

White, George.
3060.

Whitehouse, Josephine Henry.
440, 770, 1654.

Whiting, Eleanor C.
151, 682.

Whitman, Constance.
3146, 3450.

Whittaker, Helene.
1219, 1247, 2379.

Whitworth, Virginia Payne.
1807, 2080, 2174, 2199.

Widdemer, Margaret.
190, 1768.

Wiegand, Charmion Von.
947, 1721.

Wiegand, J.
3913.

Wiggin, Kate Douglas.
288, 289, 290, 1170, 2549.

Wight, Lawrence.
1404.

Wilbrandt, Adolf.
2176.

Wilcox, Grace.
3721.

Wilde, Charles F.
677, 1594, 1776, 1777, 3489.

Wilde, Oscar.
293, 445, 446, 1154, 1426, 1427, 1617, 1618,
1619, 3095, 3096.

Wilde, Percival.
63, 962, 1833, 3996.

Wilder, Thornton.
117, 526, 903, 1422, 2181, 2397, 2903, 3468.

Wilkes, Elizabeth.
2175.

Willcox, Louise C.
1286.

Willets, Jeanette.
3445.

Williams, Blanche G.
1861.

Williams, Eleanor Winslow.
3223.

Williams, George Llyonel.
3294.

Williams, Gweneira M.
1790, 1791.

Williams, Isabelle.
2746.

Williams, Jesse Lynch.
4048.

Williams, Miller.
513.

Williams, Oscar.
1823.

Williams, R.E.
2062.

Williams, Tennessee.
439, 488, 1281, 1585, 1590, 1824, 2411, 2486, 2487, 2603, 2696, 3051.

Williams, William Carlos.
2146.

Willment, Frank.
4035.

Willoughby, Edwin Elliott.
1872.

Willson, Dixie.
2100.

Wilson, Allan Doyle.
3616.

Wilson, Carolyn.
3984.

Wilson, Dorothy Clarke.
2499.

Wilson, Edmund.
861.

Wilson, Harry L.
2224, 4177.

Wilson, Leila Weekes.
1932.

Wilson, Marie Lyon.
1103.

Wilson, Meredith.
3837.

Wimsatt, Genevieve.
3208.

Wincelberg, Shimon.
1785, 4068.

Winningstad, Philip.
4153.

Winter, Mary.
3067.

Wirt, Anne Grace.
448.

Wishengrad, Morton.
3047, 3496.

Witherspoon, Frances.
2606.

Witkiewicz, Stanislaw Ignacy.
726, 2071, 3950.

Wittlinger, Karl.
852.

Wodehouse, P.G.
2756.

Wofford, Azile M.
2565.

Wolfe, Archibald John.
532.

Wolfe, Thomas.
3611.

Wolfson, Victor.
2304.

Wolman, Diana.
1612.

Wood, Charles.
645, 655, 656, 842.

Wood, Frederic T.
2711.

Woodbridge, Elizabeth.
568.

Woodford, Bruce P.
2845.

Worcester, Daisy Lee Worthington.
1386.

Worcester, Natalie S.
2063.

Worrell, Edna Randolph.
3225, 3712.

Woster, Alice.
81, 1573, 1574.

Woticky, Edward.
3868.

Wright, Doris.
3789, 3790.

Wunderlich, Lawrence.
2868.

Wymark, Olwen.
2054.

Wynand, Derk.
482.

Wyss, Johann.
3501.

Yale, Elsie Duncan.
3125, 3574.

Yeats, William Butler.
483, 1190, 1357, 1543, 1544, 2754, 3194.

York, Marjorie Ann.
1140, 1949, 2438, 3736, 3737.

Cast Analysis Index

INDEX OF CAST ANALYSES

(Check List of Abbreviations)

FULL LENGTH PLAYS

In this section are included those plays suitable for an evening's entertainment, whether called one act or several acts.

12 un. +X.
   2635.

0 m. 2 f.
   4098.

0 m. 2 f. 2 c.
   1665.

0 m. 3 f.
   1560.

0 m. 4 f.
   1802, 1803.

0 m. 11 f. 2 c.
   1555.

0 m. 21 f.
   4161.

1 m. 1 f.
   174, 1414, 1579, 3624.

1 m. 2 f.
   2854.

1 m. 6 f.
   3060.

1 m. 8 f.
   2549.

1 m. 9 f.
   724.

2 m. 0 f.
   1785, 2241.

2 m. 1 f.
   852, 2532, 2869, 3404, 4062.

2 m. 2 f.
   372, 482, 500, 1164, 1258, 1417, 1759, 1880, 3131, 4078.

2 m. 2 f. 1 c.
   48.

2 m. 3 f.
   728, 786, 1036, 2573.

2 m. 4 f.
   487.

2 m. 5 f.
   1256.

2 m. 6 f.
   510, 2663.

2 m. 14 f.
   535.

3 m. 1 f.
   873, 981, 1843, 2343.

3 m. 1 f. 1 c.
   1118, 1119.

3 m. 1 f. many c.
   962.

3 m. 1 f. +X.
   949, 950, 1638.

3 m. 2 f.
   232, 239, 240, 650, 1720, 2320, 3526, 3527, 3726.

3 m. 3 f.
   827, 928, 955, 1572, 1750, 2243, 2774, 3240, 3814, 4135.

3 m. 3 f. 1 c.
   88.

3 m. 3 f. 1 c. +X.
   2044.

3 m. 4 f.
   791, 1582, 1583, 1691, 2027, 3472.

3 m. 4 f. 1 c.
   1684.

3 m. 5 f.
   281, 382, 2967, 2968.

3 m. 7 f.
   2928, 2929, 4048.

3 m. 8 f.
   3179.

4 m. 0 f.
   3888.

4 m. 1 f.
   11, 1978, 1985.

4 m. 1 f. 1 c.
   3617.

4 m. 2 f.
   727, 930, 1139, 3160, 3198, 3826.

4 m. 2 f. 1 c.
   3182.

4 m. 3 f.
   1037, 1200, 1597, 1668, 2178, 2887, 2946.

4 m. 3 f. +X.
   79, 708, 3441.

4 m. 4 f.
   1675, 2423, 4146.

4 m. 4 f. +X.
   2827.

4 m. 5 f.
   1259, 1548, 2696.

4 m. 6 f.
   37, 3089.

4 m. 7 f.
2720, 3924, 3925.

4 m. 8 f.
4170.

4 m. 9 f.
3832.

5 m. 0 f.
3916.

5 m. 1 f.
836.

5 m. 2 f.
275, 914, 2760, 2761, 3373, 3598.

5 m. 2 f. 2 c. +X.
2202, 2711.

5 m. 2 f. +X.
3092.

5 m. 3 f.
660, 822, 1223, 2536, 3548, 4065.

5 m. 4 f.
987, 3046, 3047, 3821.

5 m. 4 f. +X.
2334.

5 m. 5 f.
225, 645, 1039, 2802, 2917, 3664, 3667.

5 m. 6 f.
3189.

5 m. 7 f.
183, 1074.

5 m. 8 f.
2160.

6 m. 0 f.
410, 748.

6 m. 0 f. +X.
1537.

6 m. 1 f.
2106, 2925.

6 m. 2 f.
722, 1524, 1552, 1935.

6 m. 2 f. +X.
2976.

6 m. 3 f.
1273, 1436, 1722, 2270, 2908, 2960, 3142,
4177.

6 m. 4 f.
220, 519, 1242, 2995.

6 m. 4 f. 1 c.
4071.

6 m. 5 f.
2220, 2793.

6 m. 5 f. 2 c. +X.
1850.

6 m. 6 f.
805, 843, 1936, 2645, 3293.

6 m. 7 f.
3609.

6 m. 7 f. 5 c. +X.
4102.

7 m. 1 f.
712, 1577, 1804, 2338.

7 m. 2 f.
1464, 1786, 3185, 4158.

7 m. 2 f. 7 c.
3451.

7 m. 3 f.
1480, 1881, 1999, 2421, 3127, 3349.

7 m. 4 f.
1327, 2749, 3710, 4068, 4178.

7 m. 4 f. 1 c.
197.

7 m. 5 f.
84, 122.

7 m. 5 f. +X.
2753, 3490, 4153.

7 m. 6 f.
3281.

7 m. 6 f. +X.
1853.

7 m. 7 f.
3080.

7 m. 8 f.
3900.

7 m. 10 f.
2064.

8 m. 0 f. +X.
3014.

8 m. 1 f.
2756, 2855.

8 m. 1 f. +X.
3885.

8 m. 2 f.
2787, 2909.

8 m. 2 f. +X.
328.

8 m. 3 f.
418, 668, 781, 825, 905, 2926.

8 m. 3 f. 1 c. +X.
1026.

8 m. 4 f.
1428, 1611, 2066, 3178.

8 m. 5 f.
813, 1080.

8 m. 5 f. 2 c. +X.
644.

8 m. 5 f. +X.
17, 1448.

8 m. 6 f.
479, 810, 2110, 2232, 2290, 2422, 2487, 2528,
3003, 3836.

8 m. 11 f.
3945.

9 m. 1 f.
2443, 29'+.

9 m. 1 f. +X.
3703.

9 m. 2 f.
1727, 2541, 3530, 3894.

9 m. 2 f. +X.
1406.

9 m. 3 f.
649.

9 m. 3 f. 2 c.
3325.

9 m. 3 f. 7 c.
958.

9 m. 4 f.
106, 1345, 1930, 3034.

9 m. 4 f. +X.
1558, 2762.

9 m. 5 f.
502, 641, 792.

9 m. 5 f. +X.
1538, 1539, 1901, 2560, 4104.

9 m. 6 f.
3155.

9 m. 6 f. 1 c.
4000, 4001.

9 m. 7 f. +X.
534, 732.

9 m. 8 f.
3308.

9 m. 9 f. +X.
2709.

9 m. 13 f.
3051.

10 m. 1 f.
1817, 2307.

10 m. 2 f. 1 c.
2778.

10 m. 2 f. +X.
2056, 3592.

10 m. 3 f.
926, 1075.

10 m. 3 f. +X.
3625.

10 m. 4 f.
63, 1483, 2592.

10 m. 4 f. +X.
3467.

10 m. 5 f.
3245, 3683.

11 m. 5 f. +X.
14, 380.

10 m. 6 f.
279, 532, 2181.

10 m. 6 f. +X.
2526.

10 m. 7 f.
488.

11 m. 7 f. 1 c.
1952.

10 m. 8 f.
1329.

10 m. 8 f. 3 c.
2849.

10 m. 9 f.
2603.

10 m. 10 f. +X.
984.

10 m. 12 f.
2578.

10 m. 16 f.
787.

11 m. 0 f.
996.

11 m. 2 f.
2488.

11 m. 2 f. +X.
3105.

11 m. 3 f.
429, 2119, 2120, 3491.

11 m. 3 f. 1 c. +X.
667.

11 m. 4 f.
453, 2065, 3800.

11 m. 4 f. 1 c.
2966.

11 m. 4 f. +X.
1820.

11 m. 5 f.
3882.

11 m. 6 f.
1330.

11 m. 8 f.
1893.

11 m. 10 f.
745.

12 m. 0 f.
842.

12 m. 0 f. +X.
2242.

12 m. 1 f.
3552.

12 m. 2 f.
3039.

12 m. 3 f.
967, 3066, 3768.

12 m. 3 f. +X.
2692, 3169, 3678, 3835.

12 m. 4 f.
2776.

12 m. 5 f.
251, 3590.

12 m. 5 f. 2 c. +X.
3813.

12 m. 5 f. +X.
815.

12 m. 7 f.
2176.

12 m. 7 f. 2 c.
376.

12 m. 8 f.
1987.

12 m. 10 f.
1702.

12 m. 17 f. 9 c. +X.
1382.

13 m. 2 f.
3181.

13 m. 2 f. 1 c.
3950.

13 m. 2 f. +X.
108, 1384.

13 m. 3 f.
3054.

13 m. 3 f. +X.
1576, 1712, 2124, 4101.

13 m. 4 f. +X.
2491.

13 m. 5 f.
3323.

13 m. 5 f. 3 un. +X.
692.

13 m. 5 f. 1 c.
1378.

13 m. 5 f. +X.
2636.

13 m. 6 f.
3510.

13 m. 6 f. +X.
2665.

13 m. 7 f.
89, 2973.

13 m. 7 f. +X.
773.

13 m. 9 f. 3 c. +X.
3532.

13 m. 11 f. 1 c.
2146.

14 m. 2 f.
4092.

14 m. 2 f. +X.
113.

14 m. 3 f.
1711.

14 m. 3 f. +X.
185, 1838.

14 m. 4 f.
1204.

14 m. 4 f. +X.
2561.

14 m. 5 f.
1659, 2072.

14 m. 5 f. +X.
242, 1157, 1640.

14 m. 6 f.
254.

14 m. 7 f. +X.
2306.

14 m. 9 f.
177, 685.

14 m. 11 f.
3471.

15 m. 1 f. +X.
    2643.

15 m. 2 f.
    32, 3668.

15 m. 4 f.
    901, 2111, 2738, 3848.

15 m. 4 f. +X.
    135, 2745.

15 m. 5 f. +X.
    2496.

15 m. 6 f.
    1347, 2780.

15 m. 6 f. +X.
    3870.

15 m. 7 f. +X.
    1243.

15 m. 8 f. +X.
    676, 2770.

15 m. 11 f. 2 c. +X.
    3868.

15 m. 14 f.
    2583.

16 m. 1 f. +X.
    1213.

16 m. 4 f.
    2512.

16 m. 5 f.
    2823.

16 m. 5 f. +X.
    142.

16 m. 7 f.
    2858.

16 m. 25 f.
    2412.

17 m. 0 f.
    1373, 2588.

17 m. 2 f.
    209.

17 m. 4 f.
    349.

17 m. 5 f. +X.
    541.

17 m. 8 f. +X.
    421.

17 m. 12 f.
    2585.

18 m. 0 f.
    379.

18 m. 1 f.
    3663.

18 m. 2 f. +X.
    255.

18 m. 3 f.
    130, 784.

18 m. 3 f. +X.
    3867.

18 m. 4 f.
    1738, 2862.

18 m. 6 f.
    3480.

18 m. 6 f. +X.
    4103.

18 m. 9 f.
    3288.

18 m. 10 f. +X.
    1557, 2360.

18 m. 12 f.
    1840.

19 m. 1 f.
    2311.

19 m. 2 f. 2 c.
    3061.

19 m. 4 f.
    1342.

19 m. 5 f. +X.
    2634.

19 m. 12 f.
    845.

20 m. 0 f.
    544, 545.

20 m. 2 f. +X.
    49.

20 m. 3 f.
    1300.

20 m. 4 f. +X.
    1086.

20 m. 10 f. +X.
    2750.

21 m. 0 f.
    3405.

21 m. 7 f. 1 c. +X.
    2668.

21 m. 8 f.
    1867.

21 m. 11 f. +X.
    1714.

22 m. 0 f.
    3056.

22 m. 7 f.
244.

23 m. 4 f.
428.

23 m. 4 f. 2 c.
93.

23 m. 6 f. 1 c. +X.
3273.

23 m. 7 f. +X.
1660.

24 m. 0 f.
280.

24 m. 7 f.
3890.

24 m. 12 f.
2527.

24 m. 20 f. +X.
3121.

25 m. 3 f.
30.

25 m. 4 f. 5 c.
3027.

25 m. 6 f.
121.

25 m. 14 f. +X.
3980.

25 m. 15 f. +X.
1934.

26 m. 1 f. 1 c. +X.
1728.

26 m. 1 f. +X.
202.

26 m. 5 f. +X.
3348.

26 m. 9 f. +X.
2037.

26 m. 11 f. 2 c. +X.
180.

26 m. 12 f.
439.

27 m. 8 f. +X.
2014.

28 m. 0 f.
112.

30 m. 8 f.
1088.

30 m. 11 f.
2074.

30 m. 12 f. +X.
3837.

31 m. 20 f.
4126.

42 m. 9 f. +X.
1334.

SHORT PLAYS

In this section are included one act plays, skits, radio scripts and most children's plays, as well as excerpts from longer works.

1 un. 1 f. 2 c.
1411.

1 un. 7 c. +X.
737.

1 un. 8 c. +X.
1479.

1 un. many c.
1861, 2615, 3445, 3730.

1 un. +X.
64.

2 un. 2 m. +X.
3986.

2 un. 2 f. 1 c.
1963.

2 un. 5 f. 4 c.
2939.

3 un.
264, 493, 1432.

3 un. 6 m. +X.
3153.

3 un. 2 f.
3920.

3 un. 8 m. +X.
3135.

3 un. 1 c.
4051, 4052.

4 un.
1998, 3222.

4 un. 1 m. 4 c. +X.
731.

4 un. 4 m.
375.

4 un. 5 m.
1959.

5 un. 4 m.
1993.

5 un. 10 c.
2294.

0 m. 1 f. 4 un
3853.

0 m. 1 f. 2 c.
648.

0 m. 1 f. 2 c. +X.
1251.

0 m. 1 f. 3 c.
3626.

0 m. 1 f. 4 c.
1466, 2433.

0 m. 1 f. 4 c. +X.
3892.

0 m. 1 f. 5 c. +X.
610.

0 m. 1 f. 10 c.
1747.

0 m. 1 f. 11 c.
2483.

0 m. 1 f. 16 c.
1004.

0 m. 1 f. many c.
1351, 2373.

0 m. 1 f. +X.
548.

0 m. 2 f.
913, 1044, 1303, 1609, 1610, 1617, 2128, 4111.

0 m. 2 f. 1 c.
670.

0 m. 2 f. 1 c. +X.
2418.

0 m. 2 f. +X.
4013.

0 m. 3 f.
211, 636, 651, 971, 1028, 1913, 1958, 2090,
2354, 2553, 2905, 3488, 4091.

0 m. 3 f. 7 un. 5 c.
1390.

0 m. 3 f. 1 c.
899, 3996.

0 m. 3 f. 11 c.
1137.

0 m. 3 f. 15 c.
1608.

0 m. 3 f. +X.
2244, 2392, 3259.

0 m. 4 f.
196, 212, 435, 1043, 2581, 2662, 3523, 3717,
3780, 3903.

0 m. 5 f.
90, 91, 92, 1090, 1099, 1100, 2328, 2402,
3374, 4009.

0 m. 5 f. 1 c.
1989.

0 m. 5 f. +X.
915, 2735.

0 m. 6 f.
21, 22, 973, 1126, 1433, 1434, 1922, 2009,
2287, 3043, 3159, 3164, 3844, 4015, 4143.

0 m. 6 f. 5 c.
2166.

0 m. 6 f. +X.
1339, 2842.

0 m. 7 f.
755, 1101, 1176, 1516, 1914, 2199, 2803,
3191, 3561.

0 m. 8 f.
97, 894, 1263, 1965, 2005, 2191, 2235, 2236,
2289, 2386, 2395, 2432, 2811.

0 m. 9 f.
896, 2007, 2010, 3435, 3436, 4107.

0 m. 10 f.
417, 1979, 2970, 2971, 3118, 3201, 3202,
3203, 3481.

0 m. 10 f. +X.
2449.

0 m. 11 f.
41, 1216, 1580, 2234, 2268.

0 m. 12 f.
879, 3932.

0 m. 12 f. +X.
1266.

0 m. 13 f.
3613.

0 m. 13 f. +X.
1267.

0 m. 14 f.
1401.

0 m. 15 f.
3614.

0 m. 16 f.
963.

0 m. 16 f. +X.
1025.

0 m. 17 f. +X.
3053.

0 m. 18 f. +X.
2192.

0 m. 23 f. +X.
2594.

1 m. 0 f.
456, 2321, 3686.

1 m. 0 f. 2 c.
607.

1 m. 0 f. 4 c.
43.

1 m. 0 f. 6 c.
2886.

1 m. 0 f. 8 c.
458, 2269, 3344.

1 m. 0 f. 14 c.
119.

1 m. 0 f. 15 c. +X.
851.

1 m. 0 f. 22 c.
3709.

1 m. 0 f. +X.
1003, 2095, 2703.

1 m. 1 f.
38, 47, 162, 163, 195, 321, 392, 546, 680,
695, 850, 990, 1151, 1152, 1177, 1195, 1280,
1314, 1435, 1467, 1525, 1585, 1624, 1649,
1839, 1896, 1954, 2158, 2459, 2484, 2562,
2597, 2610, 2644, 2666, 2677, 2771, 2870,
2961, 2966, 3313, 3419, 3464, 3529, 3802,
3807, 3845, 3968, 3970, 3978, 4093, 4128,
4140, 4145, 4157.

1 m. 1 f. 1 un.
4151.

1 m. 1 f. 5 un.
3825.

1 m. 1 f. 7 un. +X.
638.

1 m. 1 f. 8 un.
723.

1 m. 1 f. 10 un.
2437.

1 m. 1 f. 10 un. +X.
3406.

1 m. 1 f. 1 c.
62, 1386, 2186, 2930, 3727, 3728, 3729.

1 m. 1 f. 2 c.
526, 1405, 1719, 1849, 3696.

1 m. 1 f. 3 c.
1540, 3090, 3966, 4066.

1 m. 1 f. 4 c.
1083, 1418, 2364, 2382, 3842.

1 m. 1 f. 5 c.
863, 3949.

1 m. 1 f. 7 c.
1219.

1 m. 1 f. 8 c.
1988.

1 m. 1 f. 9 c.
1092, 1093, 1554, 2378.

1 m. 1 f. 10 c.
2323, 2552.

1 m. 1 f. 11 c. +X.
184.

1 m. 1 f. 12 c. +X.
821.

1 m. 1 f. 15 c.
1252, 2990, 3413.

1 m. 1 f. 17 c.
2471.

1 m. 1 f. many c.
580, 1206.

1 m. 1 f. +X.
33, 1062, 3116, 3583, 3674, 3765, 3809, 3887.

1 m. 2 f.
126, 158, 161, 200, 312, 448, 457, 512, 528,
537, 549, 617, 701, 702, 874, 881, 904, 931,
1081, 1175, 1365, 1498, 1646, 1755, 1904,
2032, 2184, 2227, 2514, 2546, 2564, 2601,
2629, 2648, 2661, 2682, 2743, 2860, 3031,
3301, 3360, 3428, 3563, 3596, 3716, 3819,
3946, 4036, 4055, 4124.

1 m. 2 f. 1 un.
2174.

1 m. 2 f. 7 un.
2145, 3652.

1 m. 2 f. 1 c.
1658, 3101.

1 m. 2 f. 2 c.
932, 1753, 4173.

1 m. 2 f. 3 c.
2398, 3926.

1 m. 2 f. 5 c.
3638, 3671.

1 m. 2 f. 7 c.
3299.

1 m. 2 f. 8 c. +X.
110.

1 m. 2 f. 9 c.
3976.

1 m. 2 f. 12 c. +X.
1703.

1 m. 2 f. many c.
525.

1 m. 2 f. +X.
2059, 2952.

1 m. 3 f.
16, 423, 647, 903, 1170, 1317, 1693, 1860,
2903, 3067, 3176, 3352, 3498, 4132.

1 m. 3 f. 7 un.
2094.

1 m. 3 f. 1 c.
2038.

1 m. 3 f. 2 c.
189, 3687.

1 m. 3 f. 19 c.
3869.

1 m. 3 f. +X.
86, 2324, 2999, 3000, 4169.

1 m. 4 f.
190, 770, 970, 1766, 1945, 2004, 2444, 2531,
2638, 3883, 4122.

1 m. 4 f. 3 c.
3487, 4011.

1 m. 4 f. +X.
301, 1292.

1 m. 5 f.
123, 555, 2097, 3971.

1 m. 6 f.
754, 870, 1167, 4022.

1 m. 7 f.
109, 539, 1917, 3069, 3320.

1 m. 8 f.
437, 898, 2789.

1 m. 9 f. 2 c.
3234.

1 m. 10 f.
635, 1500.

1 m. 12 f.
696.

1 m. 12 f. 1 un.
2790.

1 m. 15 f.
1453.

1 m. 16 f.
664.

1 m. 19 f.
4099.

2 m. 0 f.
96, 134, 325, 326, 451, 655, 687, 812, 826,
854, 883, 983, 988, 1134, 1226, 1272, 1299,
1472, 1694, 1792, 2118, 2137, 2142, 2350,
2351, 2352, 2353, 2407, 2623, 2757, 3615,
3713, 3804, 3810, 3841.

2 m. 0 f. 5 un.
3702.

2 m. 0 f. 1 c.
513.

2 m. 0 f. 1 c. +X.
1892.

2 m. 0 f. 2 c.
1793.

2 m. 0 f. 4 c.
442.

2 m. 0 f. 5 c.
1358, 4160.

2 m. 0 f. 6 c.
3211.

2 m. 0 f. 7 c.
2758.

2 m. 0 f. 8 c.
2313.

2 m. 0 f. 12 c. +X.
3649.

2 m. 0 f. 15 c.
1944.

2 m. 0 f. 21 c.
2721.

2 m. 0 f. +X.
594, 1642, 2722, 3115.

2 m. 1 f.
117, 151, 233, 234, 272, 346, 388, 441, 489,
509, 616, 829, 872, 887, 925, 972, 986, 1029,
1031, 1032, 1107, 1130, 1224, 1257, 1311,
1407, 1447, 1549, 1586, 1592, 1595, 1598,
1620, 1710, 1729, 1788, 1805, 1953, 2019,
2054, 2061, 2179, 2258, 2308, 2355, 2359,
2397, 2495, 2574, 2579, 2631, 2664, 2805,
2808, 2844, 2871, 2980, 3246, 3294, 3340,
3474, 3493, 3524, 3594, 3670, 3767, 3905,
3927, 3959, 3979, 4031, 4037, 4056, 4109,
4127, 4149.

2 m. 1 f. 1 un. +X.
2997, 3988.

2 m. 1 f. 4 un.
2799.

2 m. 1 f. 4 un. +X.
2654.

2 m. 1 f. 8 un.
4028.

2 m. 1 f. 12 un. +X.
287.

2 m. 1 f. 16 un.
1971.

2 m. 1 f. 1 c.
6, 556, 2716.

2 m. 1 f. 1 c. +X.
2914, 3536.

2 m. 1 f. 2 c.
1178, 3223, 3569.

2 m. 1 f. 3 c.
1546.

2 m. 1 f. 4 c.
604, 1709.

2 m. 1 f. 5 c.
1652.

2 m. 1 f. 6 c. +X.
3544.

2 m. 1 f. 9 c.
2702.

2 m. 1 f. 11 c.
2918.

2 m. 1 f. +X.
60, 283, 367, 672, 1113, 1645, 1968, 2155, 2156, 2157, 2575, 3194, 3228, 3612, 4086.

2 m. 2 f.
44, 45, 188, 334, 345, 379, 400, 469, 478, 514, 564, 720, 725, 757, 882, 910, 916, 924, 944, 998, 1019, 1163, 1192, 1198, 1232, 1269, 1281, 1295, 1513, 1717, 1790, 1791, 1921, 1926, 1992, 2081, 2115, 2129, 2159, 2259, 2342, 2493, 2494, 2520, 2607, 2627, 2637, 2650, 2673, 2674, 2740, 2807, 2933, 2954, 3004, 3040, 3048, 3052, 3081, 3205, 3206, 3226, 3263, 3285, 3328, 3379, 3380, 3433, 3479, 3535, 3555, 3556, 3657,

3679, 3711, 3778, 3798, 3933, 3948, 3983, 4002, 4067, 4083, 4084, 4133.

2 m. 2 f. 3 un.
4063.

2 m. 2 f. 1 c.
1455, 1676, 2614.

2 m. 2 f. 2 c.
210.

2 m. 2 f. 2 c. +X.
602, 615, 3140.

2 m. 2 f. 3 c. +X.
3239.

2 m. 2 f. 6 c.
3108.

2 m. 2 f. 7 c.
3565.

2 m. 2 f. 21 c.
3244.

2 m. 2 f. +X.
85, 333, 637, 1183, 2856, 2923, 3119, 3232, 4033, 4179.

2 m. 3 f.
55, 56, 65, 340, 361, 407, 419, 503, 529, 608, 867, 868, 978, 979, 992, 1182, 1202, 1271, 1375, 1395, 1408, 1409, 1431, 1438, 1661, 1669, 1734, 1735, 1798, 1871, 1884, 1897, 2053, 2182, 2254, 2319, 2385, 2500, 2513, 2598, 2599, 2600, 2611, 2612, 2655, 2718, 2763, 2931, 3145, 3214, 3443, 3482, 3485, 3568, 3654, 3675, 3721, 3734, 3735, 3796, 3904, 3964, 4088.

2 m. 3 f. 1 un.
228.

2 m. 3 f. 1 c.
1515, 1517.

2 m. 3 f. 1 c. +X.
612.

2 m. 3 f. 2 c.
3889.

2 m. 3 f. 2 c. +X.
1286.

2 m. 3 f. 3 c.
553, 798.

2 m. 3 f. 4 c.
3895.

2 m. 3 f. 5 c.
2932, 3399.

2 m. 3 f. 11 c.
946.

2 m. 3 f. +X.
415, 736, 1098, 1366, 1841, 2228, 2823, 3094, 3456, 3519, 4090.

2 m. 4 f.
51, 157, 253, 390, 434, 459, 506, 646, 703, 762, 943, 1011, 1012, 1156, 1262, 1328, 1507, 1514, 1518, 1746, 1787, 2149, 2173, 2190, 2387, 2394, 2525, 2593, 2621, 2622, 2657, 2736, 2741, 2899, 3009, 3310, 3337, 3362, 3748, 3827, 4072.

2 m. 4 f. 1 un.
231.

2 m. 4 f. 2 un.
3371.

2 m. 4 f. 3 un.
3688.

2 m. 4 f. 2 c.
709.

2 m. 4 f. 3 c.
2893, 3648.

2 m. 4 f. 4 c.
1374.

2 m. 4 f. 5 c.
1087.

2 m. 4 f. 11 c.
1220.

2 m. 4 f. +X.
2101, 2405, 2737, 3944, 4073.

2 m. 5 f.
705, 730, 895, 1120, 1848, 1986, 2096, 2168, 3154, 3338, 3392, 3401, 3517, 3772.

2 m. 5 f. 7 un.
2039.

2 m. 5 f. 3 c. +X.
619.

2 m. 5 f. +X.
3469, 3470, 3994, 4115.

2 m. 6 f.
496, 752, 1975, 2006, 2210, 2384, 3314,
3700, 3774, 3939, 3940, 4007, 4010.

2 m. 6 f. +X.
1398, 1942, 3298.

2 m. 7 f.
46, 1038, 2008, 2830, 3914.

2 m. 7 f. +X.
2765.

2 m. 8 f.
484, 530, 761, 2233, 3508.

2 m. 8 f. 6 c.
4114.

2 m. 9 f.
1051.

2 m. 9 f. +X.
1085.

2 m. 10 f.
3002, 3931.

2 m. 11 f.
3355.

3 m. 0 f.
351, 394, 401, 483, 508, 516, 688, 1056, 1169,
1260, 1324, 1332, 1403, 1468, 1473, 1492,
1494, 1677, 2015, 2396, 2699, 2863, 2957,
3597, 3665, 3812, 4061.

3 m. 0 f. 2 c.
3655.

3 m. 0 f. 3 c.
3645.

3 m. 0 f. 4 c.
342, 3165.

3 m. 0 f. 8 c. +X.
3650.

3 m. 0 f. 11 c.
806, 807.

3 m. 0 f. 14 c.
3282.

3 m. 0 f. 20 c.
1707.

3 m. 0 f. +X.
1946.

3 m. 1 f.
15, 40, 168, 170, 248, 511, 570, 658, 677,
710, 740, 865, 873, 911, 974, 999, 1128,
1197, 1208, 1222, 1225, 1290, 1337, 1505,
1556, 1699, 1721, 1862, 1868, 1925, 1974,
2042, 2063, 2138, 2401, 2440, 2551, 2580,
2767, 2806, 2955, 2984, 3020, 3184, 3190,
3335, 3468, 3572, 3573, 3719, 3764, 3806,
3829, 4069.

3 m. 1 f. 1 un.
1681.

3 m. 1 f. 16 un.
1014.

3 m. 1 f. 1 c.
1575, 3921.

3 m. 1 f. 2 c. +X.
1543, 1544.

3 m. 1 f. 3 c. +X.
1749.

3 m. 1 f. 5 c. +X.
504.

3 m. 1 f. 13 c.
2687.

3 m. 1 f. 24 c.
3666.

3 m. 1 f. +X.
408, 1713, 2291, 2292, 2442, 2475, 2916, 2969,
3174, 3289, 4113.

3 m. 2 f.
29, 83, 303, 318, 329, 397, 405, 542, 625,
631, 669, 675, 747, 760, 785, 848, 884, 900,
922, 1131, 1166, 1181, 1203, 1228, 1229,
1244, 1424, 1437, 1454, 1486, 1521, 1569,
1636, 1657, 1695, 1696, 1818, 1824, 1837,
1856, 1911, 1929, 2030, 2262, 2344, 2408,
2441, 2523, 2524, 2605, 2606, 2672, 2788,
2819, 2831, 2898, 2994, 3010, 3036, 3064,
3068, 3082, 3083, 3147, 3236, 3274, 3381,
3382, 3423, 3541, 3543, 3567, 3608, 3676,

3720, 3752, 3786, 3794, 3815, 3861, 3871,
3873, 4138, 4162, 4172.

3 m. 2 f. 1 un.
1430.

3 m. 2 f. 3 un. +X.
3856.

3 m. 2 f. 4 un. +X.
3341.

3 m. 2 f. 6 un. +X.
1535.

3 m. 2 f. 8 un.
274, 1671.

3 m. 2 f. 13 un. +X.
2474.

3 m. 2 f. 1 c.
313, 1907, 4021.

3 m. 2 f. 1 c. +X.
3173.

3 m. 2 f. 4 c.
1247.

3 m. 2 f. 5 c.
2540.

3 m. 2 f. 9 c. +X.
1142.

3 m. 2 f. 30 c.
2.

3 m. 2 f. +X.
262, 907, 1141, 1172, 1634, 1635, 2098,
2784, 3269.

3 m. 3 f.
18, 24, 136, 165, 216, 271, 317, 323, 330,
383, 402, 462, 466, 494, 524, 585, 592, 634,
654, 804, 809, 811, 823, 976, 997, 1017,
1046, 1055, 1148, 1214, 1265, 1288, 1323,
1362, 1383, 1393, 1412, 1413, 1420, 1422,
1450, 1481, 1512, 1519, 1520, 1616, 1718,
1767, 1778, 1811, 1906, 1912, 1923, 2050,
2079, 2109, 2185, 2276, 2300, 2301, 2331,
2347, 2380, 2381, 2434, 2436, 2456, 2465,
2469, 2485, 2497, 2563, 2616, 2646, 2843.

2956, 2989, 3093, 3106, 3322, 3428, 3446,
3558, 3659, 3682, 3742, 3770, 3891, 3929,
3995, 4047, 4054, 4057, 4060, 4119, 4131.

3 m. 3 f. 2 un.
1425.

3 m. 3 f. 1 c.
131, 4156.

3 m. 3 f. 1 c. +X.
965.

3 m. 3 f. 4 c.
571, 2728.

3 m. 3 f. 4 c. +X.
945.

3 m. 3 f. 7 c.
147.

3 m. 3 f. +X.
601, 611, 1410, 1745, 2501. 2505, 2681,
2751, 2814, 3071, 3304, 3545, 3714, 3833.

3 m. 4 f.
173, 191, 192, 227, 285, 354, 467, 721, 746,
783, 788, 862, 969, 1041, 1052, 1053, 1054,
1114, 1117, 1233, 1234, 1289, 1305, 1306,
1495, 1511, 1673, 1736, 1742, 1748, 1801,
1870, 1878, 1879, 2274, 2275, 2282, 2314,
2388, 2428, 2453, 2660, 2670, 2680, 2684,
2877, 2878, 2879, 2885, 3001, 3158, 3193,
3326, 3410, 3458, 3502, 3531, 3602, 3673,
3776, 3777, 3805, 3866, 4041, 4045, 4112,
4150, 4155.

3 m. 4 f. 1 un. +X.
840.

3 m. 4 f. 6 un.
844.

3 m. 4 f. 1 c.
1679, 2021, 2265, 2413.

3 m. 4 f. 2 c. +X.
217, 1831.

3 m. 4 f. +X.
572, 573, 653, 1015, 2260, 3055, 3133, 3880,
3960.

3 m. 5 f.
61, 66, 77, 114, 115, 371, 778, 980, 1066,
1174, 1476, 1491, 1534, 1589, 1876, 1885,
2791, 2792, 3430, 3431, 3486, 3533, 3534,
3577, 3584, 3961.

3 m. 5 f. 2 c.
1201.

3 m. 5 f. 4 c.
618.

3 m. 5 f. +X.
486, 1102, 2376, 2589, 2897, 3367, 3660.

3 m. 6 f.
471, 869, 1048, 1144, 1415, 2215, 2458,
2739, 2759, 3329, 3330, 3450.

3 m. 6 f. 1 un.
338.

3 m. 6 f. +X.
201, 1381, 1396, 2170.

3 m. 7 f.
267, 455, 2212, 2213, 2327, 2466, 3188, 3387.

3 m. 7 f. 1 c.
2216.

3 m. 7 f. +X.
2835, 3476.

3 m. 8 f.
1795, 1796, 1797, 2204.

3 m. 8 f. 6 un. +X.
3124.

3 m. 8 f. 1 c.
2463.

3 m. 9 f.
1996, 3459, 3460.

3 m. 9 f. 2 c.
3499.

3 m. 9 f. +X.
3566, 3634.

3 m. 11 f.
1103.

3 m. 11 f. 4 un.
26.

3 m. 14 f. +X.
1106.

3 m. 16 f. +X.
1255.

4 m. 0 f.
751, 769, 1073, 1127, 1129, 1625, 1648, 1700,
1763, 2055, 2070, 2121, 2154, 2446, 2746,
2848, 2981, 3183, 3195, 3334, 3388, 3611,
3757, 3828, 4032.

4 m. 0 f. 1 c.
1207.

4 m. 0 f. 2 c.
817.

4 m. 0 f. 3 c.
2363.

4 m. 0 f. 10 c.
2875.

4 m. 0 f. 16 c. +X.
266.

4 m. 0 f. +X.
432, 2358, 2652, 3075, 3604, 3773, 3987.

4 m. 1 f.
12, 28, 101, 144, 171, 203, 440, 443, 657,
977, 985, 1021, 1023, 1040, 1060, 1077,
1150, 1190, 1221, 1318, 1319, 1380, 1509,
1725, 1927, 1982, 2114, 2130, 2175, 2177,
2261, 2273, 2337, 2554, 2710, 2726, 2804,
2850, 2951, 3172, 3221, 3448, 3466, 3601,
3834, 3859, 3922, 4038, 4049.

4 m. 1 f. 1 un. +X.
454.

4 m. 1 f. 2 un.
2011.

4 m. 1 f. 13 un.
81.

4 m. 1 f. 1 c.
2695, 3874.

4 m. 1 f. 2 c.
58, 936, 1533.

4 m. 1 f. 3 c. +X.
3139.

4 m. 1 f. 4 c.
1806.

4 m. 1 f. 5 c.
2410.

4 m. 1 f. many c. +X.
1833.

4 m. 1 f. +X.
103, 140, 347, 666, 832, 1027, 1160, 2568,
2724, 2864, 3028, 3150, 3477, 3977.

4 m. 2 f.
176, 205, 263, 276, 452, 598, 803, 828, 856,
886, 964, 1020, 1071, 1123, 1124, 1235,
1283, 1343, 1359, 1363, 1475, 1508, 1561,
1607, 1615, 1726, 1807, 1858, 1910, 1939,
1961, 1976, 2051, 2092, 2131, 2518, 2522,
2542, 2873, 2882, 2934, 3074, 3100, 3120,
3235, 3260, 3261, 3386, 3429, 3497, 3635,
3639, 3680, 3681, 3838, 3847, 3851, 3943,
3982, 4050, 4130, 4137, 4139, 4176.

4 m. 2 f. 1 un.
3302.

4 m. 2 f. 1 un. +X.
2002, 2431.

4 m. 2 f. 4 un.
2972.

4 m. 2 f. 6 un.
1313.

4 m. 2 f. 11 un.
2529.

4 m. 2 f. 1 c.
830, 2348, 3599.

4 m. 2 f. 1 c. +X.
1449.

4 m. 2 f. 2 c.
3706, 3947.

4 m. 2 f. 2 c. +X.
52.

4 m. 2 f. 3 c.
2295.

4 m. 2 f. 5 c.
1184, 1451, 3141, 3421.

4 m. 2 f. +X.
67, 908, 1302, 1331, 1622, 1872, 2309, 2507,
3656.

4 m. 3 f.
82, 125, 155, 199, 292, 343, 357, 384, 422,
427, 460, 461, 586, 603, 659, 697, 921, 927,
938, 1069, 1143, 1189, 1211, 1241, 1315, 1419,
1441, 1442, 1457, 1458, 1545, 1637, 1678,
1716, 1723, 1775, 1780, 2016, 2017, 2085,
2143, 2148, 2178, 2196, 2286, 2287, 2299,
2332, 2356, 2399, 2414, 2417, 2424, 2425,
2427, 2468, 2515, 2516, 2521, 2571, 2572,
2625, 2840, 3016, 3062, 3063, 3197, 3224,
3287, 3391, 3397, 3411, 3412, 3463, 3489,

3515, 3570, 3571, 3578, 3580, 3698, 3745,
3759, 3783, 3901, 3915, 3981, 4042, 4043,
4080, 4094, 4120, 4144.

4 m. 3 f. 6 un. +X.
3537.

4 m. 3 f. 1 c.
2370, 3549.

4 m. 3 f. 3 c.
1571, 3620.

4 m. 3 f. 6 c. +X.
3291.

4 m. 3 f. 15 c.
3073.

4 m. 3 f. +X.
100, 146, 431, 583, 718, 1045, 1655, 1670,
1826, 1969, 2136, 2550, 2608, 2712, 3171,
3554, 3795, 4003.

4 m. 4 f. 8 un.
344.

4 m. 4 f. 1 c.
1340, 2907.

4 m. 4 f. 2 c.
2683.

4 m. 4 f. 4 c.
1981.

4 m. 4 f. +X.
53, 152, 475, 476, 569, 622, 838, 1063,
1360, 1485, 1644, 1704, 1784, 1937, 1938,
2083, 3779, 3973, 4014, 4082.

4 m. 5 f.
9, 75, 133, 172, 368, 382, 871, 1001, 1230,
1307, 1308, 1465, 1504, 1789, 1822, 2069,
2112, 2113, 2151, 2163, 2237, 2346, 2390,
2517, 2543, 2906, 2912, 2913, 3129, 3130,
3161, 3166, 3243, 3538, 3539, 3820, 3852,
3881, 3951.

4 m. 5 f. 6 un.
3237.

4 m. 5 f. 8 un.
2104.

4 m. 5 f. 1 c.
167, 1528, 2031.

4 m. 5 f. 2 c.
995, 3855.

4 m. 4 f.
8, 27, 116, 215, 335, 377, 465, 477, 481,
595, 596, 605, 937, 1064, 1089, 1135, 1250,
1277, 1287, 1304, 1336, 1338, 1389, 1391,
1404, 1456, 1477, 1522, 1587, 1593, 1621,
1708, 1776, 1777, 1812, 1813, 1825, 1894,
1908, 1947, 1948, 1951, 2209, 2278, 2369,
2371, 2403, 2420, 2482, 2502, 2506, 2570,
2659, 2768, 2782, 2783, 2832, 2859, 2874,
2924, 2978, 3011, 3012, 3015, 3030, 3050,
3136, 3231, 3327, 3351, 3365, 3366, 3444,

3505, 3509, 3511, 3546, 3547, 3637, 3640,
3741, 3860, 3865, 3938, 3999, 4163.

4 m. 5 f. +X.
554, 584, 620, 2091, 3238, 3724, 3997.

4 m. 6 f.
42, 581, 582, 698, 739, 989, 1049, 2377,
2462, 3350, 3591, 3792, 4148.

4 m. 6 f. 4 un.
1094.

4 m. 6 f. 11 un.
1943.

4 m. 6 f. 1 c.
2503, 2504, 2828, 3840.

4 m. 6 f. +X.
364, 1584, 2068, 2476, 2640, 3143.

4 m. 7 f.
1460, 2833, 3072, 3088, 3347.

4 m. 7 f. 7 c. +X.
1633.

4 m. 7 f. +X.
3559.

4 m. 8 f.
10, 204, 1550, 2198.

4 m. 9 f.
230, 2937.

4 m. 9 f. 7 c.
918.

4 m. 9 f. +X.
2047.

4 m. 11 f.
2221.

4 m. 11 f. 3 c.
3278.

4 m. 13 f. +X.
3788.

4 m. 15 f.
776.

4 m. 15 f. +X.
3279.

5 m. 0 f.
175, 309, 861, 912, 1496, 1497, 1601, 1629,
1823, 2041, 2153, 2225, 2245, 2246, 2477,
2669, 2996, 3689, 3701, 3863, 4027.

5 m. 0 f. 2 c. +X.
3600.

5 m. 0 f. +X.
1724, 1743, 1751, 2467, 3364, 3507, 3763.

5 m. 1 f.
20, 269, 273, 284, 350, 387, 716, 753, 808,
1155, 1264, 1488, 1493, 1754, 1842, 1890,
1898, 2133, 2336, 2435, 2892, 3032, 3107,
3109, 3111, 3358, 3452, 3494, 3618, 3849.

5 m. 1 f. 2 un.
1371.

5 m. 1 f. 3 un.
3606.

5 m. 1 f. 4 un.
3025.

5 m. 1 f. 1 c.
1484, 1899.

5 m. 1 f. 5 c. +X.
3879.

5 m. 1 f. 7 c. +X.
1440.

5 m. 1 f. 8 c. +X.
3629.

5 m. 1 f. 9 c.
3762.

5 m. 1 f. 12 c.
2393.

5 m. 1 f. 12 c. +X.
2723.

5 m. 1 f. +X.
543, 600, 780, 1016, 1321, 1352, 1603, 1604,
3495, 3672, 3862.

5 m. 2 f.
150, 277, 557, 589, 717, 1022, 1058, 1301,
1344, 1503, 1627, 1692, 1877, 2123, 2161,
2162, 2283, 2284, 2595, 2863, 2884, 2922,
2975, 2982, 3122, 3123, 3170, 3284, 3935,
4076.

5 m. 2 f. 1 un.
2630.

5 m. 2 f. 3 un.
1855.

5 m. 2 f. 6 un. +X.
3965.

5 m. 2 f. 22 un.
864.

5 m. 2 f. 1 c.
975, 2296, 3126.

5 m. 2 f. 3 c.
3907.

5 m. 2 f. 3 c. +X.
3437, 3438.

5 m. 2 f. 4 c. +X.
2704.

5 m. 2 f. +X.
258, 304, 505, 1680, 2785, 2786, 2867, 3416, 3740.

5 m. 3 f.
256, 305, 474, 480, 520, 797, 835, 1010, 1061, 1068, 1402, 1602, 1672, 1859, 1928, 1940, 2088, 2169, 2280, 2383, 2429, 2538, 2729, 2772, 2773, 2796, 2798, 2851, 2963, 3219, 3646, 3803, 3876, 3911, 3912, 4039.

5 m. 3 f. 1 c.
690.

5 m. 3 f. 1 c. +X.
831.

5 m. 3 f. 3 c. +X.
2569.

5 m. 3 f. 6 c. +X.
385.

5 m. 3 f. +X.
391, 952, 968, 1059, 1565, 1882, 2193, 2547, 2700, 2947, 3152, 3162, 3303, 3316, 3317, 3593, 3627, 3739.

5 m. 4 f.
70, 120, 206, 213, 389, 398, 497, 878, 1033, 1111, 1180, 1210, 1218, 1322, 1341, 1361, 1619, 1829, 1830, 1915, 1949, 1962, 2077, 2127, 2230, 2316, 2317, 2333, 2499, 2509, 2519, 2587, 2837, 2985, 3163, 3241, 3402, 3500, 3557, 3586, 3636, 3782, 3818, 3942, 3992, 4004, 4020.

5 m. 4 f. 1 un.
917.

5 m. 4 f. 1 c.
1187, 1844.

5 m. 4 f. 2 c.
2556.

5 m. 4 f. 3 c. +X.
953.

5 m. 4 f. 4 c.
1656.

5 m. 4 f. many c.
3393.

5 m. 4 f. +X.
7, 1050, 1316, 1705, 2285, 2544, 2667, 2800, 2801, 3332, 3333, 3641, 3642, 3822.

5 m. 5 f.
137, 221, 795, 834, 1162, 1194, 1236, 1527, 1570, 1653, 1764, 1765, 1773, 1774, 1903, 1933, 1950, 1995, 2020, 2508, 2689, 2690, 2744, 2958, 2965, 2991, 3042, 3321, 3354, 3473, 3483, 3484, 3528, 3619, 3707, 3811, 3878, 3886, 3955, 4017, 4040, 4087.

5 m. 5 f. 1 un. +X.
2691.

5 m. 5 f. 2 c.
2304.

5 m. 5 f. 4 c. +X.
3305.

5 m. 5 f. 6 c.
2941.

5 m. 5 f. +X.
76, 222, 2003, 2034, 2075, 2302, 2318, 3017, 3272, 3361, 3375, 3953, 3954, 4005, 4006.

5 m. 6 f.
111, 438, 587, 606, 802, 1002, 1136, 2211, 2222, 2249, 2533, 2534, 2943, 3376, 3506, 3585, 3587, 3850, 4018.

5 m. 6 f. +X.
1108, 1553, 3257.

5 m. 7 f.
866, 1997, 2948, 3199, 4168.

5 m. 7 f. 1 un. +X.
95.

5 m. 7 f. 3 c. +X.
624.

5 m. 7 f. +X.
226, 2255.

5 m. 8 f.
2415, 3280, 3801.

5 m. 8 f. 3 c. +X.
1562.

5 m. 8 f. +X.
2686.

5 m. 9 f.
2379, 2810, 2812, 3417, 3418, 3579.

5 m. 10 f.
3389.

5 m. 10 f. +X.
2366, 2367, 3621, 3622.

5 m. 11 f.
3385.

5 m. 11 f. +X.
74, 2368.

5 m. 12 f. 6 c.
994.

5 m. 14 f.
381, 3455.

6 m. 0 f.
153, 315, 337, 490, 628, 629, 656, 1116, 1125, 1145, 1188, 1502, 1686, 1690, 1909, 2734, 2748, 2872, 2998, 3104, 3212, 3213, 3553, 3562.

6 m. 0 f. 1 c.
495, 3296.

6 m. 0 f. +X.
    1887, 1888, 3177, 3747, 4053.

6 m. 1 f.
    332, 893, 1171, 1275, 1276, 1326, 1379,
    1706, 2880, 3149, 3307, 3440, 3603, 3695,
    3816, 3923, 3989, 4100.

6 m. 1 f. 1 un. +X.
    1875.

6 m. 1 f. 6 un. +X.
    2339.

6 m. 1 f. 11 un.
    3113.

6 m. 1 f. 1 c.
    250.

6 m. 1 f. 1 c. +X.
    2847.

6 m. 1 f. 2 c.
    2087.

6 m. 1 f. 3 c.
    538.

6 m. 1 f. 6 c.
    2647.

6 m. 1 f. 13 c.
    3084.

6 m. 1 f. +X.
    935, 1666, 1832, 1970, 3112, 3864, 4125.

6 m. 2 f.
    3, 179, 181, 300, 327, 359, 369, 632, 846,
    885, 1158, 1312, 1320, 1388, 1471, 1650,
    1663, 1697, 1698, 1808, 2071, 2288, 2472,
    2617, 2715, 3041, 3220, 3295, 3309, 3442,
    3607, 4081.

6 m. 2 f. 2 un.
    794.

6 m. 2 f. 2 un. +X.
    1377.

6 m. 2 f. 3 c.
    164, 2883, 3692.

6 m. 2 f. +X.
    139, 362, 942, 1104, 1357, 1394, 1972, 2062,
    2921, 3290, 3396, 4141.

6 m. 3 f.
    138, 265, 319, 399, 639, 665, 714, 765, 789,
    819, 857, 877, 919, 1353, 1574, 1618, 1630,
    1744, 1816, 1889, 1984, 2060, 2590, 2766,
    2993, 3192, 3217, 3336, 3370, 3407, 3550,
    3725, 3956, 4085.

6 m. 3 f. 1 c.
    3137.

6 m. 3 f. 3 c. +X.
    772.

6 m. 3 f. 4 c. +X.
    2253.

6 m. 3 f. 6 c.
    2900.

6 m. 3 f. 7 c. +X.
    3919.

6 m. 3 f. 12 c.
    929.

6 m. 3 f. +X.
    98, 297, 1297, 1459, 1489, 1730, 2164, 2345,
    2445, 2725, 2742, 2953, 3857, 3910, 4058.

6 m. 4 f.
    194, 223, 446, 473, 577, 579, 683, 684,
    729, 1217, 1279, 1532, 1701, 1815, 2125,
    2165, 2349, 2857, 2902, 3420, 3434, 3475,
    3906, 3990, 4129, 4165, 4166.

6 m. 4 f. 1 un.
    54, 3952.

6 m. 4 f. 8 un.
    3975.

6 m. 4 f. 3 c.
    219.

6 m. 4 f. 4 c.
    860.

6 m. 4 f. 5 c.
    3286.

6 m. 4 f. 22 c.
    1007.

6 m. 4 f. +X.
    599, 1261, 1536, 1606, 2281, 3447, 3589, 3610,
    3632.

6 m. 5 f.
    35, 80, 707, 759, 933, 1078, 1185, 1845,
    1846, 2305, 2326, 2426, 2940, 3029, 3078,
    3086, 3091, 3103, 3694, 3731, 3917.

6 m. 5 f. 2 un
    1731, 2838.

6 m. 5 f. +X.
    1296, 1994, 2219, 3297, 3342.

6 m. 6 f.
    295, 320, 463, 464, 734, 756, 1109, 1333,
    1423, 1581, 2018, 2200, 2201, 2374, 2685,
    2795, 2949, 3457, 3691, 3831, 3884.

6 m. 6 f. 1 un.
    1240.

6 m. 6 f. 4 un.
    2586.

6 m. 6 f. 8 un.
    742.

6 m. 6 f. +X.
    193, 758, 3058, 4096.

6 m. 7 f.
    229, 3026, 4016.

6 m. 7 f. +X.
    148, 704, 3934.

7 m. 6 f. +X.
208, 793, 1168, 3065, 3761, 3957.

7 m. 7 f.
433, 749, 750, 923, 1293, 1427, 1559, 1772,
1983, 2029, 2046, 2391, 2530, 3449, 3958.

7 m. 7 f. 10 c.
613, 614.

7 m. 7 f. +X.
1072, 1115, 1282, 1542, 2205, 3383, 3909.

7 m. 8 f.
2266, 2962, 3662, 4118.

7 m. 8 f. 2 c. +X.
3699.

7 m. 8 f. +X.
296, 890, 791, 4142.

7 m. 10 f.
2023, 2335.

7 m. 10 f. +X.
1070, 2022.

7 m. 11 f.
1246.

7 m. 12 f.
3738.

7 m. 13 f.
3941.

8 m. 0 f.
307, 358, 515, 652, 837, 1079, 1091, 1121,
1732, 2618, 2777, 3134, 3732, 4164, 4171.

8 m. 0 f. +X.
2676.

8 m. 1 f.
132, 252, 1325, 1588, 2825, 2890, 3345, 3522,
3542, 3998.

8 m. 1 f. 5 un.
3791.

8 m. 1 f. 8 un.
1042.

8 m. 1 f. 10 un. +X.
3496.

8 m. 1 f. 1 c.
260, 3102.

8 m. 1 f. 1 c. +X.
87.

8 m. 1 f. +X.
247, 278, 426, 485, 1510, 2708, 3722, 4077.

8 m. 2 f.
187, 816, 1523, 1628, 1799, 1960, 2000, 2001,
2135, 2150, 2596, 2889, 3588, 3508, 4097.

8 m. 2 f. 4 un.
2904.

8 m. 2 f. 2 c.
3514.

8 m. 2 f. 6 c. +X.
3008.

8 m. 2 f. 7 c. +X.
3265.

8 m. 2 f. +X.
406, 609, 2218, 2416, 2896, 3643, 3684, 3685.

8 m. 3 f.
522, 764, 768, 939, 991, 2389, 3156, 3207,
3258, 3339, 3704.

8 m. 3 f. 4 un. +X.
1057.

8 m. 3 f. 1 c.
2033.

8 m. 3 f. 1 c. +X.
3715.

8 m. 3 f. 2 c.
3315.

8 m. 3 f. 2 c. +X.
3690.

8 m. 3 f. 5 c.
2132.

8 m. 3 f. +X.
1452, 1664, 1809, 3384, 3408.

8 m. 4 f.
149, 445, 858, 1683, 1781, 2701, 2781, 3369,
3839, 3928.

8 m. 4 f. 1 c.
1526.

8 m. 4 f. 1 c. +X.
3984.

8 m. 4 f. 7 c.
370.

8 m. 4 f. 10 c.
715.

8 m. 4 f. +X.
94, 424, 2910, 3415.

8 m. 5 f.
824, 1688, 1828, 1836, 3875, 4023, 4030.

8 m. 5 f. +X.
1112, 1733, 2086, 2641, 2730.

8 m. 6 f.
413, 719, 1444, 1966, 2628, 2979.

8 m. 6 f. 5 un.
2430.

8 m. 6 f. 1 c. +X.
2372.

8 m. 6 f. 3 c. +X.
2824.

8 m. 6 f. +X.
259, 3630, 3937.

8 m. 7 f.
1245.

8 m. 7 f. 4 c.
3877.

8 m. 7 f. +X.
800, 1490, 2217, 2439, 2679.

8 m. 8 f.
1863, 3503.

8 m. 8 f. 3 un.
536.

8 m. 8 f. +X.
597, 686.

8 m. 9 f.
2052, 2082.

8 m. 9 f. +X.
4159.

8 m. 10 f. 1 un. +X.
288.

8 m. 10 f. +X.
290.

8 m. 11 f. 3 c. +X.
2277.

8 m. 11 f. +X.
2836.

8 m. 13 f. +X.
1758.

8 m. 17 f. 6 c.
218.

9 m. 0 f.
472, 1067, 1096, 1284, 1530, 1647, 2122,
2404, 2481, 2511.

9 m. 0 f. 4 c.
4136.

9 m. 0 f. 4 c. +X.
1769.

9 m. 0 f. +X.
1443, 1529.

9 m. 1 f.
154, 633, 859, 2450, 2479.

9 m. 1 f. +X.
733, 1631, 1800, 2478, 3230, 3266.

9 m. 2 f.
1105, 1215, 1355, 3501, 3540.

9 m. 2 f. 1 c.
2694.

9 m. 2 f. 1 c. +X.
1349.

9 m. 2 f. 2 c.
1446.

9 m. 2 f. 6 c.
560.

9 m. 2 f. 11 c.
1008.

9 m. 2 f. +X.
293, 396, 2490, 2901, 3168.

9 m. 3 f.
450, 694, 700, 889, 956, 1237, 1238, 2688,
3180, 3520, 3560, 3575, 3576, 4154.

9 m. 3 f. 3 un.
2049.

9 m. 3 f. 3 c. +X.
558.

9 m. 3 f. +X.
23, 540, 1018, 2865, 2876, 3251.

9 m. 4 f.
588, 2012, 2013, 2144, 3318, 3319.

9 m. 4 f. 2 un. +X.
3117.

9 m. 4 f. 1 c.
3661.

9 m. 4 f. 5 c.
3248.

9 m. 4 f. +X.
124, 363, 447, 565, 626, 966, 1883, 2171,
2678, 4105.

9 m. 5 f.
591, 1567, 3218.

9 m. 5 f. 4 c. +X.
2834.

9 m. 5 f. 5 c. +X.
2126.

9 m. 5 f. 6 c.
341.

9 m. 5 f. 15 c. +X.
2557.

9 m. 5 f. +X.
726, 2271, 2297, 3208, 3306.

9 m. 6 f.
1810, 2448, 3300, 4029.

9 m. 6 f. 1 un.
774.

9 m. 6 f. 1 c.
4079.

9 m. 6 f. 16 c.
3750.

9 m. 6 f. +X.
643, 763, 3518.

9 m. 7 f.
468, 2341, 3059.

9 m. 7 f. 3 un.
3897.

9 m. 7 f. 5 c.
576.

9 m. 7 f. +X.
1779, 2093.

9 m. 8 f. +X.
3858, 4008.

9 m. 9 f.
960, 1478, 3148, 4046, 4089.

9 m. 9 f. +X.
1369.

9 m. 10 f.
735, 3581, 4035.

9 m. 16 f. +X.
3414.

10 m. 0 f.
360, 796, 1392, 1967, 2194, 4019.

10 m. 0 f. 1 c. +X.
3736.

10 m. 0 f. 9 c.
1964.

10 m. 0 f. +X.
268, 1335, 2362, 3677, 3737.

10 m. 1 f.
1469, 2139, 3394, 3551, 3797.

10 m. 1 f. +X.
1462, 1687.

10 m. 2 f.
13, 738, 1400, 1814, 2464, 2693, 3037, 3038,
3492, 3516, 3967.

10 m. 2 f. +X.
1689.

10 m. 3 f.
1506.

10 m. 3 f.
957, 2256, 2451, 2713, 2714.

10 m. 4 f.
57, 779, 940, 3595.

10 m. 4 f. 5 c.
1426.

10 m. 4 f. +X.
1541, 2040, 3913.

10 m. 5 f.
623, 2036, 3525.

10 m. 5 f. +X.
674, 3751.

10 m. 6 f.
1, 1199, 2775, 3187, 3196.

10 m. 7 f.
289, 775, 1364.

10 m. 7 f. +X.
1991.

10 m. 8 f. +X.
3255.

10 m. 9 f.
237, 1980, 2147, 2203.

10 m. 9 f. 6 c.
2591.

10 m. 10 f.
2731.

10 m. 10 f. +X.
2189.

10 m. 11 f. 1 c.
1715.

10 m. 11 f. +X.
3708, 3843.

10 m. 15 f.
118.

11 m. 0 f.
1165, 1605, 1941, 4070.

11 m. 0 f. +X.
2226, 2822, 3270.

11 m. 1 f.
127, 261, 1076, 1740, 2632, 2974.

11 m. 1 f. 1 c.
1499.

11 m. 1 f. 1 c. +X.
3766.

11 m. 1 f. 2 c. +X.
1852.

11 m. 1 f. +X.
3253.

11 m. 2 f.
897, 1623.

11 m. 2 f. 1 c. +X.
839.

11 m. 2 f. +X.
3095, 3096, 4059.

11 m. 3 f.
876, 2105, 2457.

11 m. 3 f. 2 c. +X.
3138.

11 m. 3 f. +X.
99, 1278, 2779, 4034.

11 m. 4 f.
2658, 2671, 3229.

11 m. 4 f. 4 c. +X.
562.

11 m. 4 f. 7 c.
2555.

11 m. 4 f. +X.
1159, 2866.

11 m. 5 f.
2224.

11 m. 5 f. 3 un. +X.
934.

11 m. 5 f. +X.
642, 801, 1662, 2584, 3749.

11 m. 6 f.
68, 2250, 2251, 2942.

11 m. 6 f. +X.
3697.

11 m. 7 f. 8 c.
470.

11 m. 7 f. +X.
847, 4117.

11 m. 13 f. +X.
2028.

11 m. 18 f. +X.
2257.

12 m. 0 f.
2732, 3746.

12 m. 0 f. +X.
3151.

12 m. 1 f.
711, 2207.

12 m. 1 f. 1 c. +X.
3605.

12 m. 1 f. +X.
993, 1439.

12 m. 2 f.
799, 2651, 2764, 3267, 3268.

12 m. 2 f. 1 c. +X.
1641.

12 m. 2 f. +X.
2078, 3769.

12 m. 3 f.
5, 627, 743, 1770, 3356.

12 m. 4 f.
386, 2813, 3908.

12 m. 4 f. +X.
699.

12 m. 5 f.
1864, 2057.

12 m. 5 f. 12 c. +X.
1421.

12 m. 6 f. +X.
2264.

12 m. 7 f.
2915, 3902.

12 m. 7 f. 1 c.
1013.

12 m. 7 f. +X.
2102, 2103.

12 m. 8 f.
207.

12 m. 8 f. 2 un. +X.
3254.

12 m. 8 f. +X.
294, 3227.

12 m. 10 f.
373, 2438.

12 m. 12 f.
1024.

13 m. 0 f.
1082, 2357, 3167.

13 m. 0 f. +X.
3022.

13 m. 1 f.
941.

13 m. 1 f. 1 c.
501, 2992.

13 m. 1 f. +X.
814, 1348.

13 m. 2 f.
59, 1594, 2247, 2719, 2845.

13 m. 2 f. +X.
3215.

13 m. 3 f. 2 c.
841.

13 m. 3 f. +X.
241.

13 m. 4 f.
449, 2535, 2911.

13 m. 4 f. 5 un.
2613.

13 m. 4 f. 4 c. +X.
2223.

13 m. 5 f. +X.
2058.

13 m. 6 f.
3007, 3023.

13 m. 6 f. 13 un. +X.
2026.

13 m. 7 f. +X.
3019.

13 m. 8 f. +X.
575.

13 m. 10 f. +X.
593.

13 m. 11 f.
3249, 3733.

13 m. 13 f. +X.
566.

14 m. 0 f.
1931.

14 m. 1 f.
2455.

14 m. 3 f.
1294, 1531, 1782, 1783, 2231.

14 m. 3 f. +X.
1196, 3114.

14 m. 4 f.
2248, 2392, 3512, 4174.

14 m. 4 f. 5 c.
186.

14 m. 4 f. +X.
906, 2312.

14 m. 5 f. 3 c.
1821.

14 m. 5 f. +X.
2797.

14 m. 6 f. 18 c.
3110.

14 m. 8 f.
2279.

14 m. 12 f.
3651.

14 m. 14 f. +X.
3760.

14 m. 15 f. 1 un.
3723.

14 m. 23 f.
420.

15 m. 0 f. +X.
366, 1760.

15 m. 1 f.
1376, 3785.

15 m. 1 f. +X.
2498.

15 m. 3 f. +X.
310, 1612.

15 m. 4 f.
3513, 3616.

15 m. 4 f. +X.
920, 3024.

15 m. 5 f.
2197.

15 m. 6 f. 1 un. +X.
3963.

15 m. 6 f. +X.
713, 3754.

15 m. 9 f. 4 c. +X.
909.

15 m. 9 f. +X.
1006.

15 m. 10 f. +X.
3784.

15 m. 16 f.
4024, 4044.

16 m. 1 f. 5 c. +X.
1097.

16 m. 2 f.
875, 1153, 2419.

16 m. 3 f.
1752, 3132.

16 m. 4 f. +X.
888.

16 m. 5 f.
2752.

16 m. 5 f. +X.
1354, 2073.

16 m. 6 f.
1865.

16 m. 7 f.
533, 578, 1034.

16 m. 9 f.
107.

17 m. 2 f. 1 c.
1445.

17 m. 3 f.
1651.

17 m. 4 f. 2 un.
105.

17 m. 4 f. 2 c.
302.

17 m. 4 f. 2 c. +X.
1918.

17 m. 8 f. +X.
2460.

17 m. 9 f.
621.

17 m. 12 f.
3991.

17 m. 13 f. 3 c.
    336.

18 m. 0 f. 4 c.
    2229.

18 m. 1 f.
    145.

18 m. 2 f.
    3013.

18 m. 5 f.
    3077.

18 m. 6 f.
    444.

18 m. 9 f. +X.
    574.

18 m. 11 f. +X.
    2604.

18 m. 13 f.
    1463.

18 m. 19 f. 9 c.
    1212.

19 m. 2 f. +X.
    2816.

19 m. 4 f.
    4121.

19 m. 5 f. +X.
    559, 561.

19 m. 8 f.
    2815.

20 m. 0 f.
    3427.

20 m. 8 f. +X.
    3250, 3346.

21 m. 2 f. +X.
    818.

21 m. 4 f. 7 un. +X.
    3252.

21 m. 6 f. 1 c.
    2167.

22 m. 0 f.
    374.

22 m. 9 f.
    2675.

23 m. 0 f.
    1387.

23 m. 1 f.
    2140.

24 m. 1 f. 1 c.
    2263.

25 m. 2 f.
    1173.

26 m. 0 f.
    1741.

26 m. 7 f. +X.
    3936.

26 m. 11 f. +X.
    2817.

2? m. 6 f. 12 c. +X.
    3898.

30 m. 8 f. +X.
    498, 499.

50 m. 28 f. +X.
    3789, 3790.